The British Mosque

The British Mosque

An architectural and social history

Shahed Saleem

 Historic England

Published by Historic England, The Engine House, Fire Fly Avenue, Swindon SN2 2EH
www.HistoricEngland.org.uk
Historic England is a Government service championing England's heritage and giving expert, constructive advice.

The views expressed in this book are those of the author and not necessarily those of Historic England.

First published 2018

ISBN 978 1 84802 076 4

British Library Cataloguing in Publication data
A CIP catalogue record for this book is available from the British Library.

For more information about images from the Archive, contact Archives Services Team, Historic England, The Engine House,
Fire Fly Avenue, Swindon SN2 2EH; telephone (01793) 414600.

Brought to publication by Rachel Howard and Sarah Enticknap, Publishing, Historic England.

Typeset in Georgia Pro Light 9.5/11.75pt

Edited by Wendy Toole and Kathryn Glendenning
Indexed by Caroline Jones, Osprey Indexing
Page layout by Pauline Hull

Printed in the Czech Republic via Akcent Media Limited

*Frontispiece: The minbar of the Aziziye Mosque in east London. As the mosque was established by a local Turkish Muslim
community, the minbar is built in a traditional Ottoman style. [DP132048]*

Contents

Preface

The heritage of Britain, including the built environment, belongs to everyone who lives here. It is made up of local and national expressions of society throughout history.

People make places to serve their needs and express the life of their community. Historic England is committed to working with others to understand our heritage better, building on local interest and helping to stimulate debate and articulate the national context into which local achievements fit.

The research for this book revealed many remarkable local endeavours and some of their stories are told here. Places of worship are often the most visible physical manifestation of religious belief and observance. This book celebrates the contribution of mosques within Britain's complex and diverse religious landscape. It demonstrates the value and importance of documenting the contribution of local communities to this landscape while helping everyone to enjoy and appreciate our rich faith heritage.

Historic England is proud to offer the first comprehensive survey of the mosque in Britain. The emerging story explains how the mosque as a building type in Britain developed and adapted during a period of rapid social change. It also invites a debate on how the significance of mosques might be assessed as part of our national sense of place and as an integral part of our unfolding national story.

Sir Laurie Magnus
Chairman
Historic England

Foreword

As a boy brought up in a London of regimented red buses, uniform black cabs, Wren churches and a quietly confident sense that my home city was somehow the centre of the world, I treasured old travel books that showed me worlds that were utterly different. I remember especially a late 19th-century watercolour depicting a pair of nomadic Bedouin tribesmen kneeling down to pray in a desert of dark shadow and blinding light. The caption to the illustration told me that the riders had drawn a line in the sand to shape a 'mosque'. Although there were no walls or roof, much less a dome, minaret, swirling calligraphy or flowing water, this was a place of worship constructed in the mind's eye through faith alone.

When Muslims arrived in large numbers in London as I was growing up, they brought no camels with them. They were not dressed in flowing robes. They drew no lines in desert sands. And, when they did build mosques, these had none of the mystery, nor beauty nor exotic poetry of those I had seen in books that reflected a glamorous, if fairy-tale, view of Islam.

In fact, this romanticism was partly responsible for the design of the first permanent, purpose-built mosque in Britain, the sumptuous and picture-book Shah Jahan Mosque in Woking, founded by Dr Gottlieb Leitner, a Hungarian Orientalist scholar who had recently retired as the first Registrar of the University of the Punjab in Lahore, where my father was born. Leitner's architect, W I Chambers, took his inspiration from drawings of mosques he studied in the George Gilbert Scott-designed India Office library. Completed in 1889, the Woking Mosque is a Grade II* listed building today.

Most Muslim immigrants – then as now – were poor. They prayed in mosques established in very ordinary city houses. And, when local communities did find the money to build, both design and construction were simple yet underpinned, aesthetically, by what tended to look like half-remembered mosques from wherever they, or their parents or grandparents, had first set out from.

Shahed Saleem empathetically yet methodically describes and explains a sample of the many hundreds of mosques in Britain today. He explains how their appearance, whether newly constructed or inhabiting and adapting existing buildings, reflects diverse Muslim backgrounds. There are, from an architectural point of view, few outstanding mosques, but the history of communities that each conveys is brought out as an integral part of their significance.

Why, though, are there so few overtly modern mosques? The answer, it seems, is partly a desire among Muslim communities to retain a sense of identity rooted in the Indian subcontinent and to a lesser extent in the Middle East. A lack of money, meanwhile, can never be an excuse for awkward or visually poor design: one needs only to look back to the handsome, refined chapels built in city centres from the 18th century by Nonconformist Christian congregations to see how good religious architecture can be achieved at modest cost. However, it does account for the incremental nature of many mosque projects. Equally, there is little precedent for contemporary mosque design. Shahed Saleem himself has designed convincing, low-cost modern mosques, while architecture magazines have begun to publish a number of radical new designs free of domes, ogee arches and minarets.

The deeply impressive new mosque in Sancaklar, Turkey, designed by Emre Arolat Architects, conveys 'a sense of spirituality through an austere choreography of light and space'.[1] This half-buried, dune-like structure – as much a work of landscape art as architecture – is a subtle counterpoint to the big and visually aggressive mosques being built on the edges of fast-growing Istanbul. Deservedly, it won First Prize in the 2013 World Architecture Festival's Best Religious Building category. Although a highly sophisticated design, this new mosque evokes something of the pure spirit of that image of Bedouin tribesmen praying in the desert. It also implies 'a poetic religiosity that tactfully steers mosque architecture away from the proscriptive realms of politics and nationhood and redefines it anew in the context of ethics and aesthetics'.[2]

While this particular building is not a prescription for the design of new mosques in tightly packed city streets in Britain, it does help us all to acknowledge and understand ways in which religious architecture, even in conservative communities, can move on to become something truly special. With skill and care, Shahed Saleem guides us through the story of British mosque design to date. He considers mosques as a home-grown building type in their own right and places them within the broader architectural, historical and social context of modern Britain. Through this, he flags landmark mosques as well as community ones; early ones as well as distinctive ones, all of which have an impact on how we define significance locally and nationally and how that selection reflects our collective culture and its values.

Jonathan Glancey

Acknowledgements

My earliest memory of a mosque is, as a child, climbing a narrow timber staircase to a prayer room above a shop in a south London Victorian terrace. It was one of an emerging number of mosques in the 1970s formed through the ad hoc conversion of existing buildings to serve a growing Muslim community. A few years later I lay on the carpet of the new Regent's Park Mosque, gazing up into its deep blue dome, marvelling at the expanse of space – my first experience of purpose-built Muslim architecture, and what it could be.

Between these two early memories is the story of the mosque in Britain, from local grass-roots religious spaces assembled with whatever means the community could muster, to landmark buildings signifying the presence of Islam in Britain. In the years that followed I watched and assisted my parents establish the first mosque in south-east London. It started with Friday prayers in the living room at home, followed by renting local community halls, organising social gatherings, collecting funds, and eventually purchasing a house to convert into a dedicated place of worship.

This book is a testament to that pioneer generation – post-war Muslim immigrants, mostly from India, Pakistan and Bangladesh, who battled poverty, exclusion and racism, and through decades of sheer persistence, inventiveness and determination succeeded in establishing a Muslim social and religious infrastructure in Britain. Without their dedication and resilience, the material culture that this book explores would not exist.

The legacy of buildings and institutions thus established continued to grow and evolve, and gradually the original founders were joined by both newer immigrants and the next generation of British-born Muslims. Over the years of my research I travelled around the country meeting a range of people across cultures and generations, who had committed themselves to running the nation's mosques and Islamic centres. I am indebted to this community of volunteers who welcomed me, generously gave me their time, and opened up their mosques and community centres for me to visit and observe. They are too numerous to name, and I remain grateful for their support and enthusiasm for this project.

Alongside the direct observation and narrations that I gathered from the mosques, I was also dependent on the material in local planning offices and local history libraries and archives. Through this research I met many of the dedicated public servants who ensure that records are collected and maintained. They assisted me with finding sometimes obscure information and material that had not been accessed for many years, if at all. I am grateful to the professionalism and willingness of these archivists, librarians and administrators, and to the local institutions without which our unknown and underrepresented histories would be immeasurably harder to access or indeed might disappear completely.

In the interpretation of my research and the development of my themes and ideas, I received invaluable input through scholarly friends, who took the time, sometimes repeatedly, to listen to, read and comment on material as I produced it, and so helped me consider and shape my narratives. Again there are many people who took such an interest, and my particular thanks for this go to Lorraine Hamid for pushing me down this road in the first place, to Holger Adam and Jamilah Syal for being brave enough to read early drafts, to Abdool Karim Vakil and the valiant members of the Critical Reading Group for receiving and interrogating the work as it evolved, to Dr Tania Sengupta for being a sounding board and intellectual conscience, to Dr Jamil Sheriff for his enthusiasm and his own inspirational historical work, to Usamah Ward for sharing his own research and findings, and to Professor Humayun Ansari for his constant support and for his own work in preparing the foundations of British Muslim history in this country, on the back of which mine and many, if not all, subsequent projects in Muslim history are dependent.

Beyond this, I was reliant on the invaluable support I received from Peter Guillery of the Survey of London, who read each chapter as I produced it, and who not only served as a sanity-check but whose careful readings gave me balanced and insightful commentaries to work with. It was a great benefit to have the oversight of such an accomplished architectural historian.

A project such as this book cannot be delivered singularly. It has been dependent on the diligent, professional work from a team of Historic England experts from its earliest days. My thanks and appreciation go to Charlie Garratt for her project management of the commissioning stage; to Steven Baker, Anna Bridson, Alun Bull, Steve Cole, Nigel Corrie, James O Davies, Derek Kendall, Chris Redgrave and Peter Williams for their exceptional photography; to Tom Duane for preparing the distribution maps; to Jo Bradley for her help in sourcing images; to Philip Sinton, Sharon Soutar and Vince Griffin for preparing the plans and elevations; to Rachel Howard for assembling the material with such perseverance; and to Sarah Enticknap for seeing the book through to publication.

My thanks must also go to Wendy Toole and Kathryn Glendenning for their thorough copy-edits, to Pauline Hull for her design work and to Caroline Jones for preparing the index.

It is my aspiration that this book will stand as a marker in the representation of minority communities in Britain. That it has been initiated and published by Historic England is of huge importance for those who have been historically under-represented and marginalised. For the groundbreaking decisions that have enabled this, my appreciation goes to Historic England itself, and in particular Diana Evans, Rachel Hasted and Linda Monckton for championing this cause.

Indeed, it has been Linda Monckton's unwavering dedication to this project that has ensured that it has come to fruition. Her foresight in identifying the need, and then preparing the ground, was followed by her ongoing stewardship throughout. I am grateful to her for the support and the freedom she gave me to pursue the research, and for her insightful and correct interventions when necessary. I believe her work has deepened our awareness and understanding of the diversity and make-up of Britain's built heritage immeasurably.

A balanced professional life is only possible because of the security and commitment one receives at home. My parents, Abdullah Saleem Uddin and Sabiha Saleem, gave me nothing less than their total dedication, encouragement and support, and they instilled in me the confidence to pursue my ideas and aspirations, while equipping me with the tools to do this. My appreciation and gratitude to them cannot be described with words.

My own family has proved to be an enlightenment and a joy. For this my unwavering appreciation is to my wife Shahedah Vawda, who has been and remains a stimulating companion, and who is a person of rare humanity and presence of mind. For the years that I worked on this book, she carried an even greater share of domestic work than she already does, and attended to our young children in ways that I remain unaware of. And to my boys Zakaria and Ayman, my thanks to them for being such good company, and for ensuring, as children do, that we always keep ourselves and our work in perspective. This book is dedicated to them.

Publisher's acknowledgements

Many individuals have assisted in the sourcing of images and allowing them to be reproduced here. Our particular thanks go to Atba Al-Samarraie of Archi-Structure; to Tom Berndofer of DGA Architects; to Richard Biggins, Head of Conservation at Frederick Gibberd Partnership; to Ian Blake at Sutton Griffin Architects; to Tony Cain at Casson Conder Partnership Architects; to Valeria Carullo at the Royal Institute of British Architects' British Architectural Library; to Katrina Coopey at Cardiff Libraries; to David Davies at Davies Llewelyn and Jones; to Ali Omar Ermes; to Najib Gedal; to N A Godfrey; to Sarah Gould of Merton Local Studies Centre; to Kate Holliday and Tony King at the Cumbria Archive Service; to Nick Homer of F10 Studios; to Roger Hull at Liverpool Record Office; to Sophie Jonas-Hill; to Moira Jones and Stan Newens at the Gibberd Garden Trust; to Hasan-Uddin Khan and Renata Holod; to Eilis McCarthy at the London Muslim Centre Archive; to Kathryn Melia at Marks Barfield Architects; to Barry Morse at Cadenza Design; to Mehmood Naqshbandi of the Muslims in Britain website; to Jennifer Newman of the Wimbledon Society; to Lisa Pedley of White Crow Studios; to Tim Percival at Powell Dobson Architects; to Irina Porter at Images of London; to Chris Rawlings and Jackie Brown at the British Library; to Sue Reakes of Woolley Bevis Diplock; to Richard Reed at the Royal Institute of British Architects; to Jeremy Smith and Michael Melia at London Metropolitan Archives; to Parveen Sodhi of the Imperial War Museum; to Charles Toase at the Museum of Wimbledon; to Berrin Valzoglu at Umo Architecture; to Stefan Walker and Kate Boddy of Glamorgan Archives; and to Sergi Zapatero and César Cruz Gomez of Mangera Yvars Architects.

Editorial note

Mosques are reflective of and responsive to the communities they serve, therefore they are buildings that are continuously being adapted and altered, often through extensions. The descriptions of the mosques in this book, as well as the drawings and captions, reflect the mosque at the time of visiting (or at the time that the drawing was made), although the mosques may have been altered since.

Introduction – mosques and Muslims in Britain

This book tells the story of the mosque in Britain. It is a story of aristocrats and eccentrics, of sailors and immigrants, of empire and identity, a story spanning over 130 years, hundreds of buildings and thousands of lives. This story has many layers and many ways of being told, from the social, to the cultural, to the political, these narratives being both distinct and overlapping.

This book chooses to tell the story of the mosque through its buildings. It is primarily an architectural history, exploring buildings, aesthetics and urban development. But buildings are only given meaning by people who make, use and live with them, so this book also considers the social and cultural context of the mosque, investigating the processes by which it has come into being in Britain: how did mosques start, who initiated them, how have they been designed and built, how do the various Muslim communities meet their religious and cultural needs, and so on. Britain probably has the most diverse Muslim community in the world, with practically every denomination, school of thought, and ethnicity represented. The 2011 census counted the Muslim population at 2.7 million, an increase from just over 1.5 million in 2001. While churches (of all denominations) vastly outnumber mosques, standing at approximately 37,000, and weekly attendance for all Christian denominations stands at around three million,[1] mosque attendance is cited as being on a par with Church of England attendance, at nearly one million people per week.[2] Mosques, therefore, have become an established part of the urban fabric of Britain's towns and cities. The past century has seen dramatic social and demographic changes that have altered the profile and nature of religious observance in Britain and also the religious landscape. Christian practices, which once dominated British religious life, have been joined by other religious traditions to build a multifaith and multicultural society.

Muslims in Britain

There are early accounts of Muslims in Britain that date from the 16th and 17th centuries, with the first settled communities emerging from the mid-18th century[3] and the first mosques from the late 19th century. Imperial Britain had, over centuries, established multiple political, cultural and social links with its colonies, where many of its subjects were Muslim. It was as a result of these imperial projects that Muslim communities first settled in Britain, coming to the country as, for example, seamen, students and scholars. After World War II, with the advent of decolonisation, large numbers of Muslims settled in Britain from certain parts of South Asia,[4] and the Muslim population grew exponentially. Much of this immigration was from specific areas of India, Pakistan and Bangladesh, and through chain migration networks (where immigrants follow relatives and friends to new locations) whole sections of communities and their respective cultures were transported to British towns.[5] It was the social characteristics of these immigrants and the Muslim culture they brought that established the framework for post-war British Muslim culture and architecture in the subsequent decades. It was a Muslim demography and culture that was profoundly different in scale, dynamics and culture from the Muslim environment in Britain of the early 20th century.

Before the census of 2001 there was no way of accurately determining the size of the Muslim population in Britain, as previous censuses had not categorised religious affiliation. The best estimates, in 1991, concluded that the Muslim population at the time stood at one million, with 80 per cent being of South Asian (Indian, Pakistani and Bangladeshi) origin. The remainder were drawn mostly from the Arab world, Malaysia, Iran, Turkey/Cyprus, and East and West Africa.[6] With natural growth, continuing globalisation and immigration often fuelled by

Fig 1.1 (opposite)
Masjid e Tauheedul Islam,
Blackburn, a new Muslim
architectural presence
amid Victorian industrial
terraced houses.
[DP143572]

economic hardship and conflict, more immigrants arrived in Britain from other parts of the Muslim world. By the 2001 census, the percentage of Muslims in Britain who were of South Asian origin had gone down to 65 per cent, indicating the increasingly multi-ethnic make-up of Britain's Muslim population.

South Asian immigration to Britain increased rapidly after the independence and Partition of India in 1947. In 1951 the estimate for Britons of Pakistani and Bangladeshi descent stood at 5,000; by 1991 the figure had reached 640,000.[7] Muslim immigrants did not come to Britain from all over South Asia, but rather mostly from a few specific locales, namely the north Indian state of Gujarat, the Pakistani states of Punjab and Azad Kashmir, and Sylhet in Bangladesh. A number of socio-economic processes, combined with cultures of emigration, resulted in the establishment of these migratory networks. Professor Humayun Ansari explains:

Sending people away from home in search of work for extended periods was a practice that had evolved in various Muslim societies into a tradition with positive values, making emigration an indicator of affluence and status, so that individuals and families competed with each other in their capacity to emigrate. Migration thus became 'a system, a style, an established pattern, an example of collective behaviours'.[8]

The areas from which Pakistani immigrants originated – predominantly Azad Kashmir and Punjab – were areas that had 'long provided recruits for the merchant navy and British Army'.[9] Gujaratis came to Britain from the three districts of Baroda, Surat and Bharuch, which had a long tradition of migration and trading, especially with East African countries such as Kenya, Tanzania, Malawi, Uganda and Zambia.[10]

This culture of movement was encouraged through programmes of recruitment spearheaded by British industries that required workers to fill factory positions. These employers worked through agents who chose particular localities as a source of migrant labour: 'Agents and brokers were often the essential link between supply and demand, scouting villages and providing transport to the migrants' destination, arranging boarding and lodging ... their first port of call was usually their own villages and districts of origin.'[11] Thus migration networks were set up, with sponsorship and patronage provided by well-established immigrants, resulting in the establishment of chain migration networks based on kinship and friendship.[12] This process was not culture specific and has been shown to be a characteristic of economic migratory patterns historically. For Muslim migration to Britain, 'this chain mechanism was used by Turkish Cypriots, Moroccans, Yemenis and South Asian Muslims; once the bridgehead had been established by pioneers, migration grew, propelled by both push and pull factors.'[13]

Migrants settled in urban areas, following employment opportunities and to consolidate social and communal networks. Consequently Muslim communities emerged in Britain's main industrial conurbations, such as London, the West Midlands, Yorkshire and Lancashire, and Clydeside. A number of factors combined to produce the settlement patterns and emergence of Muslim communities in Britain's towns and cities: 'social support, and shared linguistic, cultural and religious traditions',[14] along with cheap housing and the experience of social and institutional racism, all played a part. The result is a British Muslim geography that is largely urban, inner city, working class and clearly defined.

The Muslim communities that emerged from the 1960s were, on the whole, 'very successful in reproducing their traditional social and cultural world[s]'.[15] The Muslims of Bharuch, Gujarat, for example, already lived in India in considerably self-contained enclaves, and now this pattern was repeated, and indeed intensified, in Blackburn, with chain migration reproducing village and kin networks.[16] This observation was not restricted to South Asian settlers: Yemenis in Britain have been described as forming an '"urban village" ... living within its own socially, linguistically and ethnically defined borders'.[17]

It was the arrival of families in the 1960s that changed the nature of Muslim communities. Prior to this demographic event, 'Indians, Yemenis and Turkish Cypriots [had] lived together in boarding houses ... sharing more or less the same religious facilities'. It was the reuniting of families that led to the gradual separation of Muslim immigrants to form 'ethnic settlements', and it was from within these distinct cultural and ethnic groupings that institutions started to form.[18] The size and concentration of the emergent Muslim communities enabled them to 'generate and sustain institutional and economic infrastructure that embodied and perpetuated specific religious and cultural norms. What emerged at the end of the 1970s was a patchwork of communities, each impressing its particular national, ethnic, linguistic and doctrinal character on the organisations it created.'[19]

This was the cultural context from which the mosque, as a social institution, emerged in Britain post 1960. Its role was as a place of practical support and cultural comfort as much as of religious provision. These mosques 'were primarily concerned with the promotion of worship and religious life, the encouragement of "fraternal" links in Muslim communities, the provision of assistance and moral support for individuals ... and the improvement of social, cultural and educational conditions'.[20] The result was that the handful of mosques that existed in Britain up to 1960 snowballed over the decades to follow.

These mosques generally instituted a particular organisational structure, much of which has been a requirement of the Charity Commission, and which has had a consequent impact on the way in which they have evolved. The mosque initiators would set up a board of trustees and a committee, which would run the affairs of the mosque. This committee would be elected by the mosque congregation at periodic intervals. The site and building would be in the ownership of the mosque, which would be registered as a charity, and therefore in the charge of the trustees. The development, evolution and in many cases architecture of the mosque would be directed and determined by the trustees and committee, who bore in mind that they needed to ensure the satisfaction of the congregation both as their duty and to maintain their positions. This may have contributed to a reluctance for the trustees and committees to stray from conventional notions of what the mosque is, or does, and what it looks like, for fear of alienating the congregation who are also their electorate and funders. This political and social dynamic has resulted in a particular type of organisational context within which mosques in Britain have developed.

Muslim social and religious life in Britain has not been exclusively confined to mosques, however, and indeed it could be argued that the mosque actually plays a somewhat limited role in the articulation of Muslim identities, which are rather intertwined with everyday social practices. Furthermore, denominations such as the Ismaili and some Sufi orders have not referred to their places of worship as mosques or masjids, but rather as jamatkhanas in the case of Ismaili, or zawiyas for Sufis. These translate more as 'meeting house' than as mosque as such, which may suggest a more extensive function than primarily congregational prayer.

The mosque has, by virtue of its physical presence in the public sphere, come to symbolise Muslim presence in Britain. Indeed, it is the mosque that has provided the opportunity for the architectural expression of Muslim identities and aspirations. For this reason this book is about the architectural and social story of the mosque and of this building type as one of the more conspicuous products of Muslim material culture in Britain. This focus on the mosque does not intend to privilege it over the myriad other forms of ritual and social practice that constitute Muslim identity; such a broader study would not be within the scope of this book.

What is a mosque?

The Muslim world is spread out like a gigantic wheel with Mecca as the hub, with lines drawn from all the mosques in the world forming the spokes. These lines converge on a city and within that city on a point. The city is Mecca, and the point is the Ka'ba at its centre.[21]

The Ka'ba, a hollow cube of granite measuring approximately 11 metres by 13 metres and 13 metres high, is the physical and spiritual centre of the Muslim world, and the location towards which Muslims pray. The Quran describes how the Ka'ba was built by Abraham and his son Ishmael when they settled in the valley of Makkah (Mecca), and although it has been rebuilt many times during its history, its origins are pre-Islamic.

A mosque, in its most elemental form, is a wall or an axis marked on the floor (not necessarily even a building) to enable prayer, in congregation, towards the Ka'ba, which takes place five times each day: at sunrise, midday, afternoon, sunset and night. The mosque as a building, therefore, is simply a prayer hall in which rows of worshippers can stand behind an imam, face the Ka'ba, and perform the prayer (Fig 1.2). The other requirement of the mosque is for a place to make the ritual ablution, the wudu (Figs 1.3 and 1.4). Before the prayer Muslims are required to wash, in clean running water, their hands, mouth, nose, face, forearms and feet, and to wipe their hair, ears and the back of the neck. The place for ablution was traditionally provided for in various ways, perhaps most characteristically with fountains in entrance courtyards.

Beyond this simple programme, all other manifestations of the mosque are cultural and

Over the centuries, from the simplest of enclosures that was Muhammad's mosque, a series of architectural elements became indicators of the building type, namely the dome, minaret, pointed arch, mihrab (niche marking out the place for the imam) and minbar (pulpit). Each element had a historical origin and in some cases had been transferred from other religious architectures. As these elements have been replicated, in some form, in almost all British mosques, it is worth briefly considering some of these origins.

The Prophet's first mosque had no mihrab, as we recognise it today, but rather a block of stone on the floor indicating the direction of the Ka'ba. The first mihrab as we recognise it today can be traced to when the Prophet's Mosque was rebuilt in 707–709 CE, some 75 years after his death. Coptic masons were employed for the reconstruction, and they fashioned a niche similar to the Coptic churches that they usually built, the difference here being that what was a devotional element in the church had now become directional. From these origins, the mihrab became the focus for decoration and emphasis and evolved into a design motif that appeared throughout the Islamic fine arts (Fig 1.5).

Alongside the mihrab will be found the minbar, perhaps best translated as a pulpit (Fig 1.6). It is used by the imam to address the congregation at

Fig 1.2
A congregational prayer under way at the Darul-Imaan Hosseinieh Foundation in Bristol. [DP035272]

Fig 1.3 (right)
Men's ablution facilities at the Manchester Islamic Centre and Didsbury Mosque. The worshipper sits on a stool, faces the wall tap and washes his hands, mouth, nose, face, forearms and feet, and wipes his hair, ears and the back of the neck. [DP137673]

Fig 1.4 (far right)
A worshipper at Masjid-e-Noor-ul-Islam, Prospect Street, Bolton, carries out the ritual ablution (wudu) before performing the prayer. [DP143402]

symbolic. The first mosque was established by the Prophet Muhammad when he migrated with some followers from Makkah to Madinah (Medina) in 622 CE. It was a place of congregational prayer, administration and the Prophet's house. Arranged as a large open prayer area with living quarters along two perimeter walls, it demonstrated the architecture of the mosque as one of utmost simplicity and served as a point of departure for all subsequent Islamic religious building. Islam spread rapidly in the decades after Muhammad's death in 632 CE and to service this expansion garrison towns were built in regions that came under Muslim rule. It was within these military facilities that buildings for prayer were erected, and so the mosque as an architectural typology began its global journey – a journey that this book picks up as it reaches Britain.

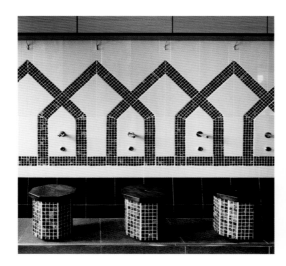

the Friday prayer, when the sermon is a mandatory part of the liturgy. The original minbar was a simple set of three steps formed from tamarisk wood in the Prophet's Mosque, where the Prophet would deliver his sermons from the top step. This evolved into a variety of stepped constructions, from the small to the large, where the imam delivers his sermon from a lower step, not occupying the top step out of respect for the absent Prophet.

Externally the mosque has come to be identified with the dome, minaret and arch. The earliest domes were small and placed over the mihrab to light the interior above the imam, before making the transition to the centre of the main worship space. The dome was used in the Middle East, well before the advent of Islam and the mosque, as a means for roofing large spaces as adequate timber was not available. When the Arabs built the Dome of the Rock at Jerusalem in the 7th century a wooden dome was used, which was the usual method for roofing churches at the time. Most domes, however, came to be built from stone or brick, and in most cases were covered with metal. Over the next centuries

Fig 1.5 (above)
The mihrab and minbar of Masjid e Tauheedul Islam in Blackburn. The mihrab and minbar can vary considerably in design across mosques, but will always have a place from which the imam will lead the prayer, and some steps from which sermons are given.
[DP143575]

Fig 1.6 (left)
A mosque can be made within the most rudimentary of spaces, such as this example at HM Prison Ford in West Sussex, where the minbar is simply a small set of wooden steps.
[AA95/04615]

Islamic buildings developed a wide variety of dome types, reflecting dynastic and religious distinctions as well as construction techniques (Figs 1.7 and 1.8).[22] The dome emerged as one of the key symbols of the mosque, and for Muslim immigrants to Britain it served as such a primary signifier that in numerous examples of British mosques domes have been incorporated into buildings even where they serve no purpose internally.

Alongside the dome, the minaret is the most famous element of mosque architecture and has acquired a symbolic significance, despite the fact that it is not a universal archetype across the historical and cultural sweep of Islamic architecture (Fig 1.9). Minarets were unknown at the time of Muhammad, and indeed the earliest mosques in Kufa and Basra, both built in 638 CE, a few years after the Prophet's death, were without minarets.[23] The first minarets are attributed to the

Fig 1.7
The dome of the purpose-built Leicester Central Mosque.
[DP137464]

Fig 1.8
The interior of the
dome of the Aziziye
Mosque in Stoke
Newington, London,
which has been
formed through the
conversion of a
former cinema hall.
[DP132044]

Fig 1.9
The minaret of the purpose-
built Sheffield Islamic
Centre and Madina Masjid.
[DP143338]

Great Mosque of Damascus, where there are three, the earliest being constructed on the northern wall opposite the Qibla (the direction of the Ka'ba). While its exact date of construction is unknown, it is generally dated as being from the early 9th century. The minaret takes the form of a square-plan tower built of stone, which is thought to derive from the traditional Syrian church tower of the Byzantine period.[24]

From this translation of Byzantine architecture to Islamic, the minaret embarked on a journey to North Africa and Spain and across the Muslim world, evolving regional styles as it did so. When the minaret came to Britain in the 1970s, the first examples at Regent's Park (*see* pp 133–47), Leytonstone (*see* pp 76–81) and Wimbledon (*see* pp 103–7) were variations of those found across Islam's architectural past.

The earliest arches in Muslim buildings were semicircular or round, and again derived from Roman or Byzantine sources. The pointed arch, which was to become characteristic of Islamic architecture, began to develop as the Muslim empire expanded from Arabia and was influenced by the world architecture that it encountered. Other types of arch that emerged were the horseshoe arch, which became common in Spain and North Africa and which had

its origins in pre-Islamic Syria, and the four-centred arch, which first appeared at Samarra.[25] Like other architectural elements, the arch has travelled to Britain as a common feature of mosques, and it is perhaps the most ubiquitous as it can be applied at a more modest scale to adapted buildings, such as within windows and doors (Fig 1.10).

Along with architectural elements, the other unifying characteristic of Islamic design is pattern-work and calligraphy (Fig 1.11). Such decoration has linked buildings and objects from all over the Islamic world for 1,300 years. What is referred to as Islamic art is not art in the European sense, but rather a form of decoration that is employed in both architecture and the applied arts. As figurative representations of God or other religious figures have always been strictly prohibited in Islam, Muslims instead developed a rich tradition of abstract, geometric and floral design. Throughout the history and geographic scope of Islamic art, similar and interlinked ideas, forms and designs have constantly recurred.[26] Islamic decoration was a medium through which artists continuously innovated and developed varieties of intricate and complex patternwork. One of the key features of this decorative practice is that it is conceptual art, where 'questions and answers are finely balanced', and where each pattern can expand and retract and can be symmetrically

Fig 1.10
The arched doorway of the
Jame Mosque, Leicester.
[DP137452]

reproduced: 'Each part of the design answers every other part and is capable of extension to infinity ... as a metaphor of eternity.'[27]

A crucial purpose of Islamic decoration has been to act as a screen to the structure of the building, which was often of a different material. The building is therefore veiled, or screened with an outer skin of decoration. It has been suggested that one function of the interlaced designs and the use of contrast as seen in much patternwork was to create the illusion of different planes, depth and three-dimensionality. Similarly, the use of different materials and textures – stucco, ceramic, stone, brick – contributes to this effect of substance. The patterned screen, therefore, is a key metaphor to convey the idea of the two-dimensional veil serving as a portal to a three-dimensional world beyond – the material world giving way to the transcendent. The surface, therefore, is a highly significant communicator in that it is the means through which this most essential message is conveyed.

Islamic decoration and calligraphy have been employed in Britain's mosques, and sit alongside the repertoire of elements described here. It is perhaps only due to financial limitations that the magnificent decorated façades and mihrabs of the Islamic world have not been paralleled. Gen-erally, decoration is used more selectively and through more achievable mediums such as paint and plastic, rather than tile or plasterwork.

The mosque throughout Islamic history has had a varied and diverse character, borrowing and adapting forms from local architectures and styles. As the Islamic city evolved, the mosque became just one of a series of typologies, including madrassas (religious schools), tombs and entrance gates, through which Muslim architectural culture would be expressed and explored. Within the mosque category itself a series of variations opened up, such as the large state mosque, the major landmark structure, the community centre complex and the small local mosque.[28] These categories included both mosques patronised by government, intended as landmarks that defined cities, and smaller mosques within neighbourhoods for everyday community use. Although Britain does have some landmark mosques, the majority are built as local community projects within Muslim populations. Some mosques built in this way, such as the East London Mosque, have since become landmarks. They may have grown from small beginnings into substantial facilities and thus have come to act as markers within neighbourhoods (Fig 1.12 and *see* pp 155–67).

Fig 1.11 (above)
The name of God is written in Arabic calligraphy over the doorway of the East London Mosque.
[DP147326]

Fig 1.12 (below)
This photograph of the East London Mosque complex c 2012 shows how it started as a single purpose-built mosque, with the dome and minarets. The London Muslim Centre, to its right, was added in 2004, and the Maryam Centre, the building under construction to its rear, was opened in 2013.
[26617/028 TQ3481/069]

Mosque numbers and locations

Britain's Muslim population covers a diverse range of denominations and ethnicities. Some religious groups are centrally organised, theologically as well as functionally, but most are not. A Muslim religious community can be led, politically and spiritually, by any person that the community sees fit, which means that mosques can be created and implemented anywhere with the most rudimentary of resources. Therefore most mosques are individual and independent community projects, and they are not tied together through any umbrella organisation or religious hierarchy. This 'portability' has allowed mosques to emerge organically and unrecorded in the numerous clusters of Muslim populations in Britain's towns and cities.

Consequently, there is no official central database that accurately lists all mosques in Britain and no chronology of mosque establishment. Perhaps the most substantial attempt at a historiography was that by Ceri Peach and Richard Gale, who led a team of academics in 2003 and listed mosques, gurdwaras and temples in Britain;[29] some were dated and all were visited. The key finding of the report was that in 1961, when Britain's Muslim population was estimated at 50,000, there were seven mosques. These numbers rose rapidly over the next 40 years, so that by 2001 the Muslim population stood at over 1.5 million and the number of mosques at 614.

There is no universal requirement for religious sites to register with the General Register Office and be included on the Register of Places of Worship and therefore this cannot be considered an accurate record of all the places of worship that actually exist. So the 614 mosques registered by 2001 was probably an underestimate, considering that the number of mosques today is thought to be around 1,500.[30] Nevertheless, the pattern demonstrated in the 2003 study offers valid insights into the spread and growth of mosques in Britain.

While some registers of mosques do exist, compiled by Muslim social organisations such as the Muslim Council of Britain or by Muslim directory services, these can very quickly become out of date because of the continuously changing mosque landscape, where new mosques are being formed and existing or temporary mosques are relocating to larger sites. Without any formal registration process, it is simply not possible to know definitively how many mosques exist in Britain at any one time.

Methodology for the English Heritage/Historic England research project

Having reviewed the available databases as part of the English Heritage/Historic England research project that resulted in this publication,[31] we found the most reliable to be the one compiled by the Muslims in Britain (MIB) website (www.muslimsinbritain.org). This is the only database where the compiler has visited a significant number of the mosques recorded, and where there is a process to continuously check the status of mosques on the list. According to the MIB database, by 2013 there were 1,577 mosques in the UK, a figure that should be taken as approximate considering the nature of the data collection.

From the listings of over 1,500 mosques on the MIB database, we filtered out the defunct mosques, and the prayer rooms (for example in hospitals), to leave a sample of around 1,300. Then we obtained aerial images of each of these mosques, which were used to identify whether a mosque was purpose-built or a conversion. This process offered a high degree of accuracy but was not watertight as some mosques may be conversions but altered to such an extent that they appear as purpose-built. However, these cases are rare and the results can be taken as accurate enough to offer a representative breakdown of the proportion of converted mosques compared to those that are purpose-built. The process showed that some 16 per cent of mosques in Britain were purpose-built, totalling approximately 200, with the remainder having been formed through the conversion of existing buildings (Fig 1.13).

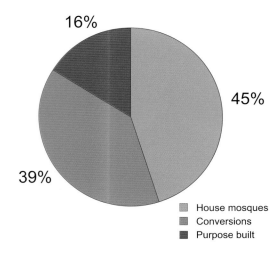

Fig 1.13
Approximate proportion of mosques by type in Britain in 2010.
[Source: English Heritage/ Historic England research project sample of around 1,300 mosques listed on the Muslims in Britain database]

Among the converted mosques, there are two broad types: the house conversion and the conversion of any other (non-domestic) building type. It is important to identify and study the house-mosque conversion separately from non-domestic conversions because the use of domestic space for religious worship is an archetypal practice. From the earliest Christian worship carried out in Roman houses to the use of houses for prayer meetings by English Nonconformist Christians from the 17th to the 19th centuries and Jewish communities in the 20th century, the idea of the house as a refuge where a minority religious group might find a safe space to practise collective worship crosses faiths and history.

The house as mosque, then, is both a continuation of this tradition and one of the earliest types of mosque formed by new Muslim communities as they settled and initiated social infrastructures. It therefore requires distinction as an important mosque type in itself, so that the particularity and intimacy of adapting domestic space to religious space can be observed.

Exploring mosque typologies

House-mosque conversions have usually undergone various degrees of internal and sometimes external adaptation, ranging in scale and extent. Non-domestic conversions have been more diverse and can encompass former warehouses, banks, public houses and churches. The extent of building work in converting buildings varies widely; some conversions may require minimal alteration to enable the building to function as a mosque, while others may involve extending, cladding and adding religious symbolism to the extent that the original building can be difficult to discern. The purpose-built mosque is one that has been built from the ground as a new mosque. It can be on a completely new site, or in some cases is the replacement of a pre-existing mosque that had been formed through a conversion. There can be further subdivision of purpose-built mosques between those that are large, landmark-type buildings and those that are designed to emplace themselves within an urban landscape.

House mosque

The conversion of the house is usually rudimentary (Fig 1.14), the emphasis being on the creation of as much open floor space as possible to accommodate the maximum number of worshippers in as unified a space as possible. Islamic symbolism will usually be limited to signage and the mihrab and minbar, which could be a simple timber structure of a few steps, with a specific prayer mat for the imam. The other main area of alteration would be the ablution facility, which could be just the extension of the existing domestic WC or bathroom facilities.

The house mosque was traditionally the first type of mosque that a Muslim community established when settling in a new urban area. Planning permission would have been required for this change of use, but in the early days might not always have been obtained due to a lack of awareness of the planning system. Funds would be collected through donations from within the community and suitable premises sourced. First, houses were the easiest properties for new immigrants to acquire when they might not be familiar with methods of commercial or other property acquisition. Second, houses would seem a natural and sensible choice for a potential mosque, having a number of rooms readily divisible into male and female spaces as well as classrooms for children's instruction, and with immediately usable washing and kitchen facilities along with the potential to be extended.

Fig 1.14
The Shahkamal Jamae Masjid in Beeston, Leeds, is an example of how a mosque can be created through the simple conversion of a house. [DP029179]

available for sale. Where a mosque grows organically into adjacent land and houses, such expansion may be combined with additions and alterations designed to denote the building's 'Islamicity'. In such cases an eclectic mix of Islamic symbolism and a local suburban vernacular can emerge. Such hybridity can also happen where the house mosque does not necessarily expand into adjacent houses or land, but where symbolic additions are applied to the existing dwelling.

If the house cannot be extended any further and is still insufficient, the mosque committee may decide to find larger premises within the locale that can accommodate demand. The next stage in the evolution of the mosque will then be to move from the house to a larger, non-domestic building that can again be converted into a mosque, or it might be to acquire a building or site that can be demolished and redeveloped into a purpose-built mosque. The house mosque, therefore, has served as the stepping stone to larger premises – usually nearby so as to remain locally relevant – to accommodate the growing community.

Fig 1.15 (above)
An improvised prayer hall created by erecting a marquee in the grounds of the Shahporan Mosque in East London, while building work was in progress.
[DP147337]

Fig 1.16 (below)
The Hanfia Mosque in Lockwood, Huddersfield, is a 2002 conversion of a former Methodist church dating from 1864.
[DP143504]

Indeed, the first mosques established in Liverpool and Cardiff between 1887 and 1946 were converted houses, and houses were also the starting point for mosques after the advent of post-war mass Muslim immigration to Britain.

As the Muslim population in an area grows, houses very quickly become too small to accommodate all the worshippers. They are extended first, perhaps, in an ad hoc manner with makeshift canopies and enclosures (Fig 1.15), and then more formally through the erection of permanent structures. In some cases, a mosque will start out as a single house and then be extended into an adjacent house or houses as they become

Non-domestic conversion

Non-domestic conversions differ from house mosques in that they can vary in status from the small local centre, which might have been the first mosque that a Muslim community established, to the larger, more established mosque that serves as a socio-religious hub for a wider Muslim community within a locale. These conversions also differ from house mosques in that they can be the second-tier mosque that a community establishes, perhaps having started from a small house mosque that has subsequently been outgrown. The conversion, therefore, can serve as the 'final destination' mosque for a given Muslim community and in this way can take on the same status as a purpose-built mosque, whereas a house mosque will generally be a stepping stone unless a community is particularly small and the house mosque fully serves its more limited needs.

Conversions can vary widely in their character according to the wide variety of buildings that serve as their starting point. In many cases, a former religious building has been adapted – usually a church or community hall (Fig 1.16). In other cases, buildings with large halls or floor areas are considered suitable for conversion into mosques, so a number of cinemas, public houses, retail premises and schools are also found as mosque conversions.

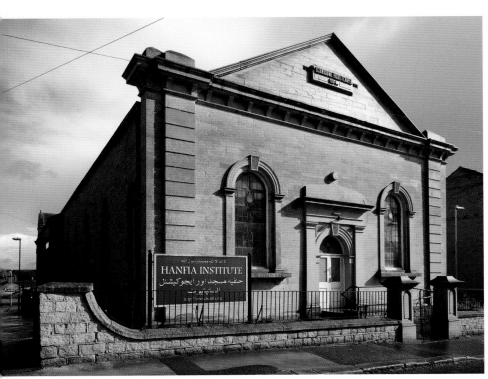

HANFIA INSTITUTE

The other main difference between such conversions and house mosques is that they offer greater opportunity for adaptation and alteration, and therefore often display architectural interventions of a wider variety and scale. As with the house mosque, the building has to accommodate the orientation of the prayer lines towards the Qibla, so while the main prayer hall must be fitted within the floor plan of the existing building, the prayer lines may run diagonally across it (Figs 1.17 and 1.18). Further to this, a mihrab is added, along with degrees of signage such as clocks showing prayer times, calligraphy, tilework, painted patternwork and perhaps doors and windows decorated with applied arches.

In some cases it becomes necessary for the converted mosque to be extended to provide more prayer space. However, this seems to happen less in conversions than in house mosques, usually because the conversion takes larger, more suitable premises at the outset. The conversion is often adapted externally with symbolic features to identify it as a mosque and as Muslim space. In these cases the adaptation can be more extensive and fundamental than with house mosques, but it similarly offers a greater or lesser degree of architectural hybridity. Where buildings to be converted are of heritage value, and may be listed, a particular engagement with the statutory authorities will take place that will inform the character of any architectural intervention and symbolic alteration.

Purpose-built

The purpose-built mosque is often the culmination of a Muslim community's mosque-development trajectory, a journey that generally starts with a house mosque or converted building that is eventually found to be insufficient to cater for the needs of a growing Muslim population and is then replaced with a larger, purpose-built facility. The purpose-built mosque is hardly ever the first mosque that a community initiates, a fact that serves to emphasise the overwhelmingly iterative and grass-roots nature of British mosque establishment.

Fig 1.17
The prayer hall of the Taiyabah Mosque in Bolton, in a converted 19th-century Sunday-school building. The direction of prayer towards the Qibla has been fitted into the hall obliquely. [DP143409]

Fig 1.18
The angled prayer lines in the Islamic Centre of England, in Maida Vale, London, a mosque formed through the conversion of a former cinema hall. [DP132090]

The purpose-built mosque has therefore presented an opportunity for already established and emerging Muslim communities to mark out spaces for religious and community endeavour, with a greater visual presence and sense of permanence than was ever achieved through house mosques or conversions, as well as introducing a new architectural vocabulary and building typology to Britain. The purpose-built mosque has altered both the urban and the cultural landscape of late 20th-century Britain, and many towns are now marked with prominent visual symbols of Britain's Muslim presence. However, not all purpose-built mosques serve as significant symbolic structures, and a distinction can be made between those that stand as landmarks, and those that are more physically emplaced within the existing urban landscape (Figs 1.19 and 1.20).

The route from house mosque to conversion and/or purpose-built mosque is the generic

Fig 1.20
*Noor-ul-Uloom Mosque,
Small Heath, Birmingham,
a purpose-built mosque
that is integrated with the
scale of its surroundings.*
[DP137713]

mosque story, a process that is organic and incremental, and often takes decades. This is not to say, however, that all mosques go through this process and evolve from house to purpose-built centre. Many mosques today will be at various stages of this process, with fundraising efforts and building proposals an almost permanent fixture on the mosque noticeboard. Most mosques will probably remain as house mosques or non-domestic conversions, albeit with ongoing extensions and adaptations, and will not become purpose-built mosques. However, the generic story holds true in that practically every purpose-built mosque in the country started as a smaller centre, either a house or other conversion, and that no Muslim community has built a purpose-built mosque as its first establishment.

Identifying patterns from this research project

The analysis of the mosques included in this research project suggests that in some towns the percentage of purpose-built mosques is higher than the national average, sometimes considerably (Fig 1.21). Interestingly, in terms of the geographic spread of these towns, they fall in the northern regions of Lancashire and Yorkshire. For example, Dewsbury, Leeds, Blackburn, Preston and Rochdale all have over 29 per cent purpose-built mosques, a figure that rises to 40 per cent for Rochdale. Indeed, Sheffield is the only northern town that has a lower than average percentage of purpose-built mosques; all other northern towns are higher than, or in the case of Manchester at, the national average of 16 per cent. As might be expected, towns with high percentages of purpose-built mosques also have a Muslim population higher than the national average, ranging from Leeds at 3 per cent Muslim to Blackburn which is almost 20 per cent Muslim. Overlaying Muslim population demographics with mosque numbers illustrates the density of mosques in relation to the density of Muslim populations. The results of this analysis suggest that northern towns such as Blackburn, Burnley and Preston have the highest number of mosques per head of Muslim population, with London having the lowest. These figures perhaps reflect the fact that London's Muslim populations are more spread out, and may congregate at fewer, larger mosques, whereas smaller towns have denser concentrations of Muslim

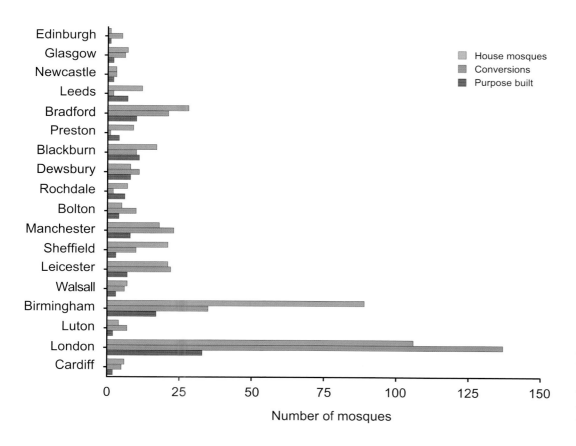

Fig 1.21
Comparison of mosque types across key towns and cities included in the English Heritage/Historic England research project.

populations, with more mosques serving very local congregations (*see* Appendix 2).

There are a range of social and geographic factors behind all of these statistics, which are not within the scope of study of this book and have only been speculated on here to introduce the overlapping demographic discourses behind mosque-making. This research suggests links between mosque establishment and cultural origin, socio-economics, settlement patterns and social histories. For example, a high concentration of Muslim residents in Lancashire towns may explain the high number of mosques, but it doesn't necessarily explain why a higher than average proportion of these are purpose built. Census results show that most Muslims in these northern towns are of Indian origin, and most of them originate from the Indian state of Gujarat. This is an unusual statistic in relation to other towns with high Muslim populations, such as Birmingham or Manchester, where the Muslim populations originate predominately from Pakistan, and where the proportion of purpose-built mosques is around the national average of 16 per cent.

In conversation about these characteristics, one local Gujarati Muslim respondent suggested that the Gujarati community was highly organised as a self-supporting social network, and that the establishment of mosques and community facilities was an important collective activity towards which resources were readily channelled within a highly devout community. It may also be relevant that the Lancashire towns faced a period of de-industrialisation when the cotton mills closed, resulting in the availability of redundant sites and buildings which could be demolished and replaced with religious facilities.

This short example shows that there are a series of overlapping factors behind the establishment of mosques in particular locations. This book does not unpack these layers in detail, but it does situate the mosque within a broader set of social and historical considerations.

Mosque geographies

To understand the geographic spread of mosques across the country, as part of this research project we chose three areas from among the areas with the highest density of Muslim population (Fig 1.22). A series of maps was produced, showing mosque locations in the key urban locations of Birmingham and the parts of the West

Midlands which lie to the west of the city; parts of southern Lancashire and the northern part of Greater Manchester; and Greater London. These maps were then overlaid with two other levels of social data: the density of the Muslim population as recorded in the census of 2011,[32] and the levels of social deprivation as recorded in the Indices of Deprivation for 2015.[33] These maps indicate how mosque locations may relate to certain sets of social criteria, from demographics to poverty. However, no distinction is made in these maps as to whether they are conversions or purpose-built. (The maps are reproduced in Appendix 2.)

The maps show that mosques are concentrated in areas of high Muslim population density, which are themselves concentrated mostly in inner-city areas where there are high levels of social deprivation. Post-war Muslim immigrants settled in such areas as they constituted a labour class working in industries, which were then often located in inner cities. The mosques they established are embedded within and serve very local communities, and the resulting pattern of mosque geographies is a result of this social and economic process.

Mosque chronology

Because of the decentralised nature of mosques, and there being no collective record of when each was established, it is not possible to compile a reliable chronology to show the rate of mosque growth. The closest attempt so far is Peach and Gale's 2003 research,[34] which proves useful to indicate a trend even though the database probably did not cover all mosques at the time. Therefore, a comprehensive chronology of mosques in Britain does not exist, and it is beyond the scope of this book to establish one.

However, what this book does do is attempt a chronology of purpose-built mosques from which a broader pattern of mosque establishment for all types can be inferred. There are two reasons to concentrate on purpose-built mosques. First, more data are available in the form of planning records and dates of approval, and this enables a date to be ascribed to the building. (Although it is often the case that the mosque is actually built some years after the date of planning permission, so this may not be an exact date, but it places the building within a period of a few years.) Second, purpose-built mosques offer a new visual language which can be

Fig 1.22 (opposite) Map of England, Scotland and Wales showing the density of the Muslim population as recorded in the 2011 Census.

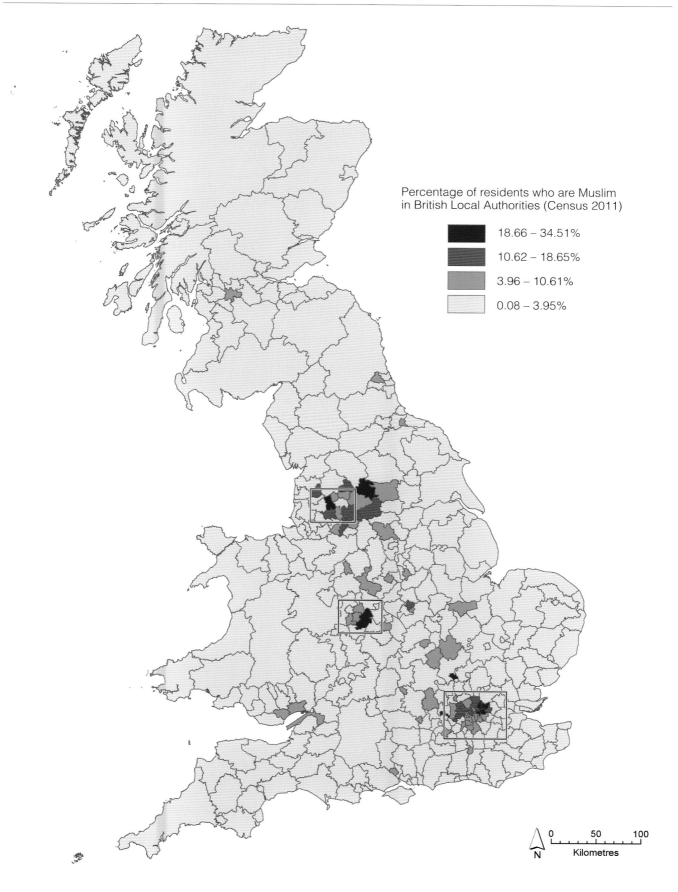

Percentage of residents who are Muslim
in British Local Authorities (Census 2011)

18.66 – 34.51%

10.62 – 18.65%

3.96 – 10.61%

0.08 – 3.95%

0   50   100
Kilometres

interpreted and from which narratives of British Muslim architecture can be constructed. This architectural story of the mosque, therefore, is based on purpose-built examples, with other types of converted building then related to this narrative.

The results of this analysis concur with statistics in Peach and Gale's study, showing that the number of purpose-built mosques grew rapidly from 1980 to 2000. What is interesting, however, is that the rate of building of purpose-built mosques declined between 2000 and 2010 from its peak in the previous decade. If these data are correct, it might suggest that mosques have reached saturation point, and that Britain's Muslim communities have, in essence, successfully established a religious and social structure through the mosque that is serving social and religious needs. However, Britain's Muslim population is known to be growing still. Perhaps it means that mosque planning permissions are more difficult to obtain than in previous decades, and that this has stifled mosque building. Or it could mean that although fewer mosques are being built, they are larger than their predecessors, so the growing Muslim population continues to have its religious needs met through a type of mosque infrastructure different from that of the previous decades. This is speculation and an area not within the scope of this study. Suffice it to say that overall, almost 90 per cent of purpose-built mosques in Britain have been built since 1980 (Fig 1.23).

This book is not intended to be a categorical survey setting out to cover as many of Britain's 1,500 or so mosques as possible. Instead, a selection has been made of mosques that are either key buildings in the historical narrative, or

are particularly interesting as examples of either converted or purpose-built mosques. Some buildings are discussed in more detail than others, which represents partly their significance and also the data that are available on a particular building. There are, of course, many interesting mosques that have not been included, but it is intended that the selection offered is diverse enough to provide a sense of the scope and character of mosques in Britain, from the simple adapted house, to other converted buildings, to the landmark new mosque.

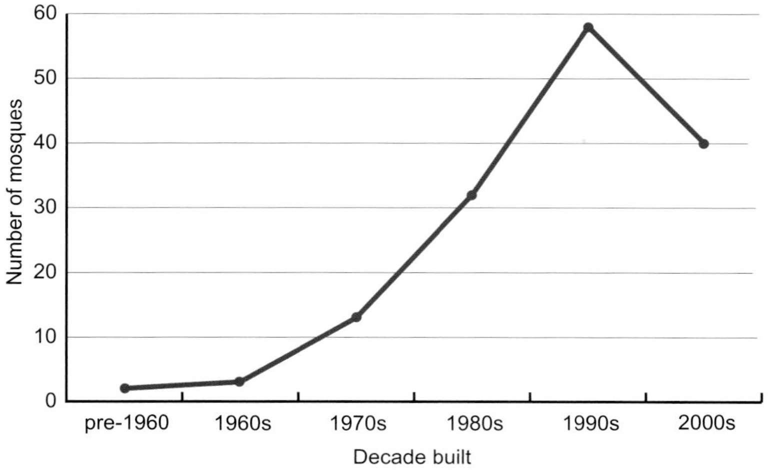

Telling the story of the British mosque

The architectural history of the mosque in Britain is told primarily through purpose-built examples. Although conversions hold as much interest and tell valuable stories in themselves, it is in the purpose-built mosques that a fuller expression of Muslim material culture can be explored, and where the emergence and evolution of architectural approaches can be observed over 130 years of mosque building.

As well as representing the diversity of types of mosque in the country, these case studies also present a cross-section of Muslim communities in Britain, and so illustrate a variety of social histories and cultural approaches.

Chapter 2 considers the early period of mosque building, from the first house mosque in Liverpool, followed by the first purpose-built mosque at Woking towards the end of the 19th century, through to two mosques in Cardiff in the 20th century. These examples are seen to constitute the first period of mosque building, from Orientalist expressions in keeping with late Victorian tastes, to the post-war modernist explorations of Cardiff, where new architectural languages were being forged.

Chapter 3 picks up from the decolonisation and Partition of India, the consequent immigration of larger numbers of Muslims from the Indian subcontinent to Britain from the 1960s, and the mosques that they built. The chapter concentrates on the formation of mosques through conversions of houses and other buildings, and covers the period from the first post-Partition house conversions from the late 1950s through to later examples in the 1970s to 1990s.

Chapter 4 looks at mosques that were being newly built at a grass-roots level from the 1970s onwards by local Muslim communities, from the

Fig 1.23
Number of purpose-built mosques per decade up to 2010.
[Source: Data taken from the author's sample of the 148 purpose-built mosques from the English Heritage/ Historic England research project which could be dated.]

London suburbs to small towns and cities. These buildings were locally resourced and meeting local needs, and they represent Muslim identities through architectures that are the direct expression of the communities that have made and used them.

Chapter 5 considers a different but concurrent development phase in the history of the mosque, looking at three landmark projects through the 1970s and 1980s that were of national and international significance, and which introduced Islamic architecture as a new discourse in Britain. Here we also see the role of the mosque within the building of Muslim social institutions of significant regional and national importance.

Chapter 6 marks a new phase of mosque building. Starting in the 1990s and continuing to the present day, a shift in the architectural outlook of the mosque is perceived and explored. Here the mosque becomes a much more literal translation of historical Islamic architectural tropes, more confident and forthright in its visual language and identity.

Chapter 7 considers mosques that have not yet been built but are planned or have remained as conceived projects, as well as others that have been built and have instigated a shift in the narrative of the mosque. These examples introduce a series of emerging themes around which the mosque is conceived. This final set of proposals suggests the direction mosques may be heading in and their future role in Muslim and wider communities.

The final chapter summarises the material presented, and introduces a series of architectural and social debates through which the mosque in Britain, and its social and architectural meaning, is explored.

In Appendix 1 examples of the different mosque types are presented and briefly described. These additional examples are intended to provide a broader picture of the mosque types that have been discussed in detail through the chapters.

Appendix 2 presents the maps described earlier in this chapter (*see* p 16), showing mosque locations in three areas of the country, overlaid with the density of the Muslim population and levels of social deprivation.

2

The first mosques

The handful of mosques in Britain before the 1960s were established by the first settled Muslim communities, which were to be found in port locations such as Cardiff, Liverpool, South Shields and east London. These communities were primarily Yemeni or Bengali ship-workers (or lascars), who had started to settle in the ports they sailed to. The Yemeni Muslim communities created their own religious network from Cardiff, through the Midlands, to South Shields. There was also a significant White British convert Muslim presence in these early years, and this influence was felt both in the establishment of the first mosques and in the organisation of the emerging Muslim institutions. Added to this were members of the Ahmadiyya[1] movement, which was founded in India in 1889, who first revived a pre-existing mosque in Woking before going on to build London's first purpose-built mosque in the 1920s – the Fazl Mosque in south London (*see* pp 35–43).

These mosques and Muslim communities before World War II were sparse and in differing ways interconnected. The subsequent chapters of this book describe how this changed after the war, when decolonisation and conflict, combined with Britain's labour shortage, galvanised mass migrations from former colonies, including from South Asia (namely India, Pakistan and Bangladesh). In the years following the 1947 Partition of India, Britain's Muslim demographic was transformed by migration and mosque building proliferated. The mosques that were initiated and built pre-Partition constitute the first phase of the story of Britain's Muslim architecture.

Case studies

1 Liverpool Muslim Institute, Brougham Terrace, West Derby Road, Liverpool, 1889
2 Shah Jahan Mosque, Oriental Road, Woking, 1889
3 Fazl Mosque (London Mosque), Gressenhall Road, Southfields, London, 1926
4 Cardiff: mid-century evolutions, 1943–1969 (including Noor-el-Islam Mosque, 1947, and South Wales Islamic Centre, 1969)

1 Liverpool Muslim Institute, Brougham Terrace, West Derby Road, Liverpool, 1889

The first recorded mosque in Britain was established in a house at 8 Brougham Terrace in Liverpool in 1889. It was not founded, as might be expected, by Muslim immigrants but rather by a group of 20 English converts to Islam. They were led by an eminent local lawyer, Abdullah William Quilliam (Fig 2.2). Born in 1856 to Wesleyan Methodist parents, he converted to Islam in 1887 after travelling through Morocco. On returning to England, Guilliam formed the Liverpool Muslim Institute in July 1887; numbering three members, they would meet in a rented

Fig 2.1 (opposite) The prayer hall in the original building of the Shah Jahan Mosque, Woking. [AA031171]

Fig 2.2 Portrait of Abdullah William Quilliam. [Courtesy of Liverpool Record Office, Liverpool Libraries]

Consequently, the group moved to a hand-some Georgian terraced house at 8 Brougham Terrace in 1889, with capacity for 100 worshippers, and established the Liverpool Muslim Institute there. With international donations, including one of £2,500 from the Emir of Afghanistan, in 1895 the house mosque was internally refurbished and the two adjacent houses at Nos 9 and 10 purchased (Fig 2.3). As the mosque was formed through the conversion of a terraced house, there was limited scope for the external application of an Islamic visual identity and the external expression of its Muslim character was limited to the use of the first-floor window, from which the call to prayer was made. Instead, the mosque was internally redesigned in a style which fused traditional Moroccan and Victorian decoration (Fig 2.4), and a large hall was built in the rear garden to serve as the main prayer hall (Figs 2.5 and 2.6).[5] The adjacent houses were used as an orphanage, a boarding school and a printing press, where Quilliam printed numerous pamphlets as well as both a weekly and a monthly journal.

Over the next two decades a Muslim community arose around Quilliam and his mosque, and through that community's efforts there emerged the first British Muslim institutions, and indeed the presence of Islam in the social and political

Fig 2.3
Front elevation of 8, 9 and 10 Brougham Terrace, which were converted by Abdullah Quilliam to serve as the Liverpool Muslim Institute in 1889.
[Author]

room in Liverpool's Mount Vernon Terrace. The little room was accessed up a 'flight of stairs in a side street'.[2] This fledgling community faced hostility, and one member recounts how neighbours would 'pelt them with stones, eggs and garbage, while shouting abuse',[3] and there was pressure from the landlady at Mount Vernon, who 'vigorously objected to a group of people who met and denied the Crucifixion on her premises'.[4]

Fig 2.4
The interior of the house mosque on Brougham Terrace after its remodelling, c 1895.
[Courtesy of Liverpool Record Office, Liverpool Libraries]

life of Britain.[6] The fame of the Liverpool Muslim Institute spread, generating widespread Muslim interest, and Quilliam was accorded the title of Sheikh-ul-Islam of the British Isles by the Ottoman Caliph – that is to say, he was made his representative in the UK.[7] In his capacity as Sheikh-ul-Islam, Quilliam made a number of diplomatic trips to Muslim countries and was known across the Muslim world.[8]

The significance of this community should not be underestimated. Liverpool was a global port city, central to the British Empire and to the slave trade. The British Empire had more Muslim subjects than Christian at this time, and with the dismantling of the Ottoman Empire and reshaping of the Middle East that followed World War I, British Muslim politics and identity were in a transformative state as soon as they emerged.

Buoyed by the growing success of the Liverpool Muslim Institute and the increasing number of converts to Islam (said to have reached 150) through his proselytising, Quilliam developed plans for a purpose-built 'cathedral mosque' in the city. An 1890s drawing of the imagined building shows a three-storey structure in North African style, complete with dome, short minaret and stepped battlements (Fig 2.7).[9] It was intended to accommodate 1,500 worshippers, included a women's gallery and printing works, and was estimated to cost £6,000. The mosque,

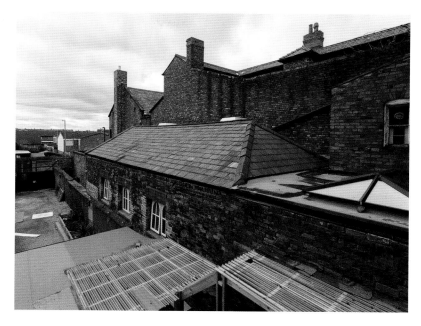

if realised, would have been the second purpose-built mosque in the country after Woking (*see* pp 26–35). Although it never came to fruition, the drawings show how Quilliam's architectural inspiration was drawn from the imposing Muslim architecture of North Africa, perhaps a remnant of his travels in Morocco.

The Liverpool Muslim Institute continued to operate from Brougham Terrace for 20 years,

Fig 2.5
The rear of the Liverpool Muslim Institute (now known as the Abdullah Quilliam Mosque), looking over the single-storey prayer hall (to the rear of No 8) that was built by Quilliam after he acquired the houses.
[Author]

Fig 2.6
The main prayer hall, which was built as a rear extension to 8 Brougham Terrace. It was refurbished and reopened in 2014.
[Author]

Fig 2.7
Quilliam's idea for a new 'cathedral mosque' for Liverpool, which was never built.
[Courtesy of Liverpool Record Office, Liverpool Libraries]

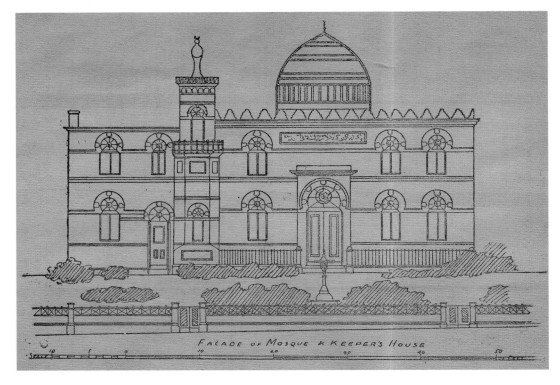

FACADE OF MOSQUE & KEEPER'S HOUSE

with a growing and established congregation of largely convert English Muslims. In 1908, Abdullah Quilliam left the city with his eldest son, Robert Ahmed, for travels in Turkey. The Institute did not survive Quilliam's departure. When he left he had given power of attorney on his properties, including the mosque and his business, to his son Bilal. Bilal did not share his father's sense of mission and quickly disposed of the properties, including the mosque, selling all three houses to Liverpool City Council and leaving the congregation without a base. Some members migrated to join the Muslim community in the newly revived Woking Mosque.

On returning to the UK several years later, Quilliam settled in his native Isle of Man, establishing links with the English Muslims of Woking, alongside some of his Liverpool congregation. He was never to return to Liverpool. He died in 1932 and was buried in Woking's Brookwood Cemetery, which incorporated the first Muslim burial ground in Britain.

Liverpool City Council converted the Brougham Terrace houses into its register office for births, deaths and marriages, and carried out internal refurbishments which meant the removal of the Islamic decoration. The prayer hall, which occupied the garden of No 8, was used as the archive store and was lined with thick concrete walls for fire and theft protection.

Throughout the building's life as the register office, this archive store was referred to by council staff as 'the little mosque', so accidentally ensuring that its heritage was never lost. This heritage was further preserved through the English Heritage listing of the three houses in 1985, which described them as a notable example of an early 19th-century terrace, as well as the 'location for what is believed to be England's first mosque ... an example of Liverpool's capacity to embrace different cultural and faith communities, and ... further historical evidence of the social and cultural diversity and tolerance which developed as a consequence of the city's function as an internationally significant seaport and trading centre'.[10]

Restoration

Towards the end of the 20th century, as interest in Britain's early Islamic history was rekindling, a local group of Liverpool Muslims formed the Abdullah Quilliam Society (AQS) with an ambition to restore the Brougham Terrace houses to the mosque and cultural centre of Quilliam's vision. In 2000 the city council vacated the premises as the terraced houses were no longer suitable for council offices. The AQS successfully negotiated a temporary lease with the council for the three houses, on the understanding that they would

Fig 2.8 (left)
The rear of the Liverpool Muslim Institute (now known as the Abdullah Quilliam Mosque) in 2016. The ground floor of No 8, to the left, has been restored and reopened as a mosque. The remainder of the building is vacant, with refurbishment works progressing incrementally. The cream-coloured building, on the right in the foreground, is a recently constructed classroom block for children's after-school religious education. [Author]

Fig 2.9 (below left)
The main prayer hall, looking towards the rear. The arched openings were restored in 2014 to replicate Quilliam's original design. [Author]

Fig 2.9 (below)
The restored arched openings to the rear of the main prayer hall. On the left, the corridor leads to the main entrance door; on the right is a glazed light well between the original house and the prayer hall. [Author]

be restored to be a mosque and a heritage centre for British Islam. Such a sizeable and ambitious project was, however, not easy to achieve, and without adequate funds being raised, the houses fell into disrepair and remained vacant.

Eventually, through the continuous efforts of the AQS, a benefactor came forward with a donation large enough to enable the ground floor of No 8 to be refurbished and brought back into use. This involved the restoration of the prayer hall to its original form, along with the reconstruction of the arches and Islamic decoration (Figs 2.8–2.10). The mosque and ground floor of No 8 formally reopened on the first day of the Muslim fasting month of Ramadan in 2014, and congregational prayers were held for the first time in over 100 years. With the re-establishment of the mosque, now known as the Abdullah Quilliam Mosque, the campaign to bring the complete terrace back into use and to create a centre for Muslim heritage in Britain continues.

Conclusion

The Liverpool Muslim Institute, as the first mosque organisation in Britain, shows how religious practice has been entwined with social endeavour from the start of Muslim institution making. It also shows how the origins of the mosque in Britain lie in the conversion and adaptation of existing buildings, and the layering of a new function over a previous one. The Institute had high ambitions and Quilliam was an effective ambassador for Islam in Britain and these are some of the reasons that the mosque at Brougham Terrace occupies a significant place in the British Muslim imagination. It is of huge importance, therefore, that the building has been returned to use as a mosque, with ongoing plans for its eventual rehabilitation.

2 Shah Jahan Mosque, Oriental Road, Woking, 1889

We none of us will ever quite recover from Kipling and the East seen through his eyes … In the centre of a very sedate, very English, very residential area, hidden partially among the leaves, rises the ornate dome of an eastern mosque.[11]

Thirty miles south-west of central London lies Woking, a comfortable town in the heart of the Surrey commuter belt. A short walk from the main railway station along a road of suburban villas, tellingly named Oriental Road, is a hard-surfaced clearing bordered by trees. In the clearing lies an oval-shaped island of grass, some 30 metres across, ringed with a low hedge. In the middle of the garden, slightly askew as it is oriented towards Makkah, stands an almost cubic structure, topped with an onion-shaped green dome and fronted by an elegant and expressive façade. This is the Woking Mosque, the first purpose-built mosque in northern Europe. Its history encapsulates colourful and eccentric aspects of late Victorian England, of empire, colony and 'going native' (Fig 2.11).

Woking and the Orientalist flourish

In his survey of the buildings of England, Nikolaus Pevsner described the Woking Mosque as:

an extraordinarily dignified little building, especially by comparison with other mock-Oriental buildings of the same date … In an Indian rather than Arabic style: onion dome on delicate rubble walls, with a decorative

Fig 2.11
The Shah Jahan Mosque, Woking, was commissioned by Dr Gottlieb Leitner, designed by William Isaac Chambers and completed in 1889.
[AA031167]

three-part frontpiece in blue and gold, as pretty as the Brighton Pavilion. The inside is a well thought-out square with a dome on squinches, three ogee niches in each wall and a sober panelled apse and preaching box.[12]

The mosque at Woking was spearheaded and commissioned by Dr Gottlieb Wilhelm Leitner, a Hungarian Jewish linguist who spent most of his working life from 1864 as Principal of Government College, Lahore, then part of British India. Leitner's ambition was to establish an educational institution in Europe which would be a centre for the culture and history of India and the Islamic world. In 1880 the site of the Royal Dramatic College in Woking became available. Leitner purchased it and proceeded to reuse the premises to set up his Oriental Institute. The enduring legacy of the institute is the mosque, which was funded by the female ruler of the Indian princely state of Bhopal, the Sultan Shah Jahan Begum, after whom the mosque was eventually named. Alongside the mosque, a two-storey building was constructed as accommodation for the imam and as a place to hold community functions and meetings. This building was named the Sir Salar Jang Memorial Hall, after the then Prime Minister of the State

of Hyderabad in central India (Fig 2.12). With two bays flanking a recessed central façade and a first-floor balcony, the building has the air of a colonial villa enhanced by Mughal-styled window and door arches, stone surrounds, fretwork and decoration.

The mosque was designed by William Isaac Chambers and completed in 1889. Chambers was an English architect who moved to Dublin in 1878 with his family and opened a practice there. In 1882 he designed a villa for himself in Dublin, which was an ornate version of the Queen Anne style, popular at the time. By the mid-1880s he had sold his Dublin business and was back in England, having set himself up in Woking. It is likely that he won the commission for Leitner's mosque because he was both a local architect and had a suitably expressive architectural style. This style had become evident through the 'stream of exuberant designs for buildings in both countries',[13] which he published in *The Irish Builder* magazine through the 1880s. It is almost certain that Chambers was aware of the work of British architects and engineers in India who were designing in an expressive language generally called Indo-Saracenic or 'Orientalist', which was widespread by the 1880s and which must have served as a

Fig 2.12
The Sir Salar Jang Memorial Hall, built alongside the Shah Jahan Mosque in 1889.
[FF000464]

conceptual reference for his approach to Leitner's commission.[14]

With Chambers' penchant for architectural flamboyance, his mosque liberally embraces Mughal architecture, the style developed by the rulers of much of South Asia from the 16th to the 18th centuries. Earlier Mughal buildings in and around Delhi display a certain classical rigour and formality. This evolved in later Mughal buildings further south around the Deccan region of India into a more expressive architectural language. While the main elements of a central large dome, large central arched portico and smaller flanking bays with arched doorways or niches remain throughout the Mughal period, in the later buildings these become noticeably more sculptural. Chambers had taken and adapted this architectural language at Woking, with a dome that is an evolution of the well-recognised onion shape into a much more spherical object (Figs 2.13 and 2.14).

The Shah Jahan Mosque also seems to take the language of late Mughal architecture in a Gothic direction in the portico's ogee archway and the trefoil-shaped arch over the main entrance door (Fig 2.15). The smaller domed cupola corner turret is a feature that occurs throughout the Mughal period. The stepped battlements, however, follow a style that originates in early Fatimid architecture found in Egypt in the 10th century. These seem to be the only real

Fig 2.13
Rear view of the Shah Jahan Mosque showing the spherical dome and rubblestone walls.
[DP148117]

Fig 2.14
Interior view of the dome of the Shah Jahan Mosque.
[DP148112]

Fig 2.15
The main entrance
to the Shah Jahan
Mosque: a land-
scaped garden leads
to an entrance
portico.
[DP148124]

instances where the architect has cross-referenced architectural languages in an otherwise faithful use of Mughal stylistic heritage.

The Shah Jahan Mosque almost perfectly captures the spirit of 19th-century 'Orientalism'. This was a time when, for curious Europeans, there was a mysterious and fantastical place called 'the East'. It was a place of strange customs, flamboyant dress and exotic women, encapsulated in a vast genre of Orientalist paintings depicting the East in theatrical ways. The Woking Mosque could be considered as the architectural equivalent of this Orientalist fantasy (Figs 2.16 and 2.17). It sits alongside other examples such as Leighton House of 1864–70, with its 'Arab Hall' of 1877–9, which could be described as outbursts of exotic flamboyance. Indeed, Woking was one in a series of buildings in Europe that embodied the characteristics of architectural Orientalism; the 1843 pumping station in Potsdam and the 1909 Yenidze tobacco factory in Dresden were two further examples, non-religious buildings that were nevertheless clothed in highly stylised and romantic Islamic architectures.

Leitner has been described as somewhat authoritarian in his control of the mosque and the Oriental Institute, and as somewhat patronising in his attitude towards South Asian Muslims: 'With little self-reflection on how British missionaries behaved in India, he declared that "the mosque is a proof of British toleration and must be used in that grateful and reverential spirit".' Leitner is also quoted as having written that 'the mosque is for the use of a select few persons' and not a 'centre of Islam in England'.[15]

Ironically, the mosque at Woking eventually did become exactly that – the centre of Islam in England. The Oriental Institute did not survive Leitner's death in 1899, and the mosque fell into disuse. It was eventually revived by an Indian lawyer, Khwaja Kamal-ud-Din, who came to London to pursue a legal case in 1912, while at heart looking for an opportunity to further the cause of Islam in the West. When in London Kamal-ud-Din learned of the existence of the mosque at Woking, and later that year made his first visit. In a letter to a colleague in India, he described how he found the mosque:

> After last Friday prayers, I and Chaudhry Zafrullah Khan went to Woking, reaching there at 5 pm. From the station we hired a carriage and reached our destination, there a polite young man agreed to show us the mosque. The courtyard and the mosque were locked. Upon my enquiry it was discovered that for years no Muslim had come here or prayed. O Allah only 20 miles from Woking is London where there are hundreds of Muslims full of national spirit, day and night. But no one came to see the mosque.[16]

In the letter, Kamal-ud-Din described what he found of Leitner's estate:

> A vast residential house, a room for keeping mementos from the East, and a small mosque to one side, which is in fact a room, five yards square. There is a very beautiful dome over it, on top of which is affixed a crescent. It has a high pulpit and a rihal [low stand] on which is placed a three-volumed copy of the Quran in large print …

Fig 2.16
Drawing of the mosque at Woking as published in The Building News (2 August 1889). The incorporation of turbanned and robed figures completes the Orientalist fantasy. [RIBA Library Books & Periodicals Collection]

In the mehrab the Surah Fatihah[17] is inscribed in Arabic. Some small plaques with the Divine names on them are on the walls. There are three or four prayer mats in the mosque. In one corner of the mosque there is some equipment for performing the wudu and in the other is a small enclosure for the Imam. In front of the mosque there is a large open courtyard, within which is a fountain occupying an area one, or one and a half, yards square. All around the courtyard is a wire fence and trees have been planted ... A few yards from this mosque is a small rest house known as the Salar Jang Memorial Hall, where a traveller is permitted to stay for a day or so.[18]

Kamal-ud-Din and his companion then proceeded to offer prayers in the mosque, in a spirit of great joy and promise at the idea of a mosque in the Western world. Kamal-ud-Din wrote:

I made a lengthy prostration, crying and pleading to be given the opportunity for the preaching and the propagation of Islam, and praying that the mosque may become a place for the dawn of the light of Islam ... This mosque in a non-Muslim land is truly 'the first house appointed for men'. What a wonder if God were to make it an Islamic centre.[19]

It was a testament to the accomplishment of Chambers' architecture that the mosque so thoroughly captured Kamal-ud-Din's imagination: Chambers had encapsulated that sense of romance and nostalgia that the Orientalist vision was meant to evoke. Having discovered the abandoned building in the forest, Kamal-ud-Din appeared as a noble reviver of Islam in a land where it had been forgotten.

Spurred by this vision, Kamal-ud-Din approached Sir Mirza Abbas Ali Beg, the Muslim advisory member of the Council of the Secretary of State for India, and they were able to acquire the mosque and memorial house from Leitner's heirs. Sir Abbas (or Abbas Ali) founded the Woking Muslim Trust, with himself, the Right Honourable Syed Ameer Ali and Thomas Walker Arnold as trustees, and Kamal-ud-Din appointed to run the mosque.[20] From here began a period of activity and growth that would see the mosque take its place at the centre of Islam in Britain in the early to mid-20th century.

Kamal-ud-Din seems to have created an open and non-sectarian Muslim organisation and mosque at Woking, even though he himself was rooted in the tradition of the Lahore Ahmadiyya movement.[21] His apparent non-partisanship resulted in the wide appeal and engagement that the mosque had during his stewardship. It is also relevant that the Lahore Ahmadiyya movement formed as a split in the main Ahmadiyya movement, as they did not accept the prophetic status of the spiritual leader Mirza Ghulam Ahmad, maintaining instead that the Prophet Muhammad was the last prophet, after whom there would be no other. This religious position was emphasised by the Woking Mosque on numerous occasions and potentially placed Kamal-ud-Din within the same doctrinal camp as more orthodox Sunni Muslims, which could be why he was able to engage leading Muslim personalities of the time in the activities of the trust.

After the revival of the mosque by Kamal-ud-Din in 1912, it seems to have played a major role as a conduit for exchange between the English world, often of high society, and Muslim culture. Indeed, it is said that in the 1920s and 1930s more than 2,000 conversions took place at the mosque. Many of the key figures of an emerging British Muslim culture were associated with the Shah Jahan Mosque. One of these was Marmaduke Pickthall, whose English translation of

Fig 2.17
Plan of the mosque as drawn in The Building News *in 1889.*
[RIBA Library Books & Periodicals Collection]

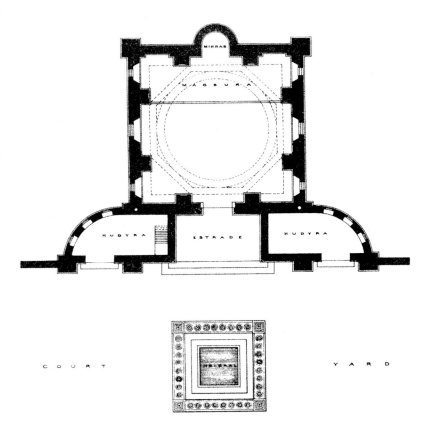

the Quran became (and remains) one of only two or three principal English versions for Muslims globally. He edited the mosque's journal, the *Islamic Review* (which ran for 60 years from 1913), and stood in as a replacement imam for Kamal-ud-Din during his trips to India, which would have been in the 1910s and 1920s. Pickthall also conducted the mosque's Taraweh prayers (late-night prayers during Ramadan). Abdullah Yusuf Ali, who had written the other main translation of the Quran into English, was a trustee of the mosque over the same period that Pickthall was working there. Both Pickthall and Yusuf Ali are buried at Brookwood Cemetery, which lies about half a mile from the Shah Jahan Mosque.

Another key personality was Lord Headley, who converted to Islam after his return to England, having spent some years from 1896 building roads in India. It is said that the imam of the Shah Jahan Mosque helped Lord Headley to understand certain passages of the Quran on which he required elucidation. After his conversion, Headley played a central role in the nascent British Muslim community and was made President of the British Muslim Society, the Woking Mosque Trust and the Muslim Literary Mission. Using his social standing among Britain's ruling class, Headley started the mosque trust and campaign that eventually led to the establishment of London's Central Mosque at Regent's Park (*see* pp 133–47). He died in 1935, before seeing the Central Mosque realised, and is also interred at Brookwood Cemetery.

The Shah Jahan Mosque became a high-profile symbol of Islam in the West, and a place where a piece of the (Indian) Muslim world could be experienced – one newspaper review wrote in 1922, 'Here, you can bathe your fevered brow in the waters of Islam.'[22] The Eid ceremony (the celebratory prayer at the end of Ramadan) held in the grounds of the Shah Jahan Mosque in 1922 was attended by prominent British converts as well as many dignitaries from Muslim countries who were posted in London. Newspaper coverage of the event illustrates the role the mosque was playing in English life at the time. One article reads:

> The scene was gorgeously spectacular to the visitor's eye, and brilliant sunshine showed up to wonderful effect the variety of colour to be seen in native costume worn by both sexes. Every race seemed to be represented. There were Arabians, Egyptians, Hindus, Afghans, Turks, Chinese, Americans, Javanese, Syrians, etc ... There was a very large percentage of English Muslims present, and the many English visitors who had been given an invitation to attend at the festival were given a cordial reception and made to feel at ease.[23]

Post-war immigration and Muslim social change

Khwaja Kamal-ud-Din died in 1936, and with Muhammad (previously Marmaduke) Pickthall passing away in the same year and Lord Headley the year before, the movement lost three of its key figures in a short space of time. The loss of the leadership and inspiration of the Woking mission was significant.[24] By the mid-20th century the London Mosque Fund, which grew from the Woking community, saw its efforts to initiate a mosque in central London take another step forward when it acquired a site at Regent's Park. With the founding fathers of the Woking mission now passed on, the centre of gravity of official British Islam therefore shifted to the new base. Over this period the Muslim population also expanded, with large-scale migrations from the former empire, which radically altered the nature and character of British Muslim society.

From the 1960s Pakistani Muslim immigrants were attracted to Woking to work in the light industries of engineering, plastic and rubber. In a pattern that was repeated across the country at the time, chain migration networks were established through which the local Muslim population grew rapidly. Of Woking's Muslim population of 4,550 recorded in 2001, 77 per cent were Pakistani.[25] As migration was largely through known links, the Muslim communities that emerged from the 1960s were 'socially and culturally cohesive and rapidly became self-contained'.[26] New Muslim immigrants were entering at the bottom of the socio-economic ladder and settling in the inner-city wards. Through disadvantage and discrimination these communities continued to suffer various forms of social deprivation, from unemployment to poor health. It was therefore inevitable that this new Muslim community would seek out the Woking Mosque and start using it as a place of support and identity. Through their numbers, the mosque's congregation was radically changed from the Muslim high society of the mosque's early years.

Through these demographic changes the Woking Mosque was retreating as a national beacon of British Islam and becoming a local mosque. Many of the mosque's founding British-based trust members were no more, and the Woking Mosque Trust, which was registered in Lahore, Pakistan, was considered too remote. It was decided that a new UK-based trust was needed. In 1964, therefore, the Woking Mosque Fund and Sir Salar Jang Memorial House was formed. The High Commissioner of Pakistan and several officials from the High Commission were appointed as trustees, with other members drawn from across Britain, so emphasising Woking's status as being of national Muslim interest.[27] A series of planning applications for new buildings followed, reflecting the increased pressure that the growing Muslim population was placing on the mosque.

In 1964 two applications were approved and built to extend the memorial house, with a new kitchen and servery on the ground floor, and five bedrooms and toilet facilities above.[28] The agent submitting the application on behalf of the mosque explained that the additional space was necessary due to the 'growing-up of the children of both sexes resident on the premises and also the need for guest rooms'.[29]

Alongside these two fairly modest expansions, a much more ambitious plan for the 'erection of 8 flats in 2 blocks and provision of 8 parking spaces'[30] was submitted, but it was refused and never built. The agent emphasised that the current memorial house was now inadequate for the needs of the congregation, hence the need for the additional facilities.[31] Despite this, the council objected on the basis that the development was too intensive, an inappropriate mix of uses, and that it would increase traffic on the access road.

The growing local Muslim population was predominantly Pakistani Sunni Muslim. With them came a growing dissatisfaction with the Ahmadiyya leadership of the mosque, despite the repeated assertions by this leadership that they were not of the persuasion that held Mirza Ghulam Ahmad as a prophet. Nevertheless, by 1966 a local group had formed a Woking Mosque Regeneration Committee, which demanded that 'control of the mosque be taken from the Ahmadiyya party in Lahore, who were appointing the Imams and spreading their literature'.[32]

The committee set out its aims quite unequivocally:

It is to our discredit that the control for running the Mosque has passed into the hands of Lahori Qadiani Movement in Pakistan, who use the mosque to propagate Mirza Ghulam Ahmed's ideas and religion, rather than for the service of the Shareeat [teaching] of Muhammad Rasool Allah and the religion of Islam ... We must change the situation ... We cannot allow the growing Muslim community of Britain to be plagued with heretical ideas ... We ask you, as our brother in Islam, to fulfil your obligation towards the Ummat of Muhammad Rasool Allah by supporting the Woking Mosque Regeneration Committee to take the control of the Woking Mosque away from the Qadiani Party in Lahore ... The affairs at the Woking mosque are so bad that there are no five times prayers, or regular Friday prayers, nor a proper school for Muslim children; and the maintenance of the Mosque is fully neglected.[33]

One day in 1968 the local congregation found that 'the Ahmadis had abandoned the mosque'.[34] The incumbent imam stayed for a few more days until he was asked to leave, and the mosque started its new life in a profoundly different and evolving British Muslim environment.

In 1972 the original mosque had a small extension built to add WC facilities. Although the building was not yet listed, this was nevertheless a sensitive and discreet addition. Minor works were also carried out to the accommodation in the memorial house.[35]

A considerably more ambitious proposal, never realised, followed two years later, with a scheme for 2 three-storey blocks of flats with 20 two-bedroom and 10 one-bedroom flats. This plan for a major residential development in front of the memorial house indicates a serious attempt by the mosque to generate income. It was refused as it was considered inappropriate, and the land was designated for primarily religious use.[36] In the early 1980s proposals for the site returned to more modest proportions. A single-storey prefabricated schoolroom and WC block adjacent to the memorial house was granted temporary approval and constructed.[37]

By the early 1990s, after local pressure, the organisational body of the mosque, the Woking Mosque Trust, had appointed local representatives to manage the mosque's affairs, so bringing it more fully into the community rather than being remotely managed. Once the management was in place, it carried out a comprehensive restoration of the mosque and memorial house, which had become neglected and were by this time in a poor state of repair.[38]

However, the pressure for space remained acute as the Muslim population continued to grow. The smaller temporary structures that had been built on the mosque site had become insufficient for the number of worshippers, and people were praying in the open air. In 1994 a single-storey warehouse on a strip of land at the north-western boundary of the mosque site bordering the railway, which had been leased to a neighbouring industrial company since 1956, was returned to the mosque.[39] This proved to be very timely as the prefabricated buildings that had been granted temporary permissions were too small to accommodate the number of people attending the mosque, and the mosque itself was already an almost impracticably small building. Constructing new buildings on the grounds of the mosque and memorial house was not the solution, as Woking District Council was determined to preserve the setting of Chambers' building, especially as the mosque had become a site of national heritage through its listing in 1984.

The council was concerned that the increased space would attract more people to the mosque, and so place additional pressures on parking and traffic congestion. The mosque, on the other hand, contested that the extra space would accommodate the activities that were already being carried out on the site, and that any increase in numbers was not due to the additional space, but rather to 'an organic growth within the community and a natural revival of interest in the religion which is occurring across the country'.[40]

After a series of negotiations between the mosque and the planning authorities concerning the traffic impact of extending the mosque facilities, landscaping and the removal of the previously built temporary structures, the change of use of the warehouse was granted permission in 2001,[41] and the mosque as it exists today was formalised. The warehouse conversion provides prayer halls, classrooms and a sports hall, and has a worshipper capacity of 2,000 (Fig 2.18). The original mosque building is very much a working mosque, with each of the daily prayers taking place here throughout the week (*see* Fig 2.1), attended by between 20 and 100 people. For the Friday prayer, when the numbers of attendees is too great for the original mosque, the warehouse is used and fully occupied.

Conclusion

The Woking Mosque has the longest and one of the most significant histories of any mosque in Britain. Architecturally, it represents the very first manifestation of the mosque as a building type, and thus the representation of Islam, in Britain and indeed in Western Europe. The mosque enabled a Muslim social organisation to develop, which played a fundamental role in the evolution of British Muslim institutions and in the establishment of Islam in Britain.

The great social changes that followed World War II, and the seismic demographic shifts in the Muslim populations of Britain, did not pass

Fig 2.18
The main prayer hall was formed through the conversion of the warehouses in the grounds of the Shah Jahan Mosque. It is used when the number of worshippers exceeds the capacity of the original building.
[AA031172]

this secluded mosque by. As social change came to Woking, the role of the mosque shifted from national beacon to place of local community need, and its administration and outlook came to reflect this new reality.

Restored and listed, the Woking Mosque is a secure part of the nation's heritage. As Muslim communities and cultures become generationally embedded in Britain, and as their histories are explored and made manifest, the Woking Mosque will always be revisited as a key starting point of Muslim architectural and institutional history in Britain.

3 Fazl Mosque (London Mosque), Gressenhall Road, Southfields, London, 1926

Nestled in the south-west London suburb of Southfields, sitting askew on its site and somewhat indifferent to its mock-Tudor surroundings, is a small, gleaming white building, taller at one end where it is topped with a green dome (Fig 2.19). Here, on the corner of the quiet residential streets of Gressenhall Road and Melrose Road, is the first mosque built in London, and indeed the first mosque built in Britain since Leitner's 1889 Woking Mosque. Completed in 1926 and named the Fazl Mosque (also known as the London Mosque), this was the first formal missionary outpost of the Ahmadiyya Muslim Community (Fig 2.20).[42]

Southfields itself is a gentle, nondescript suburb. Situated between the town centres of Wandsworth and Wimbledon, it was gradually consumed by London's suburban growth. By the 1890s, streets of Victorian terraced housing had become established to the east in Wandsworth and Clapham, while Southfields remained relatively rustic, with open fields, orchards and woodland. It was, however, a landscape that was already rapidly changing with increasing urbanisation. The establishment of Southfields station in 1889 to the south of the mosque site initiated the development of a dense grid of suburban house building on former farmland.[43] Into the 20th century the area remained a mixture of terraced streets set amid open land and large villas on grand plots.

By 1910 the immediate locality around the site had not urbanised significantly, but by the 1930s the larger villa plots were gradually filled with terraced and semi-detached housing. Post-World War II development saw the further

introduction of low-rise apartment blocks into this suburban mix.

An Ahmadiyya missionary, a Mr Siah, who had arrived in London in 1914, was tasked with finding a suitable site to establish an Ahmadiyya centre outside India. He found the current site, which comprised two detached houses and a piece of land on which a small orchard grew. The plots were purchased in 1920, and in the autumn of 1924 the foundation stone for the new mosque was laid by the head of the movement. Excavation for construction of the building did not, however, commence until the following September, when it was blessed by the London imam A R Dard, and 'a small company of Indians'.[44] It is reported that at the start of excavations Imam Dard recited 'the same prayers in Arabic as were

Fig 2.19
Exterior view of the Fazl Mosque, Southfields, completed in 1926, showing the main entrance and side façade. The design is a restrained approach to classical Mughal style which also draws on contemporary architectural trends of the period in which it was built.
[DP148054]

Fig 2.20
Photograph from The
Architect and Building
News *(1 Oct 1926, 375)
showing the recently
completed mosque set
within an orchard grove.*
*[RIBA Library Books &
Periodicals Collection]*

recited at the building of the Ka'ba', and that the
members of the community digging the ground
were 'chanting the same verses as were recited
by the Prophet Mahomed [sic] while he and his
companions were building the Medina
mosque'.[45] The cost of the land purchase and
construction of the mosque totalled £6,223 –
money that was raised in India, mostly by
Muslim women who 'took on the task after being
addressed by the head of the Movement'.[46]

The mosque was built at the southernmost
end of the site to allow for possible future expansion, while the existing houses were utilised as
offices and prayer space during construction.
Indeed, the mosque was built as a steel structure,
potentially enabling the walls to be removed
to allow for the building to be extended.[47] This
extension of the original building never materialised, however, and the community instead
accommodated its growth in a new three-storey
building erected in the grounds of the mosque
in the 1970s, and then, in the early 2000s, in a
large purpose-built mosque and complex, with a
capacity for some 6,000 worshippers, on a new
site in nearby Morden (*see* p 263).

The original Fazl Mosque (*fazl* is Arabic for
'bounty' or 'virtue') is a simple building comprising a single prayer hall measuring some 7 metres
by 10 metres, with a mihrab niche at its far end
wall, oriented south-east towards Makkah. It is
a quirk of history that the mosque was built a
few degrees off from the correct direction of the
Qibla, and when this was realised the congregation decided it had no option but to reorientate
the prayer direction within the building. The
original site plan drawing of 1925 shows the
mosque at a more acute angle than that at which
it has actually been built, which suggests that
the error came in the translation from drawing
to building. The result is that the prayer lines in
the mosque are not orthogonal with the mosque
plan, but slightly askew (Fig 2.21).

Fig 2.21
*The main prayer hall of the
Fazl Mosque, showing the
imam's mihrab niche in the
far wall. The carpet shows
the prayer lines are askew
to the end wall, as the
mosque was not built to the
correct Qibla direction.*
[DP148056]

Fazl Mosque and the emergence of the modern

The mosque, by architects T H Mawson and Sons, whose roots were in landscape and Arts and Crafts design, is carefully proportioned (Figs 2.22 and 2.23), the main prayer hall being some 5.4 metres high, with the apex of the dome approximately 10 metres high. On the side elevations, tall narrow windows with rounded arches are located within each bay between vertical piers. At each corner of the building are simple cupolas, a characteristic element of Indian Mughal architecture. The cupolas are perhaps most reminiscent of cupolas found in the Mughal architecture of the Emperor Akbar, notably on the Diwan-e-Khas in his 16th-century Fatehpur Sikri complex in northern India.

The dome and its base are, interestingly, less linked to known Indian typologies which were the primary references for the 19th-century Orientalist genre in British architecture. This is where the Fazl Mosque starts to depart from the oriental imagery that characterised its predecessor at Woking. Indeed, it is here that the idea of the Fazl Mosque as a British Islamic building influenced by contemporary trends deriving from

the Arts and Crafts Movement, which were to develop as modernism, can begin to be explored. The dome, sitting on a square base with a square buttress at each corner, can perhaps be seen to follow the domes on the twin towers of Wembley's British Empire Exhibition Stadium of 1923 and widely published at the time. That building

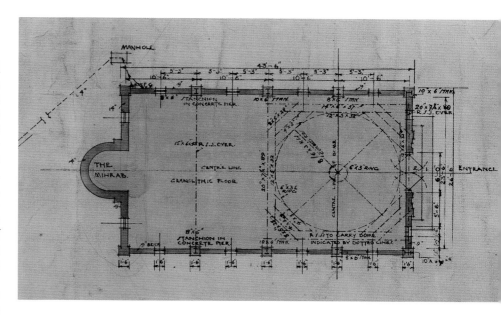

Fig 2.22
The proposed ground-floor plan of the Fazl Mosque by T H Mawson and Sons, from 1925.
[Cumbria Archives Centre, Kendal (WDB 86/2/10/1)]

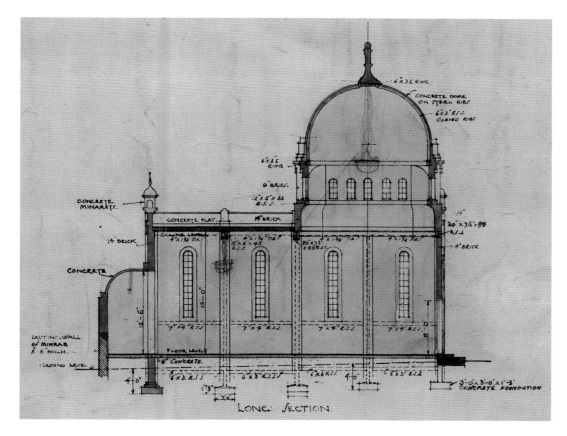

Fig 2.23
Sectional drawing of the Fazl Mosque by T H Mawson and Sons, from 1925.
[Cumbria Archives Centre, Kendal (WDB 86/2/10/1)]

was designed by the architects Sir John Simpson and Maxwell Ayrton; the latter had himself been apprenticed under Edwin Lutyens, whose work in New Delhi was seminal in westernising traditional Mughal styles. Lutyens' Presidential Palace in New Delhi, the Rashtrapati Bhavan, carries a dome which is perhaps a more direct formal reference for the dome and base at Southfields. As Lutyens' New Delhi residence was not built until 1930, it had perhaps only been seen in drawings to this date. Even so, the language of a stripped-back classicism fused with Mughal influence that Lutyens explored is also evident in the architecture of the Fazl Mosque (Fig 2.24).

The idea of the Fazl Mosque being required to negotiate its Islamic origins and its Western context is identified in a 1926 article in *Building* magazine, which reads: 'It was desirable that the traditional style used for mosques in the East should be preserved, without striking too exotic a note in a South London suburb ... It was essential that while the traditional style was maintained, the building should be adapted to the different climactic conditions and to English methods of construction.'[48]

It may also be relevant that by the 1920s the Orientalist style of the late 19th century was falling out of favour, having become associated with

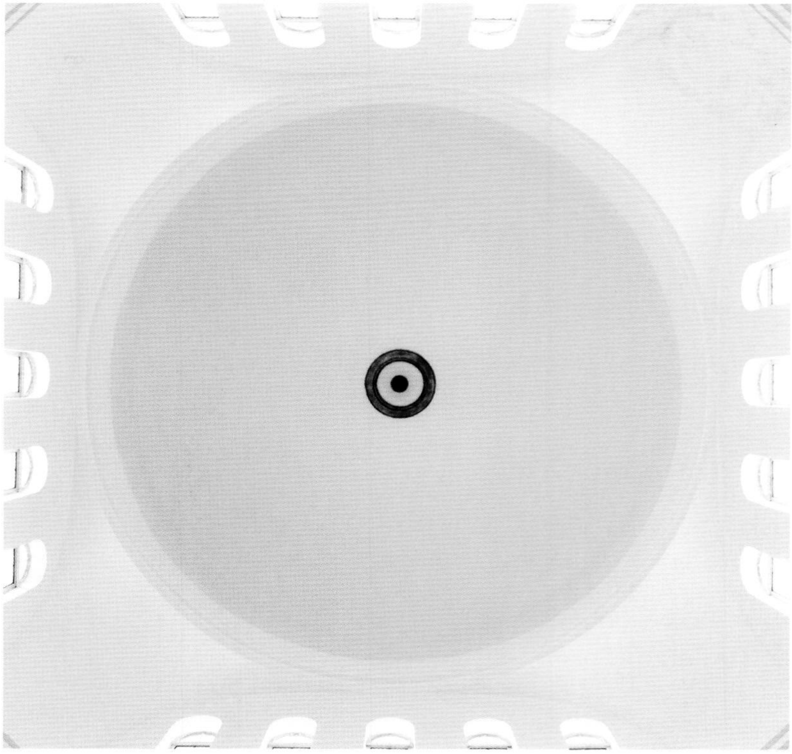

Fig 2.24
Interior view of the dome of the Fazl Mosque, a clear and unadorned feature.
[DP148057]

'theatres, cafés, seaside piers and amusement arcades' – associations that were inappropriate for places of worship.[49] So a new architectural treatment for the mosque at Southfields was an imperative for any architect aware of current trends. From contemporary accounts on the completion of the mosque, it seems that the architects were thought to have been successful in modernising the language of the Orientalist mosque to correspond better with prevailing tastes. As one local reporter wrote:

Four-square and dome-crowned, the mosque possesses the dignity of simplicity. It has no disturbing ornaments such as the western speculative builder delights in. White all over, it is embellished only by a few severe mouldings and a couple of rows of dwarf arcading ... Simplicity in outline is the dominant note. The fact that it is very inconspicuous in the midst of villas and suburban surroundings is, in itself, a tribute to the skill of the architect.[50]

The modernity of the building is also embodied in its structure, which is steel framed, encased in concrete, with brick infill panels and finished in stucco.[51] Not only was this a modern method of construction at the time, but it also allowed for future expansion – a modern consideration anticipating social and demographic change. A review in *The Builder* of October 1926 included a drawing of the mosque with its potential future extensions, showing it as being four times larger than what was already constructed.[52]

Despite its significant place in the development of Islamic architecture in Britain, being the second purpose-built mosque (after Woking) and one that presents a significantly new architectural approach, the Fazl Mosque had not been written about since the reviews in 1926 until an essay by social geographers Simon Naylor and James Ryan in 2002.[53] They emphasised the building's modernity and pointed out that the location of the mosque in the suburbs was one of the factors that allowed its architecture to be somewhat experimental, the suburbs being 'significant spaces for the adaptation and hybridisation of non-European architectural styles and forms'.[54]

The newness of the Fazl Mosque in its representation of Muslim architecture is further illustrated when considering the contemporaneous British Empire Exhibition held in Wembley in 1924–5. In this display of the countries and cultures contained within the empire, each having its own pavilion showing artefacts of that place, the Indian pavilion was typically cast in the oriental style prevalent in the late 19th century, as exemplified by the Woking Mosque. The Fazl Mosque, therefore, challenged this stylistic trope still being presented as the image of the 'East', and by doing so placed this representative language as an anachronism of a fading era.

The status of the Fazl Mosque, which played a seminal role in the social history of Muslims in Britain in the early 20th century and served as a centre and symbol of Islam in London, was reflected in its opening ceremony on 3 October 1926.[55] The ceremony was 'a grand affair, and was extensively reported in the local, national and architectural and building journals. The opening was also caught on film and relayed around the country as part of the news reels shown before feature films.'[56] The 600 or so guests who attended included many dignitaries, ambassadors, mayors, ministers and other political representatives.[57] The *South Western Star* reported: 'Crowds were present on Sunday; there were peers of the realm and members of the House of Commons, among whom half of the Wandsworth Borough Council circulated with humility. Clergymen and ministers of various denominations were present, as also was a Reverend Professor from Oxford.'[58]

However, the opening of the mosque was not without controversy. The day before the ceremony *The Times* reported that 'Emir Feisal, Viceroy of Mecca, as the representative of his father, Sultan Ibn Saud, King of the Hejaz and Nejd, will inaugurate the mosque ... At tomorrow's ceremony the young Emir Feisal will be received at the entrance to the mosque enclosure, and, proceeding to the door will unlock it with a silver key.'[59] However, at 11 am the next morning, with the ceremony due to take place at 3 pm, Emir Feisal was instructed by his father to withdraw. As *The Times* then reported, 'To the Emir's grief and disappointment, he could not perform the ceremony as he had received a telegram from his father, the Sultan Ibn Saud, the Wahabi King of the Hejaz and Nejd, forbidding him to do so.'[60]

It seems that Emir Feisal was genuinely aggrieved by the instruction from his father. The newspaper reports that he petitioned Ibn Saud to reconsider, suggesting that some misunderstanding had taken place. According to *The Times* report, the reversal was the result of 'certain Moslems in India' persuading Ibn Saud that the Ahmadiyyas 'hold heretical views and are easygoing in matters which the Wahabis (the most puritanical of Moslems) hold to be important'.[61] The paper reports that at first these efforts were unsuccessful, as the Sultan considered the benefit of a mosque in London to outweigh sectarian differences. Eventually, however, after a series of unfavourable representations of the Ahmadiyya in the Arab press, the Sultan was moved to withdraw his endorsement of the mosque.

Despite the Emir's withdrawal from the ceremony, the mosque in Southfields opened as planned in October 1926. A stable Ahmadiyya community formed around it as it continued to play a significant role in the cultural life of Islam in London. Indeed, the mosque was visited by notable figures of British Muslim culture: Khalid Sheldrake, Abdullah Quilliam (*see* pp 21–4) and Abdullah Yusuf Ali (*see* p 32) are reported to have visited the mosque on Eid festivals. It is also noted that a prominent Indian Muslim, Sir Feroze Khan Noon, attended the mosque, and in July 1935 the Saudi Crown Prince Faisal bin Abdulaziz also visited.[62]

The Ahmadiyya community itself remained relatively small through the 1920s and 1930s, 'with the majority of worshippers at the London mosque living within the surrounding areas'.[63] In fact the small mosque was sufficient through to the 1970s, when the congregation numbered fewer than 100; with no provision for a separate women's prayer space, a screen was erected to divide the building for Friday prayers.[64] An understated three-storey brick building was constructed in 1970 to replace the two houses on the site, comprising facilities for the community as well as residences for the current Caliph of the Ahmadiyya. (There is now also a TV studio and media centre, and from here the Ahmadiyya satellite channel broadcasts across the world to its estimated 20 million members.)

After the Partition of India and the creation of Pakistan in 1947, the Ahmadiyya community had moved their headquarters to a town 100 miles from Lahore. However, they faced increasing discrimination and persecution in Pakistan from vocal conservative elements of society who campaigned against them as heretics. Eventually, the movement was formally declared 'non-Muslim' by the Pakistani leader Zia-ul-Haq in 1984, and consequently the then Caliph of the Ahmadiyya relocated the headquarters from Pakistan to Gressenhall Road. Southfields thereby became the world headquarters for the Ahmadiyya Muslim Community.

The Ahmadiyya population in Britain had started to grow in the 1960s with the post-colonial migrations from India and Pakistan.[65] The increasing persecution of the Ahmadiyya in Pakistan through the 1970s precipitated further migrations to Britain, causing Southfields to grow in significance. Over the next few decades, as the community coalesced around the mosque, the requirement for more space was met through the incremental purchase of houses on surrounding streets, so that by 2011 the mosque owned 10 of these properties.[66]

The first stage in the transformation of the Ahmadiyya site from a suburban domestic idyll to the global headquarters of a faith group came in 1970 with the erection of the three-storey community centre and Caliph's residence opposite the mosque.[67] It was built in plain brick with a flat roof, simple and unadorned and, it seems, driven solely by utility rather than any notion of style or cultural identity. This was the first in a series of proposals and constructions over subsequent decades, as the Ahmadiyya attempted to shape the site to suit their growing needs and aspirations. Planning records show that the development of the site was incremental and iterative, rather than comprehensive, with no fewer than 19 planning applications for various works from 1974 to 2005.

Such a piecemeal development pattern is almost typical of mosque sites and reflects a community in a continuously changing state with evolving needs, and perhaps also a limited resource base requiring works to take place and be paid for in smaller segments rather than in a large-scale way: 'The long term aim of the community was to replace the various temporary structures – the tents, prefabricated huts and converted residential buildings – with permanent and purpose-built buildings within the Mosque site that would provide proper accommodation.'[68]

The planning applications over this 30-year period vary in terms of the scope of the proposals, ranging from the erection of a prayer hall for women in 1974, to the installation of three Portakabins to provide temporary office accommodation in 1984, to a new low-rise building fronting Melrose Road in 1998. This application was refused on the grounds of overdevelopment of the site and insufficient parking provision.[69] Looking at the planning history generally, relatively minor works have been approved while any proposal to substantially redevelop the site to increase its scope and significance has not gained planning permission. This is interesting considering that the original mosque was specifically designed with future expansion in mind. In fact, a proposal to enlarge the 1926 mosque as per the original plans was submitted in 1991 and was refused on the grounds of 'overdevelopment of site and insufficient parking provision to the detriment of the amenity of neighbours'.[70] The proposal was revised and submitted again in 1993, and again refused, a decision against which the mosque appealed unsuccessfully.[71]

Inability to redevelop the Gressenhall Road site led the Ahmadiyya to acquire a larger site in 1996 in the south-west London suburb of Morden, some 5 miles further south (see p 263). This was a 2.1 hectare site where the community successfully developed a large facility, begun in 1999 and completed in 2003,[72] which has become the main functional centre and mosque for the Ahmadiyya. Indeed, the Ahmadiyya claim that this mosque, the Baitul Futuh, is the largest in Western Europe, being able to accommodate 6,000 worshippers. However, the mosque in Gressenhall Road, with the residence of the World Leader, remains the community's spiritual home.

Proposals to develop Gressenhall Road, 2010–13

The Baitul Futuh did not dampen the desire to also redevelop the Gressenhall Road site, and revised schemes designed by Sutton Griffin Architects of Newbury were prepared from 2010 to 2013.

The first proposal showed a large circular prayer hall set back behind the 1926 mosque and almost exactly on its Qibla axis. Circular landscaping around the new prayer hall served to reinforce this axis and place the original mosque as the determining architectural object around which the new site would be configured. In this sense the proposal respected and emphasised the importance of the 1926 building. The existing facilities building was to be reclad and extended with an additional floor, and a further three-storey building was proposed on the Melrose Road frontage, which would provide residential accommodation.[73]

The proposed design was not overtly Islamic, though a series of unadorned pointed arches punctuated the elevations as both colonnades and window surrounds. A large, low dome over the prayer hall, bearing little direct association with the proportions of traditional Islamic domes, dominated. A short minaret, just taller than the roofline, was situated on the flank wall of the building fronting Gressenhall Road, hexagonal, unadorned and faced in plain render.

It is instructive to see the existing plans of the site submitted with the redevelopment application. These show how the organic growth of the facility over the 40 years since the 1970s had resulted in an arrangement that is broadly functional despite being somewhat piecemeal. This sense of ad hoc development is embodied in the fabric of many of the structures on the site, where prefabricated and timber sheet cladding indicate their temporary nature. Furthermore, apart from the original 1926 building, the current buildings do not have any aesthetic or architectural characteristics that symbolise this as an Islamic facility. The proposal sought to effect a more coherent design language across the whole site, and to introduce an architectural Islamisation through low-key symbols seen as characteristic of Muslim architecture.

The application was recommended for approval by the planning officers, but was refused by the planning committee in July 2011. The reason given for refusal was 'an increased intensification of use on an already intensively used site leading to an unacceptable impact on residential amenity'.[74]

After further consultations between the mosque and local residents, a revised scheme was submitted in November 2011 (Figs 2.25 and 2.26). With this revised proposal the main hall was reduced in width by 3 metres, resulting in an overall reduction in floor area of 19 per cent. The building was also set back from

Fig 2.25
Proposed elevations of the scheme to redevelop the land around the Fazl Mosque to create additional prayer space and facilities for the community, which gained planning permission in 2013, by Sutton Griffin Architects. [© Sutton Griffin Architects]

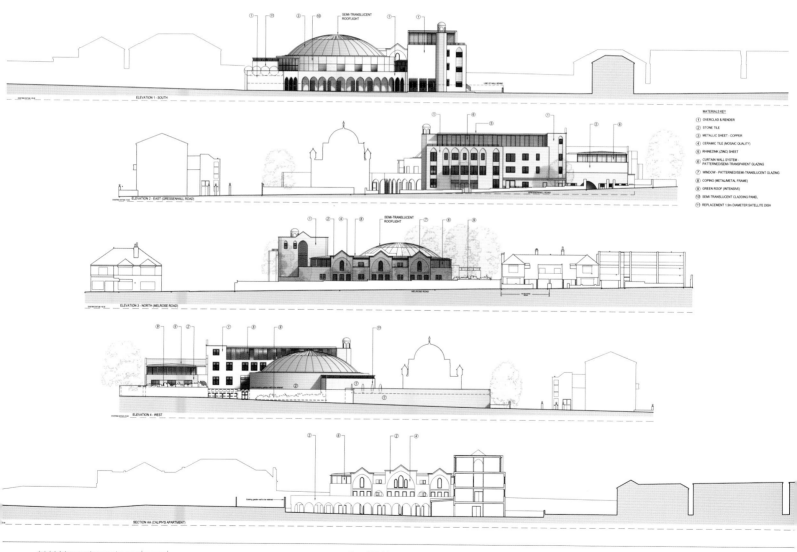

MATERIALS KEY
1. OVERCLAD & RENDER
2. STONE TILE
3. METALLIC SHEET - COPPER
4. CERAMIC TILE (MOSAIC QUALITY)
5. RHINEZINK (ZINC) SHEET
6. CURTAIN WALL SYSTEM - PATTERNED/SEMI-TRANSPARENT GLAZING
7. WINDOW - PATTERNED/SEMI-TRANSLUCENT GLAZING
8. COPING (METAL/METAL FRAME)
9. GREEN ROOF (INTENSIVE)
10. SEMI-TRANSLUCENT CLADDING PANEL
11. REPLACEMENT 1.9m DIAMETER SATELLITE DISH

ELEVATION 1 - SOUTH

ELEVATION 2 - EAST (GRESSENHALL ROAD)

ELEVATION 3 - NORTH (MELROSE ROAD)

ELEVATION 4 - WEST

SECTION AA (CALIPH'S APARTMENT)

Scale in Metres

Southfields Residence

41

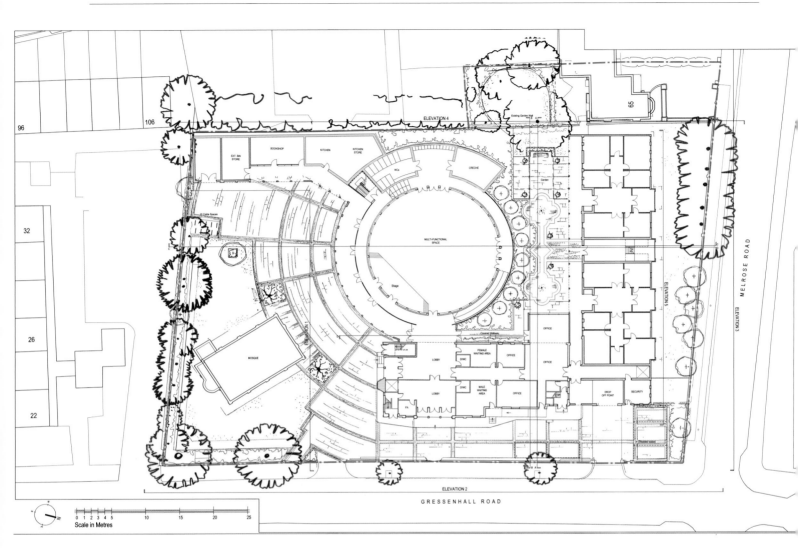

Fig 2.26
Sutton Griffin Architects'
plan of the site showing the
proposed redevelopment
around the original
mosque. (The original
mosque is shown to the
bottom left of the drawing.)
The proposals gained
planning approval in 2013.
[© Sutton Griffin
Architects]

the northern boundary, fronting the houses on Melrose Road, by 2.2 metres, and the bookshop on the western boundary was reduced by 2 metres.[75] These adjustments in scale did not impact the overall architectural language of the scheme, which remained as per the original design, and the amended proposal was finally approved in June 2013 (although at the time of writing construction had not begun).

Conclusion

The establishment of the mosque in Southfields in the early 20th century, and the subsequent history of this plot of land on the corner of Gressenhall Road and Melrose Road in a quiet London suburb, is emblematic of how an immigrant religious community has invested itself in a particular location and gradually brought about architectural and social change by reinscribing

a place with new meanings and significance. The process of organic and incremental growth, involving complex and continuous negotiations with the planning system, is also a typical pattern of the evolution of mosque sites and has become almost a generic narrative of larger mosque developments.

The 1926 Fazl Mosque remains significant as the first mosque in London and the second purpose-built mosque in Britain. Although the Woking Mosque preceded Fazl, Woking was the work of an individual and was never intended as a fully functioning community mosque. Fazl, on the other hand, was a mosque generated by a diasporic Muslim community as part of their process of establishing cultural roots in a new homeland. It could, in this way, be considered the first purpose-built community mosque in Britain, and therefore a precursor of the era of British mosque building that followed after World War II.

Fazl is also architecturally significant in that it marks a departure from the Victorian Orientalism of buildings such as the Woking Mosque, and presents instead a restrained Islamic language infused with a sense of contemporary British architecture. Considering the design of the 1924 Indian Pavilion at the Empire Exhibition, which was a somewhat oriental affair, Fazl was a radical and progressive departure and could be said to mark the end of exotic architectural representations of the 'East', and so the end of the Orientalist genre in British architecture.

Architecturally, therefore, by dampening the flourishes of exoticism, Fazl may have paved the way for modernist explorations of mosques that followed through to the 1980s. More importantly, it demonstrates how to manage references to traditional Islamic architectural symbols without recourse to pastiche or caricature, and therefore stands as an instructive reference point for ongoing mosque design in Britain.

4 Cardiff: mid-century evolutions, 1943–1969 (including Noor-el-Islam Mosque, 1947, and South Wales Islamic Centre, 1969)

No other period of English history can compare in glory with what we proudly term the 'Victorian Era', nor has any age been so fruitful in the arts of peace, in great scientific discoveries, and in all the best elements of moral, material and intellectual progress ... It has seen the sanitation of our towns, the development of a vast network of railways all over the land, the employment of the electric telegraph ... and almost every year has added to the volume and wealth of England's trade, and extended the frontiers of the British Empire.[76]

So spoke the Mayor of Cardiff on the occasion of the diamond jubilee of Queen Victoria in 1897. His city was the largest in Wales, with a population that had expanded exponentially over the previous 60 years to reach 170,000. Cardiff was a global city, being the world's largest exporter of coal, and as such was one of the hubs of Britain's Empire.

Cardiff's growth through the 19th century, like that of many of Britain's other industrial heartlands, was phenomenal. In the 18th century Cardiff remained a small town, much as it had been in the Middle Ages, but from the late

1700s transformation was on its way as the Industrial Revolution swept the country. During this time exports of coal and iron from the city boomed, and in 1839 John Crichton-Stuart, 2nd Marquess of Bute, built Bute West Dock, followed by the East Dock in 1855 and Roath Dock in 1887.[77] The area around the docks, known as Butetown, developed in the second half of the 19th century into a respectable, middle-class suburb with houses mainly occupied by sea captains and merchants.[78] With railway links from the docks to the Welsh mining valleys of Cynon, Rhondda and Rhymney, by 1900 Cardiff had become the largest exporter of coal in the world.[79]

It was the shipping trade that catalysed Muslim migration to Britain in the form of maritime workers, or lascars, and the major ports of Liverpool, South Shields, Cardiff and east London saw the emergence of the first settled Muslim communities from the mid-19th century. The East India Company had established factories in the key coastal centres of India in the 1600s, and Indian sailors provided cheap labour. Lascar settlement in Britain started in the late 1700s, and it has been estimated that the number of lascars settled in British port towns increased through the 19th century from around 500 in 1804 to 10,000–12,000 in 1855: 'Of the 7,814 lascars surveyed in 1874, 4,685 came from India and 1,440 were Arabs, 225 Turks and 85 Malays.'[80]

After its annexation by Britain in 1839, the port of Aden on the Arabian peninsula became a crucial coal refuelling station for steamships en route to East Africa, India, East Asia and Australasia. A series of droughts and famines in Yemen in the late 19th century forced people to leave villages in search of alternative livelihoods, and with major shipping companies setting up coaling depots in Aden, arduous work as stokers in the hot furnace rooms of steam ships was ready employment. The abundance of labour from the southern highlands of Yemen enabled brokers to drive down the price of Yemeni wages, so it was Yemeni lascars who were chosen above those from other parts of the empire.[81] Working the shipping lanes to the coal centres of Cardiff and South Shields, not all Yemenis returned home, and gradually Muslim communities came together in these port locations.

In Cardiff the majority of lascars were concentrated in the dock area of Butetown, and their population was estimated in the 1911 census at 700. This had swelled to 3,000 by 1919, driven by labour shortages caused by the war. Bute

Street ran from one end of Butetown to the other, connecting the docks to the heart of the capital and acting as the 'jugular vein of the Welsh economy'.[82] This district, also known as Tiger Bay, became a hub of multiculturalism as immigrants from around the world arrived and settled near the docks. Right through to the 1950s some 57 nationalities were counted among Butetown's 10,000 residents.[83] Howard Spring, a local author, described in his book *Heaven Lies About Us* the 'fascination in the walk through Tiger Bay' in the late 1930s, where people of many races 'slippered about the faintly evil by-ways that ran off Bute Street'. He continued:

> The flags of all nations fluttered on the house fronts, and ever and anon the long bellowing moan of a ship coming to the docks or outward bound seemed the very voice of this meeting place of the seven seas … It was a dirty, rotten and romantic district, an offence and an inspiration, and I loved it.[84]

The Yemeni seamen relied on a network of boarding houses that 'provided a physical, social, religious and economic base for Muslim seafarers', such as the Home for Coloured Seamen established in 1881.[85] The boarding houses also had rooms set aside for prayer, with the imam's role adopted by different seamen in turn.[86] In 1936 there were six boarding-house mosques in Cardiff, and it is reported that an early mosque was provided in a warehouse at the rear of the Cairo Café on Bute Street.[87]

The emergence of mosques in Cardiff was not simply an organic process, evolving as one might reasonably expect from the prayer rooms in the boarding houses of Butetown. Rather, it was catalysed with the outside assistance of a Muslim preacher from Yemen who came to settle and preach among the Yemeni communities, first the Yemeni community of South Shields, and then that of Cardiff. Sheikh Abdullah Ali al-Hakimi arrived in Britain from Yemen in 1936,[88] a Sufi sheikh of the Allawi Tariqa[89] who met his spiritual guide, Sheikh Ahmad al-Allawi, in Morocco in the 1920s.[90] Sheikh al-Hakimi established religious meeting houses (known as *zawiya* according to the Sufi tradition) in converted buildings in South Shields, Cardiff, Hull and Liverpool in the late 1930s, and these served to transform and project 'the largely private practice of Islam in the boarding houses into the streets'.[91] Although the Sheikh had been moving between the Yemeni communi-

ties since arriving and settling in South Shields, he relocated to Cardiff in 1938 and established premises for the Zaouia Islamia Allawoulia on Bute Street in a converted stable.[92] The arrival of Sheikh al-Hakimi invigorated the religious life of the Yemeni seafaring communities, as is described in the following account:

> Religious life was regularised and dramatised. New ritual practices were introduced and elaborate and colourful processions through the streets were organised to mark the major Muslim festivals … On these occasions many of the seamen discarded their European clothing for Yemeni dress or the Arab dress of North Africa. Special attention was given to the religious instruction of children born to seamen and their Welsh and English wives. Classes in Quranic studies were organised for both boys and girls and also for those wives who had converted to Islam.[93]

South Shields

During his stay in South Shields, Sheikh al-Hakimi had managed to establish a *zawiya* in a converted public house, the Hilda Arms, in Cuthbert Street (in around 1936). It would not have been a large place, with space for only some 60 worshippers and with the Sheikh's accommodation on the upper two floors.[94] Although there were initiatives to establish mosques in the South Shields area prior to this, none of them had come to fruition. Other than the Cuthbert Street *zawiya*, the only other mosque facilities would have been converted rooms within Arab seamen's boarding houses, which would have been in use for many years before the Sheikh's mosque.

The Yemeni community was concentrated around the Holborn and Laygate areas of South Shields, and it was in these streets that their cultural centres were formed. As with Cardiff's Butetown, post-war regeneration rewrote the urban topography of these districts, and many streets were obliterated and replaced with mass council housing. This is seen to have contributed to a dispersal of the Yemenis across South Shields, along with intermarriage and assimilation, and the community is described as having declined and disappeared after World War II. Indeed, Sheikh al-Hakimi's mosque was demolished as part of the regeneration process, along with some boarding houses.

Eventually, by 1972, a purpose-built mosque was realised in the Laygate area of South Shields, a simple two-storey building with a modest pair of minarets and a dome over the mihrab niche. In 1988 a Yemeni school for Arabic and Islamic studies was opened in a building next to the mosque, which also provided a number of apartments. As the Yemeni community declined, a new population of Bangladeshi immigrants began to settle in the South Shields area from the 1980s, and two further mosques followed, formed from a converted house and a converted church on the same street near the town centre.

Butetown mosques: realised and imagined 1938–1947

Today there are two extant mosques in Butetown: one at Maria Street (formerly Peel Street), known as the Noor-el-Islam (Fig 2.27), and one a few minutes away at Alice Street, known as the South Wales Islamic Centre (Fig 2.28). The mosque on Peel Street/Maria Street was begun in the 1940s as Sheikh al-Hakimi's first purpose-built mosque, and the one on Alice Street in the late 1960s: both have elaborate architectural histories.

Sheikh al-Hakimi started his mosque in a stable in Bute Street before his mission purchased three terraced houses at 17–19 Peel Street; before the end of 1938 he was busy submitting proposals to redevelop them into a mosque and Muslim centre. The stable-mosque

was destroyed in a World War II air raid, and the congregation moved to a new mosque, albeit a temporary structure, at the Peel Street site.[95]

However, Peel Street was not the only site where the Muslim community of Tiger Bay was attempting to establish a mosque. House conversions and new builds were also proposed by other initiators from within the Yemeni Muslim community, for example a small private mosque in the rear yard of a house on Maria Street (*see* p 49), a house-mosque conversion on Sophia Street (*see* pp 49–50), and a new-build mosque proposal on Bute Street (*see* pp 50–51). Such

Fig 2.27
The purpose-built Noor-el-Islam Mosque (1993) that replaced the 1940s mosque, on Maria Street (formerly Peel Street).
[DP137690]

Fig 2.28
The South Wales Islamic Centre, by Davies Llewelyn Partnership, opened in 1984, which replaced the purpose-built mosque that had stood on the site from 1969 to 1979.
[DP137685]

concentrated attempts to establish mosques in this part of Butetown suggest a particularly fervent period of activity, spurred by the arrival of Sheikh al-Hakimi, to establish and institutionalise Muslim space in the city.

Noor-el-Islam Mosque, 17–19 Peel Street (later Maria Street)

In total there were four proposals for the redevelopment of the houses at Peel Street. The latter two were built, with the former two remaining paper projects. Despite never leaving the drawing board, these earlier proposals provide valuable insights into the way in which Victorian houses were being reimagined as places of Muslim worship.

The first proposal, an application drawn up by Cardiff architect Osborne V Webb for the conversion of the houses and the construction of a new mosque building in the rear garden, was approved in November 1938 but never built (Fig 2.29).[96] It envisaged a new arched walkway cut through the centre of the houses from Peel Street to the rear garden, where a mosque was to be constructed. The plan of the houses would have been completely transformed, the ground floor becoming an assembly hall and classroom facing the street, with ablutions and WCs to the rear. The first floor was to be converted into 'private rooms', a kitchen and a scullery. The drawing notes that the private rooms are meant 'for praying'.

The new mosque in the rear garden would have been free-standing and approximately 12 metres by 8 metres, and is shown to almost fill the garden. It would have comprised a single prayer hall in a double-height space, reaching the same height as the Peel Street houses. The roof would have been topped with a large bulbous dome placed centrally; two smaller square cupolas or minarets at the front corners were also to be topped with a small dome.

The street-facing elevation of the Peel Street houses was to be adapted into a mix of domestic terrace with Islamised features. To each side of the façade, Victorian sash windows were to be placed at ground and first-floor level, no doubt to match the style and scale of the existing windows on the street. In the centre of the façade an ogee-arched doorway and window at first-floor level would have been flanked by column profiles topped with small domes. The pitched roof of the Peel Street houses was to be removed and replaced with a flat roof, probably to enable

the dome and minarets behind to be visible from the street.

The proposed front elevation of the mosque shows a large central arched entrance doorway, emphasised with mouldings. Rectangular windows in similar proportions to those of the Victorian houses are shown evenly arranged on the rest of the façade, and simple decoration was indicated along the parapet. The three other elevations were similarly designed, with large arched windows formally and symmetrically arranged.

The intended mosque, with its size, proportion and the scale of its architectural elements, suggests a building of some stature and independence, indifferent to the fact that it would have been squeezed into the back garden of a terrace of workers' housing and would never really be seen from any kind of distance. It could be that the mosque commissioners wanted their first mosque to be a building that demonstrated its identity and function, regardless of whether or not it would be visible.

These proposals were subsequently amended,[97] the first-floor rooms of the houses, labelled 'private rooms' on the initial application, were renamed as 'prayer rooms' with a note added that they were not to be used as residences. The central walkway through the Peel Street houses was replaced with two entrance doors, closer in scale and style to the doors they would have been replacing. The ground-floor plan was revised, the assembly room and classroom being replaced with lobby-type spaces, a kitchen and sitting room, along with the ablution facilities. The mosque itself would have remained substantially the same in the amendment, with some alterations to the parapet line. Perhaps the most significant change, however, was the direction of the Qibla, which was now in the right side, or north-eastern wall. Although the Qibla was not accurately positioned in either the initial design or the amendment, it is likely that if the mosque had been built a more accurate south-easterly direction would have been used. The prayer lines therefore would have ended up askew within the rectangular space.

By June 1939 a second application, this time unsuccessful, had been submitted for the three houses, without the purpose-built mosque in the rear garden. Its scope was restricted to the conversion of the houses to serve as a mosque.[98] It is probable that this second scheme, reduced in ambition, was a result of financial constraints that prevented the first proposal from being realised.

Fig 2.29 (opposite) Unrealised proposal for a new mosque at Peel Street by Osborne V Webb, 1937 (approved in 1938). The mosque was proposed as a new building in the garden of the terraced houses at Nos 17–19, while the houses themselves were to be converted into ancillary facilities. [By kind permission of Powell Dobson (Glamorgan RO BC/S/1/33198)] (IWM D15285)

The proposal was rejected by the local authority for reasons which are not apparent from records, but had it been implemented it would have been Britain's second recorded house mosque after Quilliam's mosque in Liverpool of 1895. The plans were prepared by T E Smith, a local architect, for the 'Western Moslem Faith', as labelled on the drawings. The building owner is specified as being Hassan Ishmael, who served as Sheikh al-Hakimi's deputy.[99]

With this proposal, the internal form of No 17 was to be retained, with a front room and back room either side of a central staircase, and a rear closet wing containing the kitchen. On the first floor the staircase would have arrived at a small landing between bedrooms. The proposal left this arrangement intact, but it widened the entrance doorway and hall, and extended the kitchen to the rear. Although the rooms were retained, they were no longer labelled with domestic uses.

Houses 18 and 19 were to be substantially altered, with all internal walls removed to create a large hall on each floor. On the ground floor this hall was labelled as the mosque, and on the first floor it was simply labelled as a large room. The first-floor hall would have been accessed from the domestic staircase of No 17, a doorway being opened in the party wall of Nos 17 and 18. The closet-wing kitchens of Nos 18 and 19 were to be extended and infilled to form a series of WC and ablution facilities.

On the front elevation, the windows on the ground and first floors to Nos 18 and 19 were intended to be bricked up to half their original size, and the entrance door to No 18 was to completely replace a window. The timber sash style was retained for the new window openings, suggesting that the mosque was attempting to maintain a stylistic congruence with the street.

This proposal demonstrates how domestic space could potentially be reshaped to create open prayer halls and ablution facilities, along with some ancillary spaces. The proposal takes three domestic layouts characterised by small cellular spaces driven by concepts of privacy, and combines them into a shared religious space driven by concepts of collectivity. This is a conceptual shift that would underpin the genre of house mosques that were to follow later in the century.

Eventually a mosque was built to replace the Peel Street houses, and it was reported in the *Picture Post* magazine for September 1943. This mosque was approved as a temporary building in March 1943 through to July 1944.[100]

ELEVATION · TO · PEEL · ST

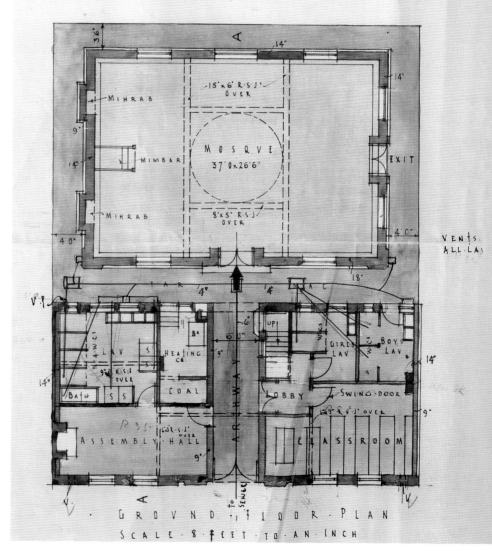

GROUND · FLOOR · PLAN
SCALE · 8 · FEET · TO · AN · INCH

The three terraced houses were cleared, and two equal-sized single-storey structures were erected, stretching from the front of the site to the back, separated by a path of approximately 1 metre. The building on the right (east) side was open plan and served as the prayer hall. The building on the left (west) side had a more varied use, with a schoolroom at the front, a residence for a 'sheikh' on the centre of the plan and ablution facilities to the rear. Both buildings were constructed using a prefabricated 'Tarran' hut system. This system was widely used during the war and was probably employed here for speed and cost. It did indeed enable the mosque to be erected quickly, between the planning approval in March 1943 and the opening that September (Fig 2.30).

The front wall was an interesting interpretation of the Peel Street terrace. The original form of the terraced house was retained, but the doors were replaced with window openings, and a new grand opening was formed on the right side of the elevation, which rose the full two storeys and was arched and emphasised with a surround. The windows were replaced with open pre-cast concrete grilles, and as the houses behind had been demolished the façade now served simply and effectively as a screen. The pitched roof was removed and replaced with a line of crenellated tiles and corbels at regular intervals along the façade. This was an interesting evolution of the first Peel Street proposal, where a new mosque was shown as a free-standing structure to the rear of the houses. It is possible that that scheme was considered too expensive, or perhaps the adaptation of the houses was too impractical.

This 1943 mosque shows what can be achieved through substantial redevelopment, in what was the first proposal for a completely new facility on the site. There is an idiosyncratic mix here of new temporary buildings, which have no symbolic expression, and the treatment of the façade, which is transformed from the front wall of terraced houses to a boundary screen signifying a mosque and alluding to traditional Islamic cities where high boundary walls conceal buildings behind.

Three years later, in November 1946, the community was in a position to replace the temporary enclosure serving as the mosque with a permanent building. A planning application for a replacement building was submitted in the name of Sheikh Hassan of 14 Sophia Street. The designs were again by Osborne V Webb.[101]

The footprint of the new mosque was the same as that of the temporary one, and it was shown on the application as a simple, rendered, flat-roofed building with domed cupolas at each corner. Arched doors and windows punctuate the façades. There was an interesting innovation in relation to the traditional styles of the earlier designs in that the cupolas were now dropped and integrated into the façade, to give a more castle-like impression. Perhaps this was a deliberate move away from the overly Mughal character of the previous mosques that Webb had been designing on the Butetown sites.

This was the mosque that was eventually built on the Peel Street site, completed in 1947. Over the next 30 years post-war clearance and redevelopment transformed the landscape of Tiger Bay around it. Photographs over this period show the mosque at first within its Peel

Fig 2.30
The Lord Mayor of Cardiff, Councillor James Griffiths, addresses the audience at the ceremonial opening of the first (and temporary) Peel Street Mosque, in September 1943. The front walls of the terraced houses have been recast into a screen wall with a full-height, arched entrance doorway.
[© Imperial War Museums (D 15285)]

Street terrace (Fig 2.31), and then standing as a lone outpost of pre-war Butetown, with the Victorian streets cleared away around it as Peel Street itself became an extension of Maria Street.

Other proposals in Tiger Bay

Over the period that the Noor-el-Islam Mosque at Peel Street was being planned and built, there was also a series of other applications to create Muslim worship space at sites around Tiger Bay. These ranged from small single-room proposals to a new-build mosque of some stature. They were mostly never built but are again illustrative of the mosque-forming activity of the Yemeni community during the mid-20th century.

17 Maria Street, 1941

A curious application was made for a small single-room structure at the end of the rear garden of a mid-terrace house on Maria Street, just one street south of Peel Street.[102] It would have measured just 5 metres by 2 metres, and been constructed of a single-skin brick wall with a flat concrete roof. It would have had one entrance door and one window facing the garden and no internal features that might have distinguished it as a mosque. In essence, this structure was to have been little more than a garden shed, but it was applied for as a 'private mosque' and approved in August 1941. The applicant was named as Ali Basha, and the proposal was designed by T E Smith, the architect of the 1939 Peel Street house mosque proposal.

10 Sophia Street, 1941

Another application for a house-mosque conversion was submitted just one week after the private mosque application at Maria Street, again by the architect T E Smith, suggesting there might have been some connection between the two projects. The applicant was Mr Sher, the secretary of the 'Moslim Community'. While the application was first approved for 10 months in August 1941, the licence was renewed continuously through to 1959, strongly indicating that the scheme was realised.[103]

This mosque was most likely the architectural manifestation of the rift that developed in the late 1930s and early 1940s between Sheikh al-Hakimi and his deputy, Sheikh Hassan Ishmael. A *South Wales Echo* newspaper article of 1955 refers to a rival mosque being set up by the latter in Sophia Street,[104] which this application most probably shows. It is possible that the proposed private mosque at Maria Street was linked to this

breakaway Yemeni group, as an urgent attempt to establish any kind of mosque to serve as an ideological base.

The house-mosque conversion at Sophia Street differed from the Peel Street house-mosque proposal in that it was for a single terraced house, while Peel Street combined three houses. The plans show the front room and rear dining room connected to form a prayer hall, the rear closet-wing kitchen retained and an ablution facility constructed in the rear yard extending from the back of the kitchen. The first floor is not shown as having any alterations and is labelled as 'existing house', suggesting that this building was to be a mixture of residence and mosque. This would also concur with the conversion being an attempt by Sheikh Hassan's new group to establish a mosque in what might have been the house of one of the group's members. They might not have had the resources in their early stages to acquire a dedicated premises.

It cannot be confirmed that this mosque was built, as the terraces have since been demolished. The proposal, however, is small and rudimentary, showing the essential alterations required to adapt domestic architecture to religious. It shows how essential the mosque was to the specific identity of the Muslim community establishing it. The diversity of the Muslim population that emerged in Cardiff is a trait that contributed to the increase in the range and number of mosques that would follow over the next decades.

34–35 Maria Street, 1944

An unrealised proposal for conversion into a mosque of two terraced houses on Maria Street was drawn up by a local firm of architects, Ivor Jones and John Bishop, for 'The International Moslem Society', of which a Haji Ali Musa is named as secretary.[105]

The houses were slightly larger than the Peel Street terraces, having three bedrooms and a staircase running front to back along the side wall, accessed from a hallway. The ground floors contained front living rooms and rear dining rooms, with kitchens in the closet wing and WCs attached to the rear wall.

The proposal retained the main body of the houses, connecting the front and rear rooms in each; in No 34 the conjoined rooms were to form a meeting room and in No 35 a mosque. The staircase at No 35 was to be removed to provide more space for the mosque room, meaning that the whole of the first floor of both houses would be accessible from the existing staircase of No 34. At the rear, a full-width extension would have been constructed, replacing one of the closet-wing kitchens and incorporating and extending the other. This rear extension would have contained the WC and ablution facilities for the mosque, and would have been accessed directly from the mosque.

On the first floor the former bedrooms were to be converted into residential uses alongside mosque uses. As it is not drawn, it can be assumed that the front elevation was to be retained as existing, which means that the mosque would have been indistinguishable from other houses in the terrace.

This was the third house-mosque proposal in Butetown and showed an emerging typology in the requirement for a prayer hall and meeting room to be the largest rooms. The series of proposals also had an element of residential provision, indicating that an imam would be living on the premises, and the living quarters would be embedded into the mosque spaces. Perhaps this was a practicality, due to limited space rather than any preference or requirement. It is not clear what the relationship was between the Maria Street house-mosque scheme and the (temporary) Peel Street Mosque that opened a year earlier: whether it was for a different Muslim group or whether another mosque was needed because of the size of the community is not known.

Bute Street 1946

The most monumental and ambitious mosque proposal in Tiger Bay to date, again designed by Osborne V Webb, the architect of the 1938 Peel Street proposal and the 1947 Peel Street (Noor-el-Islam) Mosque, remained unrealised.[106] The proposal was for a formal and ornate two-and-a-half-storey building with a large central dome and six turrets arranged along its perimeter. The Bute Street north-east-facing façade, which would have fronted the street, was to have had a large mihrab bay located in its centre, with a half-dome enclosing it. Two large keyhole-shaped windows were shown either side of the bay. The entrance to the mosque would have been on the opposite south-west façade, which was essentially the rear of the building in terms of Bute Street. The entrance door was to be a tall arch centrally placed, with surrounding ornamentation emphasising its formality. Tall keyhole-shaped windows were to be placed on either side of the door, to match the Bute Street elevation. Along the side of the mosque there was to be a single-storey WC and ablution block, separated from the mosque by a glazed covered corridor.

Along the south-western boundary of the site, effectively behind the mosque when approached from Bute Street, there were to be two ancillary buildings stretching along the site perimeter. The two-storey buildings were designed to be domestic in scale and styling, with a route through the centre of them to connect the mosque main entrance to a street running along the back of the site. These buildings were intended as a school, with a large classroom on the ground floor along with WCs for children, an office, kitchen and sitting room. The first floor was meant for a large reading and writing room in one wing, and bedrooms in another.

The Bute Street proposal followed the same design approach as the 1938 Peel Street plan, where the houses were retained along the street front and a new mosque was built behind them taking up the garden. This repetition of the houses-mosque plan suggests that a new typology could have emerged wherein existing residential and new mosque programmes would come together to form a composite architecture. With Bute Street, the 'houses' were actually to be newly built along the perimeter, rather than kept as existing as with the earlier Peel Street proposal, and an independent mosque was to be built behind them. The mosque's main entrance would have faced the houses rather than the main street, which in this instance was Bute Street. This is slightly curious in that the main frontage of the mosque, with the formal entrance door and ornamental styling, would never have been seen from the street and would only have been visible from within the gap between the ancillary facilities and the mosque. Perhaps the 1938 Peel Street plan was considered to be so effective that it was adopted as a model to be replicated in a new mosque complex.

With the Bute Street proposal, a new architectural language for the mosque was becoming much more stylised than in any previous schemes, and the design references were distinctly Mughal, with bulbous domes, rounded arches, cupolas and formal proportions. This in itself was anomalous considering that the Muslim community establishing the mosque originated in Yemen, and these architectural references were not indigenous to their homelands. It could have been that such an aesthetic language was the suggestion of the architect, who might have been more familiar with Indian styles of architecture as these were prevalent in the British imagination of its empire.

The school buildings that were proposed around the perimeter of the site were devoid of any overt Islamic stylisation, which was restricted to the arched entrance doorway and gate. These buildings were instead intended to be plain, with tall pitched roofs, rendered walls and steel-framed windows.

The Bute Street proposal was stated as being for Sheikh Hassan of 9 and 10 Sophia Street. No 10 Sophia Street was the subject of the house-mosque conversion in 1941, which suggests that the Bute Street new-build proposal was intended as the next step from the original house mosque to a grander purpose-built facility.[107] The mosque on Bute Street, however, was never built; instead the community went on to build the mosque at Alice Street that became known as the South Wales Islamic Centre (*see* pp 52–6).

The demolition and replacement of the Noor-el-Islam Mosque, Peel Street, 1988

> With its four tinted minarets and large dome, it looks totally incongruous in its modern setting; a little like a giant birthday cake ... It will be a shame to lose this fine, funny little building which has had such a lively history.[108]

This national newspaper article reports that the Noor-el-Islam Mosque was, by 1988, in a considerable state of disrepair, with crumbling brickwork, weeds and damp (Fig 2.32). The mosque committee therefore saw no option but to demolish it and replace it with a new building, and it was reported that the embassy of Saudi Arabia had promised £260,000 towards this. The replacement mosque took five years to construct – work was sporadic due to intermittent funding – and finally opened in August 1993.[109] During that period the congregation used a house as a temporary mosque, and also the mosque in Alice Street.

By the time it reopened the mosque was under the stewardship of a new Somali imam who had come to Britain to study, replacing the Yemeni imam. Noor-el-Islam became a religious centre for the Somali community in Butetown, a congregation that has diversified over the last few years with Pakistani and convert Muslims, so that the mosque now operates in three languages: Somali, Arabic and English.[110]

The 1993 mosque that replaced the 1947 building is a somewhat utilitarian two-storey brick construction, built to cover the whole site (*see* Fig. 2.27). The entrance door has been emphasised with brick banding and keystones surrounding the opening, and a timber balcony has been fitted above, which may have been intended as a place from which the adhan (call to prayer) could be issued. A dome has been placed on the centre of the flat roof; however, it is quite shallow and is therefore not easily noticeable from the street. There are no other features that identify the building as a mosque,

Fig 2.32
The Noor-el-Islam Mosque at Peel Street, photographed c 1987, shortly before its demolition in 1988.
[Courtesy of Cardiff Council Library Service]

and with grilles on the windows it has a somewhat forlorn air.

The main prayer hall is on the ground floor, with circulation spaces located around it. The lines of prayer are at an angle within the room so that worshippers are facing the Qibla. A large hall on the first floor with a central movable partition allows for additional or women's prayer space, as well as classrooms.

The terraces to the east of the mosque were acquired and replaced with four residential flats. A one-million-pound redevelopment proposal followed in 2009 to extend the mosque and provide five self-contained flats.[111] By 2017 the redevelopment plan remained unrealised and the mosque continued to raise funds.[112]

The proposal also adds a minaret to the existing building, and the part two-storey, part three-storey residential development alongside proposes a glazed curtain-wall stair core centrally placed on the front elevation, in a fairly straightforward commercial architectural style.

The description of the proposal on the website of the Noor-el-Islam Mosque offers an insight into the needs faced by the current mosque community:

> Trebling the size of the main prayer halls and expanding other areas such as the wudhu facilities ... providing a decent washroom where we can wash our Muslim dead with dignity ... educational rooms and an Islamic library so that the pure message of Islam based on the Quran and the Sunnah according to the understanding of the companions can be taught and propagated.[113]

This series of mosque proposals and buildings shows an intense period of activity and effort aimed at creating mosques in Butetown. Taken together, the proposals offer the earliest examples of the fashioning of mosques from Victorian domestic architecture and streetscapes in Britain. They encompass a range of approaches that set patterns for later mosque types, and against which later mosques can be compared.

The South Wales Islamic Centre, Alice Street, and the modernist experiment

By the 1940s Sheikh al-Hakimi had developed political ambitions and was an outspoken critic of the then regime in Yemen, becoming one of the leaders of the Free Yemeni movement which garnered much of its support from the Yemeni diaspora. The Sheikh used his base at the Noor-el-Islam Mosque to spread his political message among Yemeni seamen in Cardiff and South Shields and by 1948 was publishing an Arabic-language newspaper, *Al-Salam*, from the mosque. By the late 1940s a rival Yemeni faction, loyal to the regime in Yemen, had established itself in Cardiff led by Sheikh Hassan Ishmael, formerly for many years Sheikh al-Hakimi's deputy. Bitter rivalries continued between the factions through the 1940s and early 1950s. Even though the anti-regime Sheikh al-Hakimi returned to Yemen in 1952,[114] the feuding continued in Cardiff and in 1955 a brawl between the two groups in the Peel Street Mosque was reported in the local newspaper.[115] It was this gulf that led Sheikh Ishmael's pro-Yemeni faction to establish their own mosque, which according to the 1955 news story was initially at Sophia Street (*see* pp 49–50) before moving in the mid-1960s to Alice Street, where the South Wales Islamic Centre now stands.

The site of the Alice Street Mosque was a warehouse at the end of a street of terraced houses, within the narrow terraces of Butetown and only a few hundred metres from the Peel Street Noor-el-Islam Mosque. The first planning permission was given in May 1967 for a 'mosque, Sheikh's residence and car park',[116] and this scheme was realised two years later as the second purpose-built mosque in Cardiff and the fourth in Britain.

The applicant was named as Sheikh Ishmael and the mosque was designed by Osborne V Webb, 24 years after his first purpose-built mosque design at Peel Street. Webb's design was a radical departure from any of the mosques he had designed for the other Butetown sites, and embodied the stylistic shift that had taken place in contemporary architectural design, as well as indicating the architect's own evolution (Figs 2.33, 2.34 and 2.35).

This building was determinedly contemporary, reflecting the stylistic influences of post-war British modernism that had been emerging since the early 1950s. The plan was a simple arrangement of a circular prayer hall, and an offset rectangular two-storey residence linked to the prayer hall with a single-storey entrance lobby. The prayer hall was topped by a concrete shell roof with glazed side panels and glazed flat roof infill sections. This was a reinterpretation of the traditional dome that referenced contemporary modernist commercial and ecclesiastical architecture. The external walls of the prayer hall and lobby were rendered, and the residential block was brick-faced. The only concessions to traditional Islamic styles were found in the detailing of the entrance doors and lobby windows, which had ogee-arched frameworks. A series of smaller windows to the lobby were triangular, neither strictly traditionally Islamic nor modernist, but cleverly acceptable to both.

The Alice Street Mosque was almost immediately re-evaluated by its users as their actual requirements could now be tested within a new religious space. It is probable that the building was not built to the standard envisaged by the architect as costs were being saved throughout construction; in addition, much of the technology in relation to glazing and design would have been quite experimental and therefore prone to failure if not installed properly. For these and

perhaps a number of other functional reasons, the community soon found that the building did not quite meet their needs and a series of planning applications followed to try to amend and alter it.

In 1971 the office of O V Webb submitted a set of drawings to the council for comment,[117] proposing extension of the mosque with a covering letter outlining the reasons:

> The Mosque provided the maximum accommodation possible with the funds available at the time, but it has become increasingly obvious that the building does not fully meet the needs of the community.

Fig 2.33 (below left)
Computer-generated reconstruction of O V Webb's South Wales Islamic Centre, built in 1969 and demolished in 1979. [Visualisation by Moksud Khan at Makespace Architects]

Fig 2.34 (bottom left)
Site block plan of O V Webb's 1969 South Wales Islamic Centre at Alice Street. [Based on site plan dated May 1967 held in City of Cardiff planning file PA67/29518, by kind permission of Powell Dobson]

Fig 2.35 (bottom right)
Proposed east elevation facing Alice Street (top) and north elevation (bottom) of Webb's 1969 South Wales Islamic Centre. [Based on drawings dated May 1967 held in City of Cardiff planning file PA67/29518, by kind permission of Powell Dobson]

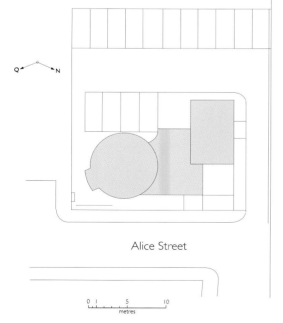

Alice Street

0 1   5   10
      metres

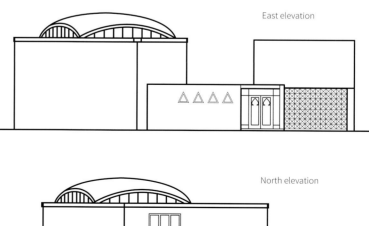

East elevation

North elevation

The present proposal is to provide a block of approx 2,000 ft sq with facilities for the instruction of children and to enable the wives to participate in worship.

The original approved drawing indicated 15 car parking spaces. The Sheik informs us that there have never been more than 6 cars parked at any time, because the majority of users live in the immediate area. The present proposal would not appear to increase the need for parking and we should be obliged if you would let us have your comments on this aspect.[118]

The proposal was never implemented, and there was no further application from the office of O V Webb. Instead in 1978 a new design proposal and application was submitted by D Comrie of 21 Dorchester Avenue, Cardiff.[119] This proposal showed additional wings of ablution facilities on each side of the building, as well as the squaring off of the main circular prayer hall. The sections and elevations showed the mosque transformed into an uninspiring series of brick boxes, with half-hearted domed turrets at each corner, a simple pitched roof replacing its concrete and glazed sculptured predecessor.

It is not clear if the 1978 proposal to extend the mosque was approved but it was not implemented and it would probably still have been insufficient for the mosque's needs. The impetus to revisit the design of the original building stemmed from inadequate space, but also from the poor quality of construction of the 1967–9 building – a result of the extremely limited resources then available to the mosque community.[120] In 1979, the community found a solution to the mosque's shortcomings when it decided to demolish it and replace it with a new building. To that end an application was submitted by Davies Llewelyn Partnership, a Cardiff architectural practice, for the demolition of the existing building and its complete replacement with a new mosque (Fig 2.36).[121] The mosque apparently chose this practice on the basis that they had an office near Butetown, and, according to the architects, members of the mosque committee simply knocked on their door one afternoon and presented them with their project.[122] The plan and general arrangement was similar to that of the demolished mosque, with the main prayer hall oriented towards Makkah, although this time it was square (Fig 2.37). An entrance lobby and ablution facilities linked the prayer hall to a residential block for the imam. The additional facilities of a women's prayer hall, of similar size to the men's hall, and a library were also provided.

The composition shows a clear arrangement of brick forms varying in height, with rounded corners and without Islamic adornment except for a small turret at each corner. These appear somewhat out of character with the modern formalism of the rest of the building, suggesting perhaps that they were included at the behest of the mosque rather than being part of the architectural concept.

In 1981, two years after the replacement mosque was approved, a subsequent application was submitted and approved for the addition of the dome.[123] The proposed elevations show the new central dome replacing the domed turrets of the approved scheme and being a more successful addition to the overall composition of the building.

Fig 2.36
Perspective view of the 1979 redesigned scheme for the South Wales Islamic Centre, by Davies Llewelyn Partnership (prior to the inclusion of a bronze dome).
[By kind permission of Davies Llewelyn & Jones]

Fig 2.37
The men's prayer hall of the
South Wales Islamic Centre.
[DP137687]

An article in the national press on the opening of the mosque in 1984 gives some clues to the struggles that the community faced over funding the building. The article reports that the total cost of the mosque was £400,000, and that work on the building had stopped two years prior to its opening with £90,000 needed to complete the roof. On hearing of the stalled project, a Yemeni businessman donated £50,000, and the Libyan government a further £100,000. Throughout the project, Iraq had donated £29,000, and Qatar and Kuwait £10,000 each; various other contributions came from Arab businessmen.[124]

After the mosque opened, the quest to add a minaret to the building continued and in 1987 the position and design of a suitable minaret was agreed as an amendment to the 1981 planning application. A letter from the architects Davies Llewelyn and Jones (formerly the Davies Llewelyn Partnership) describes the proposal:

> The minaret is 14.5m high and it is proposed to use the same Forest Royal hand made bricks as the rest of the Mosque building. Our clients have been raising finance from local people within their community to fund this feature since the completion of the mosque some four years ago.[125]

The negotiations over the siting of the minaret drew in the local MP, Alun Michael, who supported the mosque's case in a letter to the planning authorities:

> As I understand it the Mosque opened in 1984 after a number of years and going through a variety of problems to reach that far. It also acts as a cultural centre and some parts are not yet completed. The main remaining item is the minaret which is important as a visual part of the development but of course has religious and procedural importance for the community. I understand they are adamant that it is not intended to blare out noise and music from the minaret and all the necessary conditions are fully accepted.[126]

The plan and elevation of the minaret shows that the form of the mosque as it exists now is complete (*see* Fig 2.28). Its planning and financial history show its realisation to have been an iterative and negotiated process.

Within a few years of the completion of the mosque, a section of adjacent land was acquired. In 1989 a proposal was submitted to extend the mosque facility with a new-build community centre and three flats,[127] and this was subsequently approved and built (Fig 2.38). The plans show a simple and utilitarian building, faced with brickwork to match the existing mosque. On the ground floor is a community hall, kitchen, women's room and play room, and the three flats are arranged on the first floor.

Fig 2.38
View from the rear of the South Wales Islamic Centre, showing the community hall in the foreground that was added in the 1990s, designed by Varma and Griffiths Architects and Engineers.
[DP137689]

At time of writing (2017) the new extension works remained unrealised and the mosque was continuing its fundraising drive.

Conclusion

The Muslim history of Tiger Bay encapsulates one of the most significant concentrated histories of mosque establishment in Britain. Cardiff and other port towns were home to the first settled Muslim communities that emerged from the late 19th century to the mid-20th century. Cardiff, largely because of the influence of Sheikh al-Hakimi, saw Muslim identity, for the first time, make the transition from being a largely private, individual and hidden practice to being a collective, public and institutional one. Tiger Bay, therefore, was the first place in Britain where a Muslim community was attempting to use architecture to articulate its identity through a series of geographically concentrated projects.

The architectural proposals for the two mosque sites in Butetown, along with the proposals that were not built, provide the earliest examples of how Victorian working-class architecture was adjusted, shaped and appropriated to create space for Muslim social and religious life. They serve as early examples of a certain type of architectural transformation that would become typical of the hundreds of mosques subsequently formed across Britain through the adaptation of existing buildings. Furthermore, the new mosque buildings that were eventually built on each site were not only among the earliest examples of purpose-built mosques in Britain, but also remain among the most interesting and idiosyncratic examples of mosque architecture in the country.

As in many places in Britain, the Muslim communities of Butetown are growing and diversifying. The older-generation Yemeni and Somali population is decreasing and being replaced by Pakistani, Bangladeshi, new Somali and convert Muslims. Through the urban redevelopment of the 1960s, the landscape of Tiger Bay has been transformed and the Victorian terraces replaced with post-war housing. The Noor-el-Islam Mosque and South Wales Islamic Centre are looking to their futures, with major extension projects to diversify and extend the religious and social services they can provide. Since their inception, the mosque sites have never remained static, but are continuously being reimagined and transformed to adapt to the changing needs of the communities that use them.

In 2008 a proposal was submitted for a substantial extension to the mosque, doubling its capacity by extending the ground floor and adding a new first floor.[128] The scheme, which received planning permission the same year, was prepared by Davies Llewelyn and Jones, the original architects of the mosque. The extension continues the formalism of the existing building by proposing a uniform shape that is clad in patinated copper panels to read as a single formal element with a consistent surface. It is therefore a contemporary treatment that does not attempt any traditional Islamic symbolism.

A statement by the mosque as part of the design statement for the application offers some insight into its needs:

> Since 1984 and the present, Alhumdu Lillah ['praise God'], the Muslim Community in Cardiff has grown 3 fold and we find our Mosque cannot accommodate all our worshippers together on Fridays and Idd Days therefore need to expand the mosque the only way practical is to build another floor above the Mosque as our drawings show in order to carry out this work we call upon our Muslim Brothers and sisters to help donate as much as possible for this noble cause which will last us well into this new century.[129]

The endeavour for a Muslim architecture

This chapter has looked at the sites in Britain where the earliest mosques were built: Woking in 1889, Fazl in 1926 and two Cardiff sites in 1947 and 1969. Although these are only four sites representing the total mosque-building programme over about 80 years, each is significant in exploring and experimenting with the idea of what the mosque could or should be in Britain. These four sites are among very few places in the Western world where such an endeavour was taking place over this period – mosque building had so far primarily occurred in Muslim societies with Muslim histories, but was now being transplanted for the first time to the West.

The Woking Mosque was very much a product of its time: a triumphant celebration of all the exotic fantasy through which Victorian Britain culturally related to its Indian colony. It is at once a picturesque folly and an object of fascination, encapsulating a period at the end of the 19th century.

The Fazl Mosque carries the legacy of the Great War and an empire transformed. The flourish of Woking is appropriately absent, and is replaced with an austerity and restraint that draws from contemporary trends. Modernism has transformed the aesthetic landscape, and while the movement was slow to reach Britain, the 1920s had seen a shift in style that is reflected in the architecture of the mosque.

The mosques of Tiger Bay, both realised and imagined, demonstrate a design evolution that encapsulates the struggle with form-finding that would come to characterise mosque architecture of the later 20th century. This endeavour is essentially seen in the work of Osborne V Webb and Partners and the Davies Llewelyn Partnership (later Davies Llewelyn and Jones), where they open up the possibilities of what the contemporary architectural language of a mosque could be. For explorations of how a mosque could be adapted into existing domestic spaces, the various conversion proposals are particularly illuminating.

Webb's early work for Peel Street shows essentially traditional approaches to the mosque, with symbols such as domes, minarets, arches and symmetrical arrangements. The designs are difficult to locate in any particular historical genre but rather combine fairly generic Islamic motifs.

There is perhaps a creeping Mughal influence, more pronounced in the later designs, such as for the Bute Street Mosque of 1946.

After the Peel Street Mosque of 1947, Webb did not design another mosque until the South Wales Islamic Centre of 1967–9. By this time, with a career well advanced, Webb had discarded any allusions to traditionalism and opted for a decidedly modern approach, showing confidence and experimentation. While it seems the experiment did not pay off, with the building being demolished 10 years later, it nevertheless stands as the first modernist exploration of the mosque in Britain.

This precedent for exploring the idea of the architecture of the mosque without resorting to pastiche was continued in the replacement South Wales Islamic Centre by Davies Llewelyn Partnership. In their designs, strong forms are expressed in brick façades, evoking contemporary European trends. Although the customary symbols of the dome and minaret are incorporated, they are brought within the overall language of the contemporary approach.

These four examples (Woking, Fazl and the two Cardiff sites) are therefore of foundational importance in the architectural history of the mosque in Britain, not only because they were the first mosques, but also because all were profoundly different in their approaches. They are also significant because the Western mosque was a new paradigm with little precedent to draw from, and this new typology was first articulated and interrogated through these mosques, from Woking to Wales.

Although Quilliam's Liverpool Muslim Institute was not a purpose-built mosque, and therefore did not have any real opportunity to express a Muslim architecture, it nevertheless takes a rightful place in this analysis of the seminal sites of British Muslim history. Quilliam had established a social and religious organisation that advocated for the Muslim cause in Britain, and that connected parts of the Muslim world with British society. This was an endeavour that many of the mosques and Muslim organisations that followed also attempted, and as British-born Muslim communities grew through the latter part of the 20th century, interest in Quilliam and his institute was revived as he perhaps articulated an indigenously British Islam and a valuable model for negotiating the diverse cultural influences that this entailed.

3

Adaptation and transformation – a new era of mosque-making

Labour migration from South Asia (namely India, Pakistan and Bangladesh) began from the late 1950s, the general pattern being that migrants arrived as single men, often leaving families behind, with the intention of staying for a few years in Britain before returning home. This changed radically with the introduction of the 1962 Commonwealth Immigrants Act, which removed the right to come and go freely and restricted entry into Britain. The result was that what had in the past been temporary settlement from the New Commonwealth turned into permanent settlement, as migrants calculated that it was better to stay than to return home and risk not being allowed into Britain again.[1] Following on from this was the migration of dependants and families, who came to join their menfolk and settle permanently, and therefore the emergence of family units and the social networks these entailed. It was this establishment of the Muslim family in Britain that spurred a revitalisation of Muslim religious culture, and which provided a narrative around which the Muslim family and community could cohere.

As second-generation children were born and raised in Britain from the early 1960s, the need for the preservation and transmission of culture and religion became imperative. Prayer and religious classes for children were started in private houses, and the inevitable next step was the creation of dedicated places for these activities to take place. Most of the early mosques were formed from converted houses. Soon these house-mosque conversions were joined by the conversion into mosques of other buildings, often churches or community halls, and the two types of mosque formation continued side by side. The mosques created in this way were grass-roots community projects, each one an individual and highly localised endeavour by particular clusters of Muslim residents acting within the bounds of their locality.

Case studies

1 Jamia Masjid, Howard Street, Bradford, 1958
2 Bristol Jamia Mosque, Green Street, Totterdown, Bristol, 1968
3 Brick Lane Jamme Masjid, Brick Lane, Spitalfields, London, 1976
4 Leytonstone Masjid, Dacre Road, Leytonstone, London 1976
5 Ihsan Mosque and Islamic Centre, Chapelfield East, Norwich 1977
6 Kingston Masjid, East Road, Kingston upon Thames, Surrey 1980
7 Mosque and Islamic Centre of Brent, Howard Road and Chichele Road, Cricklewood, London, 1980
8 Brixton Mosque and Islamic Cultural Centre (Masjid Ibnu Taymeeyah), Gresham Road, Brixton, London, 1990

1 Jamia Masjid, Howard Street, Bradford, 1958

By 2015 there were 86 mosques in Bradford,[2] serving the city's 129,000 Muslims. The Muslim population had increased by 54,000 in the 10 years since 2001, and had risen from 16 to 25 per cent of the total population of the city.[3] Further analysis of the 2001 census shows that 89 per cent of the city's Muslims originated from Pakistan,[4] with the vast majority being from Mirpur (in Azad Kashmir) and Attock (a northern district in the state of Punjab).[5] The Muslim population of Bradford has historically been concentrated in 5 square miles of the inner city,[6] where it forms a majority. In the inner-city ward of Manningham in 2011, for example, Muslims constituted 75 per cent of the total population, while the proportion of the total population identifying as Pakistani was 60 per cent. In the neighbouring ward of Toller, Muslims made up 76 per cent, and 72 per cent of the ward's total

Fig 3.1
The minaret of the Brick Lane Mosque, which was added in 2009.
[DP153532]

population was of Pakistani origin. With the vast majority of Bradford's Muslim population originating from Pakistan, intra-Muslim multi-ethnicity in the city is very low, giving its Muslim identity an overwhelming Pakistani character. Also noteworthy is the fact that the wards with high Muslim populations are also the wards with the highest levels of poverty and social deprivation.

Furthermore, Bradford's South Asian populations of religions other than Muslim are also small, with Hindus and Sikhs jointly numbering just over 10,000 in the 2011 census, compared to 129,000 Muslims. This differs from other urban centres such as Birmingham where other South Asian religious communities are significant. 'It is this overwhelming predominance of Muslims which makes the city distinctive.'[7]

This Muslim demographic gives Bradford a particular cultural character, and informs how it is perceived in wider narratives of Britain's cities. Correspondingly, Bradford is 'represented and perceived as a venue of challenges and conflicts, especially in relation to ideas and issues connected with ethnic and religious diversity'.[8] The settlement patterns of Bradford's Muslim populations have led to the city being described as segregated or ghettoised, an idea reinforced by statistics gathered in 2005 which showed that 44 of the city's mosques were located within 7 inner-city postcodes, with 30 of the mosques within just 3 postcodes.[9]

Sociological discourses exploring Bradford's Muslim communities tend to discuss its mosques

Fig 3.2
The Jamia Masjid in Bradford's central district was the first mosque in the city. Established first at 30 Howard Street in 1958, it was incrementally extended into Nos 28 and 32.
[DP143430]

as being resources which are contested within intra-Muslim politics and identity. More so than in cities such as London, where Muslim populations are ethnically diverse, Bradford's mosques have been discussed in terms of how cultural and religious power structures are played out through them.

Bradford's first mosque was established in a converted terraced house in Howard Street in 1958 (Fig 3.2). It was established by the Pakistani Muslim Association, whose trustees 'included both West and East Pakistanis [which would now mean Pakistanis and Bangladeshis] from a variety of sectarian traditions'.[10] It was used for religious functions and also practical purposes, such as translating official documentation and addressing letters home, by those immigrants whose English was poor.[11]

Religious and cultural differences within the community, largely based on Deobandi versus Barelwi approaches, seem to have surfaced 10 years into the mosque's existence, when Pakistanis from the Punjab took control of the mosque and installed their own full-time Deobandi scholar. Over this period other mosques were forming in the city on similarly denominational lines, and a diversifying Muslim landscape was taking shape: 'Another Deobandi mosque was set up by Gujaratis from Surat, and the Bengali Twaquila Islamic Society established a mosque in two houses on Cornwall Road.'[12] The mid-1960s were also the time when a young Pir Maruf Hussain Shah, from a Sufi lineage in Mirpur, established Bradford's first Barelwi organisation, the Tabligh-ul-Islam, which opened its first mosque in Southfield Square in 1966. By 2011 the organisation was operating 17 mosques across Bradford, including the Bradford Central Mosque (*see* p 262).

In a 1994 study, Howard Street Mosque was identified as one of Bradford's 14 Deobandi mosques, of which 'seven are controlled by Pathans and Punjabis from Chhachh in Pakistan, four by Suratis from Gujarat in India – two of which by Suratis who migrated to East Africa – and three by Sylhetis from Bangladesh'.[13]

Howard Street is within 500 metres of Bradford's Town Hall, and is one of the first residential streets on the south-eastern edge of the town centre. The houses date from the mid-19th century and are of sandstone brick, with ground floors raised over semi-basements. The terrace is listed, with architectural characteristics such as stone door architraves, dentilled cornices and arched passages through the

terrace to rear access yards. It is also noted for interest as an 'unaltered, small, town house terrace at the beginning of the mid century building boom'.[14]

The reasons for this building boom can be seen in 19th-century maps of Bradford. The townscape from the western edges of the town centre is clustered with a series of textile mills and works buildings, forming the street pattern. Howard Street and its neighbouring streets of housing were within walking distance of this industrial heartland, and therefore the natural location for the mill workers to settle in the mid-19th century, and again for new immigrants to settle in the mid-20th century.

The mosque was first accommodated in a basic conversion of 30 Howard Street. Upper- and lower-ground floors were used as prayer rooms, and the first floor and roof space were classrooms or overspill prayer space. The entrance was from the rear of the house, accessed via a passageway from the street that cut through the terrace. Soon after, the mosque acquired No 28, the property next door, and was extended across both houses. The two were fully amalgamated, the separating walls between them being removed, along with all internal partitions on the lower- and upper-ground floors, and two extensive prayer halls created. As the external façades were conserved, the interiors of these prayer halls retain the traces of the domesticity of the former houses, with front doors and bay windows indicating the former domestic plan of each house (Fig 3.3).

Fig 3.3
The upper-ground-floor prayer hall of the Jamia Masjid (Howard Street Mosque), showing the original entrance door to one of the houses. The internal walls have been removed to create an open hall for prayer.
[Author]

In 1979 the next house in the terrace, No 32 on the western side of the passageway, was also purchased. The first floor was extended all the way across the three houses, over the top of the passage, to form a large additional prayer hall and classroom area (Fig 3.4). The upper- and lower-ground floors of the new house were largely unaltered from their domestic plans and used as offices for the mosque.

There was some consternation at the application to extend the mosque, the council's highways officer commenting that 'these premises are springing up like mushrooms. There is already one next to this I believe. Any extension, I feel would encourage parking and adversely affect movement close to the junction of Howard Street and Landsdown Place.'[15]

However, generally there were no planning objections, and in fact the mosque was considered

Fig 3.4
The first-floor prayer hall of the Jamia Masjid, which has been set up with reading benches for Islamic classes. The internal party walls between the houses have been removed to create as open a space as possible.
[Author]

Fig 3.5
The Qibla wall of the main prayer hall on the upper-ground floor in the converted houses of the Jamia Masjid. Two simple niches contain the imam's prayer mat and the minbar respectively.
[Author]

a way of protecting the terrace, which otherwise had an uncertain future. As the case officer commented:

Howard Street [is a] former residential terraced street. Now only a small number of properties used as such, rest blocked up.

Uncertain future of most of these terraced properties because of clearance proposals and fact that they are Listed.

Mosque occupies Nos. 28–30 at present. These are to remain whatever the future of the rest of properties.

Site, no. 32, forms the western end of the side of Howard St, so there is a great deal of logic behind the proposal.[16]

The area planning officer also commented on the future of the area:

The planning future of the Little Horton housing area is uncertain, in terms of existing properties because of the dialogue between clearance and conservation proposals. However, no. 28 and 30 Howard St – mosque – are to remain whatever the outcome and it would thus appear expedient to allow No. 32 to form an extension to the existing premises since this would not adversely affect the potential for continued housing in this area.[17]

To cater for the increased capacity of the building, an escape stairwell was added to the rear in 2003 and a larger ablution facility was provided in a new single-storey rear extension.[18] Both additions were faced with local sandstone

brick with stone features and built in a style to match the character of the listed buildings, without any Islamic embellishments.

The interior of the mosque remains largely unadorned, with a mihrab niche cut into the Qibla-facing wall on lower-ground, upper-ground and first-floor levels, indicating how the mosque has been used in each phase of its growth. Around the mihrab on the lower-ground and upper-ground floors are prayer time clocks, and framed Quranic scripts. The cut-out for the mihrab itself is a modestly decorated profile, but with no applied decorative work (Fig 3.5).

Conclusion

Howard Street Mosque was one of the first mosques created by the post-war wave of immigrants from South Asia, and it typifies such mosques by starting as a single converted house, and expanding into a terrace of interconnected spaces for religious use. It shows how domestic architecture is gradually transformed through a process of iterative alterations, and accordingly how a residential language is reinscribed with a religious and institutional one.

This mosque also demonstrates that the house mosque is not necessarily a phase on the route to mosque establishment, but can happily serve as the final destination. Some fortuity enables this: that the Qibla direction is aligned with the flank wall of the house, so that the prayer halls can make the most effective use of the space available. Also, the fact that the internal walls could be removed to such a degree as to completely open up the floor plates across two or three houses means that the open-plan prayer halls can accommodate a large number of worshippers, and can be used flexibly as classrooms.

The mosque remains at the heart of a Muslim community, and is well used. Around 170 children attend daily after-school religious education classes, attesting to the size of the local catchment. Despite insecurity regarding the fate of the terrace in the late 1970s, it has survived, with the mosque remaining embedded within it. This points to one of the consequences of numerous mosque conversions, sometimes in listed buildings, where the mosque reuse serves to retain buildings that might otherwise have been demolished. Howard Street Mosque has preserved the character of the houses, without introducing any new external visual languages. Only simple signage indicates that it functions as the key local religious institution for one of Bradford's Muslim communities.

2 Bristol Jamia Mosque, Green Street, Totterdown, Bristol, 1968

Houses were not the only types of building to be converted into mosques by newly emerging Muslim communities. Although the earliest mosques, such as Bradford's Howard Street Mosque, were created from houses, other converted buildings soon followed and proliferated alongside house conversions. Churches were amenable to conversions as they were already designated as places of worship so did not require planning permission, and they provided large halls which could be used for Muslim prayer almost from the outset, with minimal alterations.

With such conversions, architectural signification became the issue into which efforts were directed as other religious typologies were adapted and embellished with features that signalled the new Muslim use of the buildings. Bristol Jamia Mosque is one such early example, showing how a former church was transformed into the city's main mosque (Fig 3.6).

The first congregational Friday prayers in Bristol were held in 1964 at 25 Angers Road, a terraced house in the St Pauls neighbourhood. The house was owned by a young man, Mohammed Khalil Ahmed, from Faisalabad in Pakistan, who came to Bristol in 1962 to join his brother who was already settled in the city. At the time there were fewer than a hundred Asians in Bristol, mainly Sikhs and Muslims from Mirpur and Faisalabad, many of whom already knew each other from their hometowns and who were now predominantly settling in St Pauls.

The first Jummah prayers at Angers Road were attended by around a dozen people and were led by one of the community members serving as an imam.

Through the 1960s the Muslim student population in the city grew, and a room in the University of Bristol was allocated for the Friday prayer. Then in 1967 one of the local Muslims, an Iranian ex-army colonel, gathered a group of like-minded people and formed a mosque committee, with the objective of establishing a mosque in the city. On some occasions they would attend the Jummah prayers in Angers Road, and here they

Fig 3.6
Bristol Jamia Mosque from the west.
[Author]

made contact with Ahmed and enlisted his help in the movement for a new mosque. Other members of the committee were a doctoral student from Iraq and one from Pakistan.

In the same year that the mosque committee was founded (1967), it came to the attention of the group that the former St Katherine's Church on the corner of Green Street, set amid terraces of workers' housing in Totterdown, was to be sold. The church had moved to a new location nearby a few years earlier, and since then the building had been used as a British Legion Club on one floor and a warehouse on another. It was a plain rectangular building of two floors, marked out only with a steep pitched roof and Gothic pointed windows on the ground floor. Contact was made and the price negotiated at £2,500. With £700 in the mosque account, a fundraising drive was needed to secure the building. Over the weekend, Ahmed and a colleague went from Muslim house to Muslim house seeking contributions. There were 165 Muslims living in the area, and within a few days the mosque activists had raised £1,500. This was a considerable achievement as the donors were not wealthy; but as Ahmed recalled, people felt the urgent need for a mosque in their neighbourhood and gave readily.[19]

The former church was duly purchased in 1968, and Bristol's first mosque was inaugurated. To begin with, the upper floor continued to be used as a warehouse while the lower was used as the prayer hall. Very soon, however, the upper floor was cleared and brought into use as additional prayer space. Initially the number of attendees was small; Ahmed noted that religious awareness in Britain then was not as dedicated as it had become by 2011. He credited a religious revival to the Tablighi Jamaat, an Islamic movement, founded in 1927 near Delhi, whose primary mission is to revive Islam among Muslims.

Ahmed came into contact with the Jamaat while out grocery shopping one day. A group of visiting Jamaat members were enquiring about where they could stay, and Ahmed invited them to a room in his house. All 12 of the visiting missionaries stayed in the room, and invited people to pray with them. At prayer times they packed away their sleeping bags and used the room as a prayer room.

Prior to the Jamaat, as Ahmed remembers, people kept their religious observance within their own houses. But, as Ahmed experienced in Bristol, it was through the Jamaat's continuous efforts that Muslim practice as a collective and social endeavour spread. Their revivalist message reawakened Ahmed's interest in his faith, and he felt that it had a similar impact on his generation of Muslim immigrants in Britain.

Once Bristol Jamia Mosque had been set up at Green Street, a regular congregation could be established. The lower floor was used for daily and Friday prayers, and the upper floor was used for the biannual Eid congregational prayer. The mosque advertised for an imam locally in Bristol and in Gloucester, as there was a significant Muslim community there. The Gloucester Muslims originated mostly from Gujarat, to where news of the post spread, and an application came from a candidate in Gujarat who had gained his Islamic education in Madinah. The candidate was successful and was duly appointed as the imam of Bristol Jamia Mosque. Over the years the imams have either been from Pakistan, from where most of the congregation also originate, or from Gujarat.

The first application to alter the building was made in 1978.[20] It proposed retention of the existing building and replacement of the pitched roof with a flat roof and dome, and the addition of a minaret. This shows that a primary concern of the mosque was to reinscribe the building's visual identity, to move it symbolically from being a church to a mosque. None of these external alterations were required to improve the functionality of the building but were solely related to its architectural symbolism (Fig 3.7).

On this first application the dome and minaret are of a simple design, without ornamentation or embellishment. The windows have been altered slightly, with the more Gothic-style windows of the church modified to a shallower, more triangulated arch over a rectangular window that is not obviously Islamic in source.

The internal alterations and two-storey side extension from this scheme were implemented but none of the external alterations, which were also approved as part of the planning application, were carried out. Instead another application was submitted in 1979 in which the dome and minaret were made more ornate, perhaps in response to the earlier designs being considered too plain by the community. Once approved, this was the scheme that was subsequently built.

As part of the internal alterations the existing upper floor was overhauled and decorated, incorporating the now flat ceiling and dome, to formalise its use as the main prayer hall of the mosque, with a mihrab located in the south-eastern corner (Fig 3.8). Other than this, no further internal

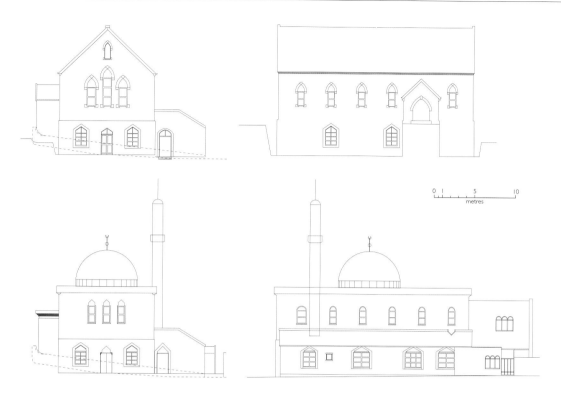

Fig 3.7
West and north elevations of the former St Katherine's Church in 1978 (it had been in use as a mosque since 1968 without any external alterations) and the proposed alterations. These included the replacement of the roof with a dome and the addition of a minaret. Although the dome and minaret were not implemented according to this scheme, the internal alterations and two-storey extension were.
[Drawings based on 1978 drawings held in Bristol City Council planning file 78/1050]

Fig 3.8
Interior view of the men's main prayer hall of Bristol Jamia Mosque, showing the interior of the dome and the mihrab in the far corner. The angles of the prayer mats show that the direction of the Qibla is askew to the building plan.
[Author]

alterations were proposed, and the halls were adapted easily to their new religious use (Figs 3.9 and 3.10). The hall on the lower floor is marked on the drawings as a social hall, for community functions and additional prayer space, and a library and office are also shown.

The two-storey extension that was added to the north-eastern side provided women's prayer space and a smaller daily prayer room, suggesting that the daily congregation was small and could be accommodated in this smaller space, leaving the main prayer hall for larger events such as Friday and Eid prayers.

The drawings showing the proposed alterations to the church were annotated in Arabic text as well as English, as they were being shown to the mosque's contacts in the Arab-speaking world in their bid to raise funds, highlighting the breadth of the fundraising exercise.

The second proposal for external alterations that was submitted in the following year showed a more stylised dome tending towards the onion shape of Mughal India, so perhaps reflecting South Asian references. The minaret remained largely plain, but with the addition of a balcony to denote the place from where the muezzin would have traditionally proclaimed the call to prayer. The dome and minaret were built in accordance with this revised design.

A series of planning applications followed over the next 30 years to carry out modest works and add facilities, illustrating the increasing requirements for space and services and a growing Muslim community. Incrementally, the

Fig 3.9 (below right)
The ground-floor plan of Bristol Jamia Mosque, showing the men's main prayer hall for Friday prayer and the smaller prayer hall for men's daily prayer to its left.

Key
1 Entrance to men's daily prayer hall
2 Entrance to men's main prayer hall
3 Men's daily prayer hall
4 Men's main prayer hall
5 Mihrab

[Rooms as used in 2013; plan based on 1978 drawing held in Bristol City Council planning file 78/1050]

Fig 3.10 (bottom right)
The lower-ground-floor plan for Bristol Jamia Mosque, with a women's prayer hall on the left adjacent to a social hall and other community functions, including residential accommodation for the imam.

Key
1 Entrance
2 Multipurpose hall
3 Store
4 Women's prayer hall
5 Women's ablution
6 Plant
7 Terrace
8 Living room
9 Bedrooms
10 Bathroom
11 Library
12 Kitchen
13 Office

[Rooms as used in 2013; plan based on 1978 drawing held in Bristol City Council planning file 78/1050]

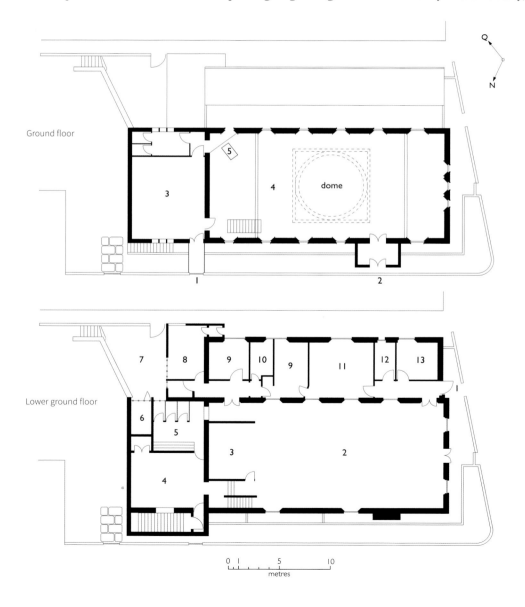

Fig 3.11
Bristol Jamia Mosque viewed along Green Street, showing the rows of terraced workers' housing among which the former St Katherine's Church had been built.
[Author]

mosque was thus adapted and extended to provide a mortuary, imam's accommodation and extensions.[21]

By 2013 the mosque was at its capacity for the Friday congregational prayer, and it was holding two Eid prayers to cope with numbers and a Muslim population that was growing and becoming more diverse. The ambition was to create more prayer space by extending the building where possible, although the scope for extension remains limited on a physically restricted site (Fig 3.11).

Conclusion

Established in 1968, Bristol Jamia Mosque was one of the earliest mosques started by the generation of immigrants from South Asia who settled in Britain after the decolonisation and Partition of India. It was unusual for its time in that it was not a converted house, as most of the early mosques were, but an existing religious building converted to mosque use. Significantly, it could well have been one of the largest mosques in Britain at the time, until eclipsed by the mosques that started being established from the 1970s.

The mosque illustrates a number of architectural strategies and social dynamics that were characteristics of mosque-making in Britain. First, it demonstrates the reuse of existing religious buildings by new religious communities, and so the reinvigoration of religious space. This phenomenon of churches and synagogues from the 19th or early 20th centuries becoming

mosques in the late 20th preserves a building's religious function often within the heart of inner-city communities. There are numerous examples where churches have been redeveloped or demolished to make way for commercial or residential uses, particularly within this working-class neighbourhood in Bristol which was once dotted with local churches and chapels. Through its conversion into a mosque, the former St Katherine's Church retains its use as a place of worship and so continues to offer a religious dimension to the neighbourhood.

The mosque's architectural alterations were modest internally but extensive in terms of visual identity, with the removal of the pitched roof and its replacement with a flat roof and dome, and the erection of a minaret. That such architectural efforts were made demonstrates how important these visual signifiers were to the Muslim community, and how important it was to reinscribe the building as a conventionally identifiable mosque. In so doing it brought a new visual dimension to the streetscape and character of the neighbourhood. It was important to the community that the Muslim presence in Bristol was demonstrated through the architectural language of the mosque, and that the mosque should serve as a visual marker for Muslims as well as non-Muslims. The desire of the community to externally adapt an existing building, adding architectural symbols derived from Islamic history so that it can signify a Muslim presence and identity, is an ambition that can be seen repeatedly in the mosques of Britain's new Muslim diasporas.

Fig 3.12
The Brick Lane Mosque in its former use as the Spitalfields Great Synagogue in 1954. The building was constructed in 1743 as a Huguenot church, used as a Wesleyan Methodist chapel from 1819, a Jewish synagogue from 1898 and a mosque from 1976.
[John Maltby/RIBA Library Photographs Collection]

Fig 3.13
The Brick Lane Mosque seen from along Fournier Street, with the 2009 minaret in the background.
[DP153534]

3 Brick Lane Jamme Masjid, Brick Lane, Spitalfields, London, 1976

Large-scale Muslim migrations from South Asia began towards the end of the 1950s, and after the early example of Bristol Jamia Mosque, further conversions of former religious or community buildings into mosques soon followed around the country. The Brick Lane Mosque is an example of a building that was originally a church, then became a synagogue and finally a mosque (Figs 3.12 and 3.13). Like Bristol, it was converted by new Muslim settlers in the area, in this case immigrants from Bangladesh, and as in Bristol they sought novel ways to signify the building's new Muslim use.

'A "deprived, dangerous and exotic" district' is how the *London Gazetteer* opens its description of Spitalfields. This no longer holds, but the area

has been 'successively known as Petty France, Little Jerusalem and Banglatown'.[22] Tower Hamlets, the London borough housing Spitalfields, Brick Lane and the Brick Lane Mosque, has become synonymous with diversity, historic poverty and a dense and multilayered mix of urban and social history.

Bounded by the global financial centre of the City of London to the west and the River Thames to the south, Tower Hamlets is one of London's smallest and most densely populated boroughs, with 206,000 people living in 8 square miles. By the 16th century there was shipbuilding along the river. By the 18th century, dense domestic industry in rows of terraced houses had taken root, to be followed in the 19th century by huge warehouses and high-walled docks along the Thames. This industrious and significant area of London was heavily bombed during World War II, when 24,000 homes and much of the industry was lost.[23] With post-war social housing building programmes, and new service industries, by the late 20th century Tower Hamlets had developed into a vigorous mix of ethnic diversity, commerce, creative industries, wealth and poverty.

In 1976 members of the Bangladeshi Muslim community in the Brick Lane area acquired a building on the corner of Brick Lane and Fournier Street to establish a mosque in the heart of the community. This handsome Georgian building, dating from 1743, had a complicated religious history to which the mosque was to add another layer (Fig 3.14). The National Heritage listing cites this building as being a 'uniquely complex instance of the "recycling" of a place of worship, its succession of religious uses encapsulating the rich migration history of East London'.[24]

Brick Lane Mosque is located in the south-eastern corner of what was known in the early 18th century as the Wood-Michell Estate. Land developers incrementally built up the estate, which now stands as a fine example of Georgian town housing, between 1718 and 1728.[25] On another site nearby, the landmark Christ Church, Spitalfields, was being erected between 1714 and 1729 and thus the religious landscape of what was then the outskirts of London was beginning to be reshaped. By 1714 the site of the Brick Lane Mosque had been purchased by Ann Fowle, a widow from Islington. It contained nine cottages, 'occupied by six weavers, a watchmaker, a clockmaker and a gardener'.[26] By 1739 the site consisted of 'four cottages ... , an inhabited building on the street and "old stables" on the corner of Brick Lane', when it was subsequently sold by Ann Fowle's granddaughter to five 'merchants of London'.[27] The £900 price for the site was provided by two members of the French Church in nearby Threadneedle Street, which was the first church of the French Huguenot community in London.

Huguenots (French Protestants) had been arriving in Britain as refugees from religious persecution from the mid-16th century. The biggest influx of refugees, some 40,000–50,000, came from France after the Edict of Nantes in 1685. Concentrated on the edges of cities, where food and housing were cheaper, the Huguenots formed distinct religious and cultural communities. In London, Spitalfields in the east and Soho in the west were the main Huguenot centres, the former because of the silk-weaving industry. By 1700 there were 14 French churches in the western suburbs and 9 in the eastern.[28]

At the newly acquired site in Spitalfields, a petition to George III in 1742 sought and gained permission to build a new church and a school 'where the children of our poor may be educated in early principles of piety towards God, of duty and loyalty to their Sovereign, and of gratitude to their benefactors'.[29] Thomas Stibbs, surveyor to the Threadneedle Street church, is accredited with the design of the building on the site. The New French Church (Neuve Eglise) opened in 1743. The school house, adjoining the church on Brick Lane (No 59), was built at the same time and housed two rooms for boys and girls, and a vestry.[30] The plan of the New French Church was that of a typical 18th-century meeting house, being a rectangle 24 metres from east to west and 16.5 metres from north to south. It had

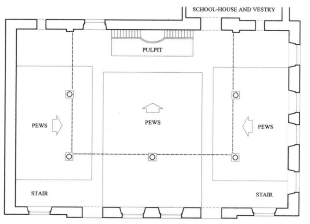

NEUVE EGLISE (NEW FRENCH CHURCH) 1743
AS RESTORED IN 1869 FOR WESLEYAN METHODIST USE

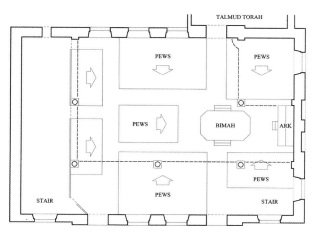

MACHZIKE HADATH (SPITALFIELDS GREAT SYNAGOGUE) 1898
AS THEN REMODELLED

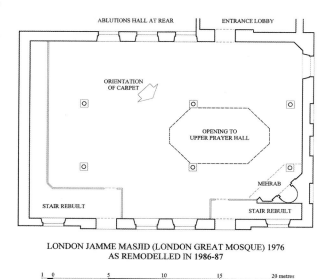

LONDON JAMME MASJID (LONDON GREAT MOSQUE) 1976
AS REMODELLED IN 1986-87

Fig 3.14
Plans showing the main hall in three of its manifestations: as a Wesleyan Methodist chapel in 1869, a synagogue in 1898 and the mosque as it was remodelled in 1986–7.
[ME00411]

a deep gallery on the south, east and west sides reached by open staircases inside the south-east and southwest angles. A reredos, placed centrally against the north wall, provided an imposing setting for the pulpit, raised above the communion table enclosure ... The plain plastered walls and ceiling were originally linked by a deep quadrant cove with groined intersections over the window arches.[31]

The building 'is bold in scale and quietly dignified in expression',[32] and was designed in an austere Palladian style, characteristic of Georgian chapel architecture of the time. It is unadorned and constructed in stock brick with stone dressings and tall round-headed windows at first-floor level fronting Fournier Street and Brick Lane. Each elevation is capped with a large brick pediment, into which a sundial is placed on the Fournier Street side and a circular window on the Brick Lane side. The original entrance of the New French Church was on Fournier Street. Two arched entrance doors on this elevation are 'recessed in a fine wooden doorcase, the reveals and soffit being panelled to match the door. The tall opening is framed by a straight-headed architrave, with plain narrow consoles supporting the shallow cornice-hood.'[33]

The Huguenots gradually became assimilated into English society through the 18th century, and the distinct religious and cultural unit that they had formed dissipated. With a declining congregation, the trustees of the New French Church gave up their premises (the church and the adjacent house at 59 Brick Lane) in 1809 on a 99-year lease to the London Society for Propagating Christianity among the Jews, a self-explanatory missionary organisation established by a Jewish convert to Christianity, the Revd J C Frey. The house at 59 Brick Lane served as a boarding house for 'a number of Jewish Children who [were] boarded, clothed and educated in the principles of Christianity'.[34]

The missionary school lasted for 10 years, and in 1819 the lease for the church and house was assigned to a Wesleyan Methodist chapel, who restored the building to 'beauty and comfort'[35] and created seating for 1,100 worshippers (Fig 3.15). In 1895 the Methodists leased the house to the London Hebrew Talmud Torah Classes, a Jewish organisation established mainly by members of the Machzike Hadath Society to promote stricter observance of religious orthodoxy: 'This community, consisting largely of immigrants from eastern Europe recently settled in East and North-east London, advocated what it considered to be a stricter standard of orthodox religious observance than that maintained in the older established Jewish community.'[36] This Jewish school had 10 teachers giving instruction to nearly 500 children.

The Methodists surrendered the lease of the church and house in 1897 to the trustees of the New French Church and left the site, and in 1898 the Talmud Torah Classes acquired the lease for the whole building. They subsequently

Fig 3.15
A coloured lithograph from c 1869 of the interior of what is now the Brick Lane Mosque's main prayer hall. This drawing depicts the building when in use as a Wesleyan Methodist chapel, which was from 1819 to 1897.
[Publisher A La Riviere, 18 Clifton St, EC London, 51 x 38 cms; it bears the signature of 'Edward Armstrong Telfer, Superintendent Minister'. London Metropolitan Archives, City of London SC/PZ/ST/02/032]

subleased the worship space to the Machzike Hadath Society to establish a synagogue. At this time a new roof was constructed, which was to provide 12 additional classrooms above the synagogue. The interior of the chapel was altered to serve as a synagogue. Part of the gallery was removed to the east for a tabernacle, and a bimah was installed and pews reorganised around it (Fig 3.16).[37]

In 1922 the synagogue bought the freehold of the building from the trustees of the New French Church at a cost of £5,750. A series of fires, reconstructions, alterations and refurbishments ensued over the next 50 years. The area's Jewish population gradually moved away, and by the 1960s it is recorded that the synagogue was little used.[38]

Bangladeshi migration to the East End

Lascar seamen from East Bengal had been settling in the East End of London since the 19th century, but this was on a relatively small scale. It was the Partition of India in 1947, followed by Bangladesh's war of independence in 1971, that spurred migration in greater numbers to Britain. This migration was predominantly from the region of Sylhet on Bangladesh's eastern border, and with chain migration patterns and the re-uniting of families, Bangladeshi communities began to emerge in Britain's cities. Settlement was primarily in London, and within London predominantly in Tower Hamlets. The 2001 census shows that 24 per cent of Britain's Bangladeshis lived in the borough, and that they formed 33 per cent of the total Tower Hamlets population, a figure which dropped slightly to 32 per cent in the 2011 census. The borough is also shown to have a 36 per cent Muslim population, which had dropped to 34.5 per cent by the 2011 census, still one of the highest concentrations in the country.

With the rapidly increasing Muslim population in the early 1970s, it was imperative that a mosque be established as a social and religious centre to serve the Bangladeshi settlers. The East London Mosque had served as the main mosque for the immediate and wider London area since 1940, and in 1975 it moved from houses on Commercial Road to a converted building on Fieldgate Street, close to the southern end of Brick Lane (*see* pp 155–67). Denominational differences have been cited as a factor in members of the Bangladeshi community wanting to set up another mosque, separate from the East London Mosque. Widening doctrinal

cleavages 'gradually led to a substantial proportion of these Bangladeshis seeking the establishment of a mosque in which they felt more at ease. In 1976 some worshippers broke away, purchased the synagogue on Brick Lane, and converted it into a mosque.'[39]

Once the building was acquired and named the Brick Lane Jamme Masjid, a series of adaptations took place to enable it to serve its new religious function. By the time the building was up and running as a mosque, the basement vaults had been converted into prayer rooms, with ablution facilities in the side rooms at their western perimeter. The vestry house at basement level was converted into a laundry, store and kitchen. On the ground floor, the Brick Lane entrance came to serve as the main entrance, which had been the entrance to the house at No 59. The domestic entrance hall therefore became the lobby to the mosque, with a new ablution area constructed in the rear yard. The hallway was already built quite generously, rather than to a domestic scale, so it served well as the main mosque entrance. The vestry house to the north of the hallway became the office for the mosque administration.

At first-floor level the mosque sought to maximise the amount of prayer floor space. The gallery over the main hall was covered save for a large octagonal opening towards its eastern end (Fig 3.17). The panelling from the synagogue gallery was reused in the mosque gallery, as was the brass handrail, and the vestry house bedrooms were converted into a prayer room and an office on this and the second floor. At third-floor level the

Fig 3.16
Interior of the main hall in use as a synagogue in 1951, showing the east wall against which the ark is placed.
[London Metropolitan Archives, City of London SC/PHL/02/1219/71/8641]

Fig 3.17
The men's main prayer hall of the Brick Lane Mosque, which also served as the main worship space for the building's former uses as a synagogue and church.
[DP147301]

Fig 3.18
Classrooms in the roof space of the main building of the Brick Lane Mosque, which were added by the synagogue c 1898 after it acquired the building.
[DP147311]

synagogue had built timber-panelled classrooms within the roof space lit by skylight windows; these were retained as classrooms for the religious education of Muslim children, or used as prayer space at times of capacity (Fig 3.18). Former bedrooms within the mansard of the vestry house were also converted into prayer space.

A series of applications and works followed over the subsequent decades, usually small in nature, for example to adapt the building to meet regulatory requirements such as fire escape provisions, and through these works various original features of the Grade II* listed building were restored. In this way the mosque negotiated the requirements of legislation and heritage to incrementally nudge the building into a functioning mosque responsive and adaptive to the needs of its congregation.

In the early 2000s the mosque appointed a London firm, DGA Architects, and embarked on a series of more ambitious proposals to adapt and upgrade the building. DGA had been working on projects locally, and had been introduced to the mosque through these. The proposals involved internal upgrading works, a two-storey rear glazed extension to 59 Brick Lane, a new two-storey annex to the rear of the mosque for study facilities, ablution and WCs, and the installation of a small mortuary behind the mihrab. Perhaps the most significant and visible proposal was for the erection of a new minaret rising to a height of 29 metres on Brick Lane alongside the main mosque building. The mosque had already tried, unsuccessfully, to gain permission for adding minarets to the building on a previous occasion.[40] However, that proposal involved adding minarets to the building itself, an idea which was not acceptable on

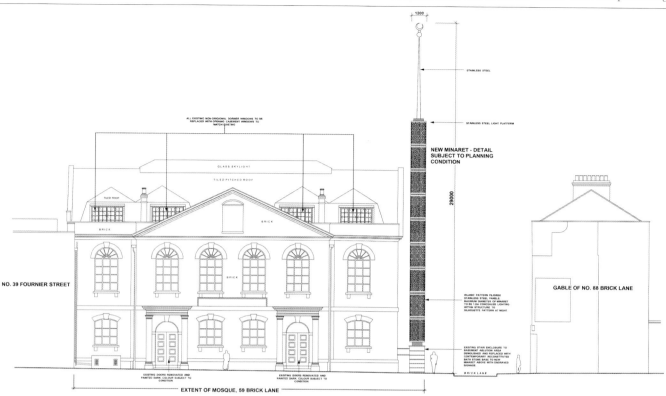

heritage grounds as the building was listed.[41] DGA instead proposed that the minaret be sited off the building, with its base serving as an entrance portal to the basement prayer space (Figs 3.19 and 3.20).

The design of the minaret represents a departure from the aesthetics that many mosques had adopted over the preceding decade, in that it does not seek to replicate a historical Islamic architecture. Instead, it offers a contemporary interpretation of a traditional architectural symbol. It is composed of a series of circular stainless steel drums, stacked on top of each other, with each drum wrapped in an arabesque

Fig 3.19
Elevational drawing along Fournier Street of the Brick Lane Mosque by DGA Architects, dated 2004. It shows the proposed design for a new minaret alongside the existing building.
[© DGA Architects, reproduced with consent]

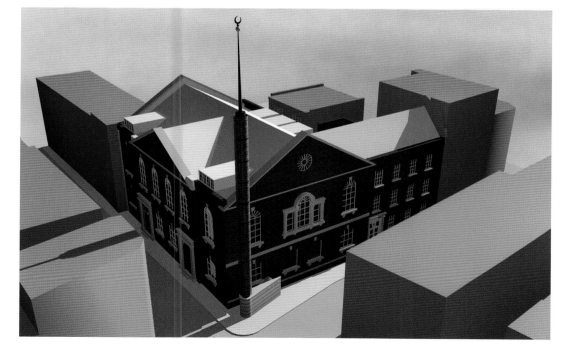

Fig 3.20
Computer-generated model of the Brick Lane Jamme Masjid by DGA Architects, 2004, showing the proposed design for a minaret alongside the existing building.
[© DGA Architects, reproduced with consent]

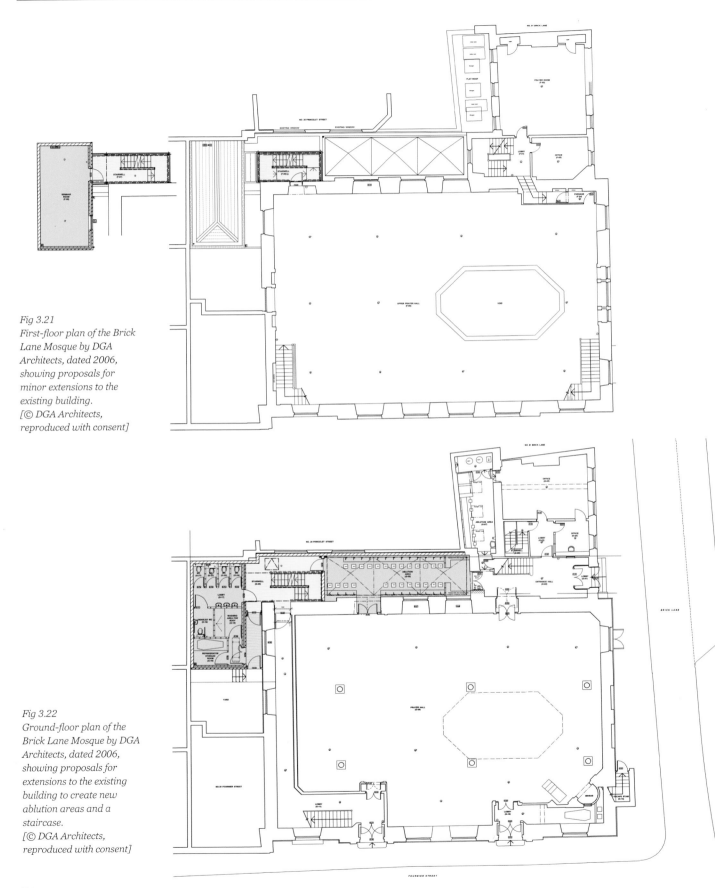

Fig 3.21
First-floor plan of the Brick Lane Mosque by DGA Architects, dated 2006, showing proposals for minor extensions to the existing building.
[© DGA Architects, reproduced with consent]

Fig 3.22
Ground-floor plan of the Brick Lane Mosque by DGA Architects, dated 2006, showing proposals for extensions to the existing building to create new ablution areas and a staircase.
[© DGA Architects, reproduced with consent]

pattern, also cut from stainless steel, which is gently lit from behind. The top of the minaret is a needle-like spire, approximately 7 metres high, topped with a crescent moon motif.

Through its design and location the minaret could be seen to be independent of the building, while still being associated with it. It was an approach which found great favour with the council's conservation officers and with English Heritage (now Historic England), who were consulted on the Listed Building application, and the scheme (Figs 3.21 and 3.22) was duly granted planning permission in 2006.[42]

Once permission was obtained, the mosque embarked on fundraising for the works, which was a slow and protracted process. In the meantime DGA Architects, through the success of their minaret design, were appointed by Tower Hamlets council to design some street furniture and signage along Brick Lane, to create a 'cultural trail' as part of the rebranding of the area as 'Bangla Town'. In this way the minaret was coordinated with other installations along the street, which further reinforced the sense of it being co-owned by the street as well as by the mosque.

The works are progressing in phases: the new ablution facilities and minaret were completed in 2009, and the remaining works are scheduled for implementation when funds become available.

The Brick Lane minaret stands as perhaps one of the most inventive and original interpretations of a customary Islamic architectural symbol that has become such an important signifier of the mosque in Britain. Through its positioning and its contemporary styling, the minaret carefully negotiates the issue of not altering a historic and listed building to such a degree that its original character is compromised, while nevertheless identifying the Islamic use of the building. It functions, therefore, as street sculpture as much as specifically a signifier of the mosque (Fig 3.23 and *see* Fig 3.1). A planning condition on the approval of the minaret situates the minaret firmly within the realm of the mosque, determining that it 'shall be removed in its entirety if the requirement for it ceases for any reason, or within 28 days of the last use of the building as a mosque, whichever is the sooner'.[43]

Conclusion

This building at the corner of Brick Lane and Fournier Street has a unique history of religious use, starting as a Huguenot church in 1743, followed by a Christian missionary school in 1809,

which gave way to a Wesleyan Methodist chapel in 1819, then a Jewish school and synagogue in 1898, and finally a mosque in 1976. This is a palimpsest of uses which is often cited as emblematic of the layering of immigrant histories in this part of London. It is a significance recognised in the council's planning report responding to the latest minaret application: 'The Mosque is one of the most important buildings in the Borough, and also in the Fournier Street and Brick Lane Conservation Area. It is grade two starred, and is an exceptional early–mid-18th-century building, and has an outstanding history of use.'[44] Brick Lane has served as the centre of the Bangladeshi community for some 40 years, and is a densely built and historic neighbourhood. The Brick Lane Mosque, with its bold minaret, encapsulates the layering of cultures and stands as a representation of the changes that the building and the area have seen and continue to go through in the second decade of the 21st century.

Fig 3.23
Looking north along Brick Lane at the Brick Lane Mosque. The minaret, added in 2009, is installed with lighting with changing colours.
[Author]

4 Leytonstone Masjid, Dacre Road, Leytonstone, London, 1976

At the same time that the Brick Lane Mosque was being established, another religious building was being converted into Muslim use, again in east London but this time in the inner suburb of Leytonstone. The Muslim population in this area had been using the East London Mosque on Commercial Road and Fieldgate Street but needed a centre close to where they lived so it could be an integral part of their community. As in Bristol and Brick Lane, reinscribing the chosen building with Muslim symbolism was one of the community's fundamental needs.

The architectural history of the Leytonstone Mosque starts with the parish church at Leyton, which has 11th-century origins and was rebuilt in the 17th and 19th centuries. As the only direct link at the time between the hamlet of Leytonstone and this parish church was a path through fields, requests were made by residents of Leytonstone for the building of a chapel of ease in their village, 'for the holding of Divine Service'.[45] By 1749 a small chapel had been built to serve the congregation. The population grew, and the chapel was expanded in 1820 by 130 seats, taking its total capacity to 580. By 1830 it was already too small for a 'population of 1,600 souls'.[46] The Vicar of Leyton issued an address appealing for a new chapel and fundraising commenced within the community.

In July 1832 the foundation stone for the new St John the Baptist chapel and burial ground was laid, and in October 1833 the premises were consecrated by the Bishop of London. The building served as a chapel of ease to Leyton until 1845, when it had its own ecclesiastical parish assigned to it. As Leytonstone's population rapidly expanded through the 19th century with the advent of the railway, further church accommodation was urgently required and a network of new churches sprang up in the locality.

The original St John the Baptist chapel continued to serve as a hall for 'Church meetings, such as the Ladies' Working Association, Parish Socials and rehearsals and concerts of the Leytonstone Choral Society'.[47] With the growth of the community, this space proved inadequate, and a member of the congregation, Mrs Elliott, offered to build a more spacious room.

The foundation stone for this new Parish Hall at Dacre Road was laid in September 1885, and the building was thereafter known as the Elliott Rooms. It was designed in a Queen Anne or Domestic Revival style, popular at the time, and with its brick faces, arched windows, buttresses and clay-tiled roof it was materially congruent with the Victorian terraced houses by which it was surrounded.

By the beginning of the 20th century this hall was insufficient to cope with the growth of the Sunday school, and a new parish hall was needed, primarily for use as a boys' Sunday school. In October 1925 space was allocated on the north side of the church, and a new hall was built. Consequently the parochial organisations gradually transferred their activities from the Elliott Rooms to the new parish hall. The Elliott Rooms gradually fell into decline, and other uses were sought.[48] In 1967 a planning application was submitted and approved for the use of the church hall as a playgroup,[49] and then in 1973 an application was refused for the use of the hall for the display and sale of fine arts and antiques.[50] Eventually, the hall was put up for sale in 1975 as its 'upkeep proved too great a drain on the parish resources'.[51]

Muslim migration to Leytonstone and surrounding areas followed the 1947 Partition of India, and grew rapidly from the 1960s onwards. By 2011, the Muslim population of the London Borough of Waltham Forest, in which Leytonstone is situated, was 22 per cent of the borough's total population, significantly higher than the national average. The Muslim population of the Leytonstone ward itself had reached almost 3,000, while the combined Hindu and Sikh population of the ward stood near to 400. Leytonstone's Indian origin population was around 1,200, compared to those of Pakistani origin, which was just under 1,000. This demographic, however, ran counter to the pattern of ethnic origin in the borough of Waltham Forest as a whole, where the Pakistani population was almost three times higher than the Indian. The Indian Muslims in Waltham Forest originated from the region of Gujarat, and were heavily concentrated in the Leytonstone area.

In the early 1970s, with no mosque in the locality, this growing Muslim community was at pains to organise congregational prayers and religious schooling for its children. The nearest mosque was the East London Mosque, then in a house on Commercial Road some five miles away (see pp 155–6). The Leytonstone Muslim community found the Elliott Rooms as a fairly run-down local hall and started to rent it for the Friday congregational prayer, children's religious classes and social events such as weddings.[52]

When the Parish put the Elliott Rooms up for sale in 1975, it was a natural step for the local Muslim community to purchase the premises and establish it as the first mosque in Leytonstone. The building was brought into use through general repairs and restoration, and used as found while plans were prepared for its extension and resignification as a mosque.

The building had a large hall 9 metres by 17 metres, with a trussed roof, which served as the main prayer hall. Conveniently, the end wall was already facing towards the Qibla so the prayer lines could be aligned with the plan (Fig 3.24). On two sides of the hall were smaller rooms, which were adapted into wudu facilities, and spare rooms, which were used as classrooms and over-spill prayer space. The building could be entered via a lobbied entrance on Dacre Road and from another lobbied entrance hall on Barfield Road.

In 1978 a planning application was submitted for the erection of an extension to include, as stated in the application, a 'flat for the priest and the provision of a minaret'.[53] The minaret was designed as a free-standing, fairly plain, brick structure in front of the original building, and intersected with a proposed boundary wall that enclosed a small front garden for the mosque. This was approved, and the work was carried out shortly afterwards. The Dacre Road building became the first architectural expression of the mosque in this part of east London (Fig 3.25). This was indeed only the third minaret in the

country, the first two being at Regent's Park (*see* pp 133–47) and Wimbledon (*see* pp 103–7).

The project was designed by Frederick Gibberd and Partners, and was the second London mosque by that practice, the first being the Regent's Park Mosque. It is somewhat remarkable that on completion of Gibberd's major landmark mosque at Regent's Park, the biggest in Britain at the time, he took on the commission for such a discreet and unacknowledged project at Leytonstone, and it says something perhaps of his profound interest in Muslim architecture in Britain. Gibberd's minaret was treated in a simple and unadorned manner, characteristic of

Fig 3.24
Interior of the men's main prayer hall of the Leytonstone Mosque, showing the simple mihrab made from two pieces of marble and how well-aligned the building is with the Qibla direction.
[Author]

Fig 3.25
The Leytonstone Mosque in 1990, when the minaret and ablution extension had been added to the front of the former church hall, which remained unaltered externally.
[By kind permission of Mehmood Naqshbandi, www.muslimsinbritain.org]

what he was perhaps keen to explore as a modernist approach to Muslim architecture.

The existing side antechambers were replaced with newly built rooms, and to the north on Barfield Road a first-floor extension was added to provide an imam's flat. To the west of the prayer hall, a further single-storey extension provided an entrance lobby and ablution facilities, and a committee room was built into the existing roof space. The works were essentially intended to modernise and improve the facilities, and to enable the building to function more effectively as a mosque and community centre than it could from the site it had inherited (Fig 3.26).

In the planning application the mosque stated that the average daily attendance was approximately 30 people, and that attendance was principally on Fridays when approximately 200 people attended. The study rooms were intended for children's classes and small committee meetings, both of which were taking place in the main prayer hall, so compromising the space as a prayer hall. In general the mosque stated that the proposals were being put forward to cope with the inconvenience now suffered by multiple uses of existing spaces and particularly of the prayer hall.

While the proposals for the side extensions were received quite pragmatically in planning terms, both by the local authority and by residents, the proposed minaret caused a prolonged and impassioned debate. As this was one of the earliest minarets in the country, this debate revealed the symbolic potency of this architectural element, new to Britain, with the emergence of a discourse of contestation that continues today.

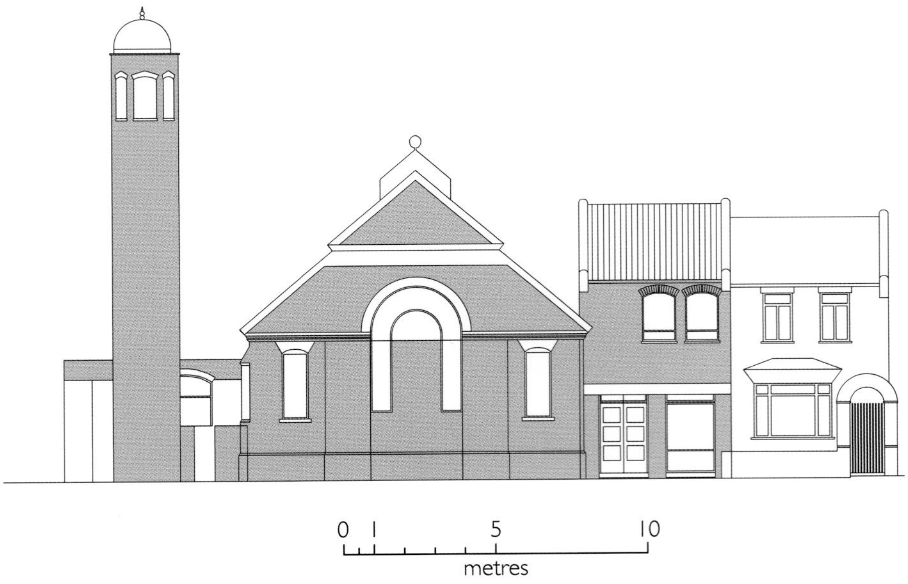

Of 23 letters of objection from local residents, 17 specifically objected to the minaret and the remainder referred to general objections based on loss of amenity, disturbance, loss of light and overshadowing.[54] One objector stated that while he had no objections to the extensions to the hall, he objected to the minaret 'in the strongest possible terms'. The objector went on to characterise the residential demography around the new mosque, and the complex issues that the minaret, from his point of view, was raising:

I, like most of my neighbours, have lived in this area of the East End of London all my life. It is an environment where I have lived and brought up my family in harmony and accord with my neighbours for over fifty years.

I have no desire to see what is at this moment a typical, quiet, East End area suddenly transformed into something out of the pages of the stories of the Arabian nights. I desire my home environment to remain what it has always been, a typical East End of London back street where a Londoner can feel he is at home. Not somewhere similar to a street in some Middle Eastern country.

The view from my house will be filled with this 50ft high, alien building that I find offensive and out of character with my home environment.

One final objection I wish to record ... is to do with the safety and well being of my wife and family ... Just as they will view their minaret as a focal point so I fear will those persons of extremist racial views who are gathering strength not only in London but in all parts of this country.

I fear these people will see the building of a minaret, an obvious alien symbol of a faith little known to them, as a challenge.

I fear they will, at the slightest pretext, take up that imaginary challenge and gather together at the Mosque protesting at what ever matter they feel is appropriate at that time. I can foresee such gatherings turning to violence with the resultant risk of injury to the person of any of the local residents, their families or visitors and of damage to their property.[55]

As with many of the objections, the letter shows the wide scope of reactions raised by local residents, addressing the symbolism of the architecture and the character of the townscape on the one hand, and fears of social conflict on the other.

Fig 3.26
Elevation showing the first stage of development in 1978 – the minaret and single-storey front extension.
[Redrawn from a drawing held in the London Borough of Waltham Forest planning file 1978/0157, by kind permission of Frederick Gibberd Partnership]

0   1   5   10
metres

Broader opposition to the minaret also centred around issues of the appropriateness of Islamic symbolism in a London residential townscape and its physical impact on neighbours. Objectors claimed that the minaret would be out of keeping with the area and alter the look of the neighbourhood as a whole; lead to a loss of light to adjacent houses and overshadow adjacent gardens; lower values of adjacent properties; lead to a deterioration in relations between residents and worshippers; be of a hideous design; destroy the pleasant environmental image; bring notoriety to the district in general; and attract more Muslims to the area as it would be one of only three minarets in London.

The objectors identified this proposed minaret as being the third in London, and one objector made a direct comparison with Regent's Park, stating that a minaret 'may be in keeping with Regent's Park, but it is definitely not here'.[56] The mosque committee, on the other hand, stated that they wanted to build the minaret 'not for the purposes of decoration, but as a symbol of the function and use of the mosque'.[57] In negotiating these positions, the planning authority decided:

The minaret is a distinctive element in the design and is seen by the applicants to be a symbol of the function and use of the building, as would be a small tower or steeple associated with a Christian church or chapel. From a townscape viewpoint the minaret is well located on the site. It has been stated that the minaret will not be used for the traditional call to prayer.[58]

The proposed extensions, alterations and minaret were subsequently approved in 1978[59] and implemented shortly afterwards. Leytonstone's is one of the first British mosque planning applications for which local response is comprehensively documented. What emerges is the potency of the minaret as a symbol provoking multiple and conflicting reactions. The discourses around and reactions to the minaret as a new architectural object in Britain, and indeed in Europe, as they were to evolve over the next 30 years can be seen in their infancy in this modest scheme in east London.

Extensions in the 1990s

Within 15 years the mosque required further space, and in 1991 an application was submitted and approved for the formation of a prayer hall in the roof space, a first-floor extension to provide classrooms, a kitchen, office and ablution area, and the provision of a small dome.[60] The proposal was designed by Associated Consulting Engineers of Stratford, London, and is an early example of a mosque designed by non-architects, a practice that was to be more commonplace in mosques that would follow in the next two decades.

The mosque stated that the additional floor space was needed to improve the quality of circulation and use of the existing building, which had 'cramped and rather undignified entrances and exits',[61] and also to improve the range of facilities, including cultural and educational activities for local schoolchildren.[62]

In terms of architectural style, the mosque committee asserted that it was trying to achieve a balance between traditional Islamic architecture and the character of the existing building and surrounding area. The first submitted proposals showed an additional floor covering the whole area, almost as high as the ridge of the existing mosque. A large dome was also included, mosaic-clad with decorated battlements lining the parapet roof line. The dome was 6 metres in diameter and 3 metres high, and was described as a symbolic feature that would draw attention to the prayer hall and complement the minaret.[63]

Local residents were vocal in their resistance to the new proposals. They objected to the planning application by citing the adverse impact of increased traffic generated by the mosque and the numbers of worshippers that the mosque was already attracting, arguing that the extended facility would increase both of these. The residents' association asserted its indignation at the volume of people attending the Friday prayer and the nature of the service, sending the council a photograph showing the 'overspill of male attendees on the pavement kneeling on prayer rugs, without shoes, in the street praying because the Mosque was full and could not hold any more attendees'.[64] The residents' association also suggested that the mosque was a cause of strained social relations between residents and mosque users, stemming from the fact that it was 'cheek by jowl with small family homes, the occupants of which are, by and large, not of the Moslem persuasion'. The association also alleged how 'little the mosque authorities would go anyway towards meeting even a simple request to stop the minaret being used as a pigeon loft'. The residents' association also intimated a deterioration in social relations should the extension work be permitted, saying, 'It is a miracle that there have, up till now, been no major clashes between the residents and the Mosque attendees', but they 'feel that if the application is granted, the residents' patience will be exhausted and there could well be a very tense situation in this area'. Finally, the residents' association requested that the mosque be relocated, asking the council to 'liaise with the mosque authorities in an effort to have the Mosque re-sited in a purpose built building', and that the nearby mosque at Lea Bridge Road be used as a replacement for this one.[65]

The planning authority did consider that the proposal amounted to a considerable overdevelopment of the site that was out of scale and obtrusive, and offered suggestions to the mosque as to how it might amend the scheme to make it more acceptable.[66] These suggestions were that the women's prayer hall should be incorporated within the existing roof void and the dome scaled down or omitted altogether.

The design was subsequently revised and made less ornate, with a plain, smaller dome and parapet capping stonework with a simple arch motif (Fig 3.27). Dormer windows in the Dacre Road elevation were also added. This revised scheme was considered more acceptable in design terms as the original form and elevations of the church hall were evident and recognisable, and the application was approved in 1992.[67] The planning report recommending approval offered a nuanced approach to a new form of architectural style, by stating that it had 'no objection to the design of a traditional mosque since it gives the building its particular identity and is an honest reflection of its function and purpose ... The revised proposals manage quite successfully to reconcile the contrasting styles of a late Victorian meeting house with a traditional mosque.'[68]

Despite the approval of the proposal to extend the mosque, residents looked for alternative ways to block the development. The residents' association submitted complaints against the planning authority's procedure in determining the application to the Council Ombudsman in an attempt to have the decision reviewed.

In mediating between the competing interests of the mosque and Muslim population and of the local objectors, Waltham Forest Council drew a fine line between matters that were planning issues and those that were not. Referring to the residents' association's complaint, the Director of Planning wrote to the Ombudsman that some of the objections were 'matters of fine detail or irrelevant in the context of the application and would not have been asked of any other applicant'. The letter continued:

> To have put these to the Mosque Steering Committee could have caused offence and in deciding not to pursue these matters with the applicants I used my professional judgement ... Many of the questions could have been interpreted as an unwarranted intrusion into the Mosque's affairs and would not have helped the LPA [Local Planning Authority] to properly consider the planning issues ... I have some sympathy with some local residents' views that [the objections] have racist undertones [and to pursue them] would have cast doubt over the impartial role of the planning officer.[69]

Within a few years the mosque had built the scheme as approved, and a two-storey extension with a small plain dome stood alongside the minaret, which left the original chapel hall visible and intact externally (Figs 3.28 and 3.29).

Conclusion

Leytonstone Mosque was established in the early phase of post-war mosque building, when Muslim communities were coalescing and settling, and their specific social and religious needs were emerging. The acquisition of the Elliott Rooms in the 1970s marked the first mosque to the east of the East London Mosque (then at Commercial Road). Through the conversion of former religious or social space, as with Bristol Jamia Mosque before it, it represented a route to

Fig 3.27
The mosque's second phase of development, the revised 1991 proposal by Associated Consulting Engineers, where a first floor was built along with an entrance portal and dome.
[Redrawn from a drawing held in the London Borough of Waltham Forest planning file 91/1068]

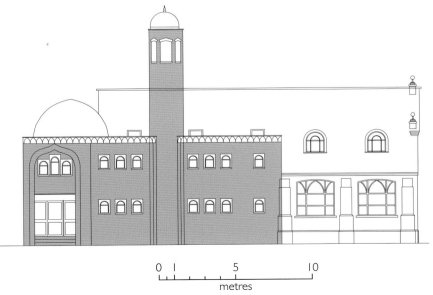

```
0   1        5         10
|__|__|__|__|_____|
        metres
```

mosque building that would be replicated across the country.

The conversion of the 19th-century parish hall, which had fallen into disuse by the 1970s, to be a significant local mosque ensured that the site retained a religious and community purpose and that its key architectural character was preserved. The pressure for space that the mosque experienced, requiring its ongoing expansion, repeated the same patterns of establishment and growth that the Church of England had experienced a century earlier.

The architectural amalgamation of mosque and church hall, with the newer functions wrapping around the hall and culminating in the new symbolism of the minaret, provides a metaphor for the overlapping of communities that the immigrant Muslim cultures brought (Fig 3.30). The resulting building is distinct in that the late Victorian parish architecture is conserved alongside new Islamic typologies that are equally distinct and prominent, resulting in a genuine and intriguing balance between the two.

Fig 3.28 (above left)
View of the south-eastern corner of the mosque, showing the original church hall building with the two-storey extension and minaret projecting forward.
[Author]

Fig 3.29 (above)
View of the Leytonstone Mosque main frontage, seen from the south along Mohammed Khan Road.
[Author]

Fig 3.30 (left)
Leytonstone Mosque main elevation, showing the front two-storey extension, minaret and dome, with the original church hall building behind.
[Author]

5 Ihsan Mosque and Islamic Centre, Chapelfield East, Norwich, 1977

At the end of the 1960s, a 37-year-old Scotsman, Ian Dallas, a noted playwright and actor, travelled from London to Morocco with a group of friends. He went to Fes, sought the imam of the historic Qarawiyyin Mosque and became a Muslim. Dallas adopted the Muslim name Abdalqadir, after a 12th-century saint and scholar buried in Baghdad. Abdalqadir went on to Meknes where he undertook religious and spiritual study under Sayyidi Muhammed ibn al-Habib, Shaykh of the Moroccan Darqawiyya branch of the Shadhiliyya Sufic order.

The Shaykh appointed Abdalqadir as his muqaddam (representative) in Britain, and instructed him to return and call people to Islam. Abdalqadir duly returned to carry out his appointed mission, both in Britain and on trips he made to the West Coast of the USA. Through this work, and his continued visits to Meknes for his own spiritual education, Abdalqadir gathered a group of Muslim converts around him, mostly English, Scottish and American, with some from other European countries.

In 1972 the fledgling Muslim group leased a few houses in Bristol Gardens, a street in the Maida Vale area of west London, and established themselves there. They also acquired some shop units in the area, so allowing themselves to become more economically self-sufficient. From this early stage, the idea of a tightly knit, community style of living for this Muslim community was being pursued.

By 1976 the lease on the Bristol Gardens houses was coming to an end, and the community, which was growing steadily, made the decision to move to the Norfolk countryside. A large country house, Wood Dalling Hall, was purchased and some 150 to 200 men, women and children that made up the convert Muslim community around Muqaddam Abdalqadir moved into the premises with the intention of setting up a 'self-supporting Muslim village'.[70] The ambitious plan for the creation of such a community could not be realised, and gradually members of the community started settling in the nearby city of Norwich and the social

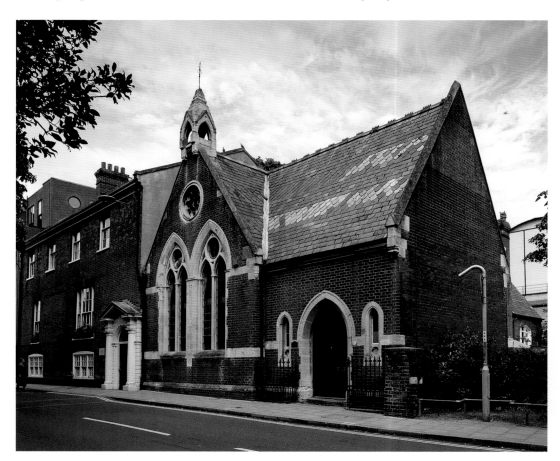

Fig 3.31
The Chapelfield East main elevation and entrance door of the Ihsan Mosque, Norwich, converted from the 1876 former school hall in 1977.
[Author]

experiment at the house in Wood Dalling came to an end. It was a natural and obvious process of migration for this mobile Muslim community.

In 1977 the community found a former Victorian school hall on the edge of Chapelfield Gardens, in the west of the city centre, and began to rent it for their religious purposes (Fig 3.31). The building dated from 1876 and was originally the St Peter Mancroft School for Boys. It had been part of a church complex that included the imposing St Peter Mancroft Chapel-in-the-Field Congregational Church, which was built in 1858 and demolished in 1972. The former school hall had previously had a variety of uses since it stopped being a school, including as a scout building and a discotheque.[71]

Within the year the Norwich Muslims were able to purchase the school hall with the help of a large contribution from an Egyptian donor, who wanted to make the gift in the name of his late mother, Ihsan. The building was duly acquired and Abdalqadir's community established the Ihsan Mosque, the first in the city. His teaching and the Muslim community he founded became established in Norwich, and as they spread their message they gained more local and international followers. In the 1990s the Norwich Muslims were joined by a group of around 20–30 converts of Afro-Caribbean descent from the Brixton area of south London, who had learned of Abdalqadir's teaching and eventually joined the Sufic order and relocated to Norwich.[72]

The school hall made an ideal conversion into a mosque without requiring any alterations needing planning permission. It consisted of a large hall approximately 30 metres long by 15 metres wide with a tall pitched roof and exposed timber trusses. The Qibla direction was in the eastern corner of the hall, at the opposite end from the entrance, which meant that worshippers could conveniently enter at the back of the hall. A small door was located in the wall where the mihrab was placed, so the imam could enter and leave from a small office and meeting room located at the western end, without disturbing the congregation (Fig 3.32).

The interior of the mosque is plainly decorated, with whitewashed walls and roof, and with the timber roof structure exposed. The mihrab is a white timber frame forming an open arch, echoing the size and shape of the existing door arches, and the minbar is a short run of timber steps. The only adornment on the walls is a large calligraphic painting hung on the eastern wall, in a 19th-century Moroccan style of calligraphy, reading 'Allah' in its centre, with the shahada (testament of faith) written around it. Reed matting is placed on the perimeter walls up to dado height, which practically allows people to lean against the walls without marking them, but also serves to soften the space. The mosque installed a women's prayer gallery at mezzanine level part way over the men's hall, so it could share the space of the main hall (Fig 3.33).

Fig 3.32 (below left)
The interior of the men's prayer hall, showing how the fabric of the original building has remained intact and been refurbished. The mihrab can be seen in the far-right corner. [Author]

Fig 3.33 (below)
The interior of the men's prayer hall looking towards Chapelfield East, showing the mezzanine floor that was inserted to form a women's prayer hall. [Author]

Fig 3.34
A door from the rear of the entrance lobby that leads to the garden, at the end of which are the ablution facilities. Many of the original features of the building have been retained such as the tiled floor, windows, doorway and door.
[Author]

Ihsan Mosque holds daily prayers, Sunday gatherings, markets and seminars and has active links with the wider Norwich community.

Conclusion

The Ihsan Mosque represents a very different route to the establishment of a mosque to that followed by most others in Britain. Most significantly, it was not set up by Muslim immigrants, as part of a wider process of settlement, community and identity formation, but was part of a religious movement by indigenous British Muslims who had converted to Islam. As that Muslim community was made up of people from quite diverse backgrounds, with no former social experience of Islam, they had to make for themselves a Muslim social and cultural context, into which their collective religious lives could be situated. The closeness of the Sufic order, therefore, may have provided a degree of this Muslim social glue that would otherwise be embedded in generational cultural practices, as with immigrant Muslim communities. In addition to this, the social experiments along the journey of the Norwich Muslims can all be seen as attempts to create a collective religious experience and culture.

The Ihsan Mosque is one of the earliest mosques in post-war Britain, established at a time when mosques were first emerging in towns and cities across the country. It started as part of the religious journey of a specific group of Muslims, and evolved into a mosque serving the wider Norwich Muslim community as it grew and diversified. The mosque remains as a valuable example and expression of a convert Muslim community that has its roots in Britain, and as the illustration of a particular religious journey spanning half a century.

The building was entered directly from the street into a convenient lobby, where shoes could be removed and the prayer spaces entered. Ablution facilities were located in outbuildings along the western boundary of the site, accessed through a small yard which ran alongside the main hall from the entrance lobby (Fig 3.34). Overall the building was ideally laid out for effective use as a mosque and as a centre for the fledgling Muslim community. With an aesthetic of modest Victorian Gothic, it had a certain civic stature, making it an opportune find.

By 2011 the Muslim population of Norwich was recorded as 2,612, which made up almost 2 per cent of the population of the whole city.[73] By 2015 the Ihsan Mosque estimated that its core congregation numbered approximately 200, from a range of backgrounds, though being mostly British-born converts to Islam. By 2015 there were two further mosques in Norwich, one noted as a 'Bangladeshi' mosque and the other as a 'Salafi' mosque,[74] which demonstrates the growth of the Muslim population of Norwich, borne out by the census figures, but also the increasing diversity of Muslims. The Ihsan Mosque community also grew an international network, in that members of the community went on to establish centres and grow communities in various countries, most notably in southern Spain and the South African city of Cape Town, where in fact Abdalqadir eventually settled. The

6 Kingston Masjid, East Road, Kingston upon Thames, Surrey, 1980

Bradford's Howard Street Mosque is an example of domestic architecture that was transformed into a place of worship and then organically adapted as the needs of the community and congregation evolved. These changes were contained within an existing architectural shell that was not altered dramatically externally as it was in a historic location and spatially restricted.

House conversions became a prevalent type of mosque, and remained an option for Muslim communities in their mosque-making endeavours for decades to follow. Kingston Mosque shows how the transformation of domestic architecture, this time in a London suburb, remained an active and dynamic architectural field 20 years after Howard Street. Unlike Howard Street, however, Kingston did remodel the external fabric and visual language of the building, resulting in a narrative illustrating the importance of architectural imagery to Muslim identities.

The Kingston Muslim Association (KMA) was founded in 1976 with the expressed aim of advancing the Islamic religion in Kingston and the surrounding area. As there are no records of Muslim settlement there, it is likely that Muslims first started arriving from the early 1960s. By the mid-1970s the KMA estimated that the Muslim population had grown to close to 1,500 people in the wider Kingston area, and believed that the need for a local Muslim centre had become evident.

To cater for its immediate needs, the local Muslim population was hiring halls for social and religious functions, such as the Tudor Hall and Surbiton Assembly Rooms. In 1977 more than 100 people attended the Tudor Hall for an Eid al-Fitr festival to mark the end of Ramadan. Friday congregational prayers, however, were not catered for and Kingston's Muslims had to travel to the mosques at either Regent's Park or Wimbledon, 'bearing expense and dislocation of work and family duties'.[75] The KMA acknowledged that while there were mosques at Woking and Southfields, these were 'either too far away or for a different sect of Muslim'. The five daily prayers were being performed in houses 'lacking the spiritual and social benefits'.[76]

One of the key aims of the KMA was to provide suitable mosque premises. It was not an easy task, and the association requested the assistance of the local council in finding a site where a mosque could be built. In June 1979 the Association found and purchased the site at 55/55a East Road (for £42,500). The site comprised a small two-storey house, similar in style and scale to the other houses along East Road. Alongside the house was a single-storey extension, which also wrapped around the rear of the house and took up much of the site.

The property had previously been used as a British Legion Club for community functions and as a bar and clubhouse. It was originally built as a small house at the turn of the 20th century before its conversion and extension to form the clubhouse.

The building provided an ideal site for a new mosque for two key reasons: first, the site already had the relevant planning permissions for continued use as a social centre, which the KMA anticipated would be sufficient to allow it to operate the mosque and community centre,[77] and second, the site had already been expanded to the side and rear to provide social space that could become prayer halls. Therefore difficult planning applications to extend the building across the site could be avoided. As the membership of the Legion had been progressively diminishing, part of the site had been rented out as storage and the KMA acquired the buildings in a considerable state of disrepair. After carrying out basic refurbishment works, the mosque opened in February 1980.

Within a year the mosque stated it was providing a range of religious and social activities for the Muslim community, comprising religious classes for children, a mothers' club, the daily prayers, youth clubs, social events, marriage ceremonies and funeral ceremonies. The Eid prayer in 1981 attracted 90 people to the mosque, the greatest number to date, comprising 60 men, 10 women and 20 children.

In May 1980 the mosque submitted a planning application for a series of works to upgrade and better organise the premises. The problems with the mosque as it stood were manifold. It could not provide separate praying areas or entrances for men and women, the floors were at differing levels and not sufficient to take the load of a full prayer room, a separate library and office were needed, wudu and WCs had to be separated from the kitchen and praying areas, and a minaret was required 'as a symbolic feature of Islam'.[78] The mosque considered that

Fig 3.35
Kingston Mosque in 1990, showing a small minaret and arched windows and openings to the lower part of the front façade – the first stages of a series of incremental changes in the transformation of the building from a British Legion Club after the mosque acquired it in 1979. [By kind permission of Mehmood Naqshbandi, www.muslimsinbritain.org]

while the minaret would not be used for calling people to prayer, it was nevertheless a symbolic feature to signify the nature of the premises; and that if it was not permitted the mosque would be 'deficient in its appearance'.

The proposals were eventually approved and carried out. A new main entrance to the rear of the building was added for male worshippers. The existing front door to the house on the front side was retained as a female entrance, for a women's prayer hall situated behind the men's on the ground floor. However, due to the increasing number of Muslims attending the mosque, the women's prayer room was eventually moved to the first floor, where the flat was converted to serve as prayer space. The domestic entrance hallway and staircase of the original house, therefore, became the route to the women's prayer room. The bathroom of the first-floor flat,

at the front of the house, was correspondingly converted into the women's wudu facilities. These elements are the only parts of the mosque complex where the domestic origins of the site are still evident.

The front of the house was significantly remodelled in the early 1980s. The bay window to the house, a key vestige of its domestic language, was removed and a new brick façade constructed across the whole frontage, uniting the house and the single-storey infill extension that was already on the site. In this way the character of the small terraced house that the site had still presented, despite its additions, was being replaced by an attempt to create a building with a larger and more institutional presence. A series of narrow, arched windows was introduced along the façade at ground-floor level, again serving to visually tie the façade together and suggest a larger, more connected building (Fig 3.35). The pitched roof over the single-storey element was removed and replaced with the minaret situated in the gap between the existing house and the adjacent house at No 53. When it was built, the minaret was one of only a few in London, and its design was somewhat plain and unadorned, with arched details that denote its Islamic symbolism.

In response to 31 consultation letters sent out regarding the original planning application, 10 objections had been received. The planning report summarised these as follows: the proposed mosque would be out of character and would not fit into the local community; lack of car parking and increased congestion; noise and disturbance; the building would be an eyesore and a monstrosity; the minaret would be obtrusive; this use was not appropriate in a residential area.[79]

Despite the objections, the planning officer recommended the application for approval, but this recommendation was not held up and the planning committee refused the proposal on 4 November 1980, to the great distress of the mosque, which was already functioning on the basis of being a community centre and thus a continued use from that of the previous occupant.[80]

The mosque appealed against the council's decision, and on 12 October 1981 the appeal was allowed and planning permission granted. The appeal inspector commented on the minaret by noting that it was lower than the ridge height of adjacent dwellings and could not therefore be considered prominent. In terms of its aesthetics, he commented:

Fig 3.36
The front elevation of Kingston Mosque, seen from East Road in 2012, showing that the first floor has been infilled, the pitched roof removed, a dome added and a minaret/clock tower has been erected in the front garden. The transformation of the building from the domestic to the religious is largely complete.
[DP181092]

While I fully appreciate that some will find the minaret an unfamiliar shape in the local architectural scene, to treat East Road as a street of special and exceptional character, deserving unusual care and protection, would seem to be unjustified. However, in this setting, it would seem reasonable to restrict the purpose of the minaret to that of symbol only.[81]

A series of planning applications and alterations followed as the mosque evolved into a larger and more complex institution, reflecting the rapid growth of the Muslim population. By 1999 it was reported in the local press that some 800 worshippers used the mosque when it was at capacity, and even then it was not sufficient and people would overspill and pray on the street.[82]

In the 25 years that followed its establishment in 1980, there were seven applications for alterations and extensions to the mosque. Soon after its inception, in 1983, the mosque applied to extend the first floor over the prayer hall to provide an imam's flat. This was refused on the grounds of loss of privacy to adjoining owners and that it would appear overbearing.[83]

In 1991 an application was approved for a single-storey rear extension, which was required to accommodate the growing congregation of the mosque.[84] By 1994 the mosque had acquired

the adjacent house at 57 East Road, and used this to provide a flat for the imam. The mosque also acquired a lease on a workshop in the rear garden of No 59, being the next house in the street. This, along with part of the garden to No 57, was changed to mosque use, and side and rear extensions built.[85] At the front of the building, the single-storey element was raised a floor and the 1980s minaret was removed.

Further Islamic icons were added in 1996, with a dome replacing the pitched roof of No 55, and although a minaret was also approved with this application, it was never built.[86] The dome is styled in a somewhat bulbous manner, and sits incongruously between tiled pitched roofs. The juxtaposition of architectural languages, from the Victorian workers' terraced housing to the mosque, creates unusual combinations of form, a typological menagerie characteristic of mosque architecture of this period. This application also saw the approval of a single-storey rear extension to both No 57 and No 59, again marking the incremental spread of the mosque across its sites.[87]

With the dome approved, the mosque then sought to complement this symbol with a 'tower', as the mosque committee described it in their planning application, perhaps choosing this description in an attempt to allay objections

Fig 3.37
The interior of the men's prayer hall of Kingston Mosque in 2012, showing the mihrab against the front wall of the building and how the arched windows are intended to give the space an Islamic character. A chandelier is used as a central feature in the place where a dome might be expected.
[DP181096]

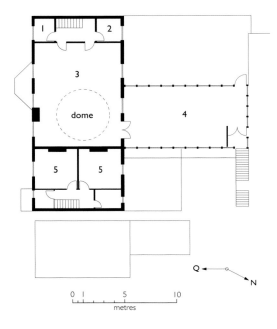

to a large, free-standing minaret. As the tower was to be much larger than the minaret approved in 1996, the mosque committee felt it should be less overtly 'Islamic' in character. The application description stated this was to be a 9-metre-high 'illuminated clock tower' in front of the existing mosque.[88]

Eight letters of objection were received, claiming the scale and design of the tower to be out of keeping with its surroundings, and stating that a clock tower is 'just another way of obtaining a minaret' and that the 'Mosque development has taken over the area – the clock tower would be further evidence of this.'[89]

A story appeared in the local press on opposition to the 'Muslim tower plan' and reported that the mosque intended to build the 'Millennium Minaret' to mark the birth of Christ. Some local residents were reported as fearing that the tower would devalue their homes, while another opined that the tower would be totally out of proportion to the mosque, 'like having one trouser leg longer than the other'.[90] A Muslim councillor explained that the minaret was a symbol for the mosque and therefore was very important for Muslims.

The proposal was approved at committee in May 2000.[91] Then, later that year permission was granted to raise the height of the tower to 12 metres, and also to remove the remaining pitched roofs on the mosque buildings and to replace them with a minaret on each side.[92] While the pitched roofs were removed and the large minaret/clock tower was built in the front yard, the smaller minarets proposed on each end of the existing building were never built and the mosque as it now stands was complete (Figs 3.36–3.39).

Conclusion

The architectural history of Kingston Mosque represents the layering and reinscribing that can take place on a site when it is acquired and shaped for mosque use. In this early stage of mosque building, the mosque as an architectural object does not appear intact. It is instead an incremental and negotiated process, responding to the evolution of the Muslim communities that it serves.

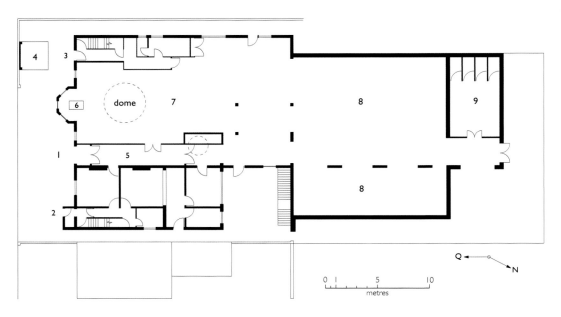

7 Mosque and Islamic Centre of Brent, Howard Road and Chichele Road, Cricklewood, London, 1980

Brent Mosque has been created in a former Congregational Church, an imposing building dating from the early 20th century which stands prominently on Chichele Road within rows of well-proportioned terraced houses built during the late 19th-century railway-led expansion of the suburb. The story of this mosque illustrates how an existing religious architecture was adapted and transformed to respond to the practical and symbolic needs of a Muslim religious community. There is also a kindred history shared by the church and the mosque as both represent the local and individual efforts of independently organised religious communities, albeit some hundred years apart.

The Congregationalist movement is one of several Protestant denominations (known as Dissenters or Nonconformists) who refused to conform to the restored Church of England in 1662, and so were subjected to persecution. The Toleration Act of 1689 permitted Dissenters to hold services in licensed meeting houses and to maintain their own preachers. Congregationalists recognise the right of each congregation to determine and organise its own affairs, and so to establish individual and autonomous churches as each community sees fit. This is a form of organisation similar to the dynamics of mosque establishment across the country.

In the middle of the 19th century, Cricklewood was a small village with nothing more than a few dwellings. The Willesden Green Metropolitan Railway Station brought accessibility in 1879 and, along with the introduction of sewers, catalysed development and house building. Towards the end of the 19th century Chichele Road was laid out by the local landlords, All Souls College, Oxford, and more housing, schools, churches and shops followed.[93]

There was a wave of Nonconformist church building in London through the 19th and early 20th centuries. The church that was to become Brent Mosque started with a group of Protestant dissenters meeting in private houses in Willesden Green from the 1810s. Records narrate that 'one of the houses belonged to the mother of Oliver Nodes who visited her each Sunday and read from the sermons of the Evangelist George Burder. They were joined by neighbours, forming the congregation which in 1820 founded the Willesden Green Independent (Congregational) chapel.'[94] By the 1830s a further five houses had been registered by Dissenters, and a series of purpose-built Nonconformist chapels – Wesleyan, Baptist, Presbyterian – had been erected by the latter part of the century. This period of expansion of Nonconformist places of worship lasted through to World War I.

Just as many mosques undergo a stepping stone route to a final institution and building, the church at Chichele Road was the culmination of a series of facilities that its Nonconformist Christian congregation had used for worship. After meeting in houses throughout most of the 19th century, the first purpose-built church came in May 1885, with the erection of a temporary iron church on the corner of Cricklewood Lane and Elm Grove. The structure had been dismantled and reused from a site in Hampstead where a new church had been built to replace it.

The temporary church was known as the 'iron hall', and served its purpose until the erection in 1893 of the Lown Hall, on Howard Road, named after Mr Richard Drury Lown, a 'first and most devoted worker in connexion with the new cause'.[95] The hall accommodated 500 people, and was intended to serve as a church and Sunday school 'until such time as a building suitable to the growing needs of the neighbourhood could be erected, and with this in view a site had been secured large enough for both the Hall and the Church'.[96] The hall was a modest two-storey building, with a large gable end and arched window facing Howard Road and triangular dormers along each side expressing an Arts and Crafts influence, common among London chapel buildings of this era. The site that had been acquired by the congregation was slotted between terraced houses and stretched between Howard Road at its north-western end and Chichele Road at its south-eastern face. The Lown Hall was built on the Howard Road side, leaving the Chichele Road site free for the future church.

The church was eventually completed in 1902 (Fig 3.40), to an exuberant design by architect Walter Wallis. It was described in *The Buildings of England* as 'an ambitious orange terracotta façade in free Gothic, with two towers'.[97] This Nonconformist church followed a century of Anglican religious building that worked through permutations of the Gothic Revival, the architectural currency of 19th-century ecclesiastical building. Much Nonconformist church building at the start of the 20th century in the north

Hindu Temple in Meadow Garth. The proposed alterations to the mosque will result in a building of distinction, which as well as

0 1   5   10
metres

held in the London Borough of Brent planning file M7245 83/0368]

apex of this gable was also to be replaced with an arched 'headstone' with Arabic inscription, which would serve to neutralise the Gothic character of the facade and reinscribe what would

The proposal was granted approval on 11 March 1983, but like Siwani's first scheme, was never implemented.

Proposals for portico, domes and mihrab, 1996 and 2002

Eventually, the alterations that were implemented were much more modest in scale, although nevertheless idiosyncratic. On 16 July 1996 permission was granted for a new domed portico at the Howard Road frontage,[112] as well as for a dome replacing the spire on the bell tower. The Howard Road frontage needed greater stature as it was by now serving as the main mosque entrance. The original doors in the Chichele Road façade that had been the main entry to the church had been closed, and worshippers arriving from that side would walk along the outside of the mosque to Howard Road and enter from there (Fig 3.44).

The portico itself is a simple red-brick, flat-roofed structure, with a ball-finial parapet, as if embattled, and two deep-green onion domes at each side with over-sized pinnacles. An identical dome is placed on top of the bell tower to replace the spire, with smaller replica domes at the four top corners of the tower. The domes are copied from Delhi's Jama Masjid, India's largest mosque, built by the Mughal Emperor Shah Jahan in 1658.

A mihrab enclosure at the Chichele Road elevation, granted permission on 27 March 2002,[113]

is again a simple red-brick rectangular enclosure, with a flat roof on which a dome is placed (Fig 3.45). Because of the lower hall and the raised level of the ground floor in the mosque, the dome sits on a flat roof some two storeys high and is a prominent visual feature on the street, marking the building out as one that has been reinscribed with a new architectural language. Of course, the dome replicas at Brent are a fraction of the size of those in Delhi, and constructed in GRP (glass reinforced plastic) rather than the individually shaped stone segments of the original. It is a process of translation that characterises mosque architecture in Britain, and one that is all the more conspicuous here because of the Gothic Revival architecture with which it is juxtaposed.

The planning report, while recognising the incongruity of the proposals, continued in its acceptance of difference on the grounds that this was consistent with what it understood as mosque design. The report stated: 'Although the

Fig 3.44 (below)
The Howard Road frontage of the mosque, showing the portico and domes that were added after being granted permission in 1996. This side of the building became the main entrance as it was at the opposite end to the direction of prayer, ensuring that worshippers did not enter in front of those praying.
[Author]

Fig 3.45 (below right)
Chichele Road frontage of the Mosque and Islamic Centre of Brent, with the extended mihrab enclosure at ground-floor level, which was granted permission in 2002, and a series of domes embellishing the existing building, which were added after they were permitted in 1996. Although there had been a series of more ambitious proposals for the building since 1980, these were the alterations that were actually implemented.
[Author]

Fig 3.46 (left)
The daily prayer hall is in the converted Lown Hall on Howard Road, which was built before the church itself. The prayer hall holds the daily prayers, while the main prayer hall in the former church is used for larger gatherings such as the Friday prayer. [Author]

Fig 3.47 (below)
The interior of the main men's prayer hall has an elaborate mihrab in the south-eastern wall which fronts Chichele Road. A false ceiling has been installed with a circular opening intended for a dome but from where a chandelier has been hung. It was installed in 2015. [Author]

extensions are not typical of the character of the area, in this case due to the unique design features of the Mosque it is considered that the design of the extensions are acceptable.'[114]

Internally, the structure and fabric of the original buildings remained largely intact, and the relationship of the church to the community hall could still be understood. On entering the building at Howard Road, the Lown Hall serves as a prayer hall on the ground floor (Fig 3.46), and a new first floor has been inserted to provide additional facilities. A door at the far end connects the hall to the main mosque in the converted church building, and here the altar has been removed and the nave cleared and carpeted to create the main prayer hall. At the far end, which is the Chichele Road elevation, a noteworthy mihrab has been constructed, a white classical portico with Corinthian columns rising to a double height, with infill panels in pastel green decorated with gold-painted diamond patterns and flower motifs. The mihrab opening is a crenellated arch, outlined in gold paint, with Arabic inscriptions reading 'Allah' and 'Muhammad' placed above it. Along the top of the mihrab Arabic inscriptions on either side read 'Bismillah-hir-rahman-ir-raheem' (I begin the name of Allah, the most kind the most merciful) and 'La-illaha-ilallah-Muhammad-ur-rasoolallah' (I bear witness that there is no God but Allah and Muhammad is the messenger of Allah), with a central circular piece reading 'Allah' (Fig 3.47).

Above the corbelled pediment sit the lower parts of the original Gothic gable windows. These have been cut short as a false roof has been inserted into the hall, into which is placed a faceted dome with a chandelier hanging into the prayer hall from its centre. This dome is only visible internally; it sits within the existing roof space and has no exterior manifestation.

The mezzanine gallery has been extended from the rear to create a women's gallery. The original timber balcony panels have been reused,

so retaining the chapel-like character of the former building. It is a character further preserved by the exposed original timber roof trusses and iron columns. Gold-painted Arabic calligraphy lines the inside face of the upper balcony, which presents a sensuous aesthetic against the more austere timber balconies. The upper level provides an opportunity to experience the fabric of the original building, with Gothic leaded windows, arched openings, concrete staircases, balconies and roof structure (Fig 3.48).

Conclusion

Brent Mosque represents a process of historical evolution and social change through the continued use of religious space for new religious traditions arriving in Britain. There is also a historical lesson in how minority religious groups establish themselves and their religious infrastructure in similar processes of grass-roots, community-based, incremental growth. The Cricklewood Congregational Church – arrived at through a gradual evolution from house, to temporary structure, to hall, to purpose-built church – represents a process that is being replicated by mosques around the country. It also illustrates how different minority religious communities follow similar strategies and trajectories in establishing their religious infrastructures.

Fig 3.48
The mezzanine gallery in the converted church is now used as the women's prayer hall, showing that original features remain in place while the space has been adapted for Muslim prayer.
[Author]

The story of Brent Mosque illuminates the significance of religious architecture and how important it is for congregations to ascribe identity through visual architectural symbols. From Siwani's unfulfilled yet striking reworking of the façade, to the cruder attempts to overwrite the church with reductive Islamic forms, to the eventual scattering of replica Mughal domes across the building, a continuous architectural negotiation through religious symbols was at play. This layering continues to the interior, where again two languages exist alongside each other.

8 Brixton Mosque and Islamic Cultural Centre (Masjid Ibnu Taymeeyah), Gresham Road, Brixton, London, 1990

Brixton became a place of settlement for Afro-Caribbean immigrants from the 1950s, and by 2001 its population was recorded in the census as being 25 per cent 'Black or Black British', a figure which remained constant over the next 10 years. By 2011 the Muslim population of the Brixton Hill ward was near to 1,000, amounting to almost 6 per cent of the ward's population.

Islam emerged in Brixton during the 1980s, heavily influenced by the American Civil Rights and Pan-African movements and key figures such as Malcolm X and Muhammad Ali. The religion offered a potent sense of empowerment, identity and direction. Within the African-Islamic movement, 'Africa had long been recognised as the Muslim continent and Islam claimed, therefore, as the natural religion of the black man'.[115]

Brixton's first mosque was established in the early 1980s by two Brixton-based Jamaican brothers who converted to Islam during a journey to the Sudan. On their return, they opened up the ground floor of their house on Bellefields Road as the first mosque 'and point of reference for West Indian Muslims and those interested in finding out about Islam'.[116] By the late 1980s the mosque relocated to another house on Ferndale Road and started to establish itself as a local Islamic centre, with a community that was rapidly growing through conversions 'on a weekly basis'.[117] This emerging Muslim community in Brixton had also made links with another group of indigenous British convert Muslims in Norwich, who would visit them regularly (*see* pp 82–4).

With the need for larger premises, the community acquired the house at 1 Gresham Road in 1990 and the mosque grew in renown and significance both for Afro-Caribbeans locally and Muslims from further parts of south London. By 1993 the mosque had been through a series of organisational changes, and the original founders, who were inspired by the Sufic teaching of the Norwich Muslims, left Brixton to relocate to Norwich and join the community there. Brixton Mosque itself acquired a new management and religious direction, and came to describe itself as 'the first Salafee Masjid in the UK', which for them meant that they aspired to follow the way of the 'pious predecessors, what they believe and how they understood the Quran and Sunnah'.[118]

Brixton Mosque at Gresham Road was established a decade after Kingston Mosque as another London house mosque, demonstrating the continued efficacy of using a house to create a place of worship. In Brixton's case, the house was built as a handsome 19th-century villa, like many across the inner suburbs of London. It had already been adapted and was being used as a community centre when the mosque took it over in 1990 and continued its transformation into a place of worship (Fig 3.49). There is a 32-year span from the Bradford house mosque at Howard Street to this one at Brixton, but the basic process of conversion remains much the same despite the time lapse. This shows that the role of the house mosque in enabling communities to quickly

set up places of worship in a rudimentary fashion remained undiminished, although by the 1990s there was also a growing body of purpose-built examples.

Mid-19th century Brixton was an area of well-proportioned town houses set within long gardens and cut through by the railway, which to the south gave onto fields interspersed with residential thoroughfares snaking out to other south London suburbs. Gresham Road was already a built-up street of varied housing stock joining Brixton town centre. After World War II significant patches of Gresham Road were opened up through bomb damage and infilled with post-war housing, resulting in the eclectic character of the street today. The mosque forms part of a terrace of three buildings, two of which are houses and one a church hall, all dating from the early 19th century and now within the Brixton Conservation Area.

The mosque building is double fronted with two bay windows, one splayed, the other square, either side of the main entrance. Architectural features are handsomely endowed, with stucco square columns to the bays, capped with straight cornices and with stone sills. The main entrance is set within a formal surround, with square columns and horizontal cornice. First-floor windows are also framed with stucco surrounds with pediments and arches. To give a formal and stately character to the house, a corbelled cornice runs along below a parapet, with a tiled

Fig 3.49
The main façade and entrance to Brixton Mosque on Gresham Road, with the men's entrance being through the front door of the house and the women's entrance in the annex to the left of the main building. [Author]

Fig 3.50 (above)
The ground-floor front room of the house, which has been set up for use as a prayer hall. The original features of the house have been retained, giving the space a residential character. [Author]

Fig 3.51 (below)
The single- and double-storey rear extension to the mosque as it appeared in 2011. The extension was completed in 2015 to provide additional prayer and community space. [DP132065]

picture rails. Some of these features have remained through the building's evolutions, particularly on the ground floor, which serves to retain the sense of a 'period house' (Fig 3.50).

From its inception as a mosque in 1990 through to 2003, the building was largely unaltered. In 2003 significant works were carried out: the central wall on the first floor was removed to create the current open-plan main prayer hall, the women's section was refurbished, and a canteen and ablution facility were added on the ground floor. In 2011 a large two-storey extension to the rear of the mosque was started to double its capacity (Fig 3.51). With pauses in the construction programme to raise funds, it was eventually completed in 2015.[119]

Through these works the existing central staircase has been retained in its original location and the original arrangement of rooms on the ground floor maintained, preserving a certain domestic feel to the space. The extension provides for an extended main prayer hall on the first floor, and community rooms on the ground floor.

Funding for all the works at Brixton Mosque has been sourced through local donations, hence the incremental nature of the works. The mosque has not come up against any major problems in planning, and has found the wider community to be generally positive towards its presence and activities.

The demographic of the locality and of the mosque's users started to change from the late 1990s as the existing and primarily Muslim convert community was joined by newly migrating Somali, Eritrean, Moroccan, Algerian and Albanian populations. It is estimated that the mosque is now used both by the convert community and new immigrant communities in approximately equal numbers. Nevertheless, the rate of conversion is still high today, as enthusiastic converts evangelise and attempt to demonstrate to friends and family what they see as the personal and social benefits of their new faith.

Brixton Mosque, therefore, stands somewhat apart in the landscape of mosques in Britain. Whereas most mosques are the initiatives of Muslim immigrants primarily for immigrant communities, Brixton Mosque was established by, and initially to serve, converts to Islam. Despite these roots, however, the mosque does not see itself specifically as an evangelical or missionary organisation seeking to gain as many converts as possible. Instead, it understands its responsibility as one of raising awareness of

roof set back behind. The house was probably built speculatively as a stand-alone dwelling for a member of London's expanding merchant or industrial middle classes. Later, a pair of three-storey semi-detached houses was built and attached to the east flank of No 1. A lower two-storey annex, attached to its western flank wall, was perhaps originally built as a garage with a room above.

On the ground floor a central entrance lobby serves a large room on each side, with a staircase to upper-floor bedrooms. Kitchens and sanitary spaces would have been to the rear of the original house. The interiors of the ground-floor rooms were originally dressed with tall timber skirtings and wide architraves around doorways, as well as cornices, arched features and

Islam and Muslims within the wider community. Indeed, during the life of the mosque Muslims have become well established within the wider community in Brixton. Through natural growth, more Muslims moving into the local area and an increasing number of families becoming religiously plural as family members convert, Islam has become a more familiar constituent of the local social fabric.

Corresponding with these social changes, the mosque has found that since the early 2000s it has become a resource used primarily by local people, rather than one drawing people in from a wider south London catchment, as was the case prior to this date. This again reflects a growing number of local converts and immigrants, and the fact that there are now more mosques in neighbouring areas to serve those populations, rather than people having to make a journey to Brixton. This increasingly local congregation has allowed the mosque to concentrate on addressing localised social issues such as religious mentoring in prisons and holding workshops on knife crime, gun crime and criminality, and using its access to engage with young people who would otherwise be hard to reach through conventional government programmes. The mosque collaborates with a local community centre to provide counselling, IT and life skills, and also English language classes. These services are provided alongside a range of religious resources that the mosque facilitates. In addition to the five daily prayers, the congregational Friday prayer and the biannual festival prayer of Eid, the mosque provides religious classes for men, women and children, religious conferences, outdoor activities, marriage counselling and a bookshop selling religious books and audio material.

The mosque has an active women's facility, situated over two floors on one side of the house. With a capacity of 150 to 200, it is often full and during conferences overflowing. It has been found that women have a different pattern of use compared to men, often attending during the day when children are at school. To respond to this, activities for women are planned by women, and include lectures and classes during the day.

The Salafee perspective of the mosque translates into its architectural expression as being one of utmost simplicity. For the mosque, and from a Salafee perspective, any kind of decoration or embellishment is unnecessary to the effective practice of the religion, and indeed could be considered as a distraction. Consequently, the

mosque is undecorated internally, the mihrab in the main prayer hall being completely unmarked and identified only by a timber three-step minbar – which simply allows the imam to follow the tradition of the Prophet during the Friday sermon – and a microphone on a stand (Fig 3.52). If the mosque were ever to construct a new building on another site, it would not consider architectural motifs that are otherwise popular with mosques, such as domes, minarets, arches or patternwork, to be necessary and would in fact avoid such embellishments.

Conclusion

Most, if not all, mosques in Britain have been founded by Muslim immigrants as part of their process of maintaining religious traditions in new places of settlement. Brixton mosque differs in that it is one of the very few mosques that can be said to have been initiated by a convert Muslim community, albeit predominantly comprising immigrants from the Caribbean. In this sense, Brixton Mosque can be seen as a particular type of indigenous Islamic institution, which serves to facilitate the religious life of Britons who have adopted Islam within a purely British context, rather than being a vehicle to transfer religious traditions brought from places of origin.

The mosque itself is a house mosque and follows the architectural pattern of the many hundreds of house mosques around the country, where a prayer hall is created by interconnecting rooms and ablution facilities are extended. As with many house conversions, much of the residential character remains, interspersed with the new religious spatial arrangements.

Fig 3.52
The interior of the men's main prayer hall, characterised by its simplicity and the absence of any decoration or embellishment. A minbar is in the far corner, alongside which the imam will lead the prayer. There is no built mihrab. [Author]

Building mosques –
new identities, new architecture

The 1980s and 1990s saw an exponential increase in mosque building across the country, as the Muslim religious infrastructure in Britain was rapidly expanding. While the house mosques and conversions of the previous chapters illustrate how the existing architectural fabric was being rewritten, it was not long before newly built mosques started to appear alongside these conversions, on a larger scale than ever before.

Muslim communities who were building purpose-built mosques faced many of the same issues as the communities who had been, and still were, converting existing buildings: how to represent their culture and identity through the mosque's built fabric, through its architecture. However, unlike with the conversions, purpose-built mosques provided opportunities for a new architectural language to be expressed, unencumbered by the limitations of existing buildings. They were able to visually signify the identities and aspirations of the Muslim communities that were building them. These early purpose-built mosques offer insights into how this question of architectural representation and identity was approached, and it is through interpreting these buildings and exploring the processes of their making that the aesthetic sensibilities and priorities of this generation of mosque-makers can be understood.

Case studies

1 Raza Mosque, St Paul's Road, Preston, 1970
2 Wimbledon Mosque, Durnsford Road, Wimbledon, London, 1977
3 Maidenhead Mosque, Holmanleaze, Maidenhead, 1985
4 Jama al-Karim Mosque, All Saints Road, Gloucester, 1986
5 Central Jamia Mosque Ghamkol Sharif, Golden Hillock Road, Small Heath, Birmingham, 1996

6 Al Manaar, Muslim Cultural Heritage Centre, Acklam Road, Westbourne Park, London, 2000
7 Shahjalal Mosque and Islamic Centre, Eileen Grove, Rusholme, Manchester, 2001

1 Raza Mosque, St Paul's Road, Preston, 1970

On the edge of one of Preston's industrial zones, where factories and warehouses give way to rows of terraced housing, is a small mosque with a significance belied by its bearing. The Raza Mosque, completed in 1970, was thought in Preston to be the second purpose-built mosque in the country, after Woking (*see* pp 26–35), but it is more likely it was the fifth, after the Fazl Mosque in south London (*see* pp 35–43), the Alice Street Mosque in Cardiff (*see* pp 52–6), and the Eagle Street Mosque in Coventry (*see* p 259). It was, nevertheless, one of the first mosques built by South Asian immigrants who came to Britain after the Partition of India. The Raza Mosque, therefore, was among the earliest expressions of a new post-war Muslim architecture.

Muslims started coming to Preston in the 1950s, and most originated from one of three specific locations: the Indian state of Gujarat, north Pakistan, and Sylhet in Bangladesh. Most came from small villages and from agricultural backgrounds, and they retained strong links with their homelands once settled in Preston. It is estimated that by 1975 there were approximately 6,000 Muslims in Preston; by 2011 this had risen to 15,000, or 11 per cent of the total population.

In the early years of Muslim arrival, when numbers were small, houses were used for daily prayers. As numbers increased, the pressure for a collective worship space increased. The first place in Preston used for collective worship was a former dance hall in Starkie Street that was

Fig 4.1
Minaret and one of the domes of Shahjalal Mosque and Islamic Centre, Eileen Grove, Manchester.
[DP137693]

rented in 1960 for Friday prayers, while daily prayers continued in private homes. There was no imam, so the Friday prayer was led by one of the community.

In 1962 the Indian Muslims started the Preston Gujarati Muslim Society and acquired a house at 24 Great Avenham Street to convert into a mosque. Due to the large number of non-Gujarati Muslims using the facility, the name was changed to the Preston Muslim Society. By 1967 a larger premises was required, which led to the acquisition of a former vicarage at Clarendon Street and its conversion into Preston's first mosque, with capacity for 500. By 1984 the existing buildings had been replaced with a large purpose-built mosque which came to be known as the Jamea Masjid.[1]

Meanwhile, the city's Pakistani Muslims, the Hanafi Sunni Muslim Circle, had already established their own place of worship in a house at 32 St Ignatius Square in the 1960s. Soon the group acquired the site at St Paul's Road and commissioned local architects George H Broadbent & Son to design a mosque; the Raza Mosque that was eventually built on St Paul's Road was their first attempt at Muslim architecture.

The basic layout of the mosque was a prayer hall for men on the ground floor of some 20 metres by 7 metres (Fig 4.2), and a similar-sized first-floor area for women's prayer and children's classes. The mosque is a simple two-storey red-brick building with a tiled pitched roof, and so conforms with local residential architecture in style and material (Fig 4.3). The ground floor is raised five steps off the ground, which the architect described as a requirement but which was rather the wish of the mosque committee as a way of physically elevating the act of prayer from the everyday. This has allowed a large formal entrance porch rising the full height of the building to be designed with a portal in a traditional Mughal style. An onion dome placed centrally on the roof is flanked by two short minarets, which appear as if chimneys topped with green plastic turbans.

Broadbent has related how, when he was asked to build the mosque in 'as near as possible to the Islamic style', he 'immediately flew to the text books to see what basically were the designs used in Islamic architecture'.[2] He relied on an 1890 publication *Architecture: Classic and Early Christian* (by T R Smith and J Slater) for its chapter on 'Mohammedan Architecture', as well as the 1889 *A Handbook of Architectural Styles* (by A Rosengarten, translated by W Collett-Sandars) for its chapter 'Mahometan Architecture'. Delhi's 17th-century Grand Jama Masjid was reproduced in these publications, and the dome of Raza takes its inspiration from this building.

Fig 4.2
The main men's prayer hall of the Raza Mosque, with a range of decorative wall hangings characteristic of the Barelwi tradition.
[DP143550]

Fig 4.3
The main frontage and
entrance of the Raza
Mosque. The plain brick
façade has an adorned
doorway and domes at roof
level.
[DP143548]

Conclusion

In this way the Raza Mosque marks the beginning of the first phase of post-war mosque building in Britain, where local communities initiated and commissioned a new mosque building, and where architects were presented with a wholly new building type. The process of referencing and sampling from historic Muslim architecture to create a new typology where an English vernacular was amalgamated with Islamic symbols was also a precursor for many mosques that were to follow. Raza Mosque, therefore, unassuming though it may be, is one of the first representative examples of post-war purpose-built British Muslim architecture, and a significant identifier of trends in the following decades.

2 Wimbledon Mosque, Durnsford Road, Wimbledon, London, 1977

Mohammed Hassan arrived in London in 1954. Originally from India, he had been displaced by Partition to Pakistan before his final migration. While working for the Greater London Council, he relocated to its regional office in the south London suburb of Wimbledon, where he joined a coalescing Muslim community. It was not long before the absence of a place where they could worship together was felt. One of the locals, Hoosen Jajbhay, was a property dealer. He purchased a house at 12 Melrose Avenue in 1964 for approximately £2,800, where the ground floor was to be used as a mosque and the first floor rented out as a flat. The Wimbledon Mosque committee was formed in 1967 to manage the new centre, with Hassan as its chairman.

Basic alterations were made, mainly to provide ablution facilities; otherwise, the house was kept as it was found. In the beginning the house was adequate for the community's needs, with ample space for Friday prayer. As the size of the gatherings increased, the mosque committee hired local halls for the Friday and Eid prayers to accommodate the increased number of worshippers. In the early days of the house mosque, any one of the community members would serve as the imam. However, the committee wanted a full-time imam and made enquiries to madrassas in Pakistan for someone with a comprehensive knowledge of Islam. In 1971, the Darul-Uloom Madrassa in Newtown, Karachi, sent a mufti, Muhammad Abdul Baqi, to serve as the resident imam at 12 Melrose Avenue and he was given a room on the first floor.

The objective now was to purchase premises that could belong to the mosque and be dedicated to its use. The mosque fund collected donations from worshippers and started looking for suitable properties. At 264 Durnsford Road, on the corner with Ryfold Road and set within Wimbledon's Edwardian streets, was an end-of-terrace house with a plot of land holding three lock-up garages. In 1971, speculating on this as a potential site, the local Muslim group submitted planning applications for a new mosque to replace the garages, proposing 'erection of a 2 storey building for use as a mosque/prayer hall, use of no. 264 for priest and provision of 5 car parking spaces'.[3] Permission was refused.

Undaunted, in 1972 the mosque committee formed the Wimbledon Mosque Building Fund, registered the institution with the Charity Commission and purchased the site. In 1973 the mosque fund appointed a local Wimbledon architect, Jack Godfrey-Gilbert, to design a purpose-built mosque for the site. Godfrey-Gilbert, a veteran of the Festival of Britain, was approaching retirement, but agreed to take on the project for fees that the mosque considered very reasonable compared to those of others. The mosque found Godfrey-Gilbert 'agreeable and sympathetic to the cause'.[4] A new application again proposed a two-storey new-build mosque to replace the garages, using the house as accommodation for what the application termed 'the priest'.[5]

In the meantime, while the planning process was under way, the end-of-terrace house was converted into a makeshift mosque so that the community could start using the premises and establish prayer. An account by the Pakistani-American architect Gulzar Haider offers a sense of the place that was created:

En route to America, on my very first Friday in the West, I prayed in a small English house on a corner lot in Wimbledon. There was no *mihrab* niche, just a depression in a side wall, a cold fireplace with a checkerboard border of green and brown ceramic tiles. A small chandelier with missing pieces of crystal was suspended asymmetrically in a corner. A rickety office chair with a gaudy plush rug draped over its back acted as the *minbar* pulpit. The prayer lines were oblique to the walls of the rooms and the congregation overflowed into the narrow hall and other nooks and corners.[6]

In January 1974 planning permission was granted[7] and building work started in 1975 with a fund of £55,000 to £60,000, which was not enough as the projected cost of the building was over £70,000. The mosque continued to approach various sources for funding as the project progressed. The costs, however, spiralled, in part due to changes being made on site, and finally reached £120,000. Funds were raised through *Qarz-e-Hasna*, a Muslim system of lending money,[8] and a large donation of £29,000 was made by a member of the Malaysian royal family, who subsequently opened the mosque in 1977.

The mosque was built without the minaret or cupolas that now adorn the corners, and was little more than a two-storey rectangular box clad with white ceramic tiles. Pairs of pointed-arched windows lined the ground and first floors, and the parapet was given a repeated arch motif. These were the only embellishments to an otherwise plain building. Perhaps it was too plain for the congregation, for on completion in 1977 a planning application was submitted by Godfrey-Gilbert for the 'addition of minaret to existing Muslim prayer hall'.[9]

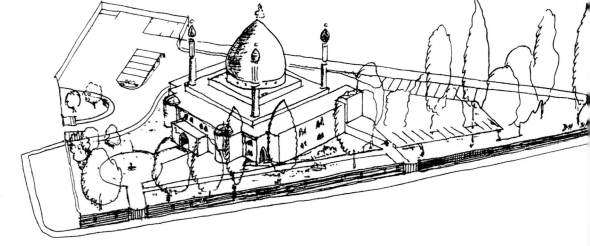

Fig 4.4
Godfrey-Gilbert's 1981 sketch proposal for a new-build mosque on former railway land near the current Wimbledon Mosque site.
[By kind permission of N A Godfrey, for and on behalf of J Godfrey-Gilbert and Partners Architects]

1974: Lock-up garages | 1977: First mosque opened | 1988: Mosque extended over site of two adjacent houses

Fig 4.5
Plans showing the development of Wimbledon Mosque.
[Based on Rondeau 1995, 71. Courtesy of the Museum of Wimbledon]

While assessing the application the borough planning officer wrote to Godfrey-Gilbert asking whether 'the proposed minaret [would] have any religious or other function such as calling worshippers to prayer either vocally or electronically',[10] to which Godfrey-Gilbert replied:

I hasten to confirm that the answer is no ... the proposed minaret is a symbol only and was not functional in any way. The reason that the Trustees of Wimbledon Mosque require the above is because a mosque is considered to be incomplete without one ... Speaking purely architecturally, I feel that one minaret will provide an important feature and will, in my opinion, improve the composition of this new development.[11]

The minaret Godfrey-Gilbert designed was a variation on the Mughal chattri on a hexagonal columnar base. The first minaret was a modest, if not diminutive, affair, placed on the Durnsford Road corner. It rises above the parapet only by the height of the chattri, some 1.3 metres.

The Mosque Trust considered the purchase of some nearby derelict railway land, between Durnsford Road and the railway, a site of approximately one acre (0.4ha). Plans were drawn up by Godfrey-Gilbert for a stand-alone mosque, in a traditional South Asian Islamic style (Fig 4.4), and were submitted to the council in February 1981.[12] The planners, however, would not allow a mosque and advocated instead a community centre for use by all regardless of religion. Mohammed Hassan promoted this idea, but it would not have fulfilled the objectives of the mosque committee, who required a place specifically for Muslim worship and learning, and so the idea was dropped.[13]

By 1981 the increasing local Muslim population required more prayer space. In 1983 the house at No 264 was converted into mosque use.[14] The Mosque Trust also acquired the next house in the terrace, 262 Durnsford Road, and started to consider the demolition of the two houses to allow for extension of the mosque. Mohammed Hassan considered that, rather than lose the houses, there might be other ways of increasing the building and explored the idea of extending the mosque to the rear above its car park. Through Godfrey-Gilbert such a design was prepared and submitted, but it was refused at planning committee and at appeal.[15]

Subsequently plans were prepared to demolish the two houses (Nos 262 and 264) and extend the mosque, and in 1985 this scheme, designed by Godfrey-Gilbert, was approved (Fig 4.5).[16] The proposal met with support from the planners, with the Director of Development advising the planning committee: 'This is an opportunity for the Council to be seen to be

Fig 4.6
The men's main prayer hall. The columns mark the line where the 1970s mosque, on the site of the lock-up garages, was extended onto the site of the two demolished houses.
[DP148107]

Fig 4.7
The Durnsford Road
frontage of Wimbledon
Mosque.
[DP148103]

Fig 4.7
The Durnsford Road
frontage of Wimbledon
Mosque.
[DP148103]

Fig 4.8
The Ryfold Road façade of
Wimbledon Mosque. The
main entrance is through
the door facing the car park
to the right of the building.
The third floor was added
in 2010.
[DP148101]

making a positive commitment towards a significant ethnic minority ... The loss of two residential units is insignificant in terms of the Borough's housing needs ... There is an alternative course of action to the conventional planning one.'[17]

By 1988 the two houses had been demolished and the extension had been completed; a line of columns in the main prayer hall shows where the two building phases meet (Fig 4.6). A larger minaret was placed in the centre of the Durnsford Road façade (Fig 4.7) at the point where the 1970s mosque met the extension. This minaret was of the same style as the earlier one, but was scaled up, with wider hexagonal tiers and a more prominent dome. With another small-scale minaret placed on the corner adjacent to the terrace of houses, this was now a building that was making its presence felt as an 'exotic' statement in an ordinary suburb.

In 2010 a third-floor roof extension was added (Fig 4.8).

Conclusion

Wimbledon Mosque, completed in 1977, was one of the first purpose-built mosques of the post-war phase of mosque building in Britain. It came at the start of a great wave of British mosque building by settling and expanding Muslim congregations that in the next three decades would realise mosques across many of Britain's towns and cities.

When Godfrey-Gilbert was designing this mosque in 1973/4, he would have had very little British mosque architecture to refer to, the only built examples being Woking (*see* pp 26–35), Fazl (in nearby Southfields; *see* pp 35–43), Raza (Preston; *see* pp 101–3), Eagle Street (Coventry; *see* p 259), Noor-el-Islam (Cardiff; *see* pp 52–6) and the South Wales Islamic Centre (Cardiff; *see* pp 46–9). Of these it is likely that only Fazl and Woking would have been known to the architect and could have been used as references. Indeed, some design reference to Fazl might be inferred in Wimbledon's use of a white exterior and green domed cupolas.

These features became particular to Godfrey-Gilbert's language of mosque architecture, and we will see them recur in his next mosque in Maidenhead. The white tile cladding was also an innovation for British mosques, and gives the building a distinctive character on a typical suburban street.

Wimbledon Mosque is one of the first of a type of religious building that introduces a previously unseen visual language into the streetscape of suburban Britain. Its incongruity in a landscape of repetitive Edwardian domesticity stands as an architectural representation of the social change that was under way in those regions where Muslims had settled, and situates this building as a key marker in the history of mosque building in the UK.

3 Maidenhead Mosque, Holmanleaze, Maidenhead, 1985

The architectural ideas of Wimbledon were transferred to the first designs of the mosque at Maidenhead, as it was the same architect, Jack Godfrey-Gilbert, who was initially employed for this purpose-built mosque. Because Maidenhead Mosque was on a less restricted site than Wimbledon, Godfrey-Gilbert was able to engage in more elaborate explorations of Islamic architecture and the representation of Muslim identity in Britain. It was, however, another designer, Ahmed Eliwa, who took over the architect's role and designed the mosque that was eventually built.

Maidenhead's mosque presents a striking image (Fig 4.9). A hexagonal prayer hall is crowned with a substantial green dome, and flanking this is a free-standing three-tiered ornate minaret, the top section of which supports a balcony, perhaps mimicking the place from where the muezzin performs the call to prayer. The building is faced in a deep red-orange brick and the roof line pronounced with decorated battlements, those on the prayer hall bearing the Arabic insignia reading 'Allah'. Window heads are triangular, with decorative mouldings. The mosque's plot of land is roughly square, approximately 30 metres by 30 metres, with the hexagonal prayer hall, measuring some 10 metres across, placed almost in its centre. The plan extends this faceted form, arcing

around the northern edge of the site to provide an overspill prayer hall, wudu facilities and an imam's flat (see Fig. 4.11). An upper storey was later added to the northern wing, to provide additional prayer space and offices.

The mosque sits on the northern edge of the town centre, facing the rear of the large council leisure centre and bordered by other community facilities, some in rudimentary structures. It is a location that has the sense of an urban left-over space, and the mosque is the most evocative building in this nondescript landscape.

Maidenhead, 34 miles west of London, grew as one of the numerous commuter towns feeding the capital after the arrival of the railways in the early 19th century. The medieval town centre was refashioned in the post-war period, ringed with a dual carriageway and its outer areas interspersed with a series of large industrial estates. In 2004 the think tank New Economics Foundation described Maidenhead as a 'clone town', in that it was part of a growing phenomenon in the UK where town centres

Fig 4.9
Maidenhead Mosque, with a green dome that replicates the dome of the Prophet's Mosque in Madinah placed over the main prayer hall. Adjacent to the mosque is an ornate free-standing minaret, modelled on examples from medieval Cairo.
[DP148062]

have undergone transformation into 'faceless supermarket retailers, fast-food chains, and global fashion outlets'.[18]

Maidenhead's industries attracted immigrants from South Asia from the 1960s, with the 2001 census recording a population of 6,118 Indians, Pakistanis and Bangladeshis constituting 4.5 per cent of the town's population. This had risen to 10,491 by 2011, which was 7.2 per cent of the total. The Muslim population increased from 3,195 in 2001 to 5,864 in 2011, almost 4 per cent of the whole. This pattern of settlement in Maidenhead determined the location of the town's first mosque, a semi-detached house at 5 Cordwallis Road, which bordered the Cordwallis Industrial Estate to the north of the town centre, where a higher concentration of Muslims lived.

Local Muslims acquired the house in 1973 and rudimentary alterations were carried out, with the rooms on the ground and first floors combined to create prayer halls and classroom space. This was the archetypal transformation of a house into a place of worship – simple, immediate and improvised – that was taking place across the country as Muslim communities settled. A community hall opposite this house mosque was hired for larger gatherings such as the Friday prayer and Eid festival prayers. This was a reuse and conversion that was carried out without planning permission, so a retrospective application was required to formalise the mosque conversion. It was submitted in 1975 and subsequently refused by the council, on grounds of traffic congestion and noise nuisance from the premises. The mosque's architect criticised the council's decision, arguing that the refusal was based on 'imaginary apprehensions', and that as most of the Muslims in Maidenhead were factory workers living locally, traffic generation was not an issue.[19]

The mosque appealed against the council's refusal and successfully overturned it in October 1976 when they were granted a two-year permission to use the Cordwallis Road house as a mosque. The search for a permanent site for a purpose-built mosque was now under way, but by the end of 1978, when the permission was expiring, no alternative site had been found. The mosque at Cordwallis Road applied for permanent planning permission, but this was refused in October 1978, a decision against which the mosque appealed again. This appeal was turned down in May 1979.[20] Some idea of the opposition to the house mosque can be seen from a letter of

objection to that application from a group of residents on Cordwallis Road. The residents argued that it was inappropriate for any 'religious sect or faith to designate a semi-detached house in a populous area as its official prayer and meeting house'. Such a permission, the letter speculated, would give the 'green light' for the 'calling to prayers of the faithful five times a day ... by shouting from the top of the mosque, the use of the premises at all times for a large number of people chanting in chorus and, even, possibly, for the subsequent building of minarets'.[21]

In June of that year, the mosque submitted an application to erect a temporary mosque, which would be no more than a single Portakabin (5.1 metres by 6.7 metres), on a different site in Holmanleaze.[22] Windsor and Maidenhead Council had designated another area of land there, on the northern edge of the town centre ring road and a few hundred metres south of Cordwallis Road, for community use. The land was to be divided to create three sites, and applications for their use were invited in September 1978 from local community groups. The Maidenhead Mosque committee was one of the applicants, the others being the Maidenhead Ivy Leaf Club and two Sikh organisations seeking to establish a gurdwara. At a council meeting it was recommended that the Ivy Leaf Club be offered the smaller plot, with the larger plots offered to the Sikh gurdwara and the mosque respectively.[23]

By August 1979 the planning application for the temporary Portakabin mosque had been approved, on the understanding that the relocation of the mosque to Holmanleaze would lead to the closure of the mosque at Cordwallis Road. The new location was seeing a clustering of community and religious group facilities, with temporary buildings also in place for Scouts and Jehovah's Witnesses. The council stressed that the permission for the Portakabin mosque was temporary, expiring at the end of 1980, and that by this time the new permanent mosque should be at least in part complete and ready for occupation.[24]

The momentum for a new permanent mosque, however, was already well established by the time the temporary permission for the Portakabin was granted in the late summer of 1979. On 5 January of that year, the mosque committee had met with the architect Jack Godfrey-Gilbert, who had already been acting for them at Cordwallis Road for the temporary permission, to work out the brief for a new mosque on the Holmanleaze site. It is likely that he had been referred to Maidenhead Mosque from

Wimbledon Mosque, as this and Regent's Park were the only other recently completed purpose-built mosques in the south of England.

Godfrey-Gilbert's design set the template to which the mosque was eventually built. On 5 January 1979, before his meeting with the mosque committee, he met the planning officers at Maidenhead Council and discussed sketches for the new mosque building. The planners had commented that the new building should reflect its function and that it was appropriate for it to incorporate the 'normal' architectural features of a mosque, such as a 'Dome and Minaret'.[25] The planners did also point out that Godfrey-Gilbert's design might elicit divergent opinions, and that it would be referred to the council's architects' panel when submitted for design review.[26]

The mosque committee set out their key requirements: that the new mosque should accommodate up to 500 worshippers; that there should be a library, mortuary room, meeting hall for social functions and flat for the imam; and also that a dome and minaret should be included in the design. Godfrey-Gilbert presented photographs of his recently completed Wimbledon Mosque, which Maidenhead Mosque's chairman had visited and found 'quite attractive'.[27] Godfrey-Gilbert suggested that the mosque be built in two phases, perhaps learning from his experience at Wimbledon; however, Maidenhead Mosque's chairman was optimistic that funds would be raised to build it in one con-tract, and they were aiming to raise £60,000 to achieve this.[28]

The mosque's optimism was derailed when it was estimated that Godfrey-Gilbert's design would cost £350,000. The mosque suggested that the building be designed to accommodate 200 people, to reduce the cost, but the architect advised that this would not meet the local Muslim community needs, and that considering the community's growth a building for 500 should be planned, even if in phased construction.[29] The mosque made a request that the budget be capped at £200,000, to which the architect set out his concerns over the compromise to the building's quality that would result, stating that phasing was the only viable option. Godfrey-Gilbert referred to his consultations with the planners, emphasising that the planning committee would 'require a well designed building which could be recognised as a Mosque having a modern oriental character with a high standard of finishings'. He went on to stress that in terms of cost, 'there is a line beyond which one cannot go if we are to provide you with a building of which you can be proud and which would be an example of good Moslem architecture which this project surely deserves'.[30]

Godfrey-Gilbert proposed a hexagonal prayer hall in the southern half of the site, with a block of facilities to its north including the main entrance lobby, with the main doorway on the western face of the building (Fig 4.10). The

Fig 4.10
Elevation of Godfrey-Gilbert's 1979 proposed scheme for Maidenhead, with similarities to his concept sketch for a new-build mosque in Wimbledon (see Fig 4.4).
[By kind permission of N A Godfrey, for and on behalf of J Godfrey-Gilbert and Partners Architects]

hexagon plan was intended to enable one side of the mosque to be parallel with the access road to the south while allowing the principal axis of the mosque to be on a line facing 'South-East, (ie towards Mecca)'.[31]

The prayer hall plan was not without controversy. In September 1979, when the design was significantly advanced, Dr Yaqub Zaki, a Muslim academic formerly known as Dr James Dickie, raised his objection to the hexagonal plan to the mosque committee. According to a letter from Godfrey-Gilbert to the chairman of the mosque committee, Zaki claimed that 'in no circumstances could a Mosque, hexagonal in plan, be permitted'. Zaki's argument was that the front row of people behind the imam must be as long, or longer than, the rows behind. This was because the front row is considered traditionally as being particularly blessed, and so a 'circular or many sided plan is therefore "discriminatory", in that people not standing immediately behind the mehrab wall do not receive the blessings'.[32]

Zaki's reasoning led the mosque to seek a second opinion by consulting the imams at Regent's Park Mosque and Wimbledon Mosque, both of whom confirmed that they knew of no reason to object to a hexagonal mosque.[33] Godfrey-Gilbert himself put forward his own defence of his plan:

> The circular and many sided mosques built all over the world, over centuries, indicate that although there may be a tradition in some areas for having a square or rectangular mosque, this is far from essential. Dr. Dickie seems to be placing undue importance on preserving certain traditions, which form no part of the Koran, and to which other Muslim authorities do not subscribe. We are informed that a mosque can be any shape whatsoever on plan and so long as it is a consecrated building it is acceptable to the Almighty.[34]

In the end the intervention from Zaki did not derail Godfrey-Gilbert's design, and the mosque decided that the objections were not substantiated enough to require a change to the shape of the prayer hall.

The exterior of the building was to be clad in white ceramic tiles, as at Wimbledon, to which Godfrey-Gilbert had referred in explaining this choice of material. A 5-metre-tall gold fibreglass dome was to be placed centrally over the prayer hall, sitting on a base with clerestory windows. The minaret was shown as free-standing, and again clad in the same ceramic tiles. It was to be topped with an onion-shaped cupola over a balcony, again of similar style to the smaller minarets at Wimbledon. The dome would have been similarly bulbous and pointed at the top, and both this and the articulation of the minaret imitated Indian Mughal architecture. The height and massing of the dome made it the dominant feature of the building, not to be 'dwarfed by the leisure centre'.[35]

The main entrance façade was designed as a blank wall punctured with the entrance doorway, which was arched in similar profile to the dome. The windows to the prayer hall were set within a moulded frame and with headers of different-coloured ceramic tiles. Despite the expressiveness of the dome and minaret, the designs otherwise struck a somewhat restrained note, with uniform cladding and little ornamentation to façades.

This proposal was submitted on 13 March 1980 and after revisions was approved on 14 October 1980.[36] The council's architects' department had taken a keen interest in the design throughout the planning process, showing a pertinent awareness of the significance of the mosque design and how it would interact with its context. In a report of May 1980, the architects' panel recommended that the scheme be refused, reasoning as follows:

> The architecture of the East will fit rather uncomfortably in Maidenhead, but if the building is to be Eastern, there is no reason why it should not be to a high and authentic standard of design, with the 'idea' consistently achieved throughout.
>
> The Mosque has rather doubtful Gothic windows and the flat and ablution block looks like a very inept and much later cheap addition with standard catalogue windows and doors.
>
> There is danger that a Seikh [sic] temple on the adjacent site could turn the area into a sort of 'Expo' site of National Pavilions. The difficulty of making it all 'fit' is immense.[37]

Drawings were revised, but the panel remained critical, responding in July 1980: 'Many of the previous Panel's comments still apply. The problem of western style windows alongside their eastern counterparts still does not appear to be completely resolved.'[38] Eventually, however, the scheme was revised enough to be considered acceptable and was granted planning permission in October.

This was not the end of the design road for the mosque. By June 1981 Egyptian architect Ahmed Eliwa, living and working in Bristol, had been appointed to amend the designs. The mosque explained to the planners that these revisions were required as the approved design by Godfrey-Gilbert was proving too expensive. However, from the revisions prepared by Eliwa it is not immediately evident where significant cost savings could have been made as the scheme was similar in scope, with an increased amount of articulation and decoration. It perhaps suggests that rather than cost being the main issue, the mosque remained unsatisfied with Godfrey-Gilbert's design.

Eliwa's design introduced a more dynamic internal plan, faceted and irregular to respond more directly to the hexagonal prayer hall (Fig 4.11). Continuous bays of windows, with decorated mouldings around triangular heads, were introduced along each of the elevations of the main building, the prayer hall retaining sets of three windows on each face of the hexagon. The dome had morphed from its fairly upright sober shape to one that bulges at its base, being somewhat a mixture of late Mughal and Russian Orthodox onion shapes (Fig 4.12). The minaret was given a hexagonal stem up to a balcony, which fanned out rather like an airport control tower, with a plain cylindrical upper part culminating in a crescent-adorned point.

The council's architects' panel was dismissive of the revisions, commenting in July 1981: 'The previous designs were difficult to accept ... but this submission has nothing to recommend it ... The minaret is more like a candlestick and much too tall ... .The building materials lack "quality" – more factory like than mosque. The whole presentation lacks finesse.'[39]

Eliwa revised his scheme and two weeks later submitted a proposal in which the exterior features had been substantially redesigned.[40] The minaret underwent the largest transformation and was now a highly ornate three-tiered structure, the lower part being hexagonal on a square base, the central part cylindrical and fluted, and the upper section a chattri-style balcony with a ring of columns before continuing with a series of decorative shapes culminating in a crescent (*see* Fig 8.7). The dome had also reverted to more classical proportions, rising vertically at its base before curving to a point (*see* Fig 4.9). Window surrounds were also ornate and articulated, with calligraphic bands along a series of window heads.

Eliwa's changes were welcomed by the architects' panel, notes by panel member Vincent Dowling indicating the extent of the dialogue between them as well as communicating panel members' views on the appropriate aesthetics for a mosque alongside their underlying disquiet:

This minaret is a great improvement on the earlier 'candlestick' design. Mr Eliwa has obviously accepted the advice that was given to him to study good examples of Saracenic architecture so that the proportions, decoration and outline of the proposed building maybe more in keeping with its tradition and purpose.

The minaret shown is a near copy of the mosque Rait-Bey [sic] in Cairo, and one cannot do better than that, although perhaps the decoration could be simplified a little to keep up with the times.

I still have the fear that a mosque in such a position by the Leisure Centre will appear like a section of Disneyland.[41]

Dowling was partly accurate in identifying the minaret as a copy of the Kait Bey Mosque in Cairo, built in the late 15th century and described by Ernest Short, a 1920s historian, as showing 'the Moslem art of arabesque at its best ... an achievement in architectural planning ... the conjunction of the rectangular church with the ornate minaret and sculpted dome'.[42] However, Eliwa's minaret is more closely aligned to the minaret that was at this time (1981) being added to the Prophet's Mosque in Madinah, in itself

Fig 4.11
Ahmed Eliwa's revised ground-floor plan as built, with a geometry that follows the hexagonal prayer hall.

Key
1 Main men's prayer hall
2 Hall
3 Entrance
4 Men's ablution
5 Kitchen
6 Women's ablution
7 Mortuary
8 Hallway of imam's flat
9 Living room
10 Kitchen
11 Bedrooms
12 Bathroom

[Based on an approved plan (dated Jul/Aug 1981) held in the Royal Borough of Windsor and Maidenhead planning file 411185, application, 13 March 1980]

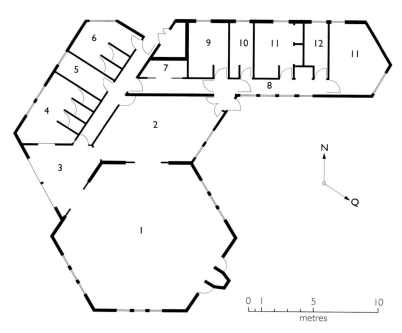

difficult to fit in at the best of times. What it really needs is a parkland setting.'[44]

Despite the council architects' ambivalence, the revised scheme was approved as an amendment to the Godfrey-Gilbert approved design on 20 August 1981. Following a period of fundraising, construction of the mosque was started in 1983 and it was completed in 1985.

Internally, the mihrab is a wide opening in the Qibla-facing side of the hexagon, shaped as an ogee arch (Fig 4.13). The face of the mihrab is tiled in Ottoman-style tilework, with blue and red floral designs and circular calligraphic inserts reading 'Ya Allah' ('Oh Allah') on the right and 'Ya Muhammad' ('Oh Muhammad') on the left. Ottoman-style tilework lines the rear of the mihrab as well as the walls of the prayer hall up to waist level. An ornate minbar is placed within the mihrab opening, with flowing profiles and gold-painted organic decoration. The interior of the dome is left plain, and a small chandelier hangs from its centre.

In 1997 a first-floor extension was added, providing more worship space, women's facilities, an office and a library. In the meantime the mosque had changed its official name to the Maidenhead Islamic Trust.

In 2013 the trust won planning permission to develop the site adjacent to the mosque into a three-storey new-build Islamic community hall and mortuary, along with a number of multifunctional teaching rooms.[45] This was the third attempt to gain planning permission for the scheme, which had initially been refused for inadequate parking provision. The new development, which started on site in 2016, is intended to extend the range of community and religious provision for the Muslim community.

Conclusion

Maidenhead Mosque is a compact and characterful building. It is a marker on the periphery of the town centre, in a location of car parks and access roads. Within this bland landscape, the building defiantly encapsulates the archetypal image of the mosque. Its Islamic motifs are derived from large landmark historic mosques of the Muslim world, referencing Mughal India, Fatimid Egypt and Madinah, scaled down to fit the scope of this modest building. The result is a building that is both unexpected and strangely endearing.

Maidenhead's mosque is the outcome of a quintessential story of post-war immigration and settlement: a Pakistani Muslim population

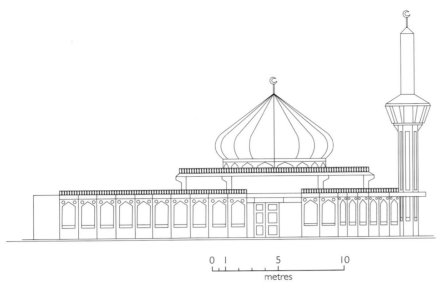

0   1   5   10
metres

Fig 4.12
Eliwa's unbuilt 1981 redesign of Godfrey-Gilbert's 1980 proposal, which introduces a more decorative and expressive style. [Based on a drawing held in the Royal Borough of Windsor and Maidenhead planning file 411185]

closely derived from Kait Bey. The echo of the Prophet's Mosque was continued through to Maidenhead's dome, which was coloured a similar green and similarly proportioned, albeit much smaller. The dome at Maidenhead has a slightly more rounded lower portion than that at Madinah, which allies it more closely to traditional Mughal and Persian dome profiles. However, the overall image of green dome and ornate minaret is a composition of elements that essentially evokes the mosque of the Prophet.

The proposal was subsequently recommended for approval, with the conditions that the mosque undertake not to use the minaret for calls to prayer and that the minaret should be inaccessible. The council's architects also stressed that the decorations had to be implemented with great care and high-quality materials for the building to be successful, noting that the 'general form, shape of the dome, minaret and the decoration are all true to type, and overall the proposed building will be a scaled down version of a typical Middle Eastern Mosque'. Further recommendations were made as regards the colour of the building, the architects' panel stating that 'colour will be important and bright light colours – particularly pinks and light blue, which are often used – should be avoided'.[43]

The issue of materiality, and the council's fear that the mosque design was bordering on absurdity, was further illuminated in a subsequent letter from the architects' panel, stating that as regards materials 'it is vitally important that these are of the highest quality. If not the whole thing could look like something from Battersea funfair. Architecturally so alien to Maidenhead, it would be

Fig 4.13
The interior of the men's main prayer hall, with an ornately tiled mihrab.
[DP148067]

settles in a town to supplement the town's industrial labour from the 1960s; it establishes a house mosque by the early 1970s in an ad hoc and rudimentary fashion; it then moves on to land leased from the council to erect a purpose-built mosque in the 1980s. This pattern of mosque building was proliferating across the country, in varying degrees, during the period. Furthermore, through its visual language, the mosque displays the borrowing of historical architectural styles and their pasting-in, scrap-book fashion, conjoining variant influences and periods into one building. Again, this approach typifies a method that was employed, in varying degrees, in the mosques built in Britain in this period.

The design process is well documented, along with comments and responses from council architects and the mosque designers, and shows how the visual language of the mosque sparked keen interest and debate from all parties. Interestingly, the planners themselves remained silent on matters of aesthetics, leaving this domain to their architects' department. It is revealing that both the council and the mosque's designers saw the only viable articulation of the mosque as being through the replication of historic styles. There is little, if any, conception that the mosque in Britain could explore a more contemporary language. Perhaps the emphasis on historical collage was partly legitimised by the period's postmodernist trend in mainstream architecture, whereby architectural history could be trawled for cursory references.

4 Jama al-Karim Mosque, All Saints Road, Gloucester, 1986

The Jama al-Karim Mosque in Gloucester has an architectural history that connects it with Maidenhead and Wimbledon. It was designed by Ahmed Eliwa, the designer of Maidenhead Mosque, from which it followed on chronologically. These three mosques were early built examples that explored the visual language of the local community mosque, and they all attempted to express a popular aesthetic through their dependency on traditional Islamic architectural references.

When the Gloucester and Sharpness Canal opened in 1827 it was the broadest and deepest canal in the world, able to ferry ships of up to 600 tonnes into the city centre. An industrial strip grew along the canal as it entered the city, culminating in warehouses built around a dock constructed in the mid-19th century. In the late 19th century Gloucester continued to be a base for industries such as farm machinery, railway stock, aircraft, timber, ice cream and printing. Inevitable industrial decline from the early 20th century was offset by an increased service sector.[46] South-east of the city centre and on the outside edge of its ring road is Barton, a swathe of 19th-century terraced workers' housing, densely packed on streets laid in grids. This gives way to 20th-century suburban housing and then to farmland. Industrial sites were situated to the north and east of this area, being easily accessible from Barton.

In 2001, Gloucester's Muslim population numbered 2,477, constituting 2.2 per cent of the total population, of which 77 per cent were concentrated in the Barton and Tredworth ward. Anecdotally, by 1966 there were some 30 to 40 Muslim households in the city.[47] The Muslim population that settled in Gloucester from the 1960s followed the general pattern of post-war Muslim immigration. People came mainly from specific areas of the Indian subcontinent, with the vast majority originating from the north Indian state of Gujarat. In 2001, 1.9 per cent of Gloucester's population was of Indian origin,[48] compared with 0.27 per cent Pakistani and 0.32 per cent Bangladeshi.

Gloucester's industry crept into the Barton residential area with a works site on the corner of Barton Street and the ring road. By the late 1970s this had become vacant, and a group of local Muslims, calling themselves the Gloucestershire Islamic Trust, who had been worshipping in a house mosque a few streets away since 1966, purchased the warehouse on All Saints Road for £10,000. This was in 1978, and straight away rudimentary adaptations were made to the building to enable it to be brought into use as the city's second mosque. The first mosque on Ryecroft Street, which by the mid-1970s had expanded into adjacent houses, was also being redeveloped at this time, and that new building was completed in the early 1980s.

A planning application was submitted in July 1981 for the 'erection of a new building to form a place of worship, teaching hall and three self-contained shops'.[49] The mosque was designed by David Williams of locally based D&G Design Consultants and comprised a two-storey building with a long brick façade running along the length of the site and replacing the existing warehouse (Fig 4.14).

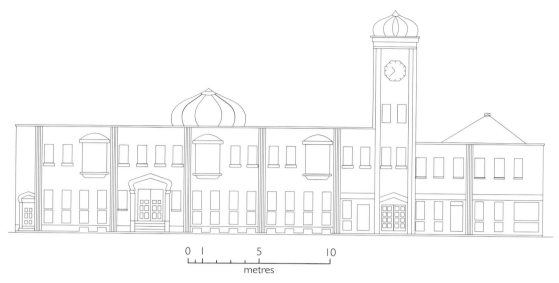

Fig 4.14
The first scheme designed
for the mosque: the
architectural language is
plainer than the final
design, although key
Islamic signifiers are
incorporated such as the
dome, minaret and arched
openings over the main
doorway.
[Based on a 1981 drawing
by D&G Design Consultants
in City of Gloucester
planning file 12265/01]

The ground floor comprised a large square main prayer hall, measuring some 15 metres by 15 metres, with an adjacent smaller women's prayer room with its own ablution facility. Three shops were to be located in the northern end of the building, where it tapers and meets Barton Road. An imam's flat was placed to the rear of the prayer hall, and a library and office to the front. This was a compact and efficient plan for an awkward site.

Curiously, three semicircular brick bays project from the first floor, shown as being for three mihrabs within a long prayer hall which is annotated as prayer halls 1, 2 and 3, even though forming one continuous space. The main elevation was to be faced in brick, with regular windows along its length at ground- and first-floor levels. Other than a squat four-centred arch and columns around the main doorway and the first-floor mihrab bays, the façade remained unadorned. A square clock tower was placed off-centre, rising to some 12 metres and topped with a Mughal-style onion dome, so denoting it as a de facto minaret. A similar but larger dome was placed in the centre of the mosque part of the development, over the long prayer hall on the first floor. Gloucester City Council's civic design committee was asked to comment on the application and responded with a single-line comment reading 'not poor enough to recommend rejection'.[50] The application was approved in September 1981.

After the approval, the Islamic Trust was introduced to Ahmed Eliwa, who was at this time working on the redesign of the Maidenhead Mosque (see pp 107–14). He persuaded the committee that the mosque as conceived by David Williams was lacking in ambition, and set about redesigning the scheme.

The result was a radical overhaul of Williams' design, with ornamentation around windows, articulated battlements, a large mihrab bay mimicking a balcony projecting from the first floor and a highly ornate three-tiered minaret, referencing Fatimid Egyptian and Indian Mughal styles and Madinah, being a replica of the minaret that Eliwa had just designed for Maidenhead. The building was also to be taller, the mosque part shown as standing at some 9 metres to the parapet versus Williams' building, which was to have been around 7 metres. The plan was also reconfigured by Eliwa: the main prayer hall was now placed on the first floor, and with the benefit of the extra height a second floor was accommodated. The main prayer hall could now also be a much grander affair, with a women's balcony, and open up to the dome placed centrally above it. A second prayer hall was placed on the ground floor to the same dimensions as the main hall above, intended for overspill prayer space – for example, on Fridays – and other social functions (Fig 4.15).

The reconfiguring of the plans to enable a main prayer hall with a considerable amount more grandeur than the previous design, along with the 'architectural Islamification' of the exterior elements, resulted in a mosque design that would unambiguously assert itself on the streetscape as a building of Muslim origin and identity. This was now a very different status claim than Williams' more modest and sedate proposal. The Gloucester Islamic Trust's mosque was intended to be a major statement in the visual landscape of Barton.

The revised scheme was submitted on 18 March 1982 as an amendment to the approval for a 'place of worship, teaching hall and three

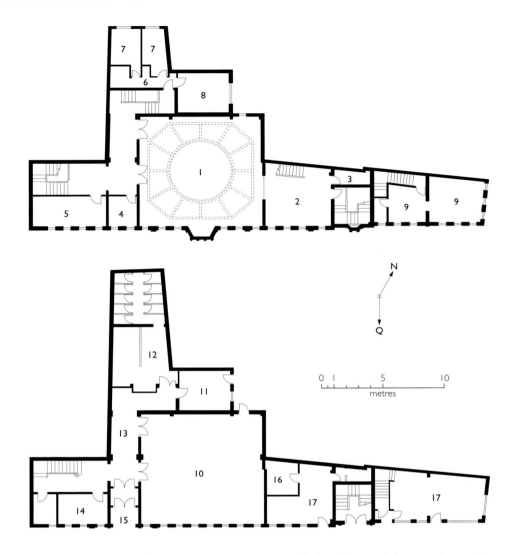

Fig 4.15
Proposed first-floor plan for
the Jama al-Karim Mosque,
Gloucester (top), showing
the Friday hall in the centre
forming the largest space.
Ancillary spaces are
arranged in the wings
filling the narrow site.
The proposed ground-floor
plan (bottom) shows how a
restricted and awkward
site is used to its best
potential to create a
functioning mosque. The
men's daily prayer hall
takes up a central position
easily accessible from the
main entrance.

Key
1 Main men's prayer hall/
*   Friday prayer hall*
2 Women's prayer hall
3 Women's ablution
4 Office
5 Library
6 Hallway of imam's flat
7 Bedroom
8 Living room
9 Storerooms
10 Men's daily prayer hall
11 Kitchen
12 Men's ablution
13 Lobby
14 Classroom
15 Main entrance
16 Storeroom
17 Shop unit

[Based on 1982 plans (with
1983 revisions) by DSW
Design Consultants
(formerly D&G Design
Consultants) in City of
Gloucester planning file
12265]

self-contained shops',[51] and approved, without fuss, three weeks later. Although Eliwa carried out the redesign, the revised drawings were submitted under the name of David Williams' DSW Design Consultants (formerly D&G Design Consultants), probably to maintain continuity with the planners and enable a smoother process. Rather tellingly, when the scheme started on site in December 1982, Williams remarked in an interview to the local press that he had found the project very difficult at the start, saying, 'I leaned on the Muslims very much. They told me what they wanted rather than me telling them what they should have.' The newspaper story commented that the mosque would have an 'Eastern Façade', and also noted that the city's other mosque on Ryecroft Street was near completion.[52]

The Islamic Trust collected funds from among themselves as well as from abroad, and started demolition of the warehouse in 1982. When funds became scant and it was clear that further revenue would be required if work was to continue, the mosque prepared a new fundraising leaflet and a handful of members journeyed to Regent's Park Mosque one Friday in a bid to raise funds from the congregation there. After the Friday prayer, the Muslim delegation from Gloucester distributed its leaflets and appealed to the central London congregation to assist with the building of their mosque. Some days later, the mosque received a call from an Egyptian Muslim businessman in London who had picked up their leaflet at Regent's Park, and who asked them to meet with him, bringing their documentation and financial reports. A group from All Saints Road duly went to London, where the meeting was held, and after reviewing the paperwork the businessman simply said, 'carry on', and there and then he promised to

abled the main prayer hall to be a square of some 10 metres by 10 metres. The lower hall on the ground floor, to the same dimensions, which was intended as secondary additional prayer space, has actually come to be used as the main prayer hall for daily prayers, with the prayer hall on the first floor being brought into use for larger gatherings. A mihrab is therefore marked on the wall of the lower hall, and a three-step minbar is also in place. Other than this, the lower hall remains unadorned, with a fairly low suspended tiled ceiling making it a somewhat utilitarian prayer space.

The upper prayer hall has a more impressive bearing, being a double-height space opening into the dome with windows in its base to admit light from above (Fig 4.17). Religious inscriptions in Arabic calligraphy decorate the inside faces of the faceted opening to the dome, from the centre of which a gold and glass chandelier hangs into the hall. The balcony front is painted timber panelling, with a series of *mashrabiya*-type latticework sections within arched openings. The mihrab is fairly plain in form, with a four-centred arch and gold-painted trimmings (Fig 4.18). It is, however, quite vibrantly decorated, with green mosaic tiling to the face and internally, along with Ottoman-style tiles lining the interior. It achieves a simple vibrancy by being set against the deep red of the carpet. The minbar is a free-standing four-stepped piece, lined with a red carpet and decorative white and gold painted timber sides and back. On either side of the mihrab, placed at high level, are framed

Fig 4.16
The front façade of the Jama al-Karim Mosque in Gloucester, seen from along All Saints Road, is a striking landmark with a decorated brick façade and an ornate minaret.
[DP148027]

Fig 4.17
Interior of the main prayer hall on the first floor, showing the men's prayer hall with the women's prayer space on the gallery above.
[DP148032]

fund all the works to completion. This anonymous benefactor suggested that the mosque be named the Jama al-Karim Mosque, from whence its name originates.[53]

By 1986 the mosque on All Saints Road was complete (Fig 4.16 and see Fig 8.8). There had been some modifications to Eliwa's design: namely, the decorative panels around the windows were built in projecting brickwork rather than as GRP (glass reinforced plastic) mouldings, as was the mihrab bay. The minaret was styled in GRP and was an exact replica of that at Maidenhead. As it was built within two or three years, it is most likely that the fabricators used the same mould for both minarets. The other addition to the scheme was four chattri-style canopies, each with a green dome, placed along the parapet, and replacing the battlements Eliwa had designed. These serve to further entangle the references to Mughal and Egyptian Islamic architectural sources.

The mosque had the good fortune to have its front wall aligned with the Qibla, which has en-

Arabic inscriptions reading 'Allah' on the right side and 'Muhammad' on the left. Other than this, the walls remain plain, without further elaboration.

Conclusion

The establishment of the Jama al-Karim Mosque followed one of the archetypal patterns of mosque development in the last quarter of the 20th century. Muslim immigrants settled in compact, working-class districts of a city, where a mixture of housing and industrial uses abounded. As industrial decline took effect in the late 1970s, warehouses and works buildings became vacant and were acquired by the Muslim communities who needed to establish places for worship. Once the warehouse was purchased, it was first used in an ad hoc way as a mosque and then redeveloped into a purpose-built facility.

The somewhat uncertain process of the mosque's design is also one that is familiar from numerous other sites. Designs were prepared and then rejected, or revised even after planning permission had been obtained. This suggests that the aesthetics and material culture of these new religious buildings were being explored and tested, both by designers and by the mosque members' own debate and consensual politics. What comes through is the mosque committee's keen involvement in and influence on the design, and that despite the new and unsure architectural ground

being trod, a definite image was being aspired to. Particular designers who were able to tap into this sensibility, it seems, could wield considerable favour among mosque commissioners, leading to the restyling of already finalised schemes, as Gloucester and Maidenhead show, as well as to repeat commissions across the country.

The Gloucestershire Islamic Trust, having successfully established the mosque on All Saints Road, has found itself within a growing and diversifying Muslim community. New Muslim immigrants from Europe, as well as from Arab and African countries, have brought cultural variety and an increase in requirements. To meet this growing need, in November 2013 the mosque gained planning approval for the replacement of a vacant adjacent warehouse with a large, low-rise extension, potentially more than doubling the footprint of the mosque. This proposal intended to provide additional prayer halls, classrooms and ablution facilities, as well as on-site car parking.

5 Central Jamia Mosque Ghamkol Sharif, Golden Hillock Road, Small Heath, Birmingham, 1996

In 1962 Abdullah Khan, a disciple of the Sufi saint Zindapir, left the mountain village of Kohat in northern Pakistan (where Zindapir lived and taught) for inner-city Birmingham to act as Zindapir's Khilafah (vicegerent) in England and teach Islam to the Muslims who were settling there. He worked alongside his compatriots in the factories around the districts of Small Heath and Sparkhill and at the same time embarked on his mission of spreading Islam among the emerging Muslim communities. He found that their religious practice was scant, with no places of prayer, no observance of Ramadan and no Friday prayer, and many of the newly arrived Muslims did not know the direction of the Qibla. His first response was to turn the ground floor of his house in Sparkhill's Durham Road into a mosque and educational space for children, while he and his family lived upstairs. Abdullah Khan set up the Tariqa (a Sufi order) at the house, and established Friday prayers, a weekly dhikr circle (for Sufi devotional practices) and a monthly spiritual gathering. These gatherings grew as Abdullah Khan 'touched the hearts of those he encountered'.[54] Gradually, the Tariqa gathered momentum until the house was no longer adequate to cater for the numbers of followers and attendees. Abdullah Khan was recognised as a spiritual guide and became known by the honorific title of Sufi Sahib.

In the 1970s, as the Tariqa grew, Sufi Sahib initiated an age-old Sufi tradition, the *jaloos* (procession) in Birmingham. This involved marching through the streets reciting part of the Muslim testament of faith, 'There is no God but Allah,' as a way of declaring one's faith in public. Since then, the *jaloos* has been an annual event in the city, marking the birthday of the Prophet Muhammad.

To find more space, Sufi Sahib moved to Warwick Road, again in Sparkhill, where the much larger ground-floor reception room was converted into a mosque. Sufi Sahib's following continued to grow, until this centre was unable to cope with the numbers. In 1983 a disused factory hall with four adjacent houses was purchased on Golden Hillock Road, Small Heath, and Sufi Sahib established the religious centre called the Darul-Uloom Islamia Rizvia,

which was able to accommodate up to 700 worshippers. Throughout the 1980s the centre flourished, providing services for the local community in conjunction with Birmingham City Council. The site was developed to provide a community centre, an employment resource centre and a boarding facility for students from outside Birmingham. As activities increased, the centre applied for planning permission to increase the size of the building. However, this proved difficult due to limited parking provision. As it happened, there was a piece of council-owned land opposite the Darul-Uloom with 35 derelict houses on it. The mosque asked whether this land could be acquired from the council, who responded by agreeing to sell it for a reduced price if it was to be used for a new mosque.

Once the site was acquired in 1990, the mosque appointed the John Manning Partnership, an architectural practice based in Luton, who had designed a few mosques already. Construction started in 1992, and in 1996 the mosque opened to the public (Fig 4.19). A prayer

Fig 4.19
The Ghamkol Sharif Mosque is a landmark building which combines Islamic forms with local materials.
[DP137779]

Fig 4.20
The central dome and chandelier in the main men's prayer hall at the Ghamkol Sharif Mosque. [DP137775]

hall is on the first floor, with a women's gallery and central dome forming a grand feature (Fig 4.20). The walls are lined in onyx and the Qibla wall adorned with photographs of holy sites and calligraphy (Fig 4.21). For the Ghamkol Sharif Mosque, expressiveness in design equated to

expressiveness of love for God. On the ground floor a smaller second prayer hall accommodates the daily prayers. The architecture of the mosque combines Islamic forms – a hexagonal minaret (Fig 4.22), arched windows and a central dome – with local materials, such as brick-faced walls and tiled pitched roofs. The building is prominently situated on a major arterial road into the city, and as such is one of a new generation of landmark mosques that emerged across residential areas with high Muslim populations during the 1990s.

The Ghamkol Sharif organisation has grown into a substantial religious and community institution on Golden Hillock Road, in the heart of Birmingham's Small Heath district. In its size, scope and ambition it rivals the Birmingham Central Mosque (*see* pp 259–60), and some would argue that it is in effect the main mosque in the city because of its size, extent of services and catchment. Through additional sites in the area, it provides a range of services for the Muslim community including education, health, care of older people and funerals.

Fig 4.21
The men's main prayer hall of the Ghamkol Sharif Mosque, viewed from underneath the women's prayer gallery. [DP137773]

Conclusion

The endeavour of Sufi Sahib and his followers since the 1960s demonstrates how a specific religious tradition was transferred from Pakistan to an English city and remained a live practice, with the representative of a Sufi saint and his Tariqa establishing local roots. Through the Ghamkol Sharif Mosque, Birmingham and Kohat became interlinked in the imagination of the followers of Sufi Sahib and Zindapir. It is not just any mosque in an English city, but rather it is one that has a specific place in a transnational religious and geographic narrative from which it derives its significance and status.

6 Al Manaar, Muslim Cultural Heritage Centre, Acklam Road, Westbourne Park, London, 2000

By the turn of the 21st century new dynamics were emerging through which mosques could be made. Over the previous two decades local mosques had proliferated, built in an impromptu and locally sourced way, and with a visual language reflecting a certain ad hoc approach. The foundation of the Muslim Cultural Heritage Centre (MCHC) in west London represented a wholly new way of creating a mosque and Islamic centre, harnessing local communities and public bodies to work together towards a shared objective.

The Muslim Communities Forum (MCF) emerged in west London in 1993 as a coalition of the multiple and varied Muslim social organi-

sations in the North Kensington area. The MCF established the Muslim Cultural Heritage Centre Trust and successfully bid for a piece of land in the City Challenge regeneration zone. (The City Challenge was a central government regeneration initiative implemented through local authorities.) The trust won some official funding on the basis that it would provide vital social and community services to the local Muslim population. The trust's feasibility appraisal identified the main beneficiaries of the centre as being 'the Muslim community living and working in the City Challenge area ... approximately 8,000 individuals from 16 Muslim nationalities. This community is one of the most deprived in terms of low educational achievement, high rates of unemployment, poor housing, lack of marketable skills, poor grasp of English and increasing social problems.'[55]

Muslims from North Africa had started to settle in North Kensington from the 1960s, attracted by cheap housing and proximity to employment opportunities in the hotel and cleaning industries of London's West End. By the 1990s, and increasingly over the next two decades, the community had become more diverse as newer immigrants settled from a range of Muslim countries so that by 2001 the Muslim population within the Goldborne ward stood at 21 per cent, compared to a borough average of 8 per cent.[56]

The wider City Challenge regeneration project involved the redevelopment of a 3.7-acre (1.5ha) former railway goods yard known as St Ervans, which bordered the railway line and the A40 flyover. A number of uses were proposed within an overall masterplan, including business, light industrial and creative facilities along with the Muslim Centre. The design brief for the site as set out in the masterplan stipulated certain guiding criteria for the new buildings, but was not prescriptive in terms of aesthetics or form.

The MCHC Trust was introduced to a renowned London practice, Chapman Taylor, and through them was able to put together some concept designs and develop a brief. The initial concept design placed flexibility as a central factor, recognising at the outset the nature of such a facility, which was to combine religious practices with community services. An entrance hall, multipurpose halls and prayer halls were therefore laid out in an interdependent way. Along with these, there was to be a women's prayer space, a library, offices and classrooms and also a café and ablution facilities. Two large halls formed

Fig 4.22
The core of the hexagonal minaret continues to ground level and is used as a circulation core for the building.
[DP137776]

Fig 4.23
Ali Omar Ermes' sketch (c 1995) of the tower of the Great Mosque of Kairouan, which was the inspiration for the tower of the MCHC. [By kind permission of Ali Omar Ermes]

Fig 4.23
Ali Omar Ermes' sketch (c 1995) of the tower of the Great Mosque of Kairouan, which was the inspiration for the tower of the MCHC. [By kind permission of Ali Omar Ermes]

Fig 4.24
The front elevation of the MCHC, with the prayer hall on the right and the community centre at the far end.
[DP148153]

the central spaces, with perimeter circulation arranged, off which other functions were placed. It was a plan that alluded to traditional hypostyle mosques of North Africa, where the user enters a large open courtyard in front of an enclosed prayer hall. The scheme was designed as a three-storey building with a simple pitched roof around an open courtyard. In later sketches a short, square minaret appears along with a hexagonal dome, suggesting that a debate was going on as to the level of Islamic symbolism appropriate in the architectural vocabulary.

The concept and brief were put to several architectural practices, and their responses were invited in order that one could be selected to develop the design and deliver the building. The MCHC Trust was not looking for just a design scheme, but for the approach of the architect, as well as the practice's past projects. One of the trustees taking a keen interest in the design process was the Libyan artist Ali Omar Ermes, who had been living in London since the 1980s. His was one of the influential voices of the commissioners who set the tone of the design process and architectural ambition of the project.

Through the selection process, the Frederick Gibberd Partnership (FGP) was eventually successful – the firm that had built Regent's Park Mosque (*see* pp 133–47) but was now without its founder, Sir Frederick (d 1984).

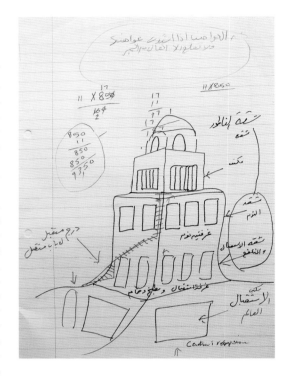

However, for Ermes, the firm was appointed despite Regent's Park Mosque, not because of it. For him, Gibberd's Regent's Park Mosque was far too 'industrial' and he sought a much 'softer' approach for the new MCHC.[57] It was the openness of the architects to the project, and their

willingness to develop the project with the client, that secured the appointment for them. That the practice had designed Britain's landmark mosque at Regent's Park was a factor that the MCHC Trust felt would be an advantage when fundraising, as trustees would be able to show that they had appointed a reputable firm with experience of mosque design in Britain.

Ermes worked closely with the architects throughout the design process up to 1996. Once FGP had been selected, Ermes invited the design team to his house for the first of a series of what he called 'awareness sessions'. Here, he showed the architects some 200 images of Islamic architecture from around the world, from Andalusia to Washington – images he had taken himself on his travels. He wanted them to know that Muslims came from a deep and varied cultural heritage, and that all Muslims shared this heritage and were also united by it.

The choice of materials for the new building was fundamental to its concept: textured and varied brickwork was to be used to offer depth

and a sense of the natural, in contrast to the concrete of Regent's Park Mosque. In terms of its Islamic symbolism, the building is muted. There is no obvious minaret, but instead a shorter tower, whose design is based on the great mosque of Kairouan, built in 9th-century Tunis. Ermes drew a sketch of the minaret for the architects, which evolved into a tower housing the caretaker's flat (Fig 4.23). A square prayer hall, almost cubic in proportion, at the eastern end of the site rises to a vaulted roof with clerestory windows, allowing light to enter into the prayer space from a high level (Fig 4.24). As domes are not traditional North African Islamic elements, there is no strong allusion to one with FGP's design. Perhaps the vaulted roof of the prayer hall and clerestory fulfil the dome's signifying function, in a language possibly inspired by the domes of the Mughal Shish Mahal in Lahore.

For Ermes the principles of Islamic architecture are light, nature, air and water, and the relationship between people and nature. These principles underlie the idea of the courtyard, which was initially open until it was decided that it could be better used as an enclosed space (Figs 4.25 and 4.26). The enclosure has a grid of glazed pyramidal lanterns reminiscent of the Topkapi Palace in Istanbul. The community facilities are located on the western edge and around the circulation core, which wraps around

Fig 4.25
The glazed central hall which serves as a multifunctional space, connecting the prayer hall (on the right) and the community facilities (on the left).
[DP148152]

Fig 4.26
The interior of the glazed central hall, which serves as overspill prayer space for the Friday prayer and as a multipurpose space at other times.
[DP148148]

the north part of the site. Each space is articulated with formal clarity, allowing the building to be read as a series of interconnected forms (Fig 4.27). The spaces allow separation of functions under normal use, with the prayer hall for daily prayers, the courtyard for social events and the community hall for meetings and gatherings. For the Friday prayer all three spaces can be opened up to create one large interconnected space, transforming the centre into a large mosque. This adaptability was at the heart of the planning strategy of the building (Fig 4.28).

Internally, the main prayer hall is a sober treatment of dark wood, with decoration and calligraphy in white plaster friezes along the walls. The mihrab is recessed into the Qibla wall, and is formed from timber with carved calligraphic panels (Fig 4.29). The women's prayer space is on an upper gallery and wraps around the sides and back of the prayer hall, with timber *mashrabiya*-style screening. The interior styling is a considered treatment of typical Islamic languages, echoing the sobriety and structure of the building overall.

Ermes' involvement was artistic as well as advisory. He designed the motif for the centre, which is a stylisation of the Arabic phrase '*Allah-u-Akbar*' ('God is the greatest'). The motif is used on the ceramic inset tiles on the front façade and as the finial on the domes (Fig 4.30). Ermes did not want to use the conventional crescent and star motif seen in most mosques, as he identified it as being specific to the Ottoman period and he sought references that were not located in a particular time and place.

The building is faced in a local stock brick, which ties it visually and materially into a London vernacular. On the street elevation the façade is decorated with patterns formed by varying depths of brickwork, banding and glazed tiles. The diamond-shaped motifs in the brickwork are taken from the Kaylan Mosque in Uzbekistan. Ermes' motif and the name of the centre in ceramic tiles are also inset into the

Fig 4.27
South and east elevational drawings by Frederick Gibberd Partnership, dated 1996, of the MCHC. The south elevation shows the street-front façade and the east elevation shows the exterior of the Qibla wall with a projecting mihrab at ground-floor level. The building was constructed according to these designs by 2000.
[By kind permission of the Frederick Gibberd Partnership]

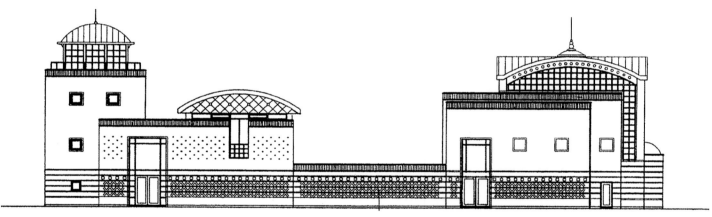

South elevation

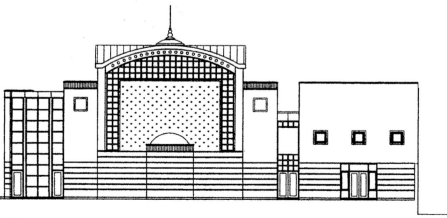

East elevation

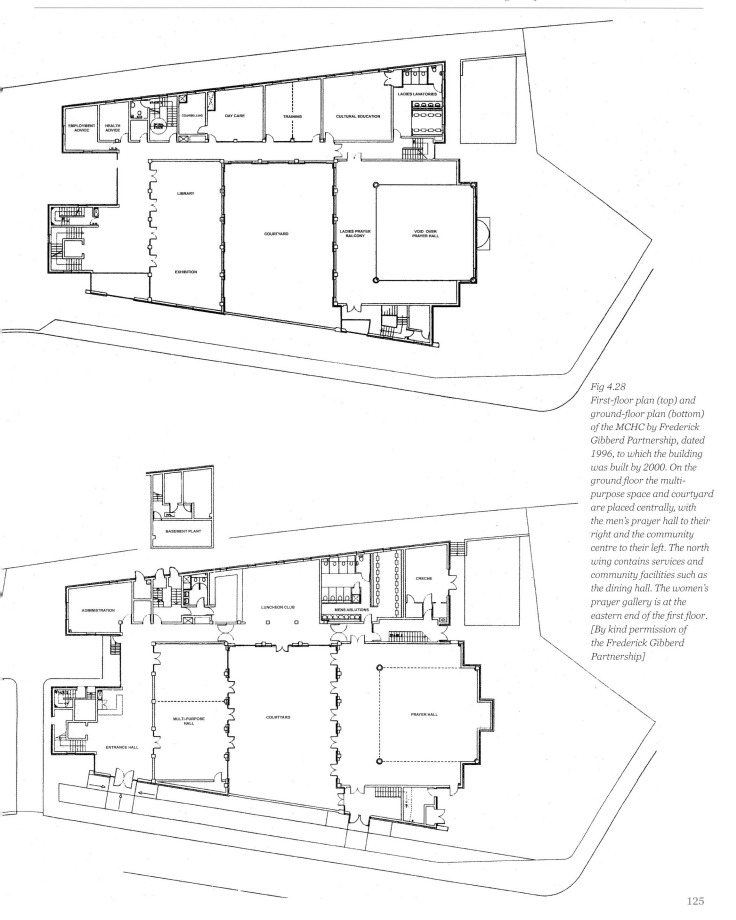

*Fig 4.28
First-floor plan (top) and
ground-floor plan (bottom)
of the MCHC by Frederick
Gibberd Partnership, dated
1996, to which the building
was built by 2000. On the
ground floor the multi-
purpose space and courtyard
are placed centrally, with
the men's prayer hall to their
right and the community
centre to their left. The north
wing contains services and
community facilities such as
the dining hall. The women's
prayer gallery is at the
eastern end of the first floor.
[By kind permission of
the Frederick Gibberd
Partnership]*

Fig 4.29
The main prayer hall with
the men's prayer space on
the lower level and the
women's prayer space on
an upper gallery that
wraps around three sides
of the main prayer hall.
[DP148145]

brickwork, adding to the earthy materiality of the façades. Along the parapets, a conventional place for Islamic decoration to be placed, a band is delineated with tile strips into which calligraphy is written with glazed tiles. The treatment of the façade oscillates subtly between the Islamic and the vernacular, following the overall language of its form.

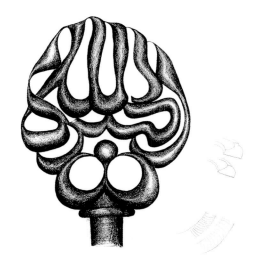

Fig 4.30
Ali Omar Ermes' sketch
(c 1995) of the Allah-u-
Akbar motif used on the
dome finials and ceramic
tiles inset into the front
façade of the MCHC.
[By kind permission of
Ali Omar Ermes]

As the MCHC is not strictly a mosque but describes itself rather as a *markaz* (a community centre with a prayer space) this discerning Islamic visual language is somewhat appropriate. It allows the building to be read as a cultural and social centre, which is a role that has been central to its agenda since its inception, and which is carried through into its daily functions. Alongside its social role, it functions as a fully operative mosque, with daily prayers and religious events duly accommodated. The range of activities hosted at the centre is diverse, from the religious to the social. There are computer classes, a supplementary school, exhibitions, diversity awareness courses for public bodies, exhibitions, charity events, women's fitness classes and so on.

Through its design, the new Muslim Cultural Heritage Centre intends to position itself firmly within British culture, both architecturally and socially. For Ermes, Islam encourages creativity, adding new ideas and not simply repeating the past. These are the concepts that he and the trustees of the MCHC wanted to impart to the new building. The centre opened in 2000, after a seven-year process of gaining political and community support, fundraising and construction.

Conclusion

The MCHC stands apart in the context of Muslim institutions on a number of levels. First, it has been brought about through collaboration between central government, local government and a coalition of local Muslim communities. From the outset it has been devised to respond to social and community needs within the Muslim population. It was not imagined, as many mosques have been, to provide an essentially religious function, and it was not established by a Muslim group bounded by communal or ethnic ties. The centre is a local-authority initiative as well as a grass-roots Muslim community initiative, and therefore straddles the boundaries of a civic, community and religious project.

In its design process and eventual architectural language, the MCHC also stands apart from most post-war mosques. It was designed by eminent architects with significant experience in the creation of Muslim space in Britain. This has resulted in a building, and an institution, that displays a level of spatial and aesthetic sophistication and an operational professionalism that set it apart from the majority of Muslim spaces and organisations that have followed more circuitous, incremental and ad hoc routes to existence.

7 Shahjalal Mosque and Islamic Centre, Eileen Grove, Rusholme, Manchester, 2001

Mosque histories can be complex and contested, and Shahjalal Mosque in south Manchester's Rusholme neighbourhood is a good example of this. The mosque was one of the city's earliest, established by the Bangladeshi community in the late 1960s. Its story is one of contest and co-operation between communities from South Asia's post-independence emerging nations, as well as within the newly arriving Bangladeshi community. By the late 1990s the mosque's history, at that point officially unrecorded, was so contested that Moulvi Mohammed Faizul Islam, one of the founder members, was moved to write an article in a local Bangladeshi newspaper setting out how the mosque had begun some two decades earlier, as an attempt to transcribe a version of events that could become the historical canon. The article was also a bid to rebut counter-

claims to the mosque's founding narrative that had recently arisen within the community.

Moulvi Mohammed was an Islamic scholar from Bangladesh who arrived in Manchester in 1963 and found employment in the local restaurant industry as a waiter. Because of his religious status, he soon became popular with the influential people within the community. In 1966 he was invited to a meeting in one of the Bengali restaurants with a few of these community initiators, where the idea was tabled for the formation of a 'mosque for the Bengalis'. The reason given was that the community could not speak in Bengali in the city's current mosque at Victoria Park, which was Pakistani-run, and due to this language barrier it also could not provide Islamic education for its children.

It was decided that a second general meeting should be called among the Bangladeshi community, where the mosque idea could gain momentum. Moulvi Mohammed describes how the leader of the meeting, Islam Chowdhury, was chosen to keep two differing Bengali community groups on board. Donations were sought and funds raised, and the project for a new Bangladeshi mosque was underway.

After this a concerted fundraising effort began within the Bangladeshi community. The mosque group would meet in the Everest restaurant in nearby Levenshulme and set out in groups to canvass support and funds. By 1968 the group had been able to purchase the former working men's club and warehouse on Eileen Grove, and carry out a rudimentary conversion for use as a mosque.

Moulvi Mohammed has narrated how inter-mosque rivalry surfaced at the first Eid prayer in the new mosque, highlighting the calming role of Malik Bakht, a member of the Bangladeshi group. He wrote:

> The Pakistanis were after us, asking why we were establishing a separate mosque. On the day of Eid they stood in Park Crescent and instructed people attending the namaz to go to the Victoria Park mosque. In response, the late Malik Bakht sat on top of a car on Plate Lane and encouraged people to come towards our mosque. I was leading the Eid prayer, I said a few words in Bengali, but some Pakistanis in the congregation interrupted and asked me to speak in Urdu. So I was forced to speak in Bengali as well as Urdu. As soon as the prayer was finished a Pakistani attending stood up asking why a different mosque was

Fig 4.31
Rear view of Shahjalal Mosque, as seen from Summer Place, showing the two-storey mosque built in 2001 comprising of the main prayer hall, domes and minaret. The mihrab is projecting from the Qibla wall with a half-domed roof.
[Author]

Fig 4.32
The interior of the dome of the 2001 main men's prayer hall: the circular chandelier and dome are situated within an octagonal opening.
[DP137708]

required. The late Malik Bakht stood up and responded to him, explaining the justification of forming the mosque. If the late Malik Bakht had not been there, then what would have happened to us is not known.[58]

Moulvi Mohammed went on to explain that, despite this rivalry, in 1968 when the Victoria Park Mosque was demolished and redeveloped, its congregation used the new Shahjalal Mosque for prayers. And indeed the Victoria Park congregation constructed new wudu facilities at the mosque and also upgraded the prayer hall. Things later seem to have turned sour once more during the Pakistan–Bangladesh war that led to the independence of Bangladesh in 1971, when the 'Pakistani' congregation 'demanded absolute custody of the mosque'. However, 'with a few unpleasant incidents here and there the final custody of the mosque went to the Bengalis'.[59] It seems that after these incidents, once the mosque was back within the control of the Bangladeshi community, a new mosque committee was formed with new members replacing the original founding group. Disheartened by the relegation of the mosque founders, Moulvi Mohammed ends his article with a plea that he wants the truth about the founding of the mosque to be revealed, and the 'false propaganda to stop'.[60]

Under the new committee the mosque embarked on a plan for redevelopment, and in the late 1990s a number of architects were approached and asked to submit proposals. One of the invited architects was Najib Gedal, originally from Libya and then established with a practice in Manchester. Although he did not win the project in the first instance, the committee was unsatisfied with the design it commissioned and returned to Gedal to revisit the scheme.

Gedal's built scheme of 2001 retained the original red-brick block of the working men's club on the western end of the site along with the shell of an adjacent brick building. A new two-storey building was constructed at the eastern end of the site, complete with dome and minaret, to serve as a new prayer hall (Fig 4.31, 4.32 and 4.33 and *see* Fig 4.1) This was linked to the former club with new ablution facilities at ground-floor level and classrooms at first-floor level.[61] A further green GRP (glass reinforced plastic) dome was placed over the stairwell on the eastern boundary, with a curved wall to match the mihrab projection on the south-eastern wall, which again is topped with a half-dome.

Further works followed, to designs by Gedal prepared in 2005. The façade of the new prayer hall was extended up to the former club to help unify the frontage, and a dome was added to the former club, again with the intention of creating

Fig 4.33
The interior of the 2001 main men's prayer hall, showing the mihrab, which is a moveable screen. A projecting bay in which the mihrab is placed receives daylight from high-level windows.
[DP137709]

Fig 4.34
The front and side elevations of Shahjalal Mosque, viewed from Eileen Grove. The former working men's club (the deep-red brick building fronting Eileen Grove) was converted into a mosque in the 1960s. The dome was added in the 2005 proposal. The central pitched-roofed building behind was faced (as part of the 2005 proposal) with a new façade that continues as the front elevation to the domed prayer hall, built in 2001. The minaret, also of 2001, is located at the eastern end of the building and completes the composition to create a new Islamic landmark.
[Author]

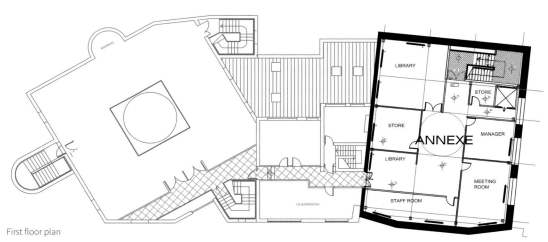

First floor plan

Fig 4.35
First-floor and ground-floor plans of Gedal's proposed additions to Shahjalal Mosque from 2005. The former working men's club building on the right (marked as the Annexe) was converted into the mosque in the 1960s. In 2001 the prayer hall to the left was added, with ablution and circulation areas infilling the space between the two. (Please note, south is to the top of these plans.)
[© Najib Gedal Architects]

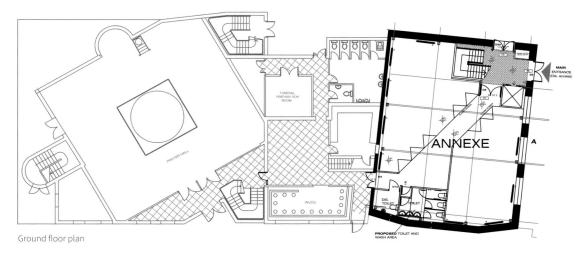

Ground floor plan

a unified whole out of the disparate building parts (Figs 4.34, 4.35 and 4.36).

Gedal drew his design inspiration from a number of sources: the domes and arches were from the Mughal period; the minaret was based on the Malwiya minaret on the Samarra Grand Mosque in Iraq; and the motifs on its finial had Moorish influences. Gedal intended the minaret to be integral to the design of the new building, as he had seen many mosques where an independently standing minaret was never built owing to lack of funds. By designing the minaret as integral, it would be seen as indispensable to the proposal and realised.[62] For Gedal, drawing from Islamic architecture's history and combining elements to form a 'contemporary structure' was a pertinent response to making new Muslim architecture in Britain.

Conclusion

The Shahjalal Mosque in Rusholme is a building with a bearing and stature that belies its roots as a simple social club; it forms a significant landmark in this off-centre residential location. The transformation of the mosque from the 19th-century building on Eileen Grove to the spiralling minaret at its other end is architecturally legible. The tiled roof of the pre-existing central building is visible behind the new brick skin which continues to form the front elevation of the mosque's prayer hall. This building shows how an assemblage of existing and new buildings have been tied together in an attempt to create a coherent architectural language along with a new Islamic identity.

Fig 4.36
The main elevation drawing of Gedal's proposal in 2005 to add a dome to the former working men's club building on the right side, and build a new façade to the existing central building that links it to the 2001 prayer hall on the left.
[© Najib Gedal Architects]

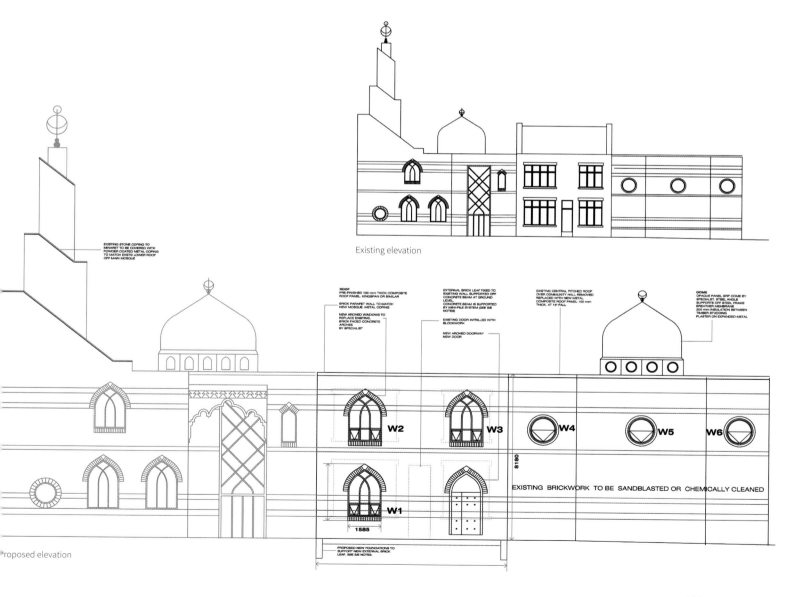

Existing elevation

Proposed elevation

5

Making Muslim landmarks and institutions

The purpose-built mosques of the late 1970s and 1980s expressed Muslim identities in architecture for the first time on a significant scale in Britain. They introduced a new repertoire of architectural symbols to the British urban landscape that directly referenced a Muslim architectural past, while also combining with local vernacular styles. This introduction of Islamic visual references brought a new aesthetic syntax to Britain's towns; traditional forms were replicated literally with a new materiality. English brick walls and GRP (glass reinforced plastic) domes replaced the more traditional materials of stone and timber from which landmarks of Islamic history were made. This was architecture of the Muslim world imitated in Britain, and it represented the pursuit of an image reflecting the personal and collective memories of Muslim users, partly based on remembered Islamic architecture from their countries of origin. It was also an expression of how Muslim buildings *should* be visualised and identified, communicating their origin and function to their own users as well as to the wider society.

Over the decades that local Muslim communities were self-building mosques and exploring their aesthetic languages, another process was also taking place. This was the building of Muslim landmarks, and through them the establishment of social organisations that would become major Muslim institutions in years to follow. These landmarks were created through a dynamic other than the highly localised and iterative processes of the many local mosques across the country. The landmark mosques were embedded within longer historical processes, involved Muslim religious leaders, diplomats and intelligentsia, and were interconnected with the early history of Muslim settlement in Britain. These projects were not conceived as local in remit, but were intended to speak to an audience regionally and globally.

Another marked difference between the landmark projects and the local mosques was the centrality of the design process, for example by the use of high-profile British architects, and thus the emergence of an architecture for Muslim buildings that became situated within the wider design and architectural discourse. The buildings were often in prominent locations, and were therefore significant additions to the image of the city. They were the visible, bold statements of the emerging public face of Islam in Britain.

Case studies

1 London Central Mosque and Islamic Cultural Centre (Regent's Park Mosque), Park Road, London, 1977
2 Ismaili Centre, Cromwell Road, South Kensington, London, 1983
3 East London Mosque and London Muslim Centre, Whitechapel Road, London, 1985/2004

1 London Central Mosque and Islamic Cultural Centre (Regent's Park Mosque), Park Road, London, 1977

During the late 19th and early 20th centuries, Britain was home to a series of influential Muslims who played a key role in shaping Islamic thought and developments in the Muslim world. Muhammad Ali Jinnah, the founder of Pakistan, came as a student in 1892, was called to the Bar, and returned in 1930 to practise law in Britain for four years. Muhammad Iqbal, revered as 'poet-philosopher of the East', arrived in 1905, studied at Cambridge and qualified as a barrister before returning [to what is now Pakistan].

Syed Ameer Ali, a well-known *Shia* scholar, came to study in 1873, married an Englishwoman and eventually settled in Britain.

Fig 5.1
The main men's prayer hall of the London Central Mosque (Regent's Park Mosque), designed by Sir Frederick Gibberd and completed in 1977. [DP148089]

Later appointed a Privy Councillor, he went on to write *The Spirit of Islam*, which had a profound influence on British Muslims as well as the Muslims of the Subcontinent. Abdullah Yusuf Ali arrived at the same time and settled in Britain to produce one of the most widely used English translation[s] of the Qur'an.

These Muslims faced a number of dilemmas concerning personal morality, codes of behaviour, types of education, forms of religious practice and cultural identity.[1]

It was from within this coterie of influential Muslims that the movement for a central mosque in London arose. They sought to establish a significant place of worship in Britain that would serve as a place for the community to perform its religious duties and would represent the Muslim presence on a national stage. With no mosque in London at the turn of the 20th century, Muslims carried out their religious events in temporary spaces. *The Times* reported on 22 December 1903 that 'members of the Moslem colony in London assembled, under the auspices of the Pan-Islamic society, in Caxton hall ... to celebrate Eed-ul-Fitr. The gathering was thoroughly representative, Persians, Turks, Indians, Moors, Egyptians, Dutch ... being present in their national costumes.' An appeal was also made at this festival for Muslims to contribute towards a Mosque Fund.[2]

This event illustrates the attempts being made in London to create spaces for Islamic worship and to establish Muslim cultural life. Around 1905, Khalid Sheldrake, a prominent Muslim convert, was conducting prayers at a house in Peckham, and after World War I the London Mosque Fund held Friday prayers at Lindsey Hall, Notting Hill Gate. It then established a prayer room in rented accommodation at 111 Campden Hill Road, naming it the London Muslim Prayer House.[3] The imam of the Woking Mosque regularly led congregations there, as did Marmaduke Pickthall (*see* pp 31–2), a prominent English convert to Islam.

The London Mosque Fund

The London Mosque Fund (LMF) itself came into being as the crystallisation of a sentiment that had been gathering among the London Muslim elite early in the 20th century. With some 100 million Muslim subjects of the British Empire who would soon be called on to fight for the Crown against fellow Muslims of the Ottoman Empire, the motivation for a London mosque was cast as being politically expedient. Syed Ameer Ali wrote in *The Times* in January 1911:

It does not require great imagination or political grasp to perceive the enormous advantages that would accrue to the empire itself were a Moslem place of worship founded in London, the hold it would give on the sentiments of the people or the addition to prestige and influence that would be gained thereby.[4]

In November 1910 the Aga Khan led a meeting at the Ritz Hotel in London, where the London Mosque Fund was inaugurated with Syed Ameer Ali as its chairman. The resolution of the fund was to raise money for the purpose of 'providing a Mosque in London worthy of the traditions of Islam and worthy of the capital of the British Empire'.[5] The fund was opened with an initial donation from the Aga Khan of £5,000. Its committee and trustees were mainly Muslims who 'hailed primarily from Western-educated classes of Indian society – namely, administrators, merchants, and professionals'.[6] There were also two 'English noblemen' appointed as trustees, Lord Ampthill and Lord Lamington, 'whose sympathy with Moslems is well-known'.[7]

Since the end of the 19th century, fuelled by political tensions as war approached, hostility towards Islam and Muslims had been high, with former Prime Minister William Gladstone denouncing the Quran as 'that accursed book' and describing the Ottoman Sultan in 1896 as 'that wretched Sultan, whom God has given as a curse to mankind'.[8] This hostility continued through to World War I, when the Ottoman alliance with Germany brought fresh doubts about the loyalty of Muslims living within the British Empire.

By 1913 overseas donations to the London Mosque Fund amounted to £7,000 from the Begum of Bhopal and £1,000 each from the Ottoman Sultan and the Shah of Persia.[9] However, progress was still slow and, despite the political climate, the London Mosque Fund turned its attention to the British government, arguing that thousands of Muslims were fighting for King and Country against Britain's enemies, which included the Ottoman Caliphate. Indeed, by the end of World War I some 400,000 Muslims had fought on the Western Front in Europe, and in Mesopotamia and Africa, and approximately 60,000 had died.[10]

The Nizamiah Mosque Trust

In this vein Lord Headley (Rowland Allanson-Winn; *see* p 32), the most prominent and influential Muslim convert at the time, wrote in 1916 to the Secretary of State for India arguing that a mosque should be built in London 'at the country's expense ... in memory of the Muslim soldiers who have died fighting for the Empire ... A gracious and spontaneous act of this kind would be returned to us an hundredfold.'[11] The British government remained unmoved, and decided instead to build a cemetery for the graves of Muslim soldiers who died in Britain. Thus the first Muslim cemetery in the country was built at Brookwood, near Woking Mosque (*see* pp 26–35), designed by an India Office surveyor and architect and complete with 'arches, minarets, and a domed gateway'.[12] The idea of a major mosque in the Imperial capital was further spurred in July 1926 when the Great Mosque in Paris was opened, funded by the French government. Syed Ameer Ali launched a fresh appeal in April 1927, reminding the 'Mahommedan subjects of the King ... and the Moslem nations in friendly relations with England of the crying necessity for a suitable mosque worthy of the position of Islam as a world religion in the metropolis of Great Britain'.[13]

In the winter of 1928 Lord Headley was invited to India by the Nizam of Hyderabad, where he explained the project to build a stately mosque in London at a cost of about £100,000.[14] The Nizam donated £60,000 towards the scheme, with the proviso that a new trust be established for these funds. The London Nizamiah Mosque Trust Fund was duly established,[15] independent of the London Mosque Fund, with Headley as its chair. It is unclear why Headley established a separate campaign for a grand mosque in London, independent of the Aga Khan and Ameer Ali's London Mosque Fund and the Woking Mosque. The first step of the new fund was to purchase a site in 1929 at Mornington Avenue, West Kensington, measuring approximately one acre (0.4ha), for £28,370.[16] The trustees appointed Sir Alfred Brumwell Thomas as their architect to design the mosque. He was known for designing three spectacular neo-baroque town halls – Belfast City Hall, Stockport and Woolwich.

Thomas's proposals were the first conception of a grand mosque for London. Although the Fazl Mosque had been completed in 1926, it was a modest building for a single community. The Nizamiah Mosque, on the other hand, was in-tended to be a monumental building to represent Islam in Britain to the world. This may have been behind the choice of Thomas as architect, given his credentials in designing flamboyant civic buildings. His proposals for the mosque do indeed depict a characteristically grandiose design, showing a monumental building in composite styles that can be traced to North Africa and Mughal India (Fig 5.2). The large onion dome, with clerestory windows in the base, is no doubt imitative of iconic Indian Mughal architecture such as the Taj Mahal. The

Fig 5.2
Sir Alfred Brumwell Thomas's unbuilt design for a mosque on Mornington Avenue, West Kensington, on a site purchased in 1929; it was grandiose in scale and style and suggested a cathedral-like plan.
[By permission of the British Library IOR/LPJ/12/468 (folio 170)]

cruciform plan of this building, however, is more resonant with Christian state architecture such as St Paul's Cathedral in London or even St Peter's Basilica in Rome, with a large central nave culminating in a central domed hall before what would be the chancel in a church, but in the case of the mosque is another nave of equal length. This proposed mosque, therefore, is a curious combination of grand Christian architecture and monumental Islamic symbols, resulting in what would have been a pastiche of epic proportions.

The estimated cost of the project stood at £187,000, but the trust only had approximately £32,000 and expected contributions from across the Muslim world never materialised. By 1932 the project had stalled and Thomas was forced to take the Nizamiah Mosque Trust to the High Court for non-payment of fees. Despite this, and through a sign of stubborn optimism, a foundation stone was laid for the Nizamiah Mosque in June 1937 by the Nizam's heir apparent, in a public ceremony well attended by dignitaries.[17] Despite this optimism, however, no further progress was made, and the outbreak of World War II stalled the development further. Eventually, in 1950, the London County Council (LCC) compulsorily purchased the Kensington site, and the project for a grand London mosque remained unrealised.

Through the 1930s the entreaties for a grand mosque had continued at the highest political levels. A changing geopolitical context was making the diplomatic benefits of a London mosque more pertinent, with Italy and Germany trying to forge alliances in the Middle East, the struggle for Home Rule gathering pace in India, and proposals for the partition of Palestine stirring up Muslims in Britain and elsewhere.[18] Despite this, however, 'government officials remained sceptical and thought it "unwise for [them] to depart in any way from an attitude of strict neutrality or commit [themselves] to giving a blessing to any such scheme as proposed until [they knew] more about it and particularly whether it [had] the backing of influential Indian Moslems" '.[19]

Muslim settlement in east London

Meanwhile, the Muslim community in the East End of London had been growing through the inter-war period, with the arrival of Indian Muslims from farming backgrounds in the Punjab and Bengal, 'merchants, peddlers, seamen, students and professionals'.[20] The need for local religious space for this growing community was recognised by the trustees of both the London Mosque Fund and the Nizamiah Mosque Trust, to the point that when the Nizam's emissary, Syed Hashimi, visited London in 1930 he commented to the LMF that Muslims in the East End 'are the people who need most to have a Mosque and some provision for the religious instruction of their children who shall otherwise inevitably drift towards irreligion'.[21] He went on to suggest that the LMF should build a mosque in the East End, and leave the project for a grand central mosque to the Nizamiah Mosque Trust.

Inevitably, a religious organisation soon emerged from within the fast-growing Muslim population in east London. The Jamiat-ul-Muslimin (J-u-M) was founded in 1934 by Indian merchants who had been pioneers in the community, helping new immigrants with accommodation and advice on employment and other matters.[22] One of the objectives of the organisation was to establish a mosque in the East End of London, an aim for which it requested the assistance of the London Mosque Fund and the Nizamiah Mosque Trust. In the early 1930s the LMF financed the hire of King's Hall, Commercial Road, for Friday prayers before it 'felt sufficiently persuaded' to approve expenditure for 'a Moslem Preacher and Prayer Room in the East End of London'.[23]

By 1940 the LMF had purchased two houses on Commercial Road for £2,800 in which a permanent mosque for East London could be established. The East London Mosque went on to become one of the foremost Muslim institutions in London, and is discussed later in this chapter (*see* pp 155–67). The first Jummah prayer was offered in this new mosque on 23 May 1941 and was preceded with an opening speech by Sir Hasan Suhrawady, the Muslim advisor to the Secretary of State for India, who had succeeded as chair of the LMF on Lord Headley's death in 1935. In his speech Suhrawady reiterated the grander vision for a monumental London mosque which would 'stand as a grand symbol of the dignity of Islam and of the power of the worldwide Muslim community, the great cathedral ... of stately dimensions, with domes and minarets in graceful Saracenic style of architecture in a conspicuous position'.[24]

Meanwhile, the campaign for a grand London mosque continued, and by the end of the 1930s it was joined by Lord Lloyd of Dolobran, then president of the British Council, who believed 'the idea of a mosque in London would serve British interests and enhance British prestige'.[25]

However, while the government would 'give the scheme of a mosque in London its "blessings" ... there was no question of contributing money towards furthering it'.[26]

By 1940 a new government was in power, with Winston Churchill as Prime Minister and Lord Lloyd as Secretary of State for the Colonies. Lloyd persuaded the Secretary of State for Foreign Affairs, Lord Halifax, and the Secretary of State for India, Lord Amery, to join him in submitting a memorandum to the War Cabinet titled 'Proposals that His Majesty's Government should provide a site for a mosque in London'.

The memorandum assembled the arguments for a London mosque that had been in circulation since Headley's appeal of 1916:

It [has been] pointed out ... not only that London contains more Moslems than any other European capital, but that in an Empire which actually contains more Moslems than Christians it was anomalous and inappropriate that there should be no central place of worship for Musulmans. The gift, moreover, of a site for a mosque would serve as a tribute to the loyalty of the Moslems of the Empire and would have a good effect on Arab countries of the Middle East.

In these circumstances, we strongly recommend that His Majesty's Government should, if possible, provide a sum for the acquisition of a site for a mosque in London.[27]

Churchill and the War Cabinet approved the recommendation on 24 October 1940. A sum of £100,000 was allocated for the purchase of a site for a mosque in London, and the announcement was duly made in Parliament on 13 November 1940.

After a search for a suitable site, a property known as Regent's Lodge, consisting of a large two-storey house on 2.3 acres (0.9ha) of land on the Outer Circle of Regent's Park, was purchased and transferred to the mosque committee on 27 November 1944. The Islamic Cultural Centre was launched with an Egyptian secretary, Shaikh Ali Abdul-Qadir, and an Egyptian imam, and alterations were made to the lodge so that it could be 'put to proper use as a cultural centre as well as a mosque'.[28] In 1961 the assets of the Nizamiah Mosque Trust, plus the proceeds from the sale of the site at Mornington Avenue in 1950, totalling £86,659[29] were amalgamated into a new fund named the Central London Mosque Trust and thus the various endeavours to establish a central mosque in London were finally consolidated.

Ramsey Omar's Egyptian Revivalism

On 1 October 1962, planners at the City of Westminster were requested to attend a private meeting by Marylebone-based architects Richardson and McLaughlan. Richardson wanted to present proposals for a grand mosque at the Regent's Lodge site. He produced a design for Regent's Park Mosque prepared by the Egyptian architect General Ramsey Omar, who had been a key figure in the modernisation of Egyptian state architecture in the 1950s (Fig 5.3). Richardson

Fig 5.3
Ramsey Omar's proposal for a new mosque (prepared in 1954) to replace the lodge house that was being used as the London Central Mosque.
[© Design Council Cabe/ London Metropolitan Archives, City of London LMA/4625/D/11/017]

explained that the design had been prepared in 1954 but had been delayed for various reasons including the Suez Crisis. Richardson and McLaughlan had been appointed by the Central London Mosque Trust to implement Omar's design. A building with 'a traditional and substantial oriental design was envisaged, the dome being some 120 feet in height and the minaret being of the order of 150 [feet] in height'.[30]

The planning officers received the proposal with considerable gravity, noting: 'It was very fully appreciated by Mr Richardson and the officers present that here was a project of major public interest and importance, not only in town planning and design terms but also in terms of international and religious relations.'[31] The architect requested that the meeting remain confidential, as the mosque did not want to attract adverse publicity at this early stage 'because of possible "international" repercussions which might arise if there were a public controversy'.[32]

Ramsey Omar's design was indeed a monumental and historic affair. It was highly reminiscent, if not outright replicative, of Fatimid mosque architecture from early 12th-century Cairo. A large hexagonal building with high walls of warm-coloured stone with tooled bands would have supported a tall dome with a diameter of 20 metres, decorated with ceramic tiles 'with an extract from the Koran around the drum',[33] all with classic Fatimid proportions. A single tall stone-decorated minaret, with three balconies along its height, would have been placed alongside the full-height entrance portico. There were to be three entrances altogether, dressed in marble and ceramics, with bronze doors treated in colour. The windows were to be infilled with stained glass 'in traditional colours'.[34]

A planning application for the new mosque was submitted on 17 September 1963, in which Richardson and McLaughlan explained the clients' design approach:

> The Trustees have felt very strongly that the Mosque should represent the Orient in London and should depict Islamic Architecture in order to enable the users of the Mosque to worship in a building with an atmosphere similar to that to which they are used to in their own countries. The design adopted and as illustrated ... is in Arabesque style and we feel sure that your Committee will agree that such a building standing in Regent's Park surrounded by trees is not inappropriate as a

partner to the adjacent Nash Terraces. The Regency Pavilion at Brighton with its adjacent buildings may be considered as an example of the happy relationship which will be obtained.[35]

The national press reported the planning application for a new mosque with some interest, but otherwise without opinion, noting that this would be central London's first mosque, that until now Muslims were praying in converted private houses, and that Woking was England's main mosque.[36] *Country Life* magazine of March 1964 pinned its colours to Omar's historicist design:

> The original Regent's liking for oriental domes, evinced in his Brighton Pavilion, and the welcome variation from monotonous rectangularity offered to London's skyline by such exotic shapes, are factors in favour of allowing the mosque ... The LCC would be acting properly and consistently with planning policy in seeking to prevent erection of such a high building in this position ... Nevertheless, this may well be an occasion when the visual interest of these exotic architectural forms, prominent as they would be, might appropriately add to the picturesque character of Regent's Park scenery while symbolising the comprehensive nature of the Commonwealth's religious sympathies.[37]

However, official opinion was less sanguine. One of the requirements of the deeds when the land at Regent's Lodge was transferred to the mosque trust was that any new mosque design be approved by the Crown Estate Commissioners and the Royal Fine Arts Commission (RFAC). There was also the statutory requirement of planning permission from the local authority. It was the opinion of the RFAC that seems to have been instrumental in preventing the granting of planning permission. The RFAC consistently objected to the scale of the proposed mosque, its secretary, Godfrey Samuel, arguing:

> The erection of the mosque of this size and scale ... would directly conflict with the agreed policy for protecting the perimeter of Regent's Park and ... the scheme should be radically reconsidered ... The Commission has no objection in principle to the adoption of an Islamic style for the building, but it does not consider the present design, either as a whole

or in its parts, is equal to the best in that tradition, nor worthy of this important site.[38]

This resistance caused some consternation among the mosque's promoters, who may have put pressure on the Mayor of Marylebone, who in turn had words with the LCC's chairman, Arthur Wicks, who then conveyed his concerns to LCC planners: 'The Mayor asserts there are unnecessary delays. An embassy is apparently involved, and the Mayor talks of consulting the Prime Minister! I think this is hot air.'[39] The situation brought in the Ministry of Housing and Local Government, prompting a letter from Whitehall to Sir William Hart, clerk of the LCC, in June 1964, affirming that no diplomatic concessions would be made for the mosque trust:

> I expect you will know something of the trouble which has been caused by the design submitted by the London Central Mosque Trust Limited for the mosque in Regent's Park. I gather that the design is just as unacceptable to the Council as it is to the Royal Fine Art Commission. We have been trying to find some way of breaking the deadlock, but so far without success.
>
> ... It is evident that for various reasons the Trustees would find it very difficult either to modify the design ... or to commission a new one. Knowing that this kind of situation might blow up into an unpleasant diplomatic incident, Dame Evelyn Sharp has asked for the advice of the Permanent Secretaries at the Foreign Office and the Commonwealth Relations Office. Both of them take the view that ... the Trustees ought to comply with the conditions which have been imposed on them, and that there are no diplomatic reasons why these conditions should be waived.[40]

Westminster's planning office replied to the Ministry of Housing and Local Government, setting out its objections to the design of the proposed mosque and stating that while the 'Islamic style' of the building was not in itself objectionable in relation to the Nash terraces, the proposal was simply too large and cumbersome 'for anything approaching a happy relationship to be achieved'. The planners noted that use of 'exotic' styles in English architecture was usually 'small in scale, having the character of follies or eye-catchers'.[41] The proposal for a new mosque at Regent's Park was eventually refused planning permission on 7 October 1964 on the grounds of its height, bulk, massing and visual impact.[42] A revised scheme in which the mosque was scaled down was sent for comment to the Crown Commissioners in early 1965. They had previously asked for the original design to be 'substantially' reduced, by around one third. The revised drawings submitted to them by Richardson and McLaughlan did not address their earlier criticism, and again failed to enlist the Commissioners' support.

Design competition 1968

After this the mosque trust embarked on a new strategy to procure a suitable design, launching an international competition in 1968. The competition brief highlighted that the RFAC had stipulated that a successful design would have to pay due respect to the Nash terraces and the character of Regent's Park. Furthermore, the trust stated its aspirations for the design, saying that the building should 'consciously express itself' as a mosque and as the central point for Muslim religious observance in London. The trust also felt that the architecture should 'conform to the classic Islamic tradition', to inspire London's Muslims and to be 'reflective of traditional Mosques in which they have worshipped in their own countries'.[43] A total of 52 designs were received, 41 of which were from overseas from 17 countries. The judging panel included Sir Robert Matthew, one of Britain's foremost modernist architects; M A Ahed, a Pakistani architect and painter; and Luis Blanco Soler, a Spanish architect.

The competition was won in 1969 by the London architect Sir Frederick Gibberd (Figs 5.4 and 5.5), with the second prize going to Marulyalı and Aksüt of Istanbul, who proposed a scheme that 'used traditional mosque themes interpreted in a modern way' (Figs 5.6 and 5.7).[44] Joint third prize was won by submissions from the Arab Bureau for Designs and Technical Consultations of Cairo, and Toan Chafai and Azebi of Rabat, both highly traditional designs reflective of the particular styles of their own countries of Egypt and Morocco. The *Architects' Journal*, reviewing the competition results in October 1969, commented that on the whole the entries 'are a disappointing collection, none really convince and few excite'. The review noted that entries from Islamic countries were 'no more successful in reinterpreting the mosque tradition than the handful from Western Europe'.[45]

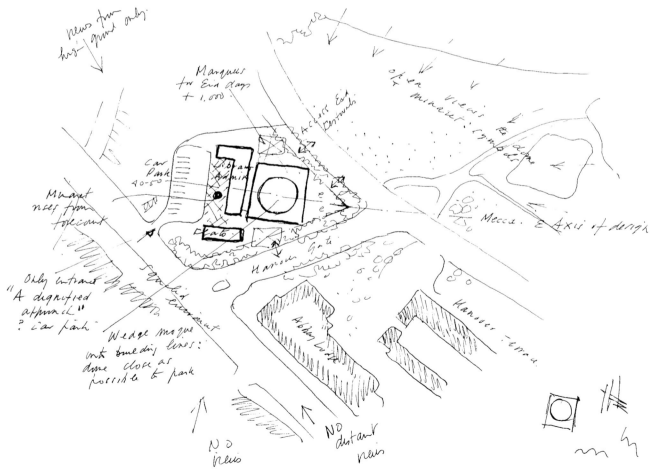

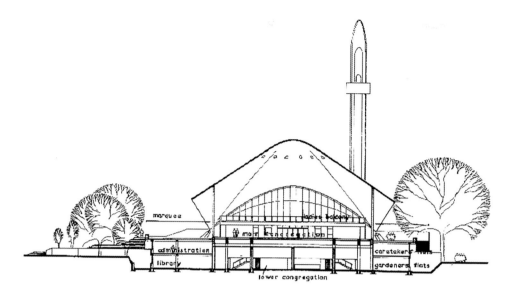

Fig 5.6
Section through Marulyalı
and Aksüt's design proposal
for Regent's Park Mosque.
[By kind permission of
Yaşar Marulyalı and
Levent Aksüt, Umo
Architecture Group]

Fig 5.7
Scale model of Istanbul-
based architects Marulyalı
and Aksüt's proposal for
Regent's Park Mosque,
which won second place in
the design competition.
[By kind permission of
Yaşar Marulyalı and
Levent Aksüt, Umo
Architecture Group]

Fig 5.8
Gibberd's proposed section drawing (c 1973), showing the courtyard and the main prayer hall, from which the scale of the dome can be understood.
[By kind permission of Frederick Gibberd Partnership]

Gibberd, modernism and the mosque

Frederick Gibberd was born in Coventry in 1908. From early in his career he was influenced by the International Style and he became one of the architects who fathered the emergence of modern architecture in Britain. Among numerous positions held throughout his career, Gibberd was a member of the influential architectural think tank MARS (Modern Architectural Research Group) founded in 1933, as well as being principal of the Architectural Association from 1942 to 1944 and a member of the Royal Fine Arts Commission from 1950 to 1970. While at the Architectural Association, Gibberd taught Philip Powell, Hidalgo Moya and Neville Conder, who were all to be in the vanguard of post-war modernism, with Conder going on to design the Ismaili Centre, which was completed in 1983 (*see* pp 148–55). Gibberd's modernist credentials, therefore, were impeccable, and these were aptly demonstrated in his other major religious building, the radical and avant garde Liverpool Metropolitan Roman Catholic Cathedral of 1962. It was undoubtedly because of this modernist legacy that Gibberd's design for the mosque, complete with dome and minaret, met with considerable disquiet from the architectural press, steeped as it was in modernist orthodoxies.

The main entrance to the mosque is off Park Road on the western boundary of the site. From here the building itself is approached across a large courtyard (Figs 5.8 and 5.9), the mosque wrapping around two sides and an accommodation block around the third. The mosque's copper dome and white cylindrical minaret rise monumentally from behind mature trees on the western edge of Regent's Park, alongside Nash's terraces (*see* Fig 8.4). This building of 1969–77 is the culmination of a multilayered and complex history that encompasses a major strand of early to mid-20th-century British Muslim history.

The plan is oriented towards the Qibla, with a large main prayer hall at its south-eastern edge having capacity for 975 worshippers (Fig 5.10 and *see* Fig 5.1). An entrance foyer forms a strip along the back of the prayer hall, returning to enclose the courtyard with offices; on the first floor a women's prayer gallery overlooks the main male prayer space (Fig 5.11) and a library is above the offices (Fig 5.12). A lower-ground floor accommodates ablutions, a canteen, car park and spaces for flexible use.

The façades are made up of a series of regular four-centred arches, common in Persian Islamic architecture, each formed from precast concrete panels and infilled with glazed curtain walling (Figs 5.13 and 5.14). A new form of dome construction was developed whereby the prayer hall was covered with a flat, reinforced concrete slab supported on four large columns, 'like a table with legs set in' (Fig 5.15).[46] The slab has a large circular hole in the centre from the edge of which rises a concrete ring beam carrying the lightweight precast concrete drum segments that

form the dome (Fig 5.16). The dome has the same four-centred profile as the wall arcades and is clad in gold-coloured copper alloy. The minaret is formed of two concentric concrete tubes cast simultaneously, with a lift in the inner one and a staircase in the outer one.[47] Gibberd's own description of the design, in an explanatory booklet issued on the scheme's completion,[48] was characteristically pragmatic, concentrating on the methods of construction and materiality and never dwelling on the symbolic meanings of the Islamic motifs.

Criticism of Gibberd's design by the architectural press, from the day he won the competition, was thinly veiled, if not outright hostile. When reviewing the competition entries in 1969, the *Architects' Journal* commented that Gibberd's arches and dome had 'come so near to plagiarism', and that the proposal that received second place, by Istanbul architects Marulyali and Aksüt, was 'very much more a legitimate product of the Modern Movement'.[49]

When the building was finally completed in 1977, *Building* magazine started its review: 'After putting up an uncompromising and hard-headed wigwam for Liverpool's Catholics, Sir Frederick Gibberd and Partners seem to have lost their nerve in designing for London's Moslems.' The article went on to describe the Liverpool Cathedral as 'one of the finest religious buildings in this country since the war', because, as the writer explained, it had managed to be

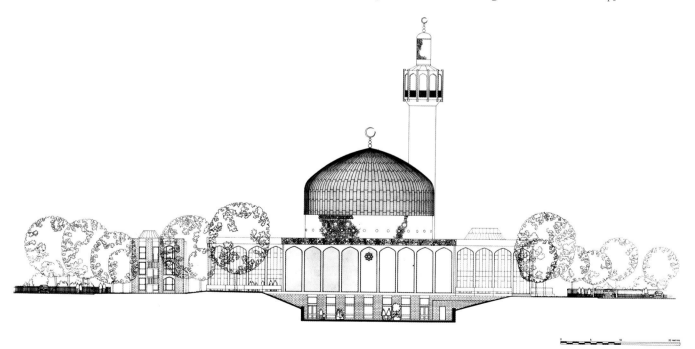

143

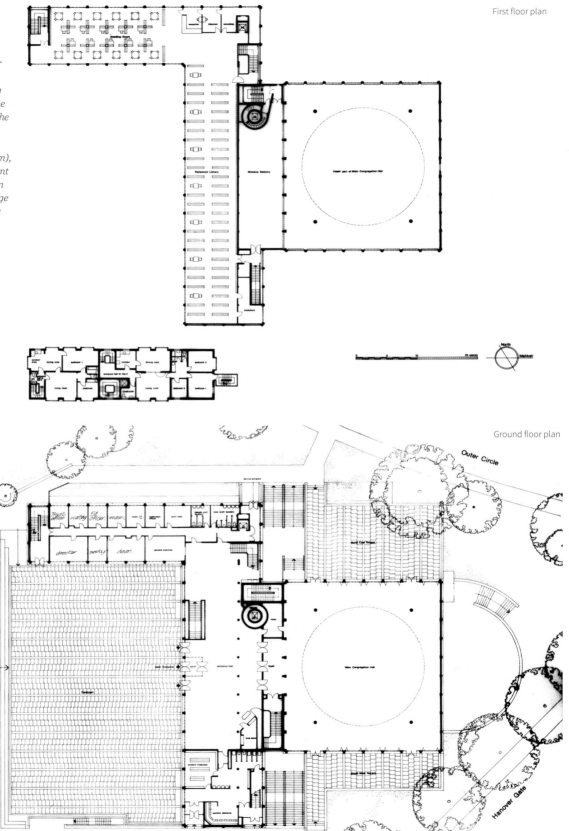

Fig 5.11
Gibberd's proposed first-floor plan (top) (c 1973), showing the women's prayer gallery to the rear of the men's prayer hall, and the library wrapping around the courtyard. The independent block is for the residential quarters. Gibberd's proposed ground-floor plan (bottom), showing the extensive front courtyard area with main entrance doors into a large foyer which leads into the men's prayer hall.
[By kind permission of Frederick Gibberd Partnership]

Ground floor plan

'convincingly religious without historicism and it's here that the Regent's Park mosque falls down'.[50]

The *Architectural Review* was even more scathing, opening its September 1977 leader by quoting Gibberd's own claim that 'everybody likes it … except other architects,' then adding, 'We can believe him.' The main objection of the *Review* was to what it called the 'decor' of the mosque, arguing that this application of motifs was a trait of Islamic buildings demonstrating that they, as a type, had failed to adapt to modern architectural programmes and considerations: 'It is not the fact that it is decorated that upsets us, or even that it is recognisably traditional in appearance, but the fact that there is

Fig 5.12
The interior of the library of Regent's Park Mosque, which overlooks the courtyard.
[DP148093]

Fig 5.13
The main entrance of the mosque viewed from the courtyard, photographed shortly after its completion in 1977.
[By kind permission of Frederick Gibberd Partnership]

Fig 5.14 (right)
Study model (c 1972) of
Gibberd's winning design
showing the glass curtain
walling set within concrete
four-centred arches, which
can be seen as built with
plain glass in Fig 5.13.
[By kind permission of
Frederick Gibberd
Partnership]

Fig 5.15 (below)
Diagrams showing the
structural strategy of
Gibberd's proposed
building – the columns
carrying the roof and dome
allow the perimeter walls to
be fully glazed and so allow
ample daylight into the
interior spaces.
[By kind permission of the
Gibberd Garden Trust]

no internal logic which ties the decor to the structure behind it. This makes it (at least for architects) a frivolous building.' However, the *Review* did bring itself to attempt some acceptance of the modernist credentials of Gibberd's design, by recognising it as a 'sober, Festival-of-Britain counterpart to the Prince Regent's Brighton Pavilion'.[51]

Gibberd, however, was clear that the symbolic language dominating the design of the mosque was central to those who would use it, commenting that the mosque committee was 'worried lest the winning design be a "modern" conception, unrecognisable as a mosque. The dome and four-centred arch are the most characteristic architectural forms of Islam; it seems that these forms could still be valid without becoming mere decorative devices.'[52]

Gibberd saw himself primarily as a functionalist, believing that architecture was formed by the three factors of function, environment and construction. In 1978 he was quoted as saying: 'I like a building to tell you how it was built.'[53] So while Gibberd had embraced traditional and

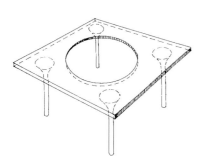

mushroom columns
supporting flat slab

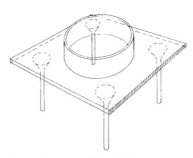

dome drum on flat slab
& mushroom columns

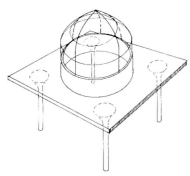

dome, drum, slab & columns

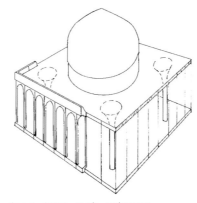

dome, drum, slab, columns.
& facade units

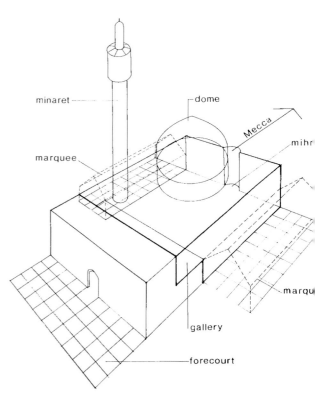

Fig 5.16
*Regent's Park Mosque
under construction in 1975.
The concrete roof top and
ring beam for the dome can
be seen taking shape.
[© Historic England.
John Laing Collection
JLP01/10/02796]*

legible Islamic symbols in the design of the mosque, his explanation of the design focused on its rationalist credentials. He said:

> If you take it [the Regent's Park Mosque design] to bits it functions very well indeed ... It was by far the most direct, simple answer to a set of problems, as an intellectual exercise. It is largely a prefabricated building, all the walls are prefabricated units which happen to have a four-centred arch. Well why not? It could have been a semi-circular arch, it didn't matter very much, either way it was structurally sound.[54]

Five years after the mosque's completion, Gibberd commented in a radio interview, perhaps as his riposte to a modernist architectural culture then seen by many as being out of touch with ordinary people, 'Had I been less interested in people and more interested in building a monument, I'd probably have been a better architect.'[55]

Conclusion

Regent's Park Mosque is unique in the history of mosques in Britain in that it was, from its inception, rooted in the world of power, diplomacy and international relations. It is also unique in that its gestation spans the longest period of any mosque, nearly 70 years from its beginnings to Gibberd's completed building.

Architecturally, the mosque encapsulates the crossroads at which it stands. It came at a time in the late 1970s when British architecture was entering a period of ideological crisis as post-war modernism lost currency and a new postmodernist architectural approach was about to emerge. Gibberd's uncomplicated use of traditional religious iconography, with his modernist emphasis on the expression of the building's structure, thwarted critics by introducing ambiguities that would carry on being negotiated in the new mosque architecture in Britain in the decades that would follow.

2 Ismaili Centre, Cromwell Road, South Kensington, London, 1983

Six years after Regent's Park Mosque was completed, another Muslim building of great significance opened two miles away in South Kensington. Standing opposite the Victorian splendour of the Victoria and Albert and Natural History museums, the Ismaili Centre, designed by the Casson Conder Partnership, was another major Islamic building on the world stage. It was built to be the UK headquarters of the Ismaili community, headed by the Aga Khan.

The Ismailis

The Ismailis constitute a major branch of Shia Islam, and the second largest Shia community in the Muslim world after the Ithna ashari (Twelver) branch. These two major Shia branches emerged after the death in 8th-century Madinah of the Prophet's descendant Ja'far al-Sadiq, who had developed Shia theology and jurisprudence. The Ismailis were followers of his second son, Ismail, while the Twelvers followed his third son, Musa.

The Ismaili followers themselves evolved various branches through time and in the 11th century a branch emerged in southern Persia under the leadership of Hasan-I Sabbah, who followed a chain of imams known as the Nizars. It is from these Nizari Ismailis that the present Ismailis have descended, now under the Imamate of the Aga Khan IV. The honorific title of 'Aga Khan', meaning lord and master, was first given to the 46th Nizari Imam Hasan Ali Shah (d 1881), by the then Persian monarch.

From the 11th century the Nizari Ismaili mission spread to the Indian subcontinent, gaining converts in the southern Pakistani province of Sind and the bordering north Indian state of Gujarat. The Hindu converts to Nizari Ismailism became known as the Khojas, a Persian translation of the Hindu term Thakur (the name by which the Hindu caste who had converted were known). These Nizari Khojas developed a distinctive religious tradition known as the Satpanth (true path), as well as the Ginans (indigenous devotional literature).[56]

In 1844 Aga Khan I was exiled from his ancestral home in Persia and travelled via Sind and Gujarat to settle in Bombay. Here he set up his darkhana (chief place of residence), and

began consolidating the Ismaili community. This process brought challenges from some parts of the Khoja Ismaili community, who did not accept the Aga Khan as Imam. A court case over leadership ensued, which was tried at the British Bombay High Court in 1861. It found in favour of the Aga Khan and recognised his overall leadership of the Ismaili community.[57]

It was during the Imamate of Aga Khan I that Khoja Ismaili merchants started to migrate to East Africa, settling first in the coastal city of Zanzibar, and then gradually moving inland over the next decades until by the mid-20th century a distinct and substantial East African Ismaili community had become established, concentrated in what is now Tanzania, Kenya and Uganda. There were also important concentrations of Ismailis in the neighbouring regions of Central and Southern Africa. With independence across East African states in the early 1960s, policies were introduced that discriminated against non-African enterprise, which impacted the economic future of East African Indians, Ismailis and others. The migration of these East African Indian communities to Britain started in 1964, culminating in the Ugandan expulsion of Indians in 1972.[58] By the late 1990s there were approximately 9,500 Ismailis in the UK, of whom 8,000 were in the Greater London area and the rest spread across major towns and cities.[59] A network of 45 Ismaili religious centres, which the Ismailis called jamatkhanas, had been established in areas of settlement.

Aga Khan III, Sir Sultan Muhammed Shah (Imamate from 1885 to 1957), had begun a process of modernising the Ismaili community in East Africa before the migration to Britain. These reforms included the increased participation of women in education, work and religious life. Women were forbidden from wearing the veil and were free to adopt colonial dress; they could lead prayers in mixed congregations, and parents were ordered to send their daughters to school. English was also adopted as the community's first language and social and economic enterprises were rationalised, resulting in the transformation of individual traders into a 'relatively modern and prosperous community'.[60]

The modernisation process stemmed from the Aga Khan's viewpoint that the Quran is a text open to interpretation, a view reinforced by the Shia tradition that the imam alone possesses esoteric knowledge of the sacred text and is therefore charged with its interpretation for the guidance of his followers 'according to changes in time and circumstances'.[61] It is a concept reflected in the 1954 memoirs of Aga Khan III, where he wrote: 'Ismailism has survived because it has always been fluid. Rigidity is contrary to our whole way of life and outlook ... even the set of regulations known as the Holy Laws are directions as to method and procedure and not detailed orders about results to be obtained.'[62]

This modernisation placed the Ismailis at a distinct advantage over other South Asian communities when migrating to Britain as they were already on the 'verge of crossing the threshold of modernity' and were 'receptive to new ideas, customs and values'.[63] The new social context in which the Ismailis found themselves in Britain presented challenges and so required a redefined strategic outlook. One of the key challenges was the maintenance of cultural and religious boundaries in a plural, liberal society where a series of identity choices were available for community members. The Ismaili community in Britain adopted social programmes to counter this threat and emphasised its identity as both Shia Ismaili and Muslim.[64]

The role of the Ismaili Centre

When the London Ismaili Centre was completed in 1983, it served as an important symbol representing the community's presence and permanence in the UK. Indeed, the role of this and subsequent Ismaili centres that would be built across the world was to consolidate and embolden a disparate community that comprised 'a multiplicity of peoples ranging in their origins from the north-west of the Arab world and Middle East, through Iran and the Indian subcontinent to Afghanistan, Central Asia and Western China. Migrations in the late 19th and early 20th centuries created a substantial presence in sub-Saharan Africa as well.'[65] One of the key aims of the centres, as later set out by the Aga Khan IV, Prince Shah Karim Al Hussani, was to enhance, facilitate and, 'indeed, encourage mutual exchanges and understanding', which would be enabled by offering facilities 'for lectures, presentations, seminars and conferences relating to the Aga Khan Development Network's areas of activity in social, economic and cultural endeavour ... [as well as to] educate wider publics about the breadth of Islam's heritage'.[66]

One of the fundamental differences between the Ismaili Centre and other Muslim buildings in Britain is that it forms part of a centrally organised network of buildings for the Ismaili community and is therefore strategically conceived and guided by the Aga Khan. The London Ismaili Centre is one of a series of centres across the world. These differ from local jamatkhanas in that they are buildings that serve to consolidate the Ismaili community in a particular country and act as 'symbolic markers of the permanent presence of the Ismaili community in the regions in which they are established'.[67] The architecture of each centre, therefore, is intended to embody the cultural positioning of the Ismaili community in a particular location: 'Architecturally unique, each building is a safeguard and a symbol of the core values of the Ismaili Muslim community.'[68]

With each Ismaili centre, the role of architecture is a paramount consideration and is one of the primary ways in which the Ismaili community culturally positions itself within each context. At the inauguration of the Ismaili Centre in Houston, Texas, in 2002, the Aga Khan emphasised that the buildings were the 'physical representation of Islamic values' and that they should 'reflect who we are in terms of our beliefs, our cultural heritage and our relation to the needs and contexts in which we live in today's world'. He also noted that no single definition of Islamic architecture exists, and that throughout its history it has 'reflected different climates, times, materials, building technologies and political philosophies'. However, the role of the centres goes beyond symbolic representation, again as the Aga Khan articulated in Houston: 'The Centre will be a place of peace, humility, reflection and prayer. It will be a place of search and enlightenment, not of anger and of obscurantism.'[69]

The Ismaili Centre and modernism

London's Ismaili Centre tested the limits of modernism, and intrigued the architectural establishment while being designed from within it. The building was designed by the Casson Conder Partnership, a local practice founded by Sir Hugh Casson and Neville Conder in 1956. Casson had made his name as Director of Architecture of the Festival of Britain, the 1951 exhibition on the South Bank that was a 'celebration of victory and modernity ... [where he realised] in three dimensions the modern picturesque approach'.[70] The project for the Ismaili Centre was led by Neville Conder and Kenneth Price of the practice.

It was a combination of the significance of this building, a major Muslim landmark in a

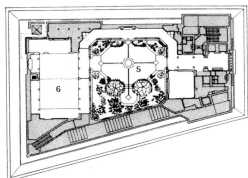

Third floor

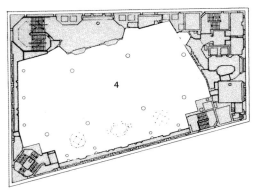

Second floor

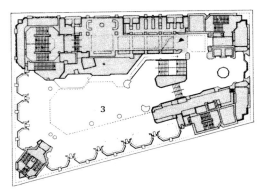

First floor

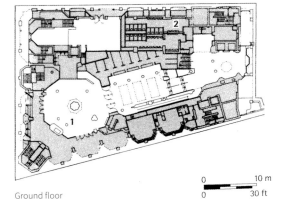

Ground floor

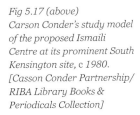

Fig 5.17 (above)
Carson Conder's study model of the proposed Ismaili Centre at its prominent South Kensington site, c 1980. [Casson Conder Partnership/ RIBA Library Books & Periodicals Collection]

Fig 5.18 (right)
The floor plans of the Ismaili Centre. The ground floor includes the main entrance foyer, with a central fountain, set back from the street and under a colonnaded entrance overhang. The first floor is organised around a large open hall for multifunctional events; the second floor is dominated by the prayer hall, and the roof garden is on the top.

Key
1 Entrance hall
2 Toilets/ablutions
3 Social hall
4 Prayer hall
5 Roof garden
6 Council chamber/ conference room

[From Holod and Khan, 1997, 47, after plans in The Ismaili Centre, London, *Islamic Publications Ltd, 1985]*

high-profile London location, and its cultural positioning 'between east and west'[71] that drew special attention. Gibberd's Regent's Park Mosque cast a shadow within which the Ismaili Centre was viewed as it tackled the same problem of 'integrating two quite different cultural, religious and aesthetic traditions into one building and expecting both sides to take the final result with complete seriousness', something that needed to be considered in relation to 'the cautionary experience of the Regent's Park Mosque'.[72]

The Ismaili Centre is prominently located, surrounded by roads including the busy route from London to the West of England, and nestled amid London's great museums (Fig 5.17). In 1977 the Aga Khan Foundation made a bid for the site, which was then owned by the Greater London Council, who had invited tenders for it. It was once occupied by the French Lycée, and was later mooted as a location for the National Theatre, but it had remained a car park since 1936.[73] For the Aga Khan, the fact that the Ismaili Centre was able to secure such a prominent London site was an indication of 'the respect the West is beginning to accord Muslim civilisation'.[74]

The bid succeeded and the building was completed in 1983. Its layout is simple and clear, arranged over four floors (Fig 5.18), with administrative and conference rooms around a roof garden at the top, a prayer hall to accommodate 1,200 on the second floor (Fig 5.19), a social hall

Fig 5.19
The Ismaili Centre's main
prayer hall, which is jointly
used by men and women.
[DP148048]

below that and an outer and inner entrance hall along with offices on the ground floor. A wide route leads from the main entrance (Fig 5.20), winding up through the building and culminating at the prayer hall; the other spaces on each floor are arranged off this route.

An Islamic garden has been created on the rooftop alongside a conference room, so continuing the tradition in Islamic architecture of an ornamental garden embedded within a sequence of spaces (Fig 5.21). This top floor is set back from the perimeter of the building and the walls canted in to meet it, the angle of the walls and the height of the garden wall being determined by the requirement not to obstruct daylight to the houses in neighbouring Thurloe Place.

This cant is continued around the building for the sake of consistency. The main mass of the building, as expressed in the flat façades of the prayer hall on the second floor, is raised off the ground on concrete columns, so allowing the ground and first floors to be treated more lightly. The building is clad with a thin skin of polished granite, which has been 'flame-stripped' to provide 'a certain sparkle when seen from the pavements' (Fig 5.22).[75] First-floor bay and oriel windows, in teak, polished steel and with bevelled glass for privacy, are a bespoke architectural element that gives the building one of its most distinctive features (Figs 5.23 and 5.24).

The interiors are restrained in ornament, with low-relief patternwork and slight variations

Fig 5.20
The main circulation
staircase of the Ismaili
Centre, with a bespoke
chandelier providing a
focal point.
[DP148041]

Fig 5.21 (above)
The courtyard garden on the rooftop of the Ismaili Centre, which references the formal and geometric designs characteristic of traditional Islamic gardens. [DP148049]

Fig 5.22 (right)
The Ismaili Centre viewed from the south-west corner, where the main entrance is situated. The form of the building is arranged as a heavily massed second floor faced in polished granite, a first floor with recessed bay windows, and part-colonnade at ground-floor level to provide permeability with the street. [DP161851]

Fig 5.23
A detail of the façade of the Ismaili Centre, showing the custom-designed teak-framed windows at ground- and first-floor levels, and the granite-faced façade with slit windows on the second floor.
[DP161850]

Fig 5.24
The interior of the first-floor circulation spaces of the Ismaili Centre, showing how the bay windows are utilised as meeting spaces.
[DP148040]

in wall colour and texture. This provides a backdrop for certain key interior elements, such as the fountain in the entrance hall, light fittings, handrails, calligraphy, commissioned artwork and bespoke furniture (Fig 5.25). The Aga Khan Foundation requested that the interiors refer more directly to Islamic principles, and they were therefore designed by Karl Schlamminger, a German Muslim who had lived and worked in the Middle East and had 'a full knowledge of the geometry, calligraphy and symbolic significance of Islamic design and pattern'.[76]

The Aga Khan himself was intimately involved with the building, engaging directly with the architects at each stage of design. He stipulated that the centre should essentially be a 'London building',[77] not necessarily derived from Islamic precedents but in keeping with their mood. As a result, Neville Conder confirmed, 'There has been no direct reference to the Islamic architecture of other countries, no use of copy books for form or pattern, although it will be obvious to all that there have been influ-

ences at work which did not have their origins in Greece or Rome.'[78]

Without reference to known types, Conder instead wanted to 'feel his way' with the client, and as the process developed he learned to 'withdraw from the design all the subtle things that had a Western emblematic significance'.[79] This led to the emergence of angles, spaces and finishes that were without precedent in his work. The review of the building in the *Architects' Journal* of November 1983, entitled 'Cross-cultural centre', separated it into Western versus Islamic references: 'The windows of the building eschewed the Western notion of transparency, becoming instead complex projecting structures in teak and stainless steel with chamfered panes of glass … the plan remains flowing and function-derived, not cellular in the Islamic manner.' The article even went as far as to determine the identity of grooves in walls: 'Even here there is a Western touch, the use of a continuous blue and white painted recessed groove to divide walls into panels, conceal construction joints and create an order of interior architecture.' The article concluded that, through this layering of alternative architectural narratives, the Ismaili Centre marks a 'threshold in the evolution of modern architecture'.[80]

This theme of interpreting the building in terms of its cultural identity ran through a series of press reviews at the time. *Building* magazine of February 1984 noted that the Ismaili Centre was planned, massed and structured as any building 'in the current western functional tradition, but the settlement of choices … has been conditioned … by certain qualities associated with traditional Islamic architecture and … by a watchful eye for the emblematic significance of shape or line'. As regards the outer faces of the building, the review noted that 'there has been no direct reference to the Islamic architecture of other countries', a point that Conder emphasised as deliberate. As there were no direct Islamic motifs, the review determined that the Muslim character of the building was contained in 'certain qualities', such as 'lightness of colour, freshness of feel, a liking for reflective and sparkling surfaces'.[81]

A review in *Building* from the previous November (1983) had picked up on the same theme of the building's multiple references but was more critical, concluding that it existed in 'an architectural no-man's land'. Commenting on the exterior of the building, the reviewer noted that it was not ' "un-western" but there are eastern bits around the back and sides in the

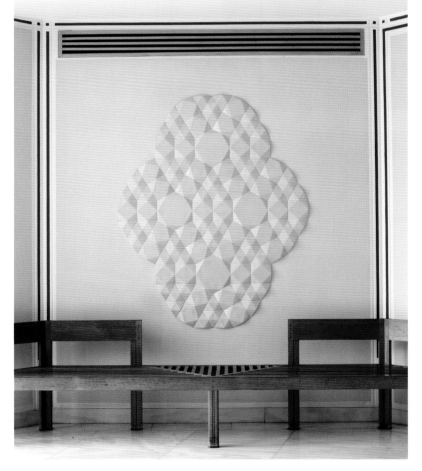

form of bow windows poking out from between the not-quite colonnades around the bottom two floors'. The end result, according to the writer, was 'a collection of parts, each laboured over and well justified – and often very pleasant indeed – as individual elements, but which never quite come together to form a coherent whole'.[82]

Despite this reservation, Conder's Ismaili Centre was generally well received, for its workmanship and attention to detail as much as for its cultural positioning. This building was decidedly modernist, but this was a modernism tempered with Islamic architectural narratives expressed in a diffuse way. The result was a manifestation of British modernism overlaid with a series of symbolic references, something that typified the practice of the Casson Conder Partnership. This shift was in step with wider changes in architectural theory and product, coming at a time when postmodernism was vigorously reintroducing historical allusions into contemporary architecture.

Conclusion

The Ismaili Centre stands apart from the built expression of the majority of Muslim communities in Britain. It challenges the idea of what a Muslim cultural and religious centre is, and how it can be represented in architecture. This is essentially because of the specific historical trajectory that the Ismaili community has followed, which resulted in a social and religious group with a form of organisation and cultural outlook substantially different from that of the majority of Muslim communities.

As a result, this is a building where the architecture plays a consciously symbolic role in being representative of how the Ismaili community positions itself within its social context. As the community is structured with a decision-making and spiritual head, the vision for the building has been clarified and explicit. This again sets the centre apart from other Muslim buildings that are otherwise community projects where decisions are often arrived at through various forms of consensus.

The Ismaili Centre is also perhaps the last example in a chain of buildings, from Woking, Fazl, Alice Street (Cardiff) and Regent's Park, to explore similar issues of design and representation. By the mid-1980s mosques had begun to proliferate, and these examples of architectural exploration were soon to be subsumed in a wave of what came to be described as pastiche mosque

design. The Ismaili Centre therefore marks the end of a strand of Muslim architecture that explored new architectural languages, an endeavour which would not be seen again until the early 21st century.

3 East London Mosque and London Muslim Centre, Whitechapel Road, London, 1985/2004

The inter-war years saw the growth of the Muslim community in the East End of London, comprising mainly Indians from farming backgrounds in the Punjab and Bengal, together with merchants, students and professionals. The new immigrants established cafés and lodging houses to serve maritime workers, as well as commercial enterprises and clothing factories. As the community expanded, so did its cultural and religious needs. To cater for this, the Jamiat-ul-Muslimin (J-u-M) was founded in 1934 with the express purpose of serving 'the cause of Islam truly by creating facilities for the observance of its principles'.[83]

The wider objectives of the J-u-M were to promote pan-Islamic interaction between London's Muslims, which it then estimated at 300, and to create 'unity, amity and general brotherhood'. The London Mosque Fund (LMF) agreed to fund an imam and the hire of King's Hall on Commercial Road for Friday prayers, duly established by the J-u-M for the Muslims of east London.[84] However, the lack of a suitable place for regular prayer was evident, and the J-u-M urged the LMF and the Nizamiah Mosque Trust to build a 'suitable, conveniently located mosque' in the East End of London.[85]

This mosque eventually came about when the LMF purchased the houses at 448 and 450 Commercial Road for £2,800, and repaired and remodelled them. They were officially opened by the Egyptian Ambassador, Sheikh Hafiz Wahba, as the East London Mosque on 1 August 1941 (Figs 5.26 and 5.27). The East London Mosque not only provided a place for prayer, but was also the genesis of a Muslim social institution that served as the template for hundreds of similar organisations that would follow across the country. The ELM provided a library, a medical service and a burial service, all of which were organised by the J-u-M based at the same address. Indeed, the J-u-M was formally

Fig 5.26
The first East London Mosque was formed from the conversion of houses at 448 and 450 Commercial Road, which the LMF had purchased by 1940, the year this photo was taken. The mosque opened in 1941. [London Metropolitan Archives, City of London SC/PHL/01/385/73/9830]

Fig 5.27
Sheikh Hafiz Wahba delivering the khutba (sermon) at the opening ceremony of the East London Mosque on Commercial Road, 1941. [ELMT/MA/02]

appointed by the LMF as the agent to run the East London Mosque, so recognising its representative role in east London.[86]

Through the late 1940s the locus of power in the East London Mosque was gradually shifting from the LMF, which represented 'cosmopolitan London Muslims',[87] to local East End community leaders represented by the J-u-M. This process was reinforced by the growing local Muslim population, as more maritime workers, mostly from Sylhet in north-east Bengal, settled in the area. In 1949 the East London Mosque Trust (ELMT) Ltd was formed with the purpose of managing the affairs of the mosque. The trust's members were the Egyptian, Saudi Arabian and Pakistani ambassadors, along with other notable figures including the judge of Calcutta's High Court, Torick Ali.[88] By the mid-1950s control of the ELMT Board of Trustees continued to shift to local East End Muslims, as the original members' attention was diverted towards the grand central London mosque scheme, which was now well under way with the establishment of the mosque at Regent's Lodge in 1944 (*see* p 137).

Relocating to Fieldgate Street

By the late 1960s the mosque at Commercial Road started to feel the limitations of the space and physical infrastructure that the ageing Georgian terrace in which it was housed could provide. In a funding letter of 14 December 1967, the ELMT chairman Suleiman Jetha noted that the mosque had spent £600 towards the 'decoration of prayer halls' and that as the 'Mosque premises are nearly 100 years old, they need repairs badly which will cost at least £1,000 or more'.[89] Jetha also noted that the Stepney area was under a Greater London Council (GLC) redevelopment scheme:

All Knowing Allah knows when the present Mosque premises will be acquired by the GLC. I, of course, cannot foretell what will be

the position at the time of acquisition a few years hence, but Muslims of London should be on their guard as forewarned is forearmed. The Committee has therefore decided to start a collection shortly under a new scheme, and Inshallah we hope to call on you.[90]

In the mid-1970s, the site of the East London Mosque on Commercial Road was indeed included in the Simms Depot Compulsory Purchase Order, to clear the site for a GLC housing scheme. The GLC agreed to relocate the mosque to a suitable site nearby, and proposed a series of alternatives. One of the sites suggested was the Brick Lane synagogue which, although it was later converted into a mosque (*see* pp 68–75), the ELMT considered to be too restricted for their needs as it seemed to have little scope for alteration and expansion. Eventually the mosque agreed to relocate to a GLC site at 43–45 Fieldgate Street in Whitechapel, lying empty following bomb damage and adjacent to the Fieldgate Street Great Synagogue. The GLC constructed a temporary single-storey building to serve as the mosque, and the ELM moved to its new premises in 1975 (Figs 5.28 and 5.29).

The forward thinking of the ELMT became evident once the mosque moved to Fieldgate

Street. Here it embarked immediately on talks with the GLC for the acquisition of a neighbouring site fronting Whitechapel Road, on which a purpose-built mosque could be constructed. By 1978 the ELMT had negotiated the purchase of the site, an additional 734m^2, for the price of £25,000, along with the GLC granting a further 652m^2 to the mosque. A design was prepared by Michael Jonas, a Potters Bar architect, for a major mosque building accommodating 2,000 people, classrooms, a library, a mortuary, imam's accommodation and shops.[91]

Jonas's site plan shows the new mosque spreading across the newly acquired Whitechapel Road site to the north and into the Fieldgate Street site of the temporary mosque to the south

Fig 5.28
The single-storey building on Fieldgate Street that the East London Mosque moved into in 1975 (the year this photograph was taken). The Fieldgate Street Great Synagogue can be seen standing to its left. [London Metropolitan Archives, City of London SC/PHL/02/1219/75/8529]

Fig 5.29
A large congregational prayer at the East London Mosque on Fieldgate Street, showing how the building itself was unable to accommodate the numbers of worshippers attending (photograph undated, c 1977–1984). [ELMT/MA/02]

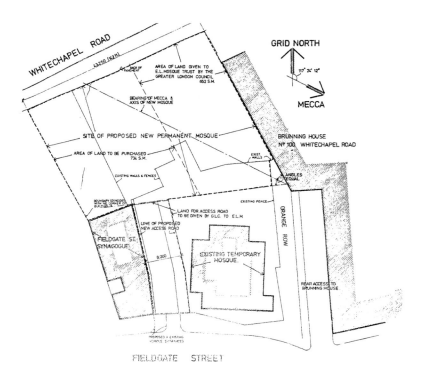

(Fig 5.30). One rendered image of the design remains and shows it to be a striking and ambitious project, particularly interesting considering that the only other purpose-built mosque of comparable scale in the country had been completed at Regent's Park a year before this design was prepared. The proposed mosque would have combined a Mughal-influenced dome and cupola-topped minaret with a three-storey façade faced in a rectangular concrete grillage, evocative of a traditional Islamic mashrabiya but also a treatment characteristic of post-war British modernism (Fig 5.31). Concrete pillars designed as twin vertical columns, unadorned except for horizontal grooves, are placed regularly along the front elevation, giving a distinctly modern tone to the building. Like Gibberd's Regent's Park Mosque, this design for the East London Mosque shows essentially a determinedly contemporary building, with a highly Islamised dome and minaret to locate it within the Muslim imagination. The plan of the building aligns it towards the Qibla, with the entrance from the street angled accordingly. The prayer halls form the bulk of the main spaces, with retail units on the ground floor and other mosque facilities and residential units on upper floors.

Jonas's proposal did not proceed beyond this early design stage. By November 1980 another scheme had been prepared by a north London collective of architects and designers – Team 3 (Fig 5.32). This was again a markedly contemporary proposal, with a four-storey glass-block wall forming the main façade fronting

Fig 5.30 (above)
Site plan of 1978 showing the temporary mosque on Fieldgate Street and marking out an area of land to the north, fronting Whitechapel Road, that the mosque acquired for expansion. [Copy of a plan held in ELM archive, reproduced here by kind permission of Sophie Jonas-Hill]

Fig 5.31 (right)
Elevation drawing of Michael Jonas's 1978 proposal for a new mosque fronting Whitechapel Road. [Copy held in ELM archive, reproduced here by kind permission of Sophie Jonas-Hill]

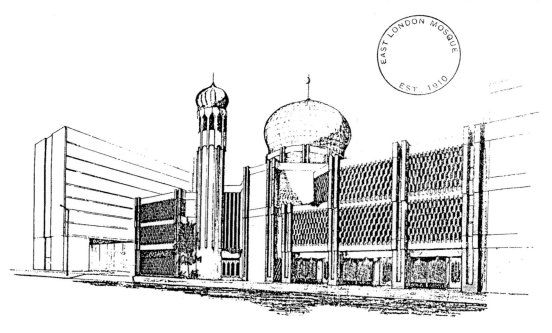

Whitechapel Road, and a four-storey entrance portico in glazed tiles, with an arch over the entrance door patterned in arabesque. A dome was to be placed over the main prayer hall, and constructed of hexagonal glass panels. A single minaret would have been located towards the rear of the building, plain in style and without decoration but with vertical strips of glass blocks along its height. A domed cupola topped with a crescent moon was perhaps the most literal concession to customary Islamic motifs.

The accommodation of the building would have been similarly ambitious, with a basement and three floors providing shops, classrooms, parking and residential units for staff. Due to the location of the Qibla, there was a strong alignment towards the corner of the site, with the central prayer hall being hexagonal to allow it a more integrated alignment with the rest of the plan, which is orthogonal to the street. The temporary mosque on the Fieldgate Street site was shown as retained, which is likely to have been a requirement of the mosque so that the site could continue in use while the new premises were constructed. The Team 3 proposal was submitted for planning permission and approved on 13 February 1982. However, it was subsequently considered unfeasible and the ELMT sought a new design.

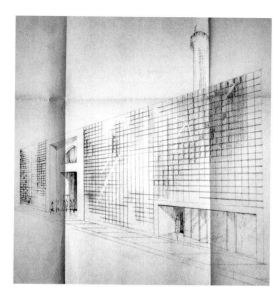

Fig 5.32
Elevation drawing of the Team 3 1980 proposal, fronting Whitechapel Road. [Copy held in ELM archive]

By June 1982 the ELMT had sought and received an outline design scheme from the Bristol architect Ahmed Eliwa, who also designed Maidenhead Mosque (*see* pp 107–14). His design (Fig 5.33) was expressly traditional, dominated by a slender ornate minaret and a large central dome with arched clerestory windows around its base. The front and side elevations were to be formed with a series of bays; there would have been a triangular arch over the upper window

Fig 5.33
The Whitechapel Road elevation of Ahmed Eliwa's 1982 proposal. [Copy held in ELM archive]

and a decorated parapet. In Eliwa's design a large square prayer hall was oriented towards the Qibla, but this did not sit within a plan aligned to the street as in the earlier designs. Here the whole building was aligned towards Makkah, meaning that the front façade would have sat askew to the street with a triangular-shaped forecourt at the front of the building.

Eliwa's design was a significant departure from the two earlier schemes, both of which had been attempting to deal with the language of the mosque in a contemporary manner. This proposal, however, abandoned any pretence of addressing contemporary architecture, opting instead for a fully traditional design. It may be that the mosque itself wanted to take a more traditional approach to its architecture and hence approached Eliwa, who recommended himself by referring to other UK mosques he had prepared designs for, including Maidenhead (*see* pp 107–14) and Gloucester (*see* pp 114–18), both of which included drawings for a built minaret and dome very similar if not identical to those in the drawings for east London.

The scope of the mosque as a place for a range of community provisions is evident in Eliwa's design. Alongside its prayer area, it was designed to contain shops, a library, accommodation, a restaurant, education space, funeral quarters and parking.[92] It is probable that the main reason the mosque committee sought to revisit the Team 3 design, which had gained planning permission, was primarily for cost reasons. When submitting his proposals to the mosque, Eliwa made the point that his scheme would provide a total floor area of 3,710m² over four floors, which is a reduction from the 4,490m² of the Team 3 scheme, which Eliwa equated to a 17.5 per cent cost saving of approximately £539,744, including the reduction of 'all unnecessary heights in basements and other floors'.[93] As the new scheme was quite a radical departure from its predecessor in terms of style, Eliwa emphasised that his approach gave 'the pure Islamic architectural appearance and functions, namely the dome and minarets', as well as a 'chance for Islamic features to be clearly seen from all sides'.[94]

The mosque responded to the scheme with some disquiet about the overtly traditional design, querying whether this would 'blend with the surroundings'[95] and opining that such a design might not be granted planning permission. In his response to their comments, Eliwa stated that 'the building has to show its identity as a mosque first and then blend with the sur-

rounding buildings'.[96] He also addressed the issue of planning by indicating that he had met with the local authorities and that the architectural language of the scheme had not been problematic.

Eliwa's scheme was not adopted by the East London Mosque, and the search continued for a suitable architect. John Gill Associates of Eltham, south London, had designed a commercial building then under construction in the City, and on noting the architects' sign board outside the project, the mosque made contact with the firm and invited proposals for their new facility. By August 1982 a completely new design had been presented to the mosque, whereby the temporary mosque was retained on the Fieldgate Street side and a new mosque set out on the adjacent site. The plan was dominated by a large, hexagonal prayer hall, with an entrance lobby aligned with it and the Qibla, leading to a skewed entrance doorway to Whitechapel Road and a small triangular forecourt on the street front. A three-storey entrance portico with a pointed-arched doorway was to dominate the façade, along with a single minaret standing independent of the building on the forecourt. The street façade was designed as a series of bays in a contemporary style with only an arch within each bay denoting its Islamic function. The dome was to be raised on a pitched tiled roof, a reference to the Dome of the Rock in Jerusalem, one of the earliest Islamic architectural monuments, dating from the 7th century.[97]

The scheme was again cost-driven, and so was more restrained than the earlier proposals, this time being arranged over basement, ground and part first floors. The architect estimated the building cost in the region of £1.1 million to £1.25 million,[98] a considerable reduction from Ahmed Eliwa's scheme, which he had estimated at £2.4 million.[99]

John Gill's proposal finally seemed to meet the mosque's complex requirements of function, cost and visual identity. With this new architectural solution, the mosque consolidated its vision of the role and function of the new centre. A brief written along with the new design stated that the aims of the 'Whitechapel Muslim Project' were:

To provide a Muslim centre for the large number of Muslims from many parts of the world, especially from Bangladesh, India, Pakistan etc now living in Tower Hamlets; To encourage and educate this large ethnic group to integrate with the host community; To promote better understanding and appreciation of Islamic teachings and culture; To provide social services and counselling to the community – especially to old persons, young children, women and handicapped persons; To organise social and cultural activities to achieve the above objectives.[100]

The document went on to note: 'For some years the East London Mosque has been under great pressure to provide community welfare and educational facilities ... to the growing ethnic Muslim Community ... [which is the] victim of general urban deprivation'. The new centre

would therefore seek to address such issues of social exclusion and community fragmentation with a range of social and religious programmes, along with 'cross-cultural events for amicable understanding between the communities and Others'.[101]

By January 1983 the scheme had been revised to provide a square prayer hall (Fig 5.34), with the front elevation straightened out along Whitechapel Road. Two further minarets were to be added to the corners of the entrance portico as a scaled-down version of the main minaret, which now had more detailed decoration. The

Fig 5.34
The interior of the main prayer hall of the 1985 mosque, with the dome centrally placed. The upper gallery to the left was used as the women's prayer space until the opening of the Maryam Centre in 2013. [Author]

proposal was approved by the local authority, the mosque was built and it opened in 1985 (Fig 5.35). Funding was continually sought through the construction of the building, from the Middle East as well as locally, and the final construction cost was approximately £1.4 million.

The new East London Mosque became a significant landmark on the Whitechapel Road, and over the next 15 years it grew and evolved into 'indisputably one of the more influential institutions of London's East End Muslim community'.[102] While addressing issues of exclusion and underachievement in its core and very local Muslim constituency, the mosque also engaged in wider communal spheres: 'Local politics provided the main arena in which it developed and exercised influence, negotiating skilfully with various dimensions of local government, seeking compromise and reaching ad hoc deals.'[103]

London Muslim Centre extension

When the mosque moved to Fieldgate Street in 1975, this part of east London, less than a mile from the City, was neglected and derelict, having suffered considerable bomb damage during World War II. The mosque helped catalyse a process of regeneration as shops and businesses followed the increase in activity and use. The site adjacent to the mosque, forming the corner of Whitechapel Road and Fieldgate Street, had served as a car park since its post-war clearance,

and the local authority was looking for a suitable use. Initially it was considered for a new fire station, which the mosque opposed, arguing that it should rather be utilised for the community.

With a rapidly increasing Muslim population, which by 2001 constituted 36 per cent of the total population of Tower Hamlets, the East London Mosque anticipated its need for expansion and the adjacent site provided a natural and ideal location. In 1998 Tower Hamlets Council was considering selling that site to a property developer to build luxury flats. The mosque joined The East London Communities Organisation (TELCO) and waged a determined struggle to prevent the transfer of the site: 'It mobilised thousands, who marched through Whitechapel demanding that the local Council allow the land ... to be purchased by the mosque and developed as a community centre.'[104] After two years of struggle over the site, a solution was found whereby the mosque was granted planning permission to build a community centre and 40 low-cost homes in collaboration with local housing associations, a solution that 'met the needs of the local residents and worshippers at the mosque'.[105]

This major extension to the mosque was to be the London Muslim Centre (LMC), envisaged as a 'vibrant community centre providing holistic and culturally sensitive services for the Muslim community of London'.[106] The aims of the centre built on the original objectives of the mosque.

Fig 5.35
The 1983 proposal by John Gill Associates for the new mosque fronting Whitechapel Road, which was completed in 1985. [Copy held in ELM archive, reproduced here by kind permission of Barry Morse, Pentar Design Partnership (formerly John Gill Associates)]

The centre focused on targeting excluded groups, in particular women and disaffected youths, and offered access to healthcare, training and advice.

The architectural challenge was to restore this significant urban block with a building that was not a mosque, but associated with one, and identifiable as an expression of Muslim culture. The Frederick Gibberd Partnership (FGP), which was also at this time designing the Muslim Cultural Heritage Centre in west London (*see* pp 121–7), was appointed as architect. Gibberd's office continued following his death in 1984, seven years after completion of Regent's Park Mosque, and the practice maintained its involvement in mosque design, led in this field by Richard Biggins, who had been at the firm since the Regent's Park project.

FGP's scheme for the LMC was arranged over eight levels, two below ground and six above. Large halls were designed on the ground floor, which would merge with the foyer of the existing mosque to form an expansive prayer space (Fig 5.36). Four retail units were also shown on the

ground floor and a range of community and office spaces were arranged across the upper levels. The roof was to be flat and landscaped, intended as an Eidgha (a large open space for the whole community to perform the twice-yearly Eid prayers). A large gateway, rising the full height of the building in the style of ceremonial entrances traditional to Persian Islamic architecture, was designed as a new entrance from Whitechapel Road. The scheme also showed the replacement of the frontage of the original mosque with a new façade that would unite both old and new developments into a coherently designed whole. Here was a plan for a nexus for prayer alongside cultural and social activities, enabling the ELM's vision of building a Muslim institution to empower communities suffering multiple levels of disenfranchisement. FGP's design for the LMC was an ambitious contemporary civic building infused with traditional Islamic architectural references, a language similar to the firm's Muslim Cultural Heritage Centre in west London.

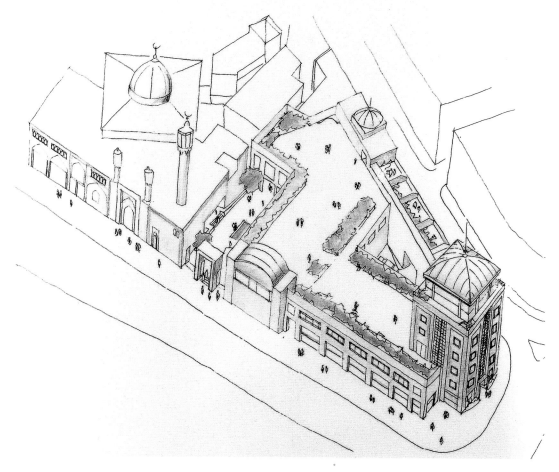

Fig 5.36
Frederick Gibberd Partnership's first proposal (c late 1990s) for the redevelopment of the corner site to create the London Muslim Centre, extending the mosque complex to include offices, shops, community services and social housing. This scheme developed into the proposal that eventually gained planning permission in 2002. [By kind permission of Frederick Gibberd Partnership]

Fig 5.37
View looking east from the corner of Whitechapel Road and Fieldgate Street, with the residential block, Mosque Tower, in the foreground and the London Muslim Centre alongside it. The minarets of the 1985 mosque are partly visible to the extreme left.
[DP147365]

Fig 5.38
View looking east along Fieldgate Street with the Maryam Centre in the centre ground. To its left is the former Fieldgate Street Great Synagogue, which closed in 2009 and was sold to the East London Mosque in 2015.
[Author]

The LMC proposal gained planning permission in February 2002 and work started on site in November that same year. Bamfords was the contractor appointed to carry out the construction, and between the February and November of 2002 it took FGP's approved design through a process of cost reduction and replanning. FGP was instructed to revise its planning-approved design, to a much simpler and cheaper scheme, which it duly produced in June 2002. Bamfords then switched architects to Markland Klaschka, who took FGP's redesigned scheme, made some very minor alterations to it, and submitted it as a revised planning application in December 2002, which was approved in May 2003.[107]

The result was a ground and first floor dominated by large halls oriented towards the Qibla so they could serve as overspill prayer space, with the rest of the accommodation arranged around them. A redesigned entrance portico in white blockwork, with an arabesque-tiled central panel, marks out the main door. The scheme retained shops on the ground floor, with office space (to let) on the upper floors facing Whitechapel Road, so effecting the commercial regeneration of this part of the street (Fig 5.37).

The London Muslim Centre extension opened in 2004. It represented the ongoing expansion of

Fig 5.39
The new entrance foyer from Fieldgate Street, built as part of the Maryam Centre development in 2013, which connects the 1985 mosque and the 2004 London Muslim Centre. The decorated tiled wall running along the entrance is the Alhambra donor wall, where names are inscribed on the tiles for a donation, which funded the development project. [Author]

Fig 5.40
The 1985 mosque's main prayer hall: a new opening connects to the extended prayer hall that was built as the ground floor of the Maryam Centre development in 2013. [Author]

Muslim infrastructure in Whitechapel and enabled the centre to dramatically increase its services and provision to the community. The complex of buildings re-established an urban grain, and represented a paradigm shift in that it marked the start of the ELM's rise to become one of the largest and most significant Muslim organisations in the country.

In 2009 the ELM embarked on its second major phase of expansion, with the construction of an eight-storey building over the original Fieldgate Street site to the south of the mosque, again designed by Markland Klaschka Architects.[108] Named the Maryam Centre and intended to provide dedicated facilities for women, this phase provided a new main prayer hall connected in one corner to the existing prayer hall, with two further halls on floors above (Figs 5.38, 5.39 and 5.40). Classrooms, offices, community services and residential accommodation occupy upper floors. With the completion and opening of the Maryam Centre in 2013, the men's prayer hall was doubled in size (Fig 5.41), and dedicated women's facilities were improved and increased. The development marked the continuing expansion of the East London Mosque and London Muslim Centre, and further reinforced its position as one of the

largest Muslim centres in the UK (Figs 5.42 and 5.43 and *see* Fig 1.12).

In 2015, the final piece of the urban jigsaw that the East London Mosque had become fell into place. The synagogue on Fieldgate Street, one of the last remaining of the once numerous synagogues in the local area, which had been closed for several years prior to this point, was purchased by the mosque for £1.5 million. The synagogue was sanguine about the loss of the building, viewing the sale as an opportunity for renewal as they could reinvest the proceeds into building new synagogues in areas where the Jewish population of the East End had settled, either further east into Essex or into the north London areas of Hendon and Golders Green.[109] The mosque appointed local practice Makespace architects (the author's firm) to start exploring the feasibility of a new mixed-use development on the site, part community, part residential and part commercial, with the possibility of including a heritage centre to record and display the local history of the area.

Funding for a wholesale redevelopment of the site, however, would be a protracted process, so in the interim, in 2016 the ELM leased the former synagogue to the National Zakat Foundation, an

Fig 5.41 (above)
The extended prayer hall on the ground floor of the Maryam Centre development, which opened in 2013. [Author]

Fig 5.42
Plan, c 2010, showing all three phases of the East London Mosque, the London Muslim Centre and the Maryam Centre. The 1985 mosque is on the top right of the complex fronting Whitechapel Road, with the Maryam Centre below it fronting Fieldgate Street. The London Muslim Centre is to the left of the mosque. This composite plan of all phases of development shows the extent of the facilities and how they have come to constitute a significant presence in the neighbourhood. [Based on an original plan held at the ELM]

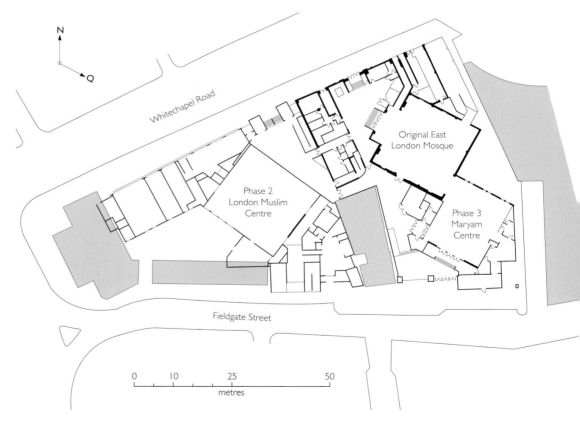

organisation that collects and distributes Muslim charitable donations, which then carried out a refurbishment of the interior of the building for its administrative purposes.

Conclusion

With the completion of the Maryam Centre, the East London Mosque and its associated facilities were reaching their physical capacity. The entire footprint of the site between Whitechapel Road and Fieldgate Street had been built over, while the Fieldgate Street Great Synagogue, embedded within the complex for 40 years, had been a pertinent reminder of the historical layers that characterise this part of east London. The combination of religious, community, social and commercial space is manifest in a plan of complex alignments and spatial arrangements. This can perhaps be read as a metaphor for the emergence of British Muslim institutions through a

strenuous, iterative and intensely negotiated process.

The new East London Mosque represented a step change in the role and function of the mosque in Britain. It was an institution rooted within, and generated from, a Muslim community that suffered from social exclusion and poverty, and it saw its key role as not only to facilitate prayer and religious observance, but also, crucially, through religion, to address the deprivations of its constituents. Built in 1985, this was the first community mosque at a scale on a par with nationally representative institutions such as Regent's Park Mosque and the Ismaili Centre. Unlike these examples, however, the ELM is embedded within a geographically local community that forms its core congregation and to which it orientates its programme. With its continued outreach work, the mosque has developed an influence beyond this locale to become a significant institution on a regional scale.

Fig 5.43
The purpose-built East London Mosque of 1985 (designed by John Gill) on Whitechapel Road (as it appeared c 2013), with the London Muslim Centre (2004; designed by Frederick Gibberd Partnership) to the right of it and the Maryam Centre (designed by Markland Klaschka Ltd) visible behind its dome. The Maryam Centre opened in 2013, completing the complex of buildings to date. [Rehan Jamil/East London Mosque]

بسم الله الرحمن الرحيم

الجامع

Central Mosque

6

New century, new historicism

The start of the 21st century heralded a new paradigm for Muslim life in Britain. The shift was precipitated through a series of unconnected, but overlapping, events. First, the national census for the first time included the category 'Religion', which enabled the most accurate determination of the size and composition of Britain's religious, and therefore Muslim, populations. The religion question, although not compulsory, had been included in the census as a result of ardent lobbying by a cross-party group of religious organisations, including the Muslim Council of Britain. Through this endeavour they were challenging the 'prevailing idea of religion being predominantly a matter for the private domain ... By gaining a category in the most comprehensive data collection exercise in the country, Muslims [had] been firmly put on the map and officially recognised as a community in their own right.'[1]

This was part of a social trend whereby religious beliefs were becoming increasingly important to people's sense of identification – not only in Britain but internationally (particularly as the dismantling of the Soviet Bloc heralded new geopolitical, and so cultural and communal, alignments from the 1990s onwards). It challenged the secularisation thesis of the 1960s which argued that through 'a combination of technological advances, philosophical rationalism and the development of consumer society, religion would overwhelmingly be removed from the public to the private sphere, becoming akin to a "leisure activity"'.[2]

Muslim religious activity in Britain over the previous two decades was a rebuttal of this thesis, with mosque numbers having increased exponentially to stand at over 600 and rising, with the Muslim population being the fastest growing religious group in the country. New immigrants, from diverse backgrounds and religions, also contributed to the persistence of religious identification, with a 1997 survey reporting that when a range of 16-to-34-year-olds was asked whether religion was very important to how they lived their lives, 5 per cent of 'Whites' agreed, compared with almost 20 per cent of Caribbeans and 65 per cent of Pakistanis and Bangladeshis.[3]

Mosque establishment, as shown in previous chapters, had been a consistent and continuous imperative of Muslim communities as they migrated, settled and became indigenous to Britain. By the turn of the 21st century the mosque, and the attendant visual culture of historical Islam that it manifested, was altering the landscape of many of Britain's towns and cities. With an architectural language new to vernacular streetscapes, mosques were described as a striking, alien and strange presence, articulating the otherness of the religious communities they served.

The second significant event was a series of incidents of social unrest in the Muslim communities of Burnley, Oldham and Bradford in the summer of 2001. In the aftermath of these disturbances, and subsequent official post mortems, notions of segregated communities and cultural conflict began to constitute the dominant discourse on Muslim communities and, in particular, the generation born in the UK.[4] With the terrorist attacks on New York's World Trade Center and the Pentagon in September 2001, this gaze on the Muslim populations of Britain intensified, with further question marks over their ability to integrate with, or even to live alongside, host communities encapsulated in the 'relentless depiction of Muslims as a fifth column within Britain'.[5] 'Stop and search' laws, along with detention-without-charge powers under new terrorism legislation, all impacted Britain's Muslims disproportionately and served to exacerbate feelings of polarisation. It can be argued that Muslim communities sought to consolidate and demarcate their religious identities as a means of support and defence, with the mosque perhaps becoming an instrument in this discourse.

Fig 6.1
Minarets over the entrance of the Suffa-Tul-Islam Grand Mosque in Bradford. [DP143566]

The actual link between social politics post 2001 and the representation of Muslim identity through the mosques built over this period is difficult, if not impossible, to determine. However, what is apparent is that from the turn of the 21st century there was an altered and intense social matrix within which the mosques of the period were placed, and within which they can be interpreted.

While mosque design as an assemblage of Islamic and local architecture continued with the mosques built in the early 21st century, where buildings were composed of historical references from disparate sources, a new phenomenon could also be observed, already emergent in the 1990s. This was the mosque as a more complete and coherent historical object, where the design was becoming more decisively Islamic and ostensibly authentic.

Case studies

1 Bilal Masjid (Markazi Jamia Masjid Bilal), Conway Road, Harehills, Leeds, 1996
2 Edinburgh Central Mosque, Potterow, Edinburgh, 1998
3 Peterborough:
Ghousia Masjid (Markazi Jamia Masjid Ghousia Ahl-e-Sunnat wal Jamaat), 406 Gladstone Street, 2006
Faizan-e-Madinah Masjid, 169–175 Gladstone Street, 2006
4 Sheffield Islamic Centre and Madina Masjid, Wolseley Road, Sheffield, 2008
5 Northolt Bohra Mosque (Masjid-ul-Husseini), Rowdell Road, Northolt, Middlesex, 2010
6 Jame Masjid, Asfordby Street, Spinney Hills, Leicester, 2010
7 Al-Jamia Suffa-Tul-Islam Grand Mosque (Bradford Grand Mosque), Horton Park Avenue, Little Horton, Bradford, 2014

1 Bilal Masjid (Markazi Jamia Masjid Bilal), Conway Road, Harehills, Leeds, 1996

The shift from the mosque as an amalgam of vernacular and Islamic styles to the mosque as a more completely Islamic object can perhaps be traced to a mosque in Leeds designed in the early 1990s and a series of mosques that followed. The Bilal Mosque in Leeds was a new-build, free-standing mosque in the inner-city district of Harehills (Fig 6.2), built by the same Muslim organisation that would later build the Suffa-Tul-Islam in Bradford (*see* pp 207–11). The

Fig 6.2
The main entrance façade of the Bilal Mosque.
[DP027128]

mosque was initially designed by Neil Bowen Architects of nearby Wakefield, and it was their first Islamic building. At some point during the design process, an Iraqi-born structural engineer based in Bradford, Atba Al-Samarraie, was introduced to the Bilal committee through some of his other mosque projects in neighbouring towns and was invited to comment on the design from the perspective of Islamic architecture. On the basis

of his observations and suggestions, the committee asked him to take on the project and amend the design to provide them with what they would feel was a more aesthetically authentic Islamic building. With this brief, Al-Samarraie set to work revising the scheme, working through the plans and elevations to bring symmetry, decoration and formality to the layouts (Fig 6.3). A hexagonal marble fountain was introduced into the

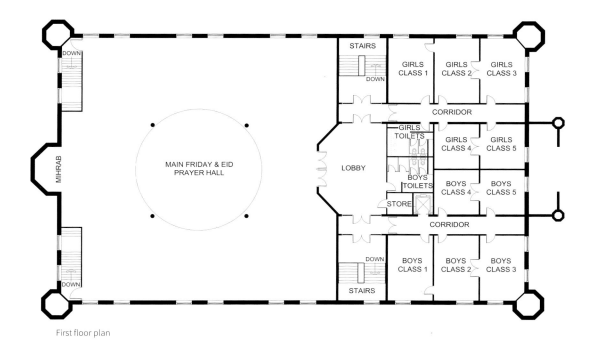

First floor plan

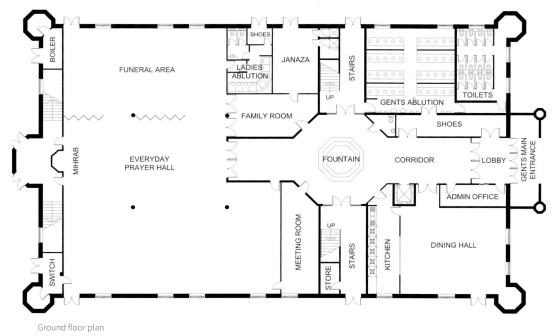

Ground floor plan

Fig 6.3
Al-Samarraie's floor plans of the Bilal Mosque, c 1993, the first floor (top) showing the men's main prayer hall and classrooms for girls' and boys' supplementary education; the ground floor (bottom) showing a range of community facilities including a dining hall and mortuary, along with the prayer hall for daily use. [Reproduced by kind permission of Al-Samarraie of Archi-Structure – Copyright]

Fig 6.4
The interior fountain on the ground floor of the Bilal Mosque, introduced to the design by Al-Samarraie in his redesign of the scheme in 1993.
[Author]

concealed by a parapet over walls punctuated by double-storey glazing, which served to situate the dome rather than leaving it somewhat awkwardly enmeshed in the pitch of the roof.

The revised scheme gained planning permission in 1993 and had been built by 1996. As in the approved drawings, the building has two hexagonal minarets at the front corners and a pair of smaller minarets flanking a double-height projecting entrance portico (Figs 6.6 and 6.7). The parapet line is decorative, and a pair of squat onion domes sit on castle-like turrets on the rear corners of the building (Fig 6.8). The walls are faced in buff-coloured Forticrete blockwork, resembling stone, with pairs of arched windows arranged along the façades. A large green dome, slightly bulbous around its middle, is off centre, so that it can be central to the first-floor prayer hall, which it dominates internally, decorated with a large chandelier (Figs 6.9 and 6.10). In the design of the Bilal Mosque, any overt references to local architectural styles and materials, as were generally apparent in mosques of this period, are gone; there is no red brick to relate to the terraced housing, and no tile or pitched roofs. The window surrounds are Islamised in shape, and are extended to read as double-storey openings in the walls.

Although Al-Samarraie had been working on additions or interventions to mosques prior to Bilal, this mosque was the first where he could

entrance lobby, leading to the ground-floor prayer hall used for daily prayers, an interiorised interpretation of the traditional mosque courtyard with ablution fountain (Fig 6.4). A larger and grander prayer hall was to be located on the first floor for larger congregational prayers (Fig 6.5 and *see* Fig 6.10). Early sketches for the exterior show a tiled pitched roof embellished with a decorated minaret. Later the roof was completely

Fig 6.5
The mihrab and minbar in the first-floor prayer hall of the Bilal Mosque, used for Friday congregational and Eid prayers.
[Author]

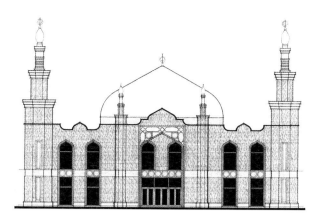

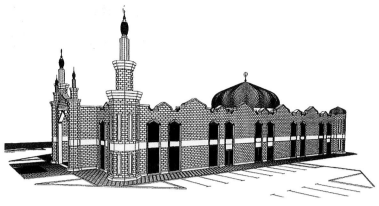

Fig 6.6 (above left) Al-Samarraie's front elevation drawing, c 1993, of the Bilal Mosque, showing the main entrance portico. [Reproduced by kind permission of Al-Samarraie of Archi-Structure – Copyright]

Fig 6.7 (above) Al-Samarraie's computer-generated design model of the Bilal Mosque, c 1993. The mosque was built to these designs and opened in 1996. [Reproduced by kind permission of Al-Samarraie of Archi-Structure – Copyright]

Fig 6.8 (left) The Qibla wall of the Bilal Mosque, showing a half-domed projection for the mihrab. [DP027129]

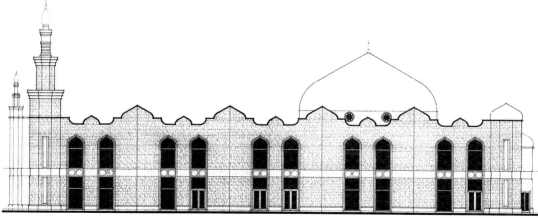

Fig 6.9 (left) Al-Samarraie's side elevation drawing, c 1993, of the Bilal Mosque, showing that the dome has been positioned so as to be situated centrally over the main prayer hall on the first floor. [Reproduced by kind permission of Al-Samarraie of Archi-Structure – Copyright]

Fig 6.10
Interior of the central
dome, with its chandelier,
over the first-floor prayer
hall of the Bilal Mosque.
[Author]

express his ideas for an Islamic architecture in Britain through a new building. The result is the first in a series of mosques that Al-Samarraie would go on to design, benefiting from the positive exposure the Bilal Mosque received from within and outside the Muslim community. In the projects that followed, Al-Samarraie was presented with a similar brief each time: to take an existing design and make it more Islamic, more authentic and more fitting for what at that time and in those communities it was felt a mosque should be.

Conclusion

Al-Samarraie's philosophy of the mosque is that it is composed of four basic elements: the minaret, the dome, the mihrab and the *bab al-sadir* (entrance door). In contemporary mosques in Britain, he acknowledges, the minaret and dome are symbolic, 'indicating the importance of the mosque to the life of the community'.[6] The practical function of the dome, to 'echo the words of the preacher and to cool hot air when it rises',[7] are largely defunct in the British context due to limitations of space, and climate. The mihrab is an indispensable element marking the direction of Makkah, and the *bab al-sadir* is the grand entrance, symbolising the importance of the mosque in the life of the town or city. Through demonstrating his understanding of these architectural elements and deploying them in a conscious and decisive way, Al-Samarraie attracted mosque committees across northern England. He has designed some 70 mosques, of which about 50 have been built.[8]

With Bilal as the precursor to this trend, the mosques would move away from the assemblage aesthetic of earlier buildings and instead seek to represent a more singular, coherent aesthetic – one that was based on a discourse of 'Islamic authenticity' – in the field of architecture.

2 Edinburgh Central Mosque, Potterow, Edinburgh, 1998

Edinburgh Central Mosque is at the southern end of the historic city centre and falls within the area of the old city which has been designated as a UNESCO World Heritage site. It is a location invested with the weight of Edinburgh's architectural heritage, a factor that has had an impact on the development of the site and situated it within a highly sensitive statutory framework against which the mosque's design was always going to be judged.

The site on which the mosque stands has a complex and layered urban history. In the 1850s it was a densely built-up area centred on a United Presbyterian Church that seated 874 worshippers. To the church's north side was a free-standing school building, and to the south an 18th-century chapel house (or vestry hall), which provided residential accommodation associated with the church. By the 1870s, what space there was between buildings was gradually being infilled, development fuelled by the growing success of Miller and Richard, a world-famous type foundry, which was immediately adjacent to the church on its eastern flank. By the 1910s the church had closed and its building, school and chapel house had been taken over by the type foundry, into which they expanded their production facilities. The foundry eventually closed in 1952, and the conglomeration of buildings became an engineering workshop.

Because of its organic growth and adaptation over a century, the site now had the character of a left-over backland industrial site, albeit with the church buildings left behind within it. New owners wanted to redevelop the site for a commercial development, but the council designated it as part of the University Action Area and so required that it be redeveloped in such a way as to integrate it into the neighbourhood.[9] This thwarted the owners' chances of gaining permission for independent commercial redevelopment, an application for such being refused in 1970.[10] The owners sought to dispose of the site, and in the early 1970s the Edinburgh Muslim community acquired the former chapel house for use as a makeshift mosque and community centre.

Realising that the adapted 18th-century building was insufficient for a growing Muslim population of residents swelled by students, the mosque successfully acquired the adjacent sprawling workshops by the end of the 1970s.

In March 1981 the mosque committee gained planning permission and listed building consent for demolition of the warehouses on the site with redevelopment of the chapel house through conversion to a place of worship.[11] As in many other mosques, space soon proved inadequate with a growing congregation and in 1984 planning permission was gained for the erection of temporary Portakabins for one year to take additional worshippers.[12] The planners were in part persuaded to grant permission by the stated intention of the mosque that the ground floor of the chapel house would be converted to mosque use that spring, which would have removed the need for the Portakabins. Funding was already flagged up as difficult, but the planner noted the mosque's commitment that the remaining phases of the conversion would proceed as funding became available.[13] Comprehensive redevelopment of the site to provide a purpose-built mosque was only a matter of time, and in 1986 an application was submitted for a new mosque and Islamic centre, designed by the Bamber Gray Partnership, an Edinburgh firm of architects.[14]

The planning report described the scheme as physically abutting and connecting to the chapel house, flat-roofed, approximately 10 metres in height and with a large central prayer hall. A single minaret was shown and there was no mention of a dome; the main walling material was to be brown brick. As the building was aligned towards Makkah, this resulted in an 'unusual relationship to the street at Potterow, and a very unsatisfactory relationship to Chapel House'.[15]

The proposal fell under the weight of this highly sensitive location, with consultations on the design sought from the Royal Fine Art Commission (RFAC) for Scotland, the Cockburn Association and the Scottish Civic Trust, as well as local residents. The RFAC for Scotland was particularly condemnatory of the proposal, stating that it had been designed to 'satisfy the needs felt by the clients who demonstrate little regard for either the urban design requirements of this part of Edinburgh, or the architectural response which might be expected for the headquarters of the Muslim community in the capital city'.[16] Along with this, the RFAC for Scotland made comment on the surrounding buildings and the damage to the setting of the chapel house. Most notably, it stated that the quality of the proposed architecture was 'too poor to justify its exemption from normal civic design criteria in the way that certain monumental buildings such as churches have broken the urban pattern in the past'.[17]

These objections were broadly in line with those of the other consultees, with particular concern being expressed over the relationship of the new building to the chapel house and whether its alignment on the site failed to contribute to the townscape by discontinuing the existing building lines. The planner noted that the applicant's architect responded 'in a very limited way to objections shown to him, explaining that his client has not allowed more substantial changes',[18] a comment which suggests something of the dynamic of the client–architect relationship.

The criticisms levelled at the proposal were, however, intended by the planning authorities to be constructive, and a generally supportive view was expressed by all parties to the building of a mosque on this location, subject to a 'satisfactory design'.[19] The planners resolved to continue negotiations with the applicant to seek ways in which the design could be improved and to work towards the successful achievement of a facility that would 'assist much in developing the life of the City's Moslem community'.[20] One of the parameters that the council laid down was that the 18th-century chapel house should remain visible from Potterow in any redevelopment of the site to form a new mosque.[21]

It was after this response to its application that the mosque sought out and appointed Basil Al-Bayati, an Iraqi architect who had gained prominence since establishing his practice in London in the 1970s. The brief that the mosque committee gave to Al-Bayati was for a place of worship to house 1,000 worshippers, a library, two function rooms, accommodation for the imam, offices and the required ablution facilities. With this Edinburgh project, Al-Bayati was faced with a number of problems: 'Primarily he had to design a building which took into consideration the severe climate of Scotland. Secondly he had to conceive a plan and decoration that would successfully blend Islamic and Scottish architectural and artistic traditions.'[22]

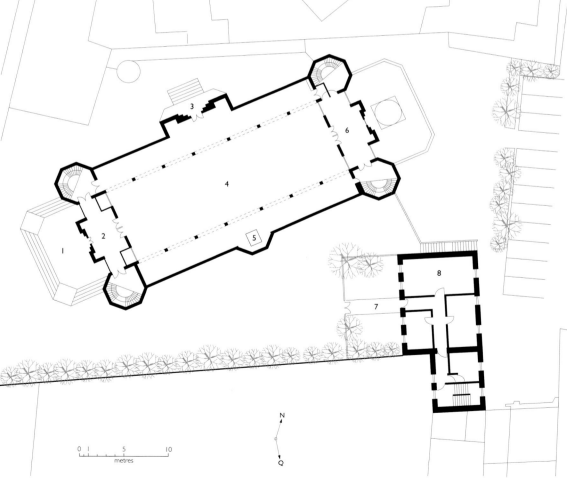

Fig 6.11
Site and ground-floor plan for Al Bayati's Edinburgh Central Mosque, showing the new mosque (as built) positioned on the Qibla axis with the original vestry building in the corner of the site.

Key
1 Forecourt
2 Main entrance lobby
3 Women's entrance
4 Men's main prayer hall
5 Mihrab
6 Lobby
7 Existing chapel house
8 Madrassa

[Redrawn from a drawing held in Edinburgh City Council planning file 1583/86/35, July 1987]

Al-Bayati was selected as the architect because much of his work addressed the challenge of blending Muslim sensibility with an understanding of the cultural context of the region in which he was designing, while also embodying what he understood as rules 'handed down by Divine Law', and how these might be translated into architecture. Al-Bayati also believed that 'in Islam, everything has an outer and an inner meaning' and that both had to be grasped before design could take place.[23] An article on Al-Bayati's work published in 1986 described it as 'an architecture rooted in traditional forms, and based on uncompromisingly strong symbols, brought to life with geometric and natural decorative patterns'.[24] He was also keenly aware of the heterogeneity of Muslim architecture, depending on time and place, writing that 'the desert experience is ... conducive to the formation of different characters from that of the city experience and this is one of the underlying causes of the diversity found in Islamic architecture.'[25] It was this architecture of contexts, symbols and meanings that Al-Bayati was to bring to Edinburgh.

By the summer of 1987 he had submitted a very much revised scheme to the council for consideration. First, to address the core concerns of building relationships and sight lines, Al-Bayati set the new mosque away from the chapel house and allowed a pedestrian route along the south side of the site to enable the historic building to be experienced. Although the proposed mosque remained aligned towards Makkah and so was positioned askew on the site, it had enough space around it to allow it to take up this position in a comfortable way (Fig 6.11).

The revised proposals were roundly welcomed by the planners and consultees, almost all of whom commended the new design. The planners concluded that Al-Bayati's proposal was an 'interesting and competent building', the only reservation being one of scale to the surrounding context. This concern was, however, offset by the planners' opinion that the new mosque was 'sufficiently interesting to stand on its merit in this circumstance'.[26] Planning permission was granted in August 1987 and work started on the new building. However, funding soon dried up and a partially completed building was left on the site for several years. Work did finally recommence towards the end of the 1990s and the mosque was eventually completed in 1998.

Al-Bayati had infused the design with what could be described as a Scottish Baronial influence, with monumental octagonal corner towers and turret-like structures, and a single octagonal minaret emerging as a continuation of one of the towers, serving to signify the mosque (Fig 6.12). The large turrets on three of the four corners of the mosque are topped with tiled, straight-sided conical roofs, which replicate a feature that can be seen in traditional architecture in Edinburgh and is itself derived from Scottish castles

Fig 6.12
The street-facing façade of Edinburgh Central Mosque, showing the monumental entrance portal flanked by a minaret and turret to evoke a Scottish Baronial style of architecture.
[DP143546]

Fig 6.13
The rear façade of Edinburgh Central Mosque, which combines traditional Islamic and Scottish references into an overall composition.
[DP143545]

Fig 6.14
The men's main prayer hall of Edinburgh Central Mosque, with the mihrab and minbar visible behind the columns to the right.
[DP143543]

(Fig 6.13). The Kufic scripts wrapping around the towers, reading '*Allah*', have been likened to the chequered patterns of Scottish tartan. These towers flank a monumental entrance portico rising the full height of the south-western façade with a series of recessed pointed arches on squinches, distinctly reminiscent of 11th-century Seljuk architecture.

The main entrance into the mosque (used as the women's entrance) is actually on the north-west façade, directly opposite the mihrab on the south-east wall, and visually connected to it by a straight axis where the roof is higher than over the rest of the main prayer hall. However, this façade does not form the street frontage, so is not completely practical as a main entrance. To address this, another entrance is located on the south-western façade, facing Potterow. This serves practically as the main entrance, and is thus articulated with the large and deep entrance portico (*see* Fig 6.12). This is approached via a platform stepping up from the street, 'in recognition of its importance as the first step in getting to the mosque area'.[27] The main men's prayer hall is on the ground floor (Figs 6.14 and 6.15), with a women's prayer area on a galleried mezzanine level, accessed from stairs that spiral up the corner towers, another castle-like feature. A basement

Fig 6.15
The recessed arches forming the mihrab and minbar of Edinburgh Central Mosque. [DP143541]

and attempts a genuine re-articulation of this language within a traditional Islamic architectural narrative. Through this hybridisation there emerges a new set of forms and languages that can be seen as analogous to the adaptation and evolution of Muslim cultures within their new Western contexts.

Edinburgh Central Mosque, as the city's main mosque in a prominent position, is a significant public building, and has set itself a high bar with its bold ambition to negotiate an Islamic history, with a contemporary Scottish Muslim identity, in a profoundly historic location.

3 Peterborough:

Ghousia Masjid (Markazi Jamia Masjid Ghousia Ahl-e-Sunnat wal Jamaat), 406 Gladstone Street, 2006

Faizan-e-Madinah Masjid, 169–175 Gladstone Street, 2006

Two of Atba Al-Samarraie's commissions following from the Bilal Mosque were new mosques on the same street in Peterborough.

With the dawn of the Industrial Revolution and the development of the rail system in Britain, the major trading and market town of Peterborough began steadily to transform into an industrial centre. Easy access to both London and Doncaster by railway made it a regional hub. In addition, natural clay deposits in the area made it an ideal location for the production of bricks, and Peterborough became the biggest brick-producing town in Britain up to the mid-20th century – the local London Brick Company produced the bricks that were used in many of the country's landmarks.

The population of Peterborough has grown much more quickly than the national average in recent years due to immigration of both Europeans and large numbers of Muslims from Commonwealth countries. As a result, the city as a whole has a far higher percentage of Muslims, at 6 per cent, than the national average of 3 per cent. But in certain areas, such as Millfield in the Central ward and New England in the Peterborough North ward, the Muslim population was close to 48 per cent in the 2001 and 2011 censuses.

It is in the Peterborough North ward that two substantial mosques on the same street are to be found, both completed in 2006.

accommodates further function halls, a kitchen, library and ablution facilities. Offices and other ancillary facilities are placed in a single-storey block to the north-east of the main prayer hall.

The mosque is faced in sandstone, a building material ubiquitous in Edinburgh's historic centre, which again serves to tie the building into the existing architectural fabric. The chapel house was shown on the approved planning drawings as to be converted into a mortuary in its cellars and a madrassa on its upper floors. This conversion, however, was never implemented and the historic building remains vacant.

Conclusion

Edinburgh Central Mosque is one of the early complete and coherent expressions of Muslim architectural heritage in Britain and marks a departure from the ad hoc mosques of the previous 25 years. Here the mosque is conceived in totality, as a single object that has a series of symbolic readings and historical references. This is a direction that mosque architecture in Britain was to take in the subsequent decade, and Edinburgh represents a precursor to this trend.

The mosque is also unique in that it actively engages in a local Scottish architectural tradition

Fig 6.16
The main prayer hall in the house at 46 Gladstone Street, Peterborough, which was used as the original mosque on the site; the prayer hall was extended by combining the rooms on the ground floor and then building into the garden. [DP153524]

Fig 6.17
Proposed east elevation (facing Gladstone Street) for the new Ghousia Mosque, c 2002. [Reproduced by kind permission of Al-Samarraie of Archi-Structure – Copyright]

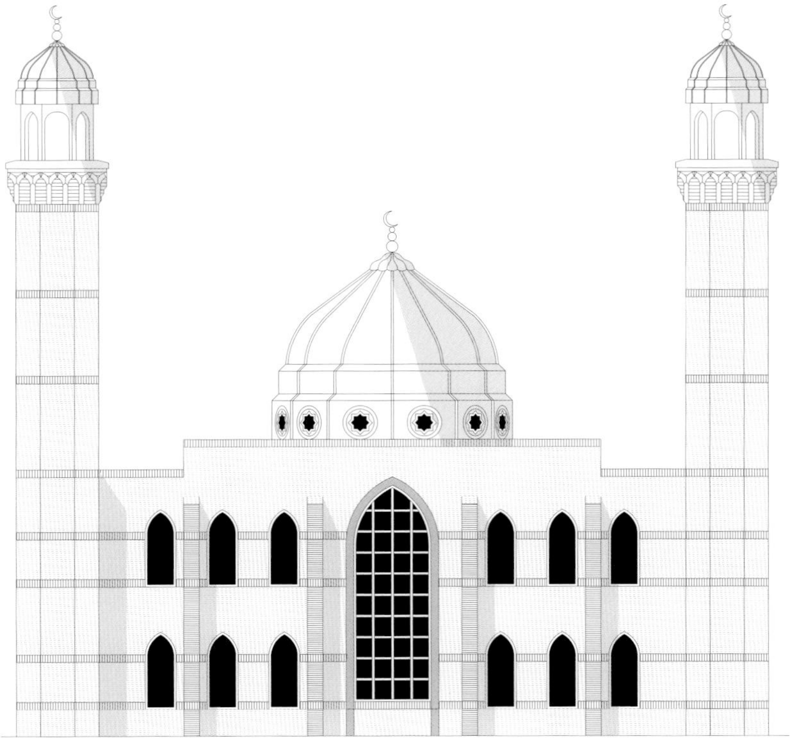

Ghousia Masjid

The Muslim community of Peterborough predominantly comprised immigrants from Mirpur, Kotli and Jhelum in north Pakistan, who had been arriving in the city since the late 1960s. The city's first mosque was established in 1967 in a converted house at 60 Cromwell Road, in the northern part of the city centre where the newly arrived Muslims were settling. However, the Muslim community was growing rapidly and by the early 1990s a detached house (46 Gladstone Street) had been purchased from a local vicar and converted into a mosque, and some of the Cromwell Street congregation moved to worship there.

As the Muslim community grew, the house mosque was extended in stages until it occupied the whole of the site to a depth of some 30 metres, over ground and first floors. On the ground floor all the internal walls were removed, and with an extension to the rear, one long, open prayer hall was created (Fig 6.16). A timber-panelled mihrab was built into the south-eastern corner of the room, reflecting the angle of the prayer lines due to the oblique alignment of the house in relation to Makkah. On the first floor the bedrooms were interconnected or knocked through to form prayer halls and classrooms, right through to the back of the site.

The site adjacent to the house comprised three terraced houses, garages and a car park. While the house was being extended to its maximum potential, the mosque anticipated that it would need larger premises. With this pressing need in mind, it purchased the adjacent land, demolished the buildings and appointed Atba Al-Samarraie to design a purpose-built mosque on the cleared site.

The key design requirements the mosque presented to the architect were for minarets, a dome and a large chandelier (Fig 6.17). The council was largely supportive of the scheme although it was concerned at the height of the minarets, advising that they should remain lower than the height of the city's cathedral spires. The planning application for the mosque was submitted on 8 April 2002 and approved on 30 October of the same year. Fundraising followed, with building starting soon afterwards, and the mosque was completed and opened in 2006. The original house mosque on the adjacent site has been retained for ongoing community use (Fig 6.18).

Ghousia Mosque is a simple building, square, two tall storeys high, with a central dome and a pair of hexagonal minarets on the corners of the eastern façade, fronting Gladstone Street (Fig 6.19). There is a large car park to the north of the mosque, into which elevation the main entrance is placed. The external walls and minarets are faced in a buff wire-cut brick, which gives a clean, crisp impression, with horizontal banding of glazed dark green brick in soldier courses spaced at approximately 2-metre heights along the façades. Windows with pointed arches line both storeys, with the horizontal banding aligned to form the head of each arch. The main entrance comprises two sets of double doors, marked with a full-height brick portico with twin pointed arches. Within the arches, on the

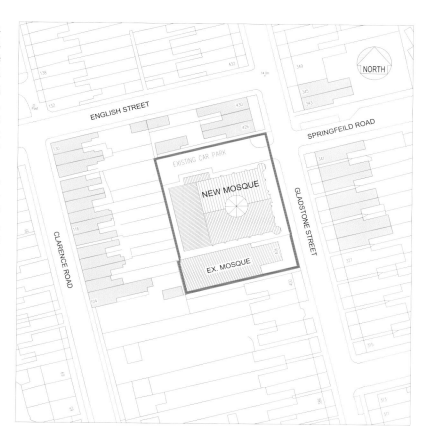

Fig 6.18
Site plan showing the site of the new Ghousia Mosque occupying all the available land, with the existing house mosque retained adjacent. [Reproduced by kind permission of Al-Samarraie of Archi-Structure – Copyright]

Fig 6.19
The main entrance façade of Peterborough Ghousia Masjid with a monumental entrance portal fronting on to the entrance forecourt and car park. [DP147358]

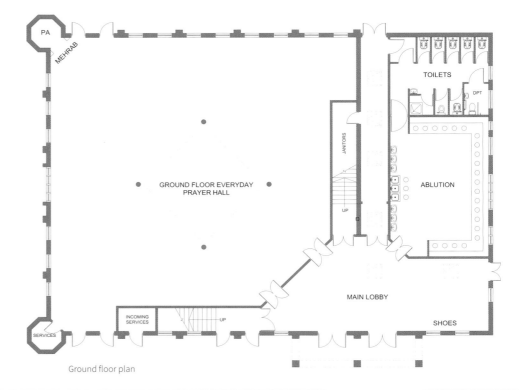

Fig 6.20
Proposed ground-floor plan for Ghousia Mosque, c 2002. The mihrab is neatly fitted into one of the corner minarets. [Reproduced by kind permission of Al-Samarraie of Archi-Structure – Copyright]

PA

MEHRAB

TOILETS

DPT

JANITORS

GROUND FLOOR EVERYDAY PRAYER HALL

UP

ABLUTION

MAIN LOBBY

INCOMING SERVICES

UP

SERVICES

SHOES

Ground floor plan

Fig 6.21
The men's ablution facility at Ghousia Mosque. [DP153517]

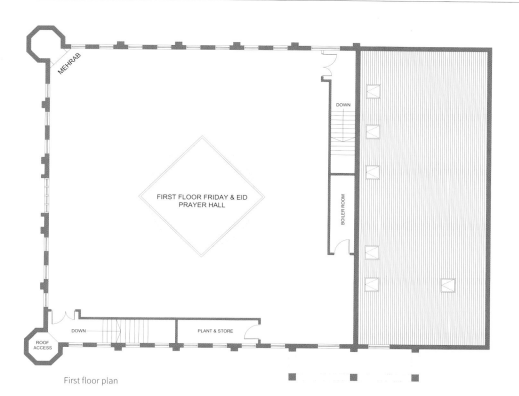

First floor plan

Fig 6.22
Proposed first-floor plan for Al-Samarraie's Ghousia Mosque, c 2002. [Reproduced by kind permission of Al-Samarraie of Archi-Structure – Copyright]

Fig 6.23
The interior of Ghousia Mosque, showing the upper-floor gallery with the centrally placed dome and chandelier. [DP153522]

face of the wall, are placed a pair of large circular motifs, reading 'Allah' on the right, and 'Muhammad' on the left. Decorated battlements line the parapet walls, and the minarets are topped with faux chattris, with green panel infill where traditionally there would be an open balcony. Their domes are green and circular with crescent pinnacles. The main dome, placed centrally on the main building, is a similar green and rises over a drum with circular star motifs. In style, it echoes the dome of the Prophet's Mosque in Madinah.

Due to the orientation of the site, the Qibla is effectively at 45 degrees to the orthogonal plan of the mosque. The main prayer hall occupies two thirds of the ground-floor plan, and is to the left of the main entrance lobby (Fig 6.20). To the right, and occupying the rest of the plan, are the WCs and wudu facilities (Fig 6.21). The mihrab is in the south-eastern corner of the prayer hall, and is combined with the corner minaret in this location. A second prayer hall is located on the first floor (Fig 6.22) immediately above the ground-floor main prayer hall. This first-floor hall has a square balconied opening in its centre that visually connects it to the hall below and above which is placed the dome. A large chandelier hangs from the centre of the dome through the opening between the first and ground floors. The dome itself is painted white, with Quranic inscriptions in black lettering lining the inside base (Fig 6.23).

Fig 6.24
The mihrab and minbar of Ghousia Mosque. [DP153519]

Fig 6.25
Ghousia Mosque, seen from Gladstone Street, is a striking landmark and a new architectural language in the street scene. [DP147363]

Generally, the interior decoration is fairly plain, the only embellishments being at the mihrab and in the supporting columns within the prayer hall, which are in a Corinthian style with a marbled effect and gold-painted head and base. These classical inflections are continued through to the mihrab, which has pairs of similarly styled columns on each side of the arched opening from within which the imam leads the prayer. The minbar is an elaborate cushioned and decorated piece, with the sense of being a ceremonial chair raised one step up. Fairy lights are strung around the columns and across the top of the mihrab, a typical Barelwi characteristic (Fig 6.24).

Both the first house mosque and the purpose-built mosque are situated within the urban grain in the same way as mosques in many towns across Britain, within inner-city, working-class housing areas where immigrants have traditionally settled and where the Muslim population is most concentrated (Fig 6.25). The mosque committee has a concern, based on demographic trends, that as Muslim populations become more affluent, those inner-city, working-class residents who have provided the congregation will move to better housing in outer suburbs, so depopulating the local Muslim community. This is a trend that the mosque can already see happening here and that has been observed in other towns. The fear, therefore, is that one day the mosque will no longer have the thriving congre-gation that is its lifeblood. To counter this possible scenario, the mosque is seeking to expand its services and facilities. It has purchased two adjacent houses, and is intending to acquire and redevelop further sites to create housing for older Muslim people. The idea, which has council interest, is that older people fare better if they can stay within their communities than if they are relocated and potentially isolated. The mosque has also purchased a church a few minutes away, which will serve as a community centre and a centre for Muslim funeral services, as well as be a place where prayers can be made and the deceased be visited prior to burial. Through these initiatives, the mosque is starting to diversify its range of social provision and thereby increase its built stock and the way it reshapes the city.

The mosque has seen an increase in the number of young people visiting since the new building was completed. Educational achievement among the Muslim youth in the area is

low, and in an attempt to begin to address this, the mosque provides supplementary educational classes and youth facilities. Sermons and speeches are delivered in Urdu and English, and young people are actively encouraged to attend.

The Muslim community in Peterborough is diversifying. It is increasingly made up of recent immigrants from other Muslim countries, in particular from Afghanistan, which has provided new congregants for the mosque, while immigrants from Pakistan are coming mostly to join family members already there.

The mosque caters for around 5,000 to 6,000 Muslim residents, and has an active membership in the region of 1,000. It has also expanded its presence in the community through a closed radio system, whereby local people can purchase receivers and listen to sermons and prayers within their homes. This technology is seen as mitigating the fact that there is no dedicated women's space within the mosque, providing women instead with a direct link to religious services.

Faizan-e-Madinah Masjid

This mosque is on a large site on the corner of Gladstone Street and Link Road, formerly that of a works building surrounded by streets of compact terraced housing close to the town centre (Fig 6.26).

As with Ghousia Mosque further along the same road, Atba Al-Samarraie was appointed as the designer for this project because the mosque committee had become aware of his mosque designs in Dewsbury, Bradford and Leeds. The committee visited some of Al-Samarraie's other mosques and developed their brief and aesthetic requirements accordingly, remaining heavily involved in the internal layouts. It was the Suffa-Tul-Islam Mosque in Bradford (*see* pp 207–11) in particular that led to his appointment for this scheme. Indeed, the mosque committee asked Al-Samarraie to design a mosque which would be 'as unique as Suffa-Tul-Islam',[28] as it would be one of the first purpose-built mosques in

Fig 6.26
The Faizan-e-Madinah Mosque is on the former site of a semi-industrial works building, surrounded by terraced housing, as this 2002 plan shows. [Reproduced by kind permission of Al-Samarraie of Archi-Structure – Copyright]

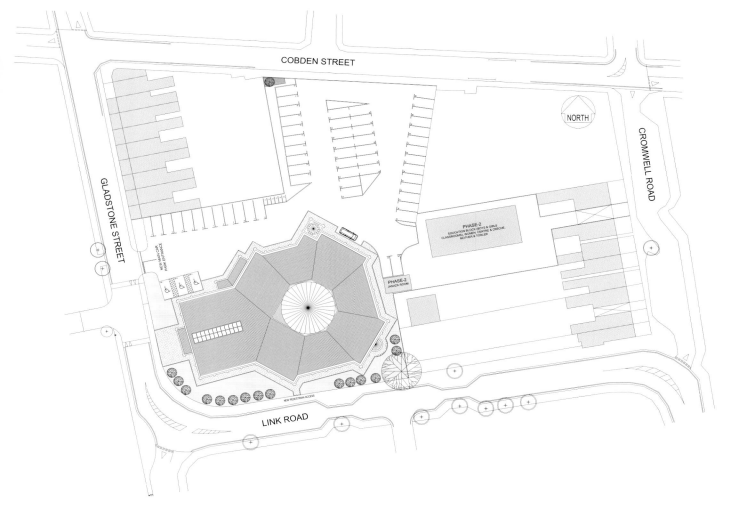

on 13 September in the same year. The building was completed and opened in 2006.

The exterior elevations are ordered with vertical grey-brick piers, between which are placed arched windows with stone surrounds (Figs 6.27 and 6.28). The mosque commissioners had asked for a unique feature on the elevations, to which Al-Samarraie responded by adding a band of glazed bricks around the parapet in Arabic Kufic script representing the Muslim testament of faith. Al-Samarraie finds that mosque clients who originate from Pakistan usually request more than one minaret and dome, as did the committee of Faizan-e-Madinah, perhaps a reflection of their familiarity with Mughal architecture; however, with this mosque he suggested only the single minaret and dome, arguing that this made the building distinct from Suffa-Tul-Islam, Bradford (Fig 6.29).

The ground plan is dominated by and organised around the main prayer hall, which is octagonal so as to allow a geometric shape with one side aligned towards the Qibla. As Al-Samarraie explained, it gave him 'the opportunity to replicate the elevations on all sides in the true style of Islamic Architecture, relying on geometric patterns and symmetry and clean-cut lines'.[30] A rectangular wing extends to the west of the hall, with an office, ablutions, WCs and staircases (Fig 6.30). A single square minaret is

Fig 6.27
The Faizan-e-Madinah Mosque, Peterborough, viewed from Gladstone Street, near to its junction with Link Road – a landmark religious building bringing a new architectural language to a residential townscape.
[DP147353]

Peterborough. The brief given to the designer was that the mosque should cater for men, women and children, and have capacity for future growth. Al-Samarraie drew his inspiration for the design from his 'early childhood memories of Baghdad and Iraq', which is the case for most of the mosques he designs.[29]

The planning application for the new mosque was submitted on 12 January 2000 and approved

Fig 6.28
The main entrance façade of the Faizan-e-Madinah Mosque on Gladstone Street.
[DP147355]

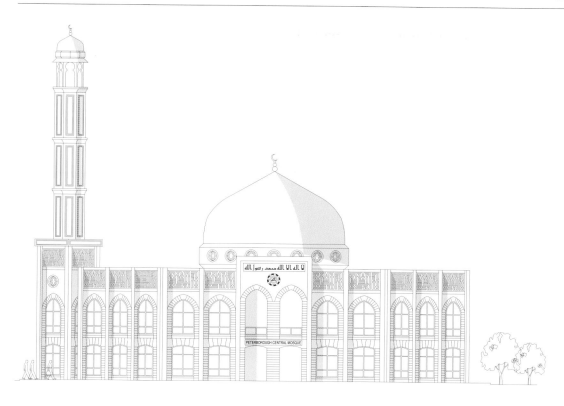

Fig 6.29
Proposal drawing (c 2000) of the main entrance elevation to Gladstone Street for the Faizan-e-Madinah Mosque. [Reproduced by kind permission of Al-Samarraie of Archi-Structure – Copyright]

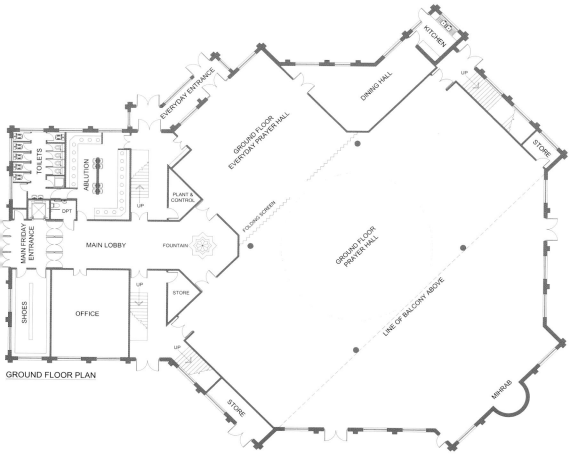

GROUND FLOOR PLAN

Fig 6.30
Proposed ground-floor plan (c 2000) of the Faizan-e-Madinah Mosque as it was built. It is arranged as a large octagonal prayer hall with the mihrab in the bottom right, and the entrance to the building through a block to the left. [Reproduced by kind permission of Al-Samarraie of Archi-Structure – Copyright]

Fig 6.31 (right)
Ornate entrance doors
from the lobby into the
men's main prayer hall.
[DP147395]

Fig 6.32 (far right)
The mihrab of the Faizan-
e-Madinah Mosque was
designed as an approximate
replica of the mihrab of
the Prophet's Mosque in
Madinah, which marks
the spot from where
Muhammad is believed
to have led prayers.
[DP147399]

placed on the northern corner of the octagon, which rises to the height of the main building and continues as an octagonal minaret with a large chattri-style domed balcony. The first floor contains further classrooms and a balcony prayer hall overlooking the main hall. A large green dome is placed centrally over the main prayer hall, so maintaining the geometric order of the design. The interior is mostly plain, with decorative focus on the interior of the dome, the mihrab and main entrance foyer (Fig 6.31). The mihrab is an approximate replica of that at the Prophet's Mosque in Madinah (Fig 6.32).

Conclusion

Ghousia and the Faizan-e-Madinah mosques are striking and significant urban presences in an area of small, low-rise, terraced workers' housing. Their stories mirror those of many other mosques in Britain which have either evolved from a house mosque extended to its limits before a new facility is built adjacent to it, or have been built to replace a house mosque on another site. The Muslim demography of Peterborough also repeats patterns of settlement of Muslim communities across the country, where they have become concentrated in inner-city, working-class districts as their migration was largely drawn to provide labour in the local industries of the city. The fact that the purpose-built mosque is built adjacent to the house

mosque demonstrates how important it is for it to remain a local facility, rooted within its congregation.

These mosques were designed and built in the early 2000s, coming after the first wave of mass mosque building in Britain which saw the construction of religious buildings characterised by iterative design and construction. That piecemeal process was primarily due to funds being raised as the mosques were being built and over extended periods of time. The two purpose-built mosques in Peterborough, however, are some of the first in a new phase of mosque building where the mosque is conceived and designed as a complete and 'Islamic' object, without any stylistic reference to local architecture and style.

4 Sheffield Islamic Centre and Madina Masjid, Wolseley Road, Sheffield, 2008

The City of Sheffield is built across several valleys on the edge of the Peak District National Park in the north of England. Its recent history is the archetypal story of industrial growth and post-industrial decline followed by regeneration programmes. From the 1850s to 2001 Sheffield's population expanded from around 130,000 to around 550,000. This growth was founded on expertise in iron, steel and silver-plating, for which Sheffield gained international renown.

These industries attracted inward migration throughout the 20th century, including from the northern areas of Pakistan in the 1950s and 1960s. By 2001 the Muslim population of Sheffield constituted approximately 4.4 per cent of the total population, with the vast majority originating from Pakistan. Sheffield Islamic Centre, the biggest mosque in the city, is located to the south of the city centre in the residential area of Nether Edge, where the Muslim population rises to nearly 12 per cent.

The site on which the mosque now stands previously housed a Co-op store with three storeys and a basement, which had closed and been purchased in 1977 for £40,000. It was then converted into a mosque and community centre for the local Muslim community, and it functioned as such until it was demolished to make way for the new mosque, which was completed in 2008 (Fig 6.33). Before 1977 the local Muslim population used prayer rooms in other local community centres, shifting between halls as bookings permitted.

The converted Co-op store in the south of the city was not, however, the first mosque in Sheffield. The north and north-east of the city housed the majority of the South Asian and Muslim populations because the steel industry was located in these areas, and it was here that the first house mosques were established in the 1960s. South Asian Muslim migration to the city was mostly from Pakistan or Bangladesh, with a limited Indian Muslim community.

Even so, the converted Co-op store was the largest mosque at the time and provided prayer space for approximately 450 people. With the ground floor being open plan, it was also a multi-use space, with funeral and day-care facilities. Children's classes were spread over all four floors, including the basement, which the mosque recognised as inadequate for teaching and as poor-quality space. The converted Co-op, along with the other houses being used as mosques in the 1980s and 1990s, were proving too small and, apart from the lack of space for prayer and education, Muslim burial rites could not be carried out within a fully Muslim context but had to be arranged through mainstream funeral providers not fully attuned to the culturally specific needs of the community. For example, many bodies are sent for burial in Pakistan or India, and therefore need to be stored for a few days before being sent. It was preferable during this period for the body to be kept in the mosque, where prayers could be held. These were the core reasons behind the formation of a purpose-built centre: a need for additional and better-quality space for prayer, community facilities, Islamic education and burial.

Non-religious community services have always been central to the role of the mosque, even from its early days as a converted shop, as these were seen as the link back into the community. The facilities that the mosque was able to develop with the new building, such as health care, day care, citizens' advice, clinics from the local hospital, and councillor surgeries, enabled

Fig 6.33
The main entrance façade of Sheffield's Madina Mosque, with a large entrance portico rising the full height of the façade fronting onto the mosque's car park.
[DP169305]

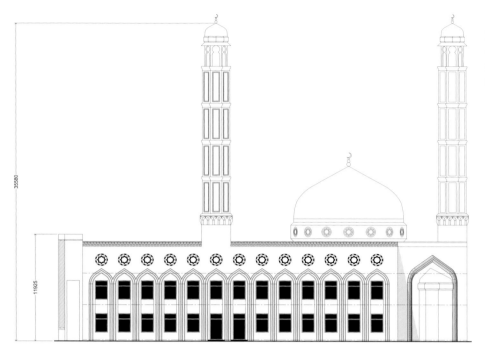

Fig 6.34
Al-Samarraie's c 2003
proposal drawing of the
western elevation of the
Madina Mosque, showing
the main entrance. The
mosque was built to these
designs and opened in 2008.
[Reproduced by kind
permission of Al-Samarraie
of Archi-Structure –
Copyright]

It was the second-generation, British-born Muslims' childhood experiences of using the early mosques that informed their approach to determining the needs of a new mosque. As one of the members recollects:

> We grew up hating coming to mosques ... because you walked in, you saw shoes, you saw a dingy place, it wasn't nice, it wasn't welcoming, it wasn't a great place to study, and when you came in the one thing that was obvious was, you couldn't understand the imam that was talking to you, because he was talking in a pure Urdu, Punjabi or whatever it was, and you were sat there looking at his face thinking, OK. And that is where we were coming from. Even though our parents loved that, and my dad was spellbound by some of the stuff, I was at the complete other end because I couldn't grasp it. It was like you go home, and your mum speaks in your mother tongue and you answer back in English.[31]

the mosque to remain part of the community which was one of its founding objectives. The old Co-op building, although refurbished and altered for increasing services and facilities, was never sufficient and was always short of space.

Looking for a new larger site, the mosque purchased a nearby former cinema in the early 1990s with a view to moving the mosque to these premises. However, as the cinema was Grade II listed it could not be altered to a sufficient and practical degree to enable it to function as a mosque. The site was subsequently sold, and the mosque decided that a more professional and formal route to a new building was required, so the mosque committee decided to enlist the skills of the younger members of its community. To this end, a development committee was set up in 1997 to pursue the idea of a new mosque. The group was made up of six volunteers from the younger Muslim community of Sheffield, children of the first immigrants, who had by now become educated adults and begun entering professions. They were given a free rein by the mosque elders to push forward the project for a new purpose-built mosque. Not wanting to become enmeshed in the mosque's internal politics, the development committee was given a point of contact with the mosque and promised no other interference. This formal relationship was beneficial; the development committee consulted with the mosque committee, but acted otherwise on its own agenda and direction.

This second-generation Muslim group consulted with the older generation to understand the Asian community's mentality and usage, expectations that were partly determined by traditional cultural values. They required a prayer hall, and funeral and washing facilities. The development group then filled in the pieces, focusing, for example, on children and education, looking at the low achievement of Muslim youth and wanting to use the mosque as a place in which to address this.

The first thing the mosque development group did when it was set up in 1997 was to approach the council about where the most appropriate location for a new mosque would be. The council responded by presenting seven potential sites. Along with six new sites, one of the options was the current Co-op building together with an adjacent site on Wolseley Road that was owned by the council. This was left-over space, with some car parking and vacant land, characteristic of inner-city areas where long-since abandoned small local industries may have once stood. It was the most difficult site due to the need for highway closures, land clearance and the removal of old foundations. However, the mosque chose this site for the simple reason that it could not allow the community to split, and felt that it was more important to remain within the community than move to a potentially better site, dislocated from the congregational base. Because of the nature of its use, the mosque needed to be within walking distance of its community.

The development committee became aware of the Bilal Mosque in Leeds, designed by Atba Al-Samarraie, recently completed and hailed as an exemplary mosque for its design, finishes and facilities. The group visited the Bilal Mosque and were told about Al-Samarraie, and subsequently visited him to discuss their ideas for a new mosque. In total 15 designers – some Muslim, some not – were asked for proposals and ideas. Al-Samarraie was preferred for what the mosque felt was his innate Islamic knowledge that came from his background as an Iraqi Muslim. The sense of naturalness with the mosque type and Muslim spatial culture demonstrated by Al-Samarraie was not something the mosque felt in any of the other designers. Furthermore, he had already designed several mosques and was working at the time for a large construction company, Bullen Construction, which not only gave him a certain professional credibility but also offered a potential contractor to carry out the build if necessary.

The other reason for choosing Al-Samarraie was his background. The mosque had a vision of looking to the Middle East and North Africa, for example Morocco and Tunisia, for design concepts as these were considered places of Islamic heritage. The development committee, as young second-generation Muslims of South Asian parentage, consciously wanted to stay away from Indian and Pakistani aesthetic influences, preferring instead the regional influences of the Maghreb and Middle East. They found more aesthetic congruence with their own tastes in design from these regions.[32]

Al-Samarraie presented a concept design that was immediately well received, the image of the mosque it presented concurring with their visions and aspirations. The original design had twin minarets over each of the two main entrances, as is characteristic of traditional South Asian Mughal architecture, and was perhaps a way of appealing to the Pakistani community for whom Al-Samarraie was designing. However, with the development group leaning more towards Middle Eastern influences, these minarets were replaced by designs for the two that now rise from the building (Figs 6.34 and 6.35 and *see* Fig 1.19).

The development group wanted a building of stone but felt this would not be acceptable both in planning terms, as the local material is predominantly brick, and because of the additional cost of stone. The group looked through multiple mosque photographs to choose types

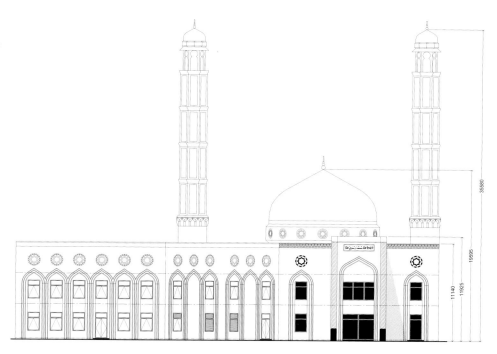

and preferences and were particularly inspired by examples of recent mosques from the Gulf region, such as the Sheikh Zaid Mosque in Abu Dhabi. The group wanted simplicity, without too many colours, and a high quality of construction in brickwork and detailing. The twisted columns at the main entrance, constructed from a special brick, exemplify this concern with craft and are a feature subsequently requested and implemented by other mosques. Due to the length of time it was taking for planning approval to come through, ideas were brought to the mosque from Al-Samarraie's other projects. For example, the parapet details were brought from the Suffa-Tul-Islam Mosque in Bradford (Fig 6.36).

Fig 6.35
Al-Samarraie's c 2003 proposal drawing of the Wolseley Road elevation of the Madina Mosque. [Reproduced by kind permission of Al-Samarraie of Archi-Structure – Copyright]

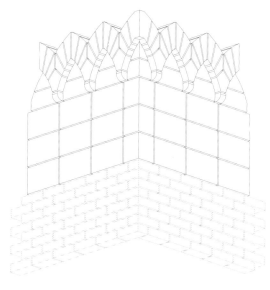

Fig 6.36
Al-Samarraie's c 2003 detailed drawing of the parapet of the Madina Mosque, showing how traditional Islamic design was being utilised in the building. [Reproduced by kind permission of Al-Samarraie of Archi-Structure – Copyright]

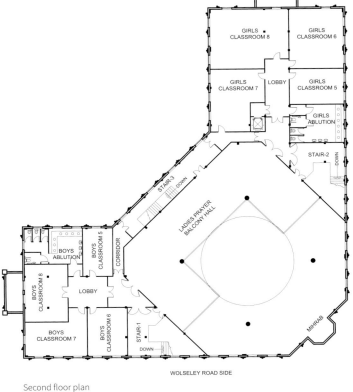

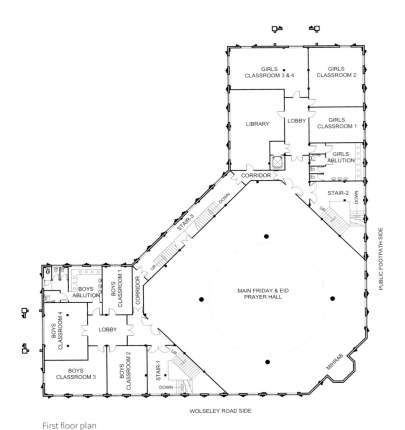

First floor plan

Second floor plan

Ground floor plan

Fig 6.37
Al-Samarraie's c 2003
proposed floor plans for the
Madina Mosque.
The second-floor plan (above
right) shows the women's
prayer gallery, which overlooks
the men's Friday and Eid
prayer hall on the first floor.

The first-floor plan (above left)
shows how the men's Friday
and Eid prayer hall dominates
and organises the plan.

The ground-floor plan (left)
shows how the building is
configured around the large
men's prayer hall used for
everyday prayers, with the
main entrance to the building to
its left side.

[Reproduced by kind
permission of Al-Samarraie of
Archi-Structure – Copyright]

The first planning application was granted in September 1998, for a new mosque to replace the existing building on the Wolseley Road site. Al-Samarraie's design placed a hexagonal prayer hall in the south-east corner of the site, with two wings projecting to its north and west. This configuration would allow a geometrically shaped prayer hall while accommodating the oblique angle of the Qibla. Through subsequent revisions, the prayer hall became more rectangular due to the acquisition of some additional land adjacent to the site. The two wings would contain the other facilities: day-care centre, classrooms, administrative areas, mortuary, kitchen and women's prayer spaces. The dome was proposed as turquoise GRP (glass reinforced plastic) standing at 23 metres high, with the tallest minarets at 35 metres. The remainder of the site was to be used for car parking.

The planning recommendations confirmed that planning policy supported community facilities such as places of worship within housing areas and also supported 'good design and innovation'. Furthermore, planning policy encouraged 'design which reflects the ethnic and cultural needs of the city's residents'. The planning officer noted that the mosque design found 'considerable support in the Muslim community. Among other residents there has generally not been widespread objection.' To situate, and perhaps justify, the introduction of a traditional Islamic design in Sheffield, the officer commented that 'similar designs have been erected in Bradford, Wakefield and Manchester', and that 'overall the building with its features and details is a good architectural design which is acceptable in the location'.[33]

The 1998 project was never commenced; instead, a revised scheme for a larger building was submitted in 2003 (Fig 6.37). The design and traditional Islamic character of this new scheme were largely similar to the plans approved in 1998.

Al-Samarraie described this new proposal's design as 'traditional Islamic architecture, having long arched windows and fenestration complete with dome over the main hall, 2 minarets ... and a smaller half-dome covering the mehrab'. He acknowledged that the design and appearance of the mosque would 'contrast with the established character of the area ... This dominant effect is normal for religious and community buildings (of any religion) throughout the world.' In justifying the minarets, Al-Samarraie argued that 'the principle of imposing (vertical) features on places of worship is established in many religions

and cultures and this element is an essential part of any Islamic Mosque design'. He also explained that the brickwork chosen for the exterior façades would sympathise with the local buildings (Fig 6.38), and that the gold and green colours of the dome were 'dictated by religious tradition', as were the height and proportions of the minaret in relation to the mosque. To demonstrate the point that this mosque would not generate undue traffic, the design statement listed 20 mosques within a 5.5km radius of the site to affirm that the users of this new mosque would be local; anyone from slightly further afield who might drive would find other mosques to go to.[34]

However, this 2003 proposal met with more considered design critique from the council, with a planners' design review meeting commenting:

Concern was raised over the quality and design of the building. Appears to be a pastiche of traditional architecture, and the quality of some of the materials appear poor. For example the dome/minarets are in green GRP ... Urban design officers happy to work with the architect to develop the design, but the current scheme is considered poor.[35]

Despite these concerns, and largely because the stylistically similar design had been approved in 1998, this amended scheme with the extended footprint on the northern wing was approved in August 2003.

Construction started in October 2004, under one contract from start to finish, at £3.6 million. When the building was watertight, halfway through construction, the mosque ran out of money and for eight months work stopped, with the builder owed around £1.1 million. A loan agreed by Yorkshire Bank was disapproved by the community, who wanted instead Islamic financing for the project. HSBC's Amanah Islamic banking product was just launching in the area, so the mosque shifted its account to that bank and was able to raise the £1.5 million needed to complete the project. Construction duly recommenced and was completed in 2008, when the mosque opened (Fig 6.39).

Fig 6.39
Interior of the main prayer hall of Sheffield Islamic Centre, showing the mezzanine women's gallery on the right and the dome above.
[DP143327]

Conclusion

Sheffield Islamic Centre marks a shift in the way grass-roots community mosques were procured for two key reasons. First, great consideration was given to selecting the appropriate designer as the person who would deliver the aesthetic vision of the commissioners. As with the other mosques described in this chapter, the design was conceived as a complete Islamic building, without any formal reference to local architectural languages, and it was one of the new wave of 21st-century mosques built in this way.

Second, the building was procured by a British-born Muslim generation, and again this was a new phenomenon in the demographic of those commissioning mosques. The organisational and aspirational culture of the commissioners represented a step change from the first-generation immigrants who had been building post-war mosques up to this date. This group had successful examples of mosques in Britain to refer to, which was a factor in determining a brief for the new mosque. Quality, user experience and design became criteria for directing how the mosque should be built, with the emphasis not solely on the establishment of a space for prayer. This generational shift also brought more definite ideas on aesthetics and architecture through which a more conscious connection with an Islamic heritage was sought.

5 Northolt Bohra Mosque (Masjid-ul-Husseini), Rowdell Road, Northolt, Middlesex, 2010

The Bohra religious community of London traces its scriptural and cultural roots to Fatimid Egypt. It was there in the 11th century that the Mustali sect of Shia Islam emerged from a split in the ruling Fatimid class. The contest was over which of two sons, Al-Mustali and Nizar, would succeed their father, the Caliph Al-Muntasir, who died in 1094. Those followers who accepted Al-Mustali formed the Mustali sect, while those following Nizar became known as the Nizaris, from whom the Nizari Ismailis descend (*see* p 148). When Fatimid rule eventually came to an end in Egypt in 1171, the Mustali branch relocated and survived in Yemen. Mustali belief is that the caliph's grandson and successor as spiritual leader, Abu'l-Qasim al-Tayyib, was taken into Occultation (hiding) at a young age, but that he remains alive and will return at a divinely appointed time. In the interim, the community is led by a lineage of religious leaders known as the Dai.[36]

From the 11th century, Mustali missionaries had been gaining a foothold in India, via the trading ports in the north-western state of Gujarat. The Indian converts became known as the Bohras, a term that is a loose translation of the Gujarati term *vahaurau*, meaning trader. By the 16th century the Bohra community in Gujarat was substantial and the centre of Mustali power had moved from Yemen to Sidhpur, a town in north Gujurat. By the late 16th century a split had occurred between Da'ud ibn Qutb Shah and Sulayman, both claiming leadership of the community, which endures to this day without any significant dogmatic differences. The followers of Da'ud became known as the Dawoodi Bohras and remained in India, while the Sulaymani seat of power was in Yemen.[37] In the 1920s the headquarters of the Dawoodi Bohra community moved to Bombay (now known as Mumbai), where it remains.

Prompted by the Rajputana famine of 1869, Dawoodi Bohra traders started to migrate along the shipping routes from Gujarat to East Africa. The Bohras travelled with the Malabari Arabs, settling first in Madagascar and Mombasa before starting to move inland during the 20th century. After World War II young East African Indians were encouraged to study in the UK, and as they held British Colonial passports a pattern of immigration began that continued through to the 1980s. Within the last 30 years, Bohra immigration has also occurred directly from the communities of India and Pakistan, to constitute a community in Britain that now stands at around 3,500 members. This community is served by seven Bohra mosques, located in Birmingham, Bradford, Leicester, Manchester and London (where there are three).[38]

In the 1970s Dr Sayedna Mohammed Burhanuddin, the Dai (spiritual leader) of the Dawoodi Bohras from 1967 until his death in 2014, made his first visit to London. This would have given much moral support to the newly arriving Bohra immigrants who had begun settling in the city. It was on this visit that the Dai initiated the idea of starting a community centre, and a former church on Lillie Road in the west London district of Fulham was purchased and converted into the first mosque and community centre for the Dawoodi Bohra in Britain. Elementary alterations were carried out to enable the building to

perform in its new role, and it served community functions as well as being a place for congregational prayer.

With new and increased migration of members of the Bohra communities from South Asia, as well as continued migration from East Africa, the London Bohra community grew rapidly and the place of worship at Lillie Road proved too small. In 1980 the Bohra community purchased a former Jewish boys' club in nearby Hanwell, with a view to establishing a larger centre. The site was surrounded by privately owned semi-detached houses, and this new religious and community centre caused considerable objections, to the point where the local authority closed the premises under the Control of Pollution Act 1974 – the objections being that there were 'amplified chanting, the dumping of rubbish and car parking difficulties'.[39] With a larger site required for a Bohra community that continued to expand, and local opposition, the Bohra sought the assistance of Ealing Council (the local authority) in finding a site for a purpose-built facility. In 1986 Ealing identified a former industrial site, known as the Sadia site, on the edge of an industrial estate in the district of Northolt that had been vacant for five years. The Bohra were invited to purchase this site, which they did, selling their current site at Lillie Road to the council.

London's Dawoodi Bohras called on the services of Aliasger Jivanjee, an architect based in Karachi and himself a Dawoodi Bohra. He had gained renown among the community for having designed a series of community buildings throughout the diaspora. As a child, Jivanjee, along with his parents, had been among the wave of immigrants from Tanzania to the UK. He completed his architectural education at the Polytechnic of Central London and went on to work with the US practice SOM on the Hajj Terminal in Jeddah for a year before spending the next three years working under Hassan Fathy in Cairo. With Fathy, one of his projects was the restoration of the Al-Hakim Mosque, the 10th-century Cairo mosque which is one of the great monuments of Islamic and Fatimid architecture. From here Jivanjee started to work on educational and community buildings for the Bohra community in Surat and Karachi, and through these projects settled in Karachi and established his practice.

Jivanjee's design concept for the Northolt Mosque was rooted in the principles of Fatimid architecture, which he considers as being the root of the Bohra literary and architectural

Fig 6.40
A view across the mosque car park of one of the two terraces of houses that were built as part of the mosque development at Northolt. The houses are occupied by congregants, and have doors in the rear garden wall into the mosque site. Housing is an integral part of the complex and continues the tradition of creating a mahalla (neighbourhood or community).
[DP195267]

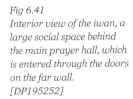

Fig 6.41
Interior view of the iwan, a large social space behind the main prayer hall, which is entered through the doors on the far wall.
[DP195252]

heritage, a connection that is pursued in the 'modern culture and lifestyle of the community'. For Jivanjee it is through contemporary community buildings that the Fatimid tradition can be 'revitalised to retain its continuity for future generations'.[40]

The guiding principle for the Northolt site was that the mosque should be part of a *mahalla* (a neighbourhood or community), and should not stand alone as an independent facility. With the Sadia site being within an industrial estate and already separated from residential areas of any kind, let alone areas where Bohra communities resided in any density, it was proposed that 22 houses would also be constructed on the site, so enabling the mosque to 'generate' its own community. Accordingly, the plan of the site developed with the houses arranged in two terraces on the south-western and north-western perimeters and the mosque building set behind them, within the site and oriented towards the Qibla (Fig 6.40).

The proposal received planning permission in July 1987 and a protracted period of fundraising began. Construction took time, but the project was complete by 2010.

The mosque itself is designed around three main organising elements that are arranged in sequence: the ceremonial entrance portico, the *iwan* (enclosed courtyard) and the *bait-us-salat* (prayer hall). A requirement of Bohra belief is that the prayer hall must be built on solid earth without any buildings or services such as pipework beneath. A large *iwan* serves as a community hall between the entrance and the *bait-us-salat*. It rises the full height of the building and is lit with three octagonally pyramidal rooflights, perhaps alluding to domes (Fig 6.41). This central enclosed courtyard is galleried at its upper level, off which are located a series of classrooms for children's religious instruction. The Bohra emphasis on communality is exemplified with a large kitchen and dining area in the basement directly underneath the *iwan*, known as the *mawaid*. During religious gatherings the centrality of communal eating is enacted in this space, with several attendees at a time eating from a number of thalis (shared large dishes). These religious and social spaces are laid out over four floors, and the floor plans show how this conceptual arrangement has been achieved (Figs 6.42–6.45).

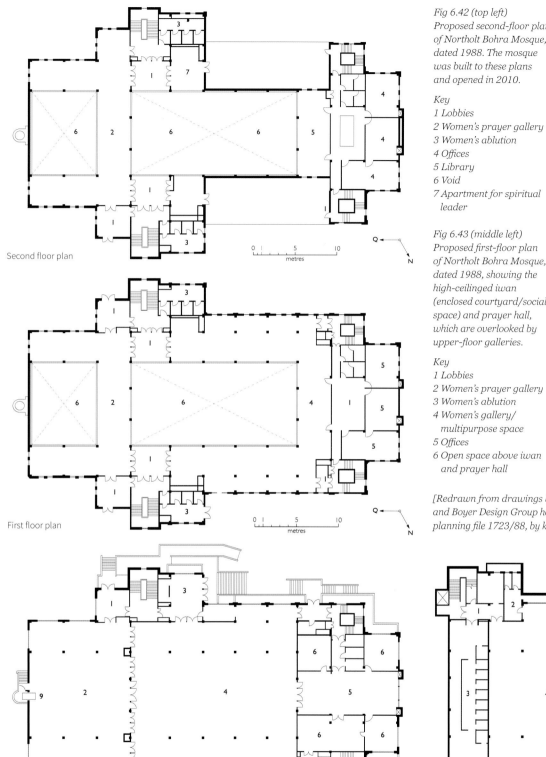

Second floor plan

First floor plan

Ground floor plan

Fig 6.42 (top left)
Proposed second-floor plan
of Northolt Bohra Mosque,
dated 1988. The mosque
was built to these plans
and opened in 2010.

Key
1 Lobbies
2 Women's prayer gallery
3 Women's ablution
4 Offices
5 Library
6 Void
7 Apartment for spiritual
  leader

Fig 6.43 (middle left)
Proposed first-floor plan
of Northolt Bohra Mosque,
dated 1988, showing the
high-ceilinged iwan
(enclosed courtyard/social
space) and prayer hall,
which are overlooked by
upper-floor galleries.

Key
1 Lobbies
2 Women's prayer gallery
3 Women's ablution
4 Women's gallery/
  multipurpose space
5 Offices
6 Open space above iwan
  and prayer hall

Fig 6.44 (bottom left)
Proposed ground-floor plan
of Northolt Bohra Mosque,
dated 1988, showing how
the main prayer hall (2)
combines with the iwan (4)
to create a large space for
prayer and gathering.

Key
1 Women's entrance
2 Men's main prayer hall
  (bait-us-salat)
3 Men's main entrance lobby
4 Enclosed courtyard used
  as multipurpose hall (iwan)
5 Ceremonial entrance hall
6 Offices
7 Burial shrine
8 Entrance lobby
9 Mihrab

Fig 6.45 (below)
Proposed basement floor plan
of Northolt Bohra Mosque,
dated 1988, dominated by
an open-plan dining hall and
large kitchen.

Key
1 Lobbies
2 Women's WC
3 Men's ablution
4 Dining area (mawaid)
5 Kitchen

[Redrawn from drawings by Aliasger Jivanjee & Associates
and Boyer Design Group held in the London Borough of Ealing
planning file 1723/88, by kind permission of Aliasger Jivanjee]

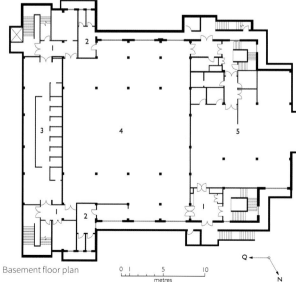

Basement floor plan

During construction of the mosque complex, Amatullah Aisaheba, the wife of the Dai, passed away while visiting London. She was buried in a specially designated room alongside the main prayer hall, and this mausoleum has duly become a place of Bohra pilgrimage. Mausoleums to spiritual guides are common in South Asia and across the Muslim world and have an elaborate and significant architectural history, but this is a type that has not translated to Britain in the same way that the mosque has. The shrine in the Masjid-ul-Husseini, therefore, is perhaps the first Muslim expression of this type in Britain, and potentially a precursor of more to come as the first generation of spiritual leaders who have settled in Britain begin to pass away.

The organisation of the building follows that of Fatimid architectural principles, and so cements the link between the contemporary Bohra community and its spiritual roots. The building's functions are further expressed in its external form, so it reads as a heavily massed front section with a monumental entrance portico, and a slimmer *iwan* middle portion, which widens again at the south-eastern, Qibla, end to accommodate the prayer halls. This results in a tripartite arrangement also characteristic of Fatimid architecture. Two short minarets are placed on either side of the prayer hall block, which are formed from two tiers of rectangular towers, each topped with a balconied, domed 'kiosk'. The minarets are derived from the Mosque of Al-Juyushi, built in the 11th century on a hill overlooking the cemeteries of Cairo (Fig 6.46). Jivanjee became familiar with this Fatimid structure while working in the city and, impressed by the presence of the medieval Cairene mosque on its hilltop location, sought to bring this feature to Northolt.

Three materials are used in the exterior facing of the mosque: red sandstone, buff sandstone and a yellow stock brick. The buff sandstone is a

Fig 6.46
South-west side elevation of Northolt Bohra Mosque, showing one of the two minarets inspired by medieval Cairene tomb architecture.
[DP195265]

direct reference to the Al-Hakim Mosque, which is faced in the same. The red sandstone was requested by the planners in order to break up the massing of the building; it is used on the minarets as well as on the ceremonial entrance portico that rises the full height of the front façade. The yellow stock brick is used on the central *iwan* section, and again can be read as a way of connecting the building to a local materiality and context, as the houses surrounding the mosque have been faced with the same brick.

Jivanjee makes the point that Fatimid decoration is very important to contemporary Bohra architecture and design,[41] and this is carried through at Northolt in the clean lines and bold Kufic calligraphic script, both in the writing of '*Allah*' over the main entrance door and in the inscription above the mihrab. The monumental entrance portal is also distinctly Fatimid in concept, with a large pointed arch resting on columns, all formed from red sandstone block-

work (Fig 6.47). All windows are round-arched and articulated with stone surrounds, those on the ground floor being larger and so exhibiting the taller storey height. A decorated red sandstone parapet follows the roofline, serving to tie the distinct forms of the building together.

Internally the halls are fairly plainly decorated, with moulded classical pilasters, cornices and panelling embellishing the structural elements. The main prayer hall rises the full three storeys of the building, with two upper galleries which are used as a women's prayer area overlooking the main hall. These galleries are fronted with balustrades of carved teak (Fig 6.48). The mihrab is again kept quite plain, being little more than the whitewashed wall with a round-arched opening decorated with geometric patternwork surrounds (Fig 6.49). The use of classical articulation, the teak balconies and the gold-painted decoration on white walls are characteristics that can also be seen in the

Fig 6.47
Main elevation of Northolt Bohra Mosque, showing the full-height entrance portico in red sandstone.
[DP195263]

Fig 6.48
View across the
main prayer hall,
with the men's area
on the ground floor
and women's
galleries above.
[DP195256]

Bohra mosques of Gujarat.[42] This influence on the interiors from traditional Bohra mosques in India, juxtaposed with the Fatimid-inspired exterior massing and styling, gives this building an idiosyncratic character that is a result of its Indian cultural roots combined with its Cairene ideological roots.

The 22 terraced houses to the north-western and south-western perimeter of the site are vernacular in style with no religious or Islamic articulation, instead employing stock brick, tiled pitched roofs and timber windows. Jivanjee explains this as a conscious decision, and one that the planners encouraged, to enable the perimeter buildings of the site to speak a more parochial language, so leaving the mosque hidden away behind this vernacular screen to celebrate the 11th-century North African roots of its community.[43]

Conclusion

When it opened in 2010, the Masjid-ul-Husseini at Northolt was unique for a number of reasons. First, it was the religious centre of a denomination that was not only a minority within the wider UK population, but also a minority within the British and indeed global Muslim community. The Shia Bohra are also distinct in that they constitute an ethnic group as well as a religious group, which is unusual in the spectrum of Muslim denominations, where different persuasions may be regionally dominant but are very seldom, if ever, specific to one ethnic group.

The migration pattern of the Shia Bohra was different to that of the majority of post-war South Asian immigrants in that they arrived in Britain from East Africa from largely entrepreneurial backgrounds and formed business communities; the majority of South Asian immigrants originated from rural backgrounds, and settled into industrial and working-class neighbourhoods. As a result, of this, and the sheer fact that their numbers were, and remain, relatively small, the Shia Bohra did not consolidate into residential clusters, as some other Muslim communities did. Instead, the Bohra moved their religious facility from place to place around west London, accessible to the dispersed community, before finding a permanent home in Northolt.

The Northolt site, on the edge of the industrial estate and suburban housing and alongside the Grand Union canal, was in danger of being isolated from the community, anathema to the traditional concept of the mosque embedded within a dense and close-knit Bohra *mahalla*.

Fig 6.49
The mihrab in the main men's prayer hall is a curtained opening in the Qibla wall.
[DP195257]

What the Northolt complex does to counter this isolation is to create a neighbourhood by encircling the mosque with houses, resided in by members of the Bohra community, with each house having a direct link from its small rear garden into the mosque enclosure. Unlike most, if not all, other mosque sites, the Masjid-ul-Husseini is a mixed-use religious and residential development that creates a self-sufficient and enclosed religious neighbourhood.

The Masjid-ul-Husseini marks a further departure from British mosques of the late 20th century in that its design is a conscious attempt to create an architectural and cultural link with the community's origins in 11th-century Fatimid Cairo. Aliasger Jivanjee has deliberately introduced an architectural language that is either a literal translation of Fatimid motifs, or a variation of them. The architectural lineage of the mosque serves to symbolise, and therefore reinforce, a religio-cultural lineage and continuity. It is notable that the Bohra mosques of India do not display this adherence to Fatimid form, and are instead more Mughal influenced, or follow local vernacular building styles. This Indian influence was transported to the Bohra mosques in East Africa, so expressing the ethnic heritage of the migrant community. The 'Fatimidisation' of the Bohra mosque is therefore something that is happening in the contemporary Bohra diaspora, including recent projects designed by Jivanjee for the US, Kenya and Singapore as well as Northolt. Jivanjee has explained that he has introduced the Fatimid minaret from the Mosque of Al-Juyushi into the Bohra mosques that he is designing.[44]

In its materiality, therefore, the mosque is a complex representation of the confluence of the Bohra ethnic heritage and religio-cultural ideals. The Indian-inspired interiors refer to a heritage that is temporally and experientially closer, while the Fatimid form and exterior detailing reconnect the community with its religious and existential origins. It may be that this connection to origins has become more prescient due to the migrations of the Bohra. The first of these was the migration of members of the Bohra community from their home in Gujarat through the late 19th and early 20th centuries to East Africa, and then from East Africa to Britain from the 1970s. Without emphasis on its origins in architecture, the culture of the Bohra, as a small minority community, might be under threat, so it is through the architecture of the mosque and residential complex that the Bohra attempt to pass on and maintain their culture and traditions.

6 Jame Masjid, Asfordby Street, Spinney Hills, Leicester, 2010

The Spinney Hills area of Leicester, just over a mile east of the city centre, has a 71 per cent South Asian population, of which approximately 50 per cent are Muslim. Although religious and ethnic demography varies across the city, Leicester remains the most multicultural place in Britain, where almost 40 per cent of the population was non-White in 2001. The eastern inner-city suburbs of Leicester are streets of densely packed terraced housing, interspersed with sizeable industrial sites. The textile industries located here drew migrants to settle in the area, as current demographics show. The site of the Jame Mosque is one such post-industrial location, having originally been industrial premises flanked by a terrace of houses and a small public square (Figs 6.50 and 6.51).

In the late 1970s local Muslims purchased a building in Asfordby Street that had been part of the Imperial Typewriting Company and converted it into a mosque. Their aim was for the mosque to serve the existing Muslim community from South Asia and East Africa and to accommodate community growth as immigration continued. Today the mosque is attended by around 400 to 500 people each daily prayer, which swells to 2,500 for the Friday prayer. East African Muslims were arriving in the 1970s and joining an existing South Asian Muslim community who had been settling in Leicester since the 1960s. The majority of Indian Muslims had migrated from Gujarat.

In the process of the conversion, the existing building was partially demolished, along with an adjacent terraced house owned by the mosque, to make way for a new mosque in due course. A first redevelopment proposal in 2008 was designed by the local firm Apt Design, who concentrated on building up the Asfordby Street elevation with decoration and motifs, leaving the rest of the existing building with modest interventions. After this scheme gained planning permission in October 2008,[45] the mosque committee was dissatisfied, feeling that its new building could be more ambitious. Members were familiar with the new architecture of the United Arab Emirates, and its demonstrativeness impressed them. After making some enquiries, an architectural practice was found in Sharjah, in the UAE. The practice, Architectural Academic Office, was a branch of a firm originating in Cairo. An example of their particular expertise could be seen in one of their completed projects, the Al Noor Mosque in Sharjah, which was designed as a replica of the Blue Mosque in Istanbul. Such examples of their work led the Jame committee to decide that the practice had suitable skills and experience to turn the Jame Mosque into a landmark with a visual identity befitting a major mosque. After initial brief and concept discussions in Sharjah, an architect travelled to the Leicester site before starting the design work in earnest. The approved scheme was worked up so that the decorations and ornamentation could be enhanced and refined. The mosque was keen that the materials and colours of the new building should fit in with the local context, so the neutral colour scheme and muted materiality of stone was chosen as a way of blending with the surroundings, in preference to the reflective or bolder materials such as marble that the architects were more used to.

There were several designs for each of the mosque elements before the final schemes were chosen. The mosque committee referred to literature on traditional Islamic architecture, and particularly mosques that had been built in the Emirates, as inspiration for the Jame design scheme.

Following a relatively quick construction period for a mosque project, suggesting a smooth fundraising effort, the mosque opened in 2010.

Fig 6.50
Leicester's Jame Mosque,
seen along Baggrave
Street, stands as a
landmark in a low-rise
residential neighbourhood.
[DP137460]

Fig 6.51
The Jame Mosque as
seen from Atkinson Street:
traditional Islamic
architecture sits within a
19th-century residential
townscape.
[Author]

Fig 6.52
YYM Services' 2008
proposed floor plans
for the Jame Mosque.
YYM Services were
the project engineers
implementing AAO's
designs on site. The
first-floor plan (top)
shows classrooms
arranged off a
central corridor with
a common meeting
room at the end. The
ground-floor plan
(bottom) shows how
the main prayer hall
occupies as much
space as possible,
with the main
entrance hall to the
left of the prayer hall,
accessed from
Asfordby Street.
[By kind permission
of YYM Services Ltd]

First floor plan

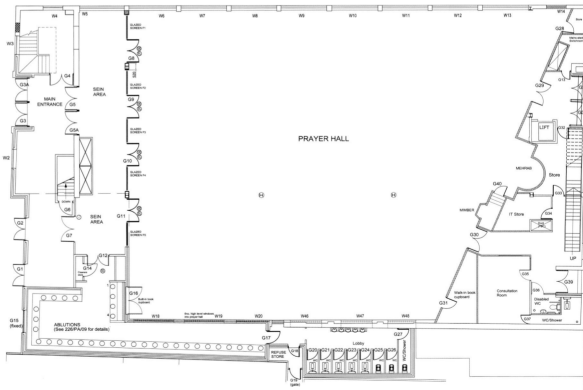

Ground floor plan

The new mosque is distinctly Fatimid in its styling, evoking the architecture of medieval Cairo. Architectural Academic Office employed a number of Egyptian architects, which may go some way to explain the Fatimid influence. As the two-storey building was built on the partially demolished foundations of the former industrial building, the axis of the prayer hall remains the same and the prayer lines are therefore obliquely aligned within (Fig 6.52). Internally the mosque is carefully and lavishly decorated (Fig 6.53). Marble-inlaid cladding faces the walls and columns. The mihrab is clad in marble with a pointed-arch-shaped recess for the imam and flanking walls lined with bands of alternating coloured marble, a characteristic of Fatimid styling (Fig 6.54). The ceiling of the main prayer hall is made up of a series of panels that are aligned towards the Qibla, so mitigating the fact that the building is not properly aligned. On the first floor there is a meeting room and classrooms are arranged off a central corridor (Fig 6.55).

Minarets rise on each of the four corners and are square up to the first balcony above the main building parapet line, from where they continue

Fig 6.53
The entrance lobby of the Jame Mosque, with the decorated doors to the men's main prayer hall. [Author]

Fig 6.54
The mihrab in the main prayer hall of the Jame Mosque. The minbar is built into the wall and located to the right, with a concealed entrance. [Author]

Fig 6.55
One of the first-floor
classrooms of the Jame
Mosque.
[Author]

Fig 6.56 (below)
The Jame Mosque spans a
residential block between
Baggrave Street (on the
left of this image) and
Asfordby Street (on the
right of this image).
[Author]

Fig 6.57 (below right)
The main entrance to
the Jame Mosque on
Asfordby Street: two
minarets flank a large
entrance portico over
which is placed a dome.
[Author]

parepets are decorated with traditional battle-ments (Fig 6.56). Full-height entrance porticos adorn the street fronts to north and south (Fig 6.57 and *see* Fig 8.11).

Conclusion

As with the other mosques in this chapter, the Jame Mosque overtly and completely signals itself as Islamic through a replication of traditional Islamic architecture. The degree to which design was important is shown in the fact that the com-missioners travelled overseas to source what they felt was the required expertise. This is a building where the quality of design and execution was fundamental to how it communicated its mission and purpose. Each element was coordinated, from interior design to the external treatment. This is one of the new generation of mosques since 2001 where what is understood to be a fully Islamic idiom is deployed with very few concessions to local architectural style and language.

as octagonal and then fluted circular sections. The tops are adorned with ovoid pinnacles, reprising the late 15th-century Kait Bey Mosque in Cairo. Towards the front of the mosque there is a dome, which again follows Fatimid form and is characteristically patterned with raised-profile latticework. Along the flank wall facing the public space a full-height columnar arcade is broken by a patterned storey band and the

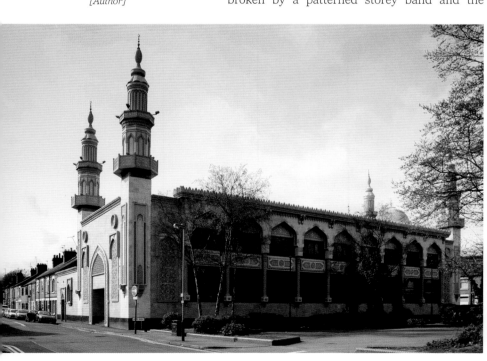

7 Al-Jamia Suffa-Tul-Islam Grand Mosque (Bradford Grand Mosque), Horton Park Avenue, Little Horton, Bradford, 2014

This imposing landmark mosque is set within a zone of parkland, playing fields and terraced housing on the edge of the Little Horton district of Bradford, south-west of the town centre and where the city's first house mosque on Howard Street can also be found (*see* pp 59–62).

Little Horton's religious diversity has a long history, with a large number of religious dissenters having settled in the area – the first Presbyterian meeting house in the area was recorded in 1688. During the late 19th century German cloth merchants arrived and established a chapel on Great Horton Road. After World War II, Eastern European immigrants established communities in the area, followed by large numbers of immigrants from South Asia from the 1950s. By 2001, 42 per cent of the population was of Pakistani or Bangladeshi origin.[46]

The land on which the mosque stands was the site of a disused railway line and a railway station that had operated until the 1950s, adjacent to the Horton Park Cricket ground. It was acquired by the Suffa-Tul-Islam religious organisation from the council in late 1998, with a symbolic foundation stone being laid in January 1999. Planning permission was obtained in October 1999 and building work proper started in 2002.

Suffa-Tul-Islam is a Sunni Sufi religious mission that traces its origin from the Prophet Muhammad, through historic lineages of teaching known as the Qadiri and Naqshbandi traditions. According to this understanding, traditional Islamic knowledge was passed down through a continuous chain of *ijaza* (permissions), through spiritual guides known as sheikhs. The mission was started in 1850 by Sheikh Mohamed Hayaat in Tangrot, a small fishing town on the border of Pakistan and Kashmir, now under the Mangla dam. After this the mission split, with half moving to Dangri, further up the mountains in Kashmir, and the other half south to Punjab. The mission moved to the UK in 1983 when a descendant of Sheikh Hayaat, Sheikh Mohammed Habib Ur Rehman, arrived in Bradford. He now serves as the spiritual leader of the movement, with his base in a former textile mill in Shearbridge Road, Bradford, just

over a mile from the new mosque in Horton Park Avenue. The centre in Shearbridge Road serves as a school, where students train to become Islamic scholars, and a mosque. While the main headquarters is in Bradford, Suffa-Tul-Islam has influence in five or six countries, including Belgium, the Netherlands, the UAE and Pakistan. It is expected that the chain of teaching and spiritual knowledge will continue in Bradford.[47]

Little Horton was one of three sites in Bradford that the Suffa-Tul-Islam organisation was considering when seeking land for a purpose-built mosque. The need to expand was precipitated by a growing Muslim community and increasing attendance at the Shearbridge Road centre, and the aspiration to implement new services and to offer a leadership role as an 'integrated Islamic establishment'.[48] Alongside prayer space, the organisation wanted the new mosque to provide religious schooling, supplementary schooling, adult learning and extensive women's provision for religious, social and educational needs.

This is the second mosque that the group has built, the first being the Bilal Mosque in Leeds in the 1990s (*see* pp 170–4). Atba Al-Samarraie was the architect for the Bilal Mosque, and the organisation approached him again to design the new building in Bradford. Suffa-Tul-Islam wanted a building that would 'look like a mosque, that was iconic, that stood out and said I am a mosque'. As far as they were concerned, most of the mosques in the UK at the time did not look the way mosques should.[49]

Al-Samarraie presented the organisation with a watercolour image of an imposing new mosque, complete with domes and minarets resplendent in a pink-red sandstone. The concept was well received, and agreed as the basis for the new design. It was intended that the red sandstone would be sourced from Scotland, but the colour turned out not to be the correct shade of pink. Eventually the mosque sourced the colour it wanted from Agra in India, and representatives travelled there to approve the samples and place the order. While in Agra the mosque members found some traditional screens in stone patternwork and were so impressed with them that they directed that they should be used for the balconies of the minarets.

To research mosque design, Suffa-Tul-Islam members visited other mosques in the Midlands and north of England, including some of Al-Samarraie's other mosques, and then formulated their own brief. They were heavily involved in devising the internal layouts, while leaving the overall external details to the architect. As construction took a long time, new design ideas could be introduced as they were conceived; these were largely confined to the detailing and patternwork. For example, the 99 names of Allah, along the parapet in decorated tiles, were a later design detail agreed by the mosque.

With building work taking place as funds were collected in seven phases, over more than a decade, the mosque eventually opened in 2014. It was a principle of the mosque that no money should be borrowed for its construction, and

*Fig 6.58
Al-Samarraie's first-floor plan (c 2001) of the Suffa-Tul-Islam Grand Mosque, showing the large men's and women's prayer halls with the classrooms to their left. [Reproduced by kind permission of Al-Samarraie Archi-Structure – Copyright]*

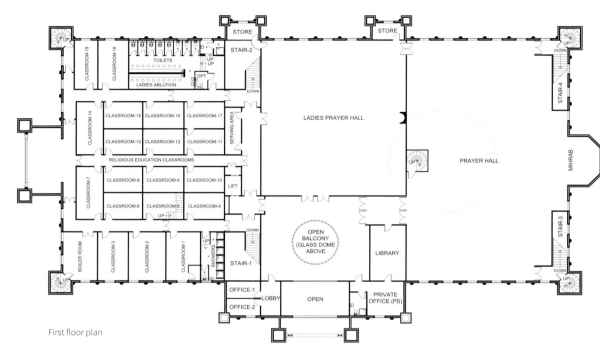

First floor plan

*Fig 6.59
Al-Samarraie's ground-floor plan (c 2001) of the Suffa-Tul-Islam Grand Mosque, showing the large men's and women's prayer halls arranged on the centre and right side of the plan, and ablutions and dining on the left. There are two major entrances to the building, one on the south-west façade which faces onto the road, and the other on the north-west façade fronting onto the mosque car park, which leads through the ablution areas. [Reproduced by kind permission of Al-Samarraie Archi-Structure – Copyright]*

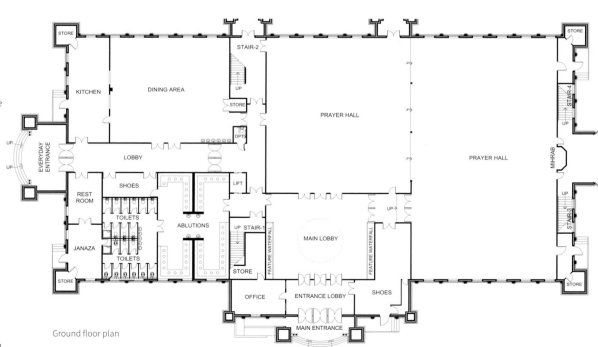

Ground floor plan

Fig 6.60
The Suffa-Tul-Islam Grand Mosque as it is seen when approached from the south-east along Horton Park Avenue. The mihrab projection can be seen on the south-eastern façade rising up its full height, and the triple domes and multiple minarets are also visible.
[DP143565]

also that the building should be an incremental process, reflecting the efforts made in procuring the building and also an exercise in *sabr* (patience) – a key Muslim value.[50]

The presence of the mosque is enhanced by the fact that it stands in a relatively open area of Little Horton with no buildings around it, and this also makes it unusual as mosques in the UK are usually found within urban neighbourhoods. It is a large rectangular building, with a short side aligned to the Qibla (Fig 6.58 and 6.59), and stands three storeys high to the parapet. It has a tall minaret on each corner, and entrance porticos on three sides, with a projecting mihrab niche on the south-eastern elevation taking the form of a five-sided niche and rising the full height of the building (Fig 6.60). The north-east and south-west entrance porticos are emphasised with a quartet of minarets, the inner pair smaller (Fig 6.61). The building hosts a total of

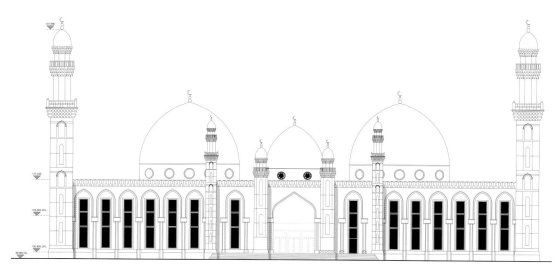

Fig 6.61
Al-Samarraie's c 2001 drawing of the south-west elevation fronting Horton Park Avenue. The mosque was built to these plans.
[Reproduced by kind permission of Al-Samarraie Archi-Structure – Copyright]

14 minarets – probably more than any other mosque in the country. Large green plastic domes adorn each side of the roof (Fig 6.62), with a third smaller dome, faceted with reflective bronze glass panels, over the main entrance (Fig 6.63).

Al-Samarraie states that his mosque designs are based on his childhood memories of Baghdad, and the Suffa-Tul-Islam Grand Mosque in Little Horton can be seen to reflect North African and Middle Eastern traditional forms. It is dominated by full-height entrance porticos and square minarets that continue to rise as hexagons after the first balcony, seemingly a combination of Fatimid and Abbasid styles (Fig 6.64). However, there is also a distinct Mughal flavour to the mosque, which is instilled in large part through its materials and also through some stylistic inflections. The façade panels of red Agra sandstone give the mosque a distinctively north Indian character (Fig 6.65). They are of the same material used for some of the most well-known Mughal landmarks, such as

the Red Fort and Jamma Masjid in Delhi, as well as Agra's own Red Fort. Further, the arches over the main entrance porticos are detailed with an ogee inflection, making them distinctly more Indian than the pointed window arches lining the elevations (Fig 6.66 and *see* Fig 6.1).

Conclusion

The Suffa-Tul-Islam Grand Mosque in Little Horton was a project of great ambition, both architecturally and institutionally. It marks a type of mosque establishment different from the majority of post-war mosques. Rather than a local community building – a mosque for itself and its local congregation – it is one of the centres of an organised mission, with clear religious objectives.

The commissioners of this mosque have intentionally sought an architectural language that, for them, replicates archetypes of traditional mosque design. Their aim has been to create a building that wholeheartedly reflects

Fig 6.62
The view from the top of the minaret on the northern corner of the Suffa-Tul-Islam Grand Mosque, showing the expanse of the building and the twin green domes, each of which contain meeting rooms. [Author]

Fig 6.63
The south-west façade of the Suffa-Tul-Islam Grand Mosque, fronting Horton Park Avenue. [DP143563]

what they identify as authentic Islamic heritage in a more accurate way than mosques in Britain have hitherto been able to do. This is a vision of the mosque as an architecture of uncompromising historicism, where its aesthetics are wholly located in those of centuries-old Muslim cultures from disparate global locations.

It was the ability of the Suffa-Tul-Islam organisation to access design expertise through Al-Samarraie, the quality of materials obtained from suppliers in India, and its own internal management and procurement procedures to co-ordinate in phases that allowed it to implement its vision for what a mosque should be in Britain, and how it should appear.

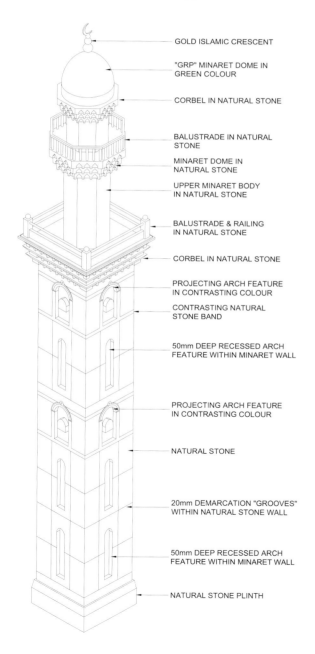

- GOLD ISLAMIC CRESCENT
- "GRP" MINARET DOME IN GREEN COLOUR
- CORBEL IN NATURAL STONE
- BALUSTRADE IN NATURAL STONE
- MINARET DOME IN NATURAL STONE
- UPPER MINARET BODY IN NATURAL STONE
- BALUSTRADE & RAILING IN NATURAL STONE
- CORBEL IN NATURAL STONE
- PROJECTING ARCH FEATURE IN CONTRASTING COLOUR
- CONTRASTING NATURAL STONE BAND
- 50mm DEEP RECESSED ARCH FEATURE WITHIN MINARET WALL
- PROJECTING ARCH FEATURE IN CONTRASTING COLOUR
- NATURAL STONE
- 20mm DEMARCATION "GROOVES" WITHIN NATURAL STONE WALL
- 50mm DEEP RECESSED ARCH FEATURE WITHIN MINARET WALL
- NATURAL STONE PLINTH

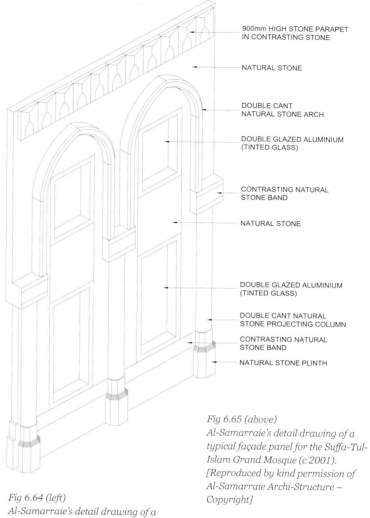

- 900mm HIGH STONE PARAPET IN CONTRASTING STONE
- NATURAL STONE
- DOUBLE CANT NATURAL STONE ARCH
- DOUBLE GLAZED ALUMINIUM (TINTED GLASS)
- CONTRASTING NATURAL STONE BAND
- NATURAL STONE
- DOUBLE GLAZED ALUMINIUM (TINTED GLASS)
- DOUBLE CANT NATURAL STONE PROJECTING COLUMN
- CONTRASTING NATURAL STONE BAND
- NATURAL STONE PLINTH

Fig 6.65 (above)
Al-Samarraie's detail drawing of a typical façade panel for the Suffa-Tul-Islam Grand Mosque (c 2001). [Reproduced by kind permission of Al-Samarraie Archi-Structure – Copyright]

Fig 6.64 (left)
Al-Samarraie's detail drawing of a typical minaret for the Suffa-Tul-Islam Grand Mosque (c 2001). [Reproduced by kind permission of Al-Samarraie Archi-Structure – Copyright]

Fig 6.66 (below)
Detail of the inscriptions over the south-west entrance to the Suffa-Tul-Islam Grand Mosque. [DP143567]

7

New narratives

The story of the mosque told so far describes how mosque establishment emerged from two phases of predominantly South Asian Muslim migration to Britain – before and after India's independence. Before India's independence a handful of mosques were built in Britain, mostly in port locations, to serve Muslim communities coalescing as a result of imperial trade and politics. Following World War II (and after India's independence and Partition), larger-scale migration from the wider Commonwealth was required to supply Britain's industry and service sectors, and this included significant numbers of Muslim immigrants from India and Pakistan who formed settled communities. These communities established mosques initially in converted buildings before going on to build new ones. The first wave of purpose-built, post-war mosques were effectively self-designed and built, reflecting the immediate symbolic needs of the communities that created them. Theirs was an architecture described as ambivalent or hybrid, in which Islamic idioms were combined with local vernacular forms, resulting in a visual language for mosques that oscillated between domestic and foreign in an improvised way.

By the turn of the 21st century the mosque in Britain had developed a visual language that was envisaged as being a more authentic replication of traditional Islamic form, and the attempts of late 20th-century mosques to combine local vernacular and Islamic styles seemed to have been supplanted by a new singular expression of Muslim identity. Mosques were now being designed by Muslim designers with experience in mosque architecture, either in Islamic countries or in Britain. In itself this indicates that commissioning communities were becoming more discerning about the quality and significance of Islamic design in their buildings. It also shows that communities were able to access levels of expertise previously unattainable, and that they made considerable efforts to source and select a designer who would deliver a mosque that would reinforce their sense of self-identity.

The shift can be seen as reflective of a series of social changes within Muslim communities in Britain. First, the skills base within these communities had expanded as labouring immigrants who settled in the earlier period of the 1950s and 1960s were joined by entrepreneurial and professional classes, particularly following the East African migration of the 1970s from countries such as Kenya, Tanzania, Malawi, Uganda and Zambia. Also, the earlier immigrants' children, who were born and educated in Britain, began to bring skills to their communities that enabled more professional forms of planning, organisation, procurement and decision-making. Sheffield Islamic Centre (*see* pp 188–94) is a prime example of this shift, where the children of steel workers were given the task of delivering the new mosque, and in their manner of doing so achieved a building which stands as a marker to the new phase of mosque architecture in Britain.

Both Sheffield and other related mosque designs are highly traditional in a way that may be intended as being more 'Islamically authentic'. The buildings are not only fully designed with reference to Islamic architectural histories before they are built, but are also executed in higher-quality materials and with a higher degree of craftsmanship than had been the case at earlier mosques. For example, Sheffield utilised new forms of brickwork, taking a vernacular English building material and fashioning it to convey Islamic identities, and for the Suffa-Tul-Islam Mosque in Little Horton, Bradford (*see* pp 207–11), the committee travelled to Agra to source the exact shade of pink sandstone wanted for the mosque, and during these travels brought back stone lattice balconies to be used on the minarets.

This search for architectural quality and authenticity may demonstrate a number of things. First, it may signal the greater financial security of the Muslim congregation, and an

Fig 7.1
The Shahporan Mosque, London.
[Author]

increased adeptness at fundraising. In turn, this may point to a community that is better organised and more able to negotiate the formal channels of building procurement, planning and finance. Second, the mosques also represent the emerging prominence of key British mosque designers, individuals who have tapped into the aspirations and expectations of mosque commissioners and who are able to encapsulate and deliver this through the representation of particular visual and material cultures.

The result has been a new type of historicism, where Islamic architectural history is replicated through direct references, in a more complete way than with the earlier phase of mosques. So, for example, the minaret at Northolt directly references a specific medieval Cairene mosque (Al-Juyushi) that has relevance to that Muslim denomination's history (*see* p 198). Edinburgh Central Mosque was designed as a series of classical Islamic historical references carefully composed into a building that manifests these references with a vernacular edge (*see* pp 175–9). Leicester's Jame Masjid is a carefully executed replication of Fatimid styling and patternwork (*see* pp 202–6). It seems that the increased ability of communities to access skills and capabilities has allowed them to pursue and implement what they envisage as a more authentically historic representation of the mosque in Britain.

By the end of the 20th century Muslim communities had become embedded within the fabric of Britain's social and cultural life, and had diversified in terms of ethnicity, age, language, social history, class, politics and religious outlook and forms of practice. The result was a diverse and vibrant British Muslim culture that identified with a common Muslim heritage. As the needs of these communities evolved, new mosques continued to be conceived to meet and reflect their aspirations. A series of mosque projects, some recently built and some still in progress, are presented here to consider how the next generation of mosques may develop, and how they will build on expressions of Muslim identity and architecture that the buildings of the last century have laid down.

Case studies

1 Lewisham Islamic Centre, Lewisham High Street, Lewisham, London, 2000
2 Shahporan Masjid and Islamic Centre, Hackney Road, Bethnal Green, London, 2014

3 Masjid Alhikmah and Community Centre, Nelson Street, Aberdeen (in progress, 2017)
4 North Harrow Community Centre (Salaam Centre), Station Road, North Harrow, Middlesex (in progress, 2017)
5 Cambridge Mosque, Mill Road, Romsey Town, Cambridge (in progress, 2017)

1 Lewisham Islamic Centre, Lewisham High Street, Lewisham, London, 2000

The Lewisham Islamic Centre has a notable history as it is the only mosque known in Britain to have been started by a woman. Dr Sabiha Saleem had graduated from the Osmania University in the Indian city of Hyderabad, and had spent some years in New York in the 1950s on medical training. After this, she intended to spend time gaining work experience in London before returning to Hyderabad. Dr Saleem, however, never returned to live in India, and instead married her husband Abdullah in London, settling in south-east London to run a GP practice.

By the mid-1960s she had two small children, who were growing up fast, and who are the older siblings of the present author. Dr Saleem and her husband were very conscious that their circle of Muslim friends and community was small and fragmented. Their concern was that if the next generation grew up without a sense of their Muslim heritage and religious awareness, they would lose touch with their identity and face unknown difficulties and an uncertain future.

The only Islamic facilities she could find were weekend religious classes at the Islamic Cultural Centre in Regent's Park, which had been a mosque since the mid-1940s (*see* pp 133–47). When it no longer became practical to make the 16-mile journey from her house to central London every week, Dr Saleem decided to start Islamic classes in her house for her children and a handful of other Muslim children of family friends, with one of the parents taking the classes. This type of arrangement continued through the late 1960s, providing some kind of teaching for the small number of children. In 1973 Dr Saleem heard of a religious teacher who was giving classes for children at his house in Streatham, still a 10-mile journey, but she found this the best arrangement for her children.

In the meantime, Dr Saleem and her husband were holding the Friday congregational prayer in the front room of their house in Bromley, where perhaps 10 to 15 people would attend, the imam being a local religious preacher. When numbers increased, they started to hire a local hall in Catford, where the Friday prayer was regularly held. With the help of her husband and a group of friends, she organised functions in hired halls celebrating religious auspicious days such as the *Mawlid* (the birthday of the Prophet Muhammad) and *Miraj* (his ascent to heaven). Gradually the group also initiated a Sunday school in a local church hall, where local children could benefit from religious and cultural classes as well as seeing themselves as part of a Muslim community.

In the late 1970s Dr Saleem first noticed that there was a considerable number of Muslim names in her local phonebook. The Muslim population was growing, but still there was no centre, and no mosque to serve them. She decided it was time to bring the community together and create an institution that would foster this. With the assistance of her husband, she wrote to all the Muslim names in the phone book inviting them to a meeting to discuss establishing a centre, and sent the letters by post or hand-delivered them herself.

With 400 letters sent, four people attended the meeting in Dr Saleem's house. Along with some of her family members, those present formed a community centre initiative. The chairman of the new Muslim organisation was an English convert from Kent, Eric Siddiqui, who had responded to Dr Saleem's call. Further meetings were held and incrementally more local Muslim residents became involved. The fledgling group contacted the Union of Muslim Organisations, the only umbrella group for Muslim community groups at the time, for advice on setting up an institution. On their advice a constitution was drafted, charity registration was obtained, and the Lewisham and Kent Islamic Centre was born.

While the group continued to organise events in local hired halls, it was now also looking for a building to become its base. In 1984 premises were found in the form of a family house at 336 Brownhill Road in Catford. Money was raised from the local Muslim community, and fund-raising trips were made to Regent's Park Mosque to raise donations from the congregation there, with Dr Saleem enlisting her children to carry donation boxes. Through such endeavour, funds were raised and the house purchased. After some basic alterations, this was to become the

first mosque in south-east London, and very quickly its congregation grew with the rapidly expanding local Muslim population. Dr Saleem remained as secretary of the Lewisham and Kent Islamic Centre, perhaps the only woman to date to hold such a position in a British mosque. The original founding committee remained in place, running the centre until the early 1990s when, with a growing congregation, the house became too small for the demands placed upon it, and larger premises were sought. Gradually the founding members of the mosque stepped down and were replaced by a new committee, and in 2000 a new location was found for the centre to move to where it could cope better with the increasing numbers of attendees.

This new premises was a former nightclub at the end of a shopping parade at 363–365 Lewisham High Street (Fig 7.2). The building provided a large room that became the prayer hall (Fig 7.3), and ancillary space that could serve as classrooms. The congregation quickly increased, until around 2,500 people were attending the Friday prayers and 100 to 250 each daily prayer. It is estimated that some 8,000 people have converted to Islam at the new mosque, and the convert community makes up around 30 per cent of the congregation.

Fig 7.2
The Lewisham Islamic Centre, facing onto Lewisham High Street. The mosque started as a conversion of a 1960s single-storey, red-brick building at the end of a shopping parade (left in this photo), and has gradually acquired the adjacent buildings in the block.
[DP153540]

The Lewisham Islamic Centre, as it became known, developed a series of community services targeting Muslim youth, keenly aware of the need to provide social support in inner-city London. A primary school was established, delivering the national curriculum as well as religious education to 62 pupils (Fig 7.4), along with a supplementary school for religious classes, with 300 children and 12 students of *hifz* (the traditional practice of memorising the Quran). In addition, the mosque set up football clubs, a Scout programme, swimming sessions, youth clubs, marriage counselling, legal services, and outreach and community cohesion projects.

Very soon the mosque was looking at developing its site to create more space and become a landmark building. The site was, however, restricted, and suitable expansion was proving difficult. Within a few years an adjacent building in the terrace came up for sale and the mosque instead dedicated its resources to acquiring it, intending to expand into it. In subsequent years, the mosque purchased each adjacent site as it became available, so that by late 2014 it had acquired all the properties in the terrace. With the extra space, the Islamic Centre was able to provide a bookshop, gym, travel agency and restaurant (Fig 7.5), so diversifying its methods of engagement with the Muslim community, and it was now able to start thinking of a comprehensive redevelopment as a long-term project.

With the prospect of the mosque becoming an urban landmark and a significant social centre now seeming achievable, ideas for the redevelopment of the site were drawn up by different designers. These proposals sought to replace the cluster of terraces with a new urban form, of a scale and design that would mark it as a local architectural landmark, and change the character of the streetscape. By 2014 two projects had been prepared, although neither had been taken forward owing to lack of sufficient funding. Instead, to meet the mosque's ongoing needs, a series of smaller alterations and additions were made to the complex of buildings. While such works met the mosque's immediate needs as they arose, the ambition remains for a landmark mosque and community centre to be built eventually.

Conclusion

Through realisation of its ambition to acquire and redevelop a site, and to provide purpose-built facilities from which to offer a range of services to the Muslim and wider community, the Lewisham Islamic Centre has secured its place as an indispensable local community organisation of significant impact. The centre is one of a number of institutions emerging in London and across the country, from humble beginnings, to provide religious, social, educational and commercial services at a regional level. The trajectory of the centre over the decades typifies the growth of those mosques that evolve into regional centres. Lewisham illustrates the step-by-step process of this growth, and indicates where the future may lie for such institutions.

2 Shahporan Masjid and Islamic Centre, Hackney Road, Bethnal Green, London, 2014

Makespace, the author's east London-based architectural practice, had been working on Muslim buildings for almost a decade by the time its first designed mosque, the Shahporan Masjid on east London's Hackney Road, was completed. The east London boroughs of Tower Hamlets and Hackney, on the borders of which the mosque is situated, have had a rich and varied history. The locale itself had been designated as the Hackney Road Conservation Area for its varied historic townscape, fine urban grain and layers of building types and styles.

Hackney Road forms one of the key routes from the City eastwards, through districts characterised by a mixture of working-class housing and light industry, interspersed with older town houses. The original Shahporan Mosque was formed through the conversion of 444 Hackney Road in 1996, a modest though handsome Grade II listed end-of-terrace residence dating from the early 19th century. The project of 2011 to 2014 involved refurbishment of the house mosque (Fig 7.6) and the construction of a new three-storey rear block, facing onto Treadway Street (Fig 7.7). This more than doubled the size of the mosque, with a new main prayer hall (Fig 7.8) and additional prayer and community spaces.

The new three-storey mosque brought a new building type to this historically layered and rich

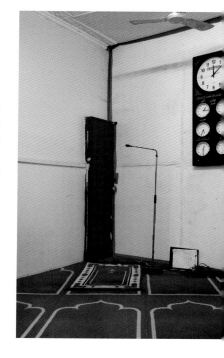

Fig 7.6
The temporary mihrab used at the Shahporan Mosque during the refurbishment and works on the new building. [DP147342]

Fig 7.7
The new Shahporan Mosque under construction, alongside the existing Grade II listed building, which was refurbished in 2011. The marquee at the front of the original building is a temporary prayer hall used during the building works (see Fig 1.15). [DP147336]

Fig 7.8
The mihrab in the
Shahporan Mosque's newly
built main prayer hall.
[Author]

Fig 7.9
The new Shahporan
Mosque building (right)
alongside the existing
Grade II listed terraced
house (left). The new
entrance has been placed
centrally to link the old and
new parts of the building.
[Author]

environment, a new typology which represented the most recent phase of East End migration and introduced a new set of visual references. The physicality of the mosque encapsulated this layered environment: the existing listed house was preserved and refurbished, complete with Victorian lettering carved into its flank wall, while the new building attached to it matched it in height and presence but signified the contemporary cultural and global changes that had brought it into being (Fig 7.9 and *see* Fig 8.12).

For us as the architects, this dense urban context meant that any new building on an infill site needed to be embedded into its environment, and by virtue of this have a dialogic relationship with its history and place. The aim for the mosque, a combination of old and new, was for it to be aware of its context and to belong to its place, while at the same time being a provocative presence signifying change and adaptation, reflecting London's culture as an ever-changing, fluid and dynamic urban and social matrix.

With this aim in mind, intact and literal historical references, as had characterised much of mosque architecture in post-war Britain, were not sufficient. These would have been an attempt

to locate the building in another mythic time and place, and they would ultimately have fallen short of the aesthetic standards required by any new building. However, abandonment of the visual tropes of Islam would also be a failing, as the reality of the mosque was that it had been initiated by diasporic Muslims who did identify with and draw comfort from narratives of religion and culture that were located outside the European world view.

The scheme, therefore, conceived the whole façade as a single sign, as the space in which these multiple narratives would take place. The façade was treated as a large pattern, the inspiration for which was tilework on a complex of palaces from 13th-century central Anatolia. However, unlike the historicist attempts of other recent mosques to replicate Islamic architecture literally, on the Shahporan Mosque the pattern is not re-created whole or intact, but is instead enlarged so that only its corner and parts of the top and side appear on the façade (Fig 7.10 and *see* Fig 7.1). The rest of the tile pattern has to be imagined as occurring outside the frame of the façade. In this way, the idea of history as something that can be preserved and replicated is replaced with the idea of history as a process, with imperfections and absences, where narratives which are temporally and geographically distant go through a process of re-creation each time they are invoked in a new time and place.

A metal mesh was applied on the main stone pattern to unify the façade into one composition and allow light to pass through the windows. This idea of a perforated screen relates to traditional *mashrabiya* fretwork, which is widespread in historic Islamic architecture (Figs 7.11 and 7.12). The pattern fretwork on the Shahporan Mosque is a replica of that found on the windows of the 1889 Woking Mosque (*see* pp 26–35). In this way, the visual language references another British mosque, so creating a dialogue within British Islamic history, and detaching it from reliance on more distant geographies.

Conclusion

The Shahporan Mosque is intended to present a careful choreography between the history of Muslim architecture in Britain, and cultural and identity needs. It is also a manifesto for a Muslim architecture that is rooted in its contemporary British context, physically and culturally, from where it claims both difference and belonging.

Fig 7.10
The façade and main entrance of the new Shahporan Mosque along Treadway Street.
[Author]

Fig 7.11 (below left)
The main prayer hall of the Shahporan Mosque, with the front windows looking through the metal lattice screen to the street.
[Author]

Fig 7.12 (below)
An upper-floor window in the new Shahporan Mosque building, with metal lattice screening.
[Author]

3 Masjid Alhikmah and Community Centre, Nelson Street, Aberdeen (in progress, 2017)

Makespace has been able to further its approach to new mosque architecture with a subsequent project for a new mosque in the northern Scottish city of Aberdeen. The first mosque in the city was established in 1978, and had been formed through the conversion of a former bank and three adjoining terraced houses. No external alterations were carried out to signify the building as a mosque, and internal alterations were also very limited, to the extent that the houses were not interconnected as might be expected, but remained separate, each accessed by its own front door. This made the building difficult to use as a

Fig 7.13
Artist's impression of the first proposal for the Alhikmah Mosque in 2012. [By kind permission of the Alhikmah Foundation]

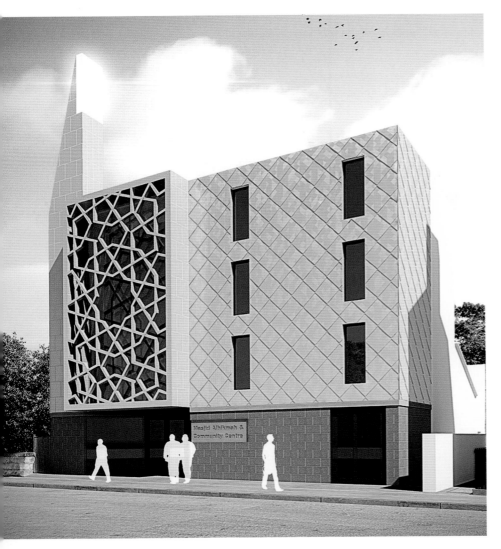

place of worship and hampered its development into an effective community centre. However, despite its limitations, which were exacerbated as the Muslim population grew, it was still the only mosque in the city 30 years later.

Since its emergence as an oil and gas centre in the 1960s, Aberdeen has developed into a cosmopolitan city, with a diverse Muslim community. Part of the reason for the lack of a new mosque was the transient nature of a large section of this Muslim population, many of whom were posted to Aberdeen for a few years from Muslim countries, or were studying in the highly regarded universities of the city, before returning home. However, by the turn of the 21st century, a significant Pakistani and Bangladeshi settled Muslim community had emerged, with second-generation Scottish Muslims rooted in Aberdeen. With growing instability in Muslim countries, more Arab and African migrants working in the oil industry also settled in the city, so further swelling the Muslim population and diversifying the community.

These demographic changes only intensified the pressure on the existing mosque, until eventually a group of the city's young Muslim professionals, frustrated at the lack of progress, decided to come together to form a completely new mosque that would cater for the needs and expectations of the Muslim community. The committee that formed in 2011 to deliver the new mosque was a reflection of the city's cosmopolitan character. It was set up by two Aberdonian Muslim brothers of Pakistani heritage, and its members comprised professionals working mostly in the oil and gas industries, hailing from countries such as Malaysia, Nigeria, Egypt and Pakistan.

A former warehouse on the edge of the city centre was acquired by a local business family in 2011 and pledged as the site for the new mosque. The Masjid Alhikmah organisation was duly formed and registered as a charity with a carefully drafted constitution and operating structure. The committee was keenly aware of the need to bring the city's Muslim population along with its vision for a new mosque, and so embarked on a sophisticated public relations and outreach programme, approaching the community and spreading the message of the mosque through carefully organised and executed strategies. The Alhikmah team used project management and marketing strategies borrowed from the commercial worlds in which its members operated. Threats were analysed, a brand identity was created, a website and promotional videos were produced and a complete vision of a new mosque was delivered to Aberdeen's Muslims along with a project programme, funding targets, milestones and a deliverable design.

Alhikmah selected Makespace as the project's architects on the basis of the practice's previous mosque work, in particular the design for the Shahporan Mosque in Bethnal Green. For Alhikmah, the vision of a contemporary mosque architecture as espoused and realised by Makespace delivered the message that the team wanted to promote – that Muslim architecture in Britain is contemporary and connected to its Muslim past, and that it reflects a Muslim identity that is British, modern and in dialogue with wider society.

The mosque itself was to be a former warehouse conversion with a front new-build element, a familiar mosque type. While interiors were carefully planned, they were to remain simple and practical. The façade was to be treated as the main signifier and identifier of the building and its identity, and it was here that the ethos of the founders was to be expressed.

The project started on site in late 2014 and the first phase, the building shell, was completed in late 2015. The mosque then stopped work and continued to fundraise before starting the internal fit-out. Once additional funds were in place, a new contractor was appointed for the next phase of the construction and work started on the internal fit-out in April 2017, with the aim of completing the whole project and opening the building in July 2017.

The design process that led to the final proposal was extensive, and a series of ideas for articulating the mosque's identity on the street front were worked through. The first significant proposal (in 2012) was for a three-storey building with a copper-clad façade, an arabesque pattern screen over a large window, and an angular minaret-style pinnacle (Fig 7.13). This scheme was considered too large and costly for the mosque, and perhaps also too exuberant for what was a relatively quiet residential street. The proposal was subsequently revised to present a two-storey building in a much more restrained visual language (Fig 7.14). This time granite cladding was to be used on the ground floor, to respond to the ubiquitous and characteristic use of granite in buildings in Aberdeen. Half of the façade would be taller than the rest of the building, and would carry a large Islamic pattern to act as a signifying element. After consultations through planning, this scheme was slightly revised to reduce the height of the patterned

Fig 7.14
The revised proposal for the Alhikmah Mosque that was submitted for planning permission in 2012. [By kind permission of the Alhikmah Foundation]

Masjid Alhikmah

Fig 7.15
The proposed design for
the Alhikmah Mosque that
eventually gained planning
permission in 2013. The
local authority had
required a reduction in
the height of the façade.
[© White Crow Studios Ltd,
reproduced by kind
permission of the Alhikmah
Foundation]

*Fig 7.15
The proposed design for
the Alhikmah Mosque that
eventually gained planning
permission in 2013. The
local authority had
required a reduction in
the height of the façade.
[© White Crow Studios Ltd,
reproduced by kind
permission of the Alhikmah
Foundation]*

*Fig 7.16
Detail of the front façade
of the Alhikmah Mosque,
showing the decorated
concrete façade panels with
individually made and
coloured ceramic stars.
[Author]*

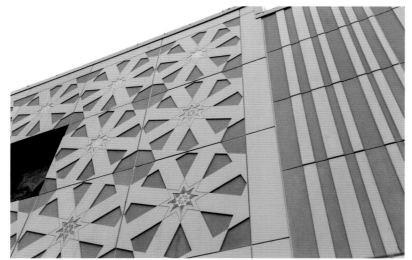

element of the façade (Fig 7.15). As executed, the single large pattern was also replaced with a series of tiles fabricated from GRC (glass reinforced concrete) with a repeated Islamic pattern (Fig 7.16). In the centre of each tile there is a ceramic star, each one individually made and coloured by the London-based ceramic artist Lubna Chowdhary. In this way the design sought to bring craftsmanship into the architecture of the mosque, to invoke the way that traditional Muslim architecture relied on artisanship in its decoration.[1]

The final mosque design (which received planning permission in 2013) departs from the use of conventional Islamic signifiers. There are no traditional symbols such as the dome and minaret, but instead the façade is an interplay of identifiably Islamic pattern and regular bands of granite, a material which characterises the city (Fig 7.17). The design creates a pattern rooted in Islamic tradition, but in which the influence of contemporary architecture can also be discerned, a subtle interplay of sources that points to the dialogue between cultures.

Conclusion

The Alhikmah Mosque differs from most mosques in that it is not a facility that has emerged organically from within a particular ethnic community, but instead it has been consciously set up and planned as a strategic response to a dire need, namely the lack of any kind of mosque development in the city for over 30 years. It is also different in there being a degree of patronage – the site was acquired by a local family of property developers, who then donated it to the mosque organisation. The mosque committee that formed to deliver the project is not based in a particular community with shared ethnicities or origins, but is instead a cosmopolitan collection of individuals who form a multicultural Muslim community.

This collaboration of individuals, the organising structure, the use of commercial-world strategies and the involvement of a patron also affected the design process and outcome. Rather than the aesthetics being dictated by a wide congregation, in the Aberdeen mosque the design represents the aspirations and ideals of the founding members. The design of the new mosque is also part of a wider discourse on social

Fig 7.17
The front façade of the
Alhikmah Mosque (under
construction), with granite
blocks at ground-floor
level to echo the vernacular
and familiar material in
Aberdeen, set alongside
a contemporary use of
concrete in the decorated
façade panels of the
first floor.
[Author]

positioning and identity. The founding group considered locality and place, alongside a recognition and expression of a Scottish Muslim identity, as core values to be embodied in the mosque aesthetic. The result is very different from the new historicist mosques built in the first decade of the 21st century. The Islamic identity of the mosque is signified primarily through the structuring of Islamic decoration within an overall modernist approach, and the proposed design interweaves this Muslim tradition with local materials and styling rather than seeking to replicate the aesthetics of an Islamic past.

4 North Harrow Community Centre (Salaam Centre), Station Road, North Harrow, Middlesex (in progress, 2017)

Set among the seemingly endless suburbs of North Harrow, amid nondescript rows of semi-detached houses thrown up for the burgeoning lower-middle classes of 20th-century London, is the centre for the Shia Ithna'ashari Community of Middlesex (SICM). It is housed in a series of single-storey prefabricated structures that once served as the West Harrow School. The school moved and the SICM rented the buildings from 1989, sharing the site with an Irish community centre and pub. Eventually the SICM was able to purchase the entire site from Harrow Council when it was put up for sale in 1990.

The Shia Ithna'ashari are communities of Shia Muslims originating in the Indian subcontinent, mainly in the states of Gujarat, Maharashtra, Rajasthan and Hyderabad. Following migratory patterns prevalent among communities on the west coast of India through the 19th century, many members of the Ithna'ashari community settled in East Africa, in Kenya, Tanzania, Malawi, Uganda and Zambia. A small group of Shia students from East Africa arrived in London in the mid-1960s, and soon made links with other Shia students from Pakistan, India, the Middle East and Persian Gulf countries. This formative multi-ethnic group of Shia Muslims organised social events according to their religious calendar, and so developed a social and religious network across London.

With instability in East Africa in the early 1970s, many Asians from the region relocated to Britain, and the Harrow Shia community expanded with these newly arriving members. The requirement for holding religious and other community functions became more regular as the community grew, and the SICM was established in North Harrow to meet this growing need. At first, iftar functions (the meal to break the fast during Ramadan) were held in individual houses and then in hired halls in and around Harrow, where, by the early 1980s, more than 100 Shia families lived. Soon gatherings were being held every Friday evening, and then on religious occasions, but it was only after a long process of lobbying of the local council by the SICM that the former West Harrow School could be leased for the community, before eventually being bought.

Once the centre had a permanent home, it was able to increase and regularise its activities: for example, a special prayer programme on Thursday evenings, Friday lectures, Quran reading, religious anniversaries, children's religious and supplementary school classes, sports and leisure clubs, burial facilities and daily prayers. Activities are centred on religious traditions and practices, and are supplemented with social and leisure pastimes for community members. Although daily prayers are also held, it is notable that the centre is never described as a mosque or masjid as the SICM believe that in order for a space to be a mosque it must fulfil certain criteria, one of which being that the building must be established as a permanent place for prayer. The buildings occupied by the SICM were considered as temporary from the start as it was always the intention to redevelop the site. Indeed, even when the buildings were part of the school they were intended to be only semi-permanent structures. Therefore, although the halls serve as prayer halls and other religious activities take place as in any other mosque, the facility is described by the community as the North Harrow Assembly Hall.

This concept of 'meeting place', rather than mosque, is carried through into the proposed redevelopment of the Assembly Hall, which gained planning approval in January 2011.[2] This permission was not easily won. The initial scheme submitted for planning approval in 2008 was refused at the planning committee in 2009 after 700 people demonstrated against the proposal.[3] The revised scheme was approved two years later, in 2011, after many design concessions and intense public and political petitioning of local councillors by the Muslim community across denominations.

Work started on site in 2014, with an original project build cost in the region of £8 million (later rising to around £13 million). The construction programme was originally set at three years, although this was subject to funding, as monies were to be raised as the project progressed on site. At time of writing (2017) the work was still ongoing, but the mosque was able to remain in the prefab units on site during the build.

The North Harrow Community Centre, also called the Salaam Centre, has been designed by Mangera Yvars Architects, an Anglo-Spanish firm who won a competitive interview to design the scheme in 2005. Their proposal is billed as a radical reinterpretation of Muslim space and bears none of the conventional hallmarks of literal Islamic symbols, such as domes, minarets and pointed arches, that characterise almost all other expressions of Muslim architecture in Britain. Instead, the design is for a fluid, wave-like building, evoking Islamic traditional visual references only obliquely, and aesthetically situating itself more within the genre of international parametric architecture than habitual Islamic buildings (Fig 7.18).

Fig 7.18
Visualisation of the street frontage of the proposed Salaam Centre on Station Road, which gained planning permission in 2011.
[© Mangera Yvars Architects]

In terms of its programme, the Salaam Centre is not described anywhere in its own literature as a mosque, which is consistent with the descriptions of the North Harrow Assembly Hall. Instead, the facility is promoted as a 'shared space for the community',[4] which will be open to all, so not specifically for the use of the Shia Ithna'ashari community. A prayer hall will be provided on the ground and first floors, to hold up to 700 worshippers (Figs 7.19 and 7.20). To emphasise the central theme of openness, the prayer hall will be visible from outside. Apart from this space, the

Fig 7.19
Proposed ground-floor plan for the Salaam Centre (2010), showing how the prayer hall does not dominate the plan, and equal amounts of space are being given to the gallery and café.

Key
1 *Entrance*
2 *Prayer area*
3 *Exhibition space*
4 *Agora Piazza*
5 *Dining*
6 *Rear garden*
7 *Garden of contemplation*
8 *Garden of discovery*
9 *Kindergarten*
10 *Car park*

[Based on an original drawing © Mangera Yvars Architects]

Fig 7.20
Proposed section drawing for the Salaam Centre (2010), which shows the scale of the proposed development, with a double-storey, below-ground gym.
[© Mangera Yvars Architects]

Fig 7.21
Visualisation (2010) of how the proposed Salaam Centre will appear at night.
[© Mangera Yvars Architects]

centre is billed to be for open use by all, with its stated aims being:

> To fulfil the physical, intellectual and spiritual needs of people from all walks of life, age and gender ... [fostering] an environment of warmth, thought and creativity through the open interaction of users at the Centre, be it during a workout at the gym, a book club in the library or over coffee at the cafeteria. The Salaam Centre can become a place to enjoy with friends and family, a resource for work on projects and shared dreams, and ultimately a space to develop oneself and the community.[5]

This idea of the centre dissolving boundaries between it and the outside world is reiterated in the architects' design statement, where the North Harrow Community Centre is described as a 'purely civic space', where 'the diversity of the programme has led to a rich and complex layering of spaces and this in turn will give us unexpected but meaningful encounters'.[6] The design statement also outlines the idea of providing accessible spaces for new social encounters and interaction. It is intended that through its design the building will 'stimulate cultural discourse' and 'explore subtle relationships and social juxtapositions between functions and user groups ... [through] open fluid spaces where activities are blurred and overlapped'.[7]

The architects' vision is for the building to be seen as a 'fluid landscape reminiscent of landscapes of the Levant and the Indus Valley', through a 'suggestive' architectural narrative that enables the building to be '"of its time" while incorporating the richness and variety of Eastern culture'.[8] To realise this vision, the building's curves will be manifested through a cladding band at first-floor level, which is to be made up with fibre-cement patterns generated from 'fractal geometries'. The result will be a decorative façade that could be read as referring to Islamic traditions of patternwork, but equally could be situated as contemporary ornamentation without any implicit Islamic connection (Fig 7.21). This is an ambiguity that can be applied to the aesthetic language of the building as a whole: while it can reference Islamic sources, such as in the placement of gardens around the centre and

the façades, these references have been through such a process of reinterpretation that the connections to traditional Islamic aesthetics and the other expressions of Muslim architecture in Britain are abstracted to the point that the Salaam Centre will almost sit outside the current genre.

Indeed, this idea of forging a new path for British Islamic architecture by breaking ties with the current aesthetics of the mosque genre is echoed in the concept and programme of the centre. As one trustee of the centre states, it will 'take us to the next level in the evolution of Muslim centres in the West'.[9] Indeed, with 5,000m² of floor space, half of which will be contained in two basement levels, and with an estimated cost of £13 million, the Salaam centre is vying to be the biggest, most ambitious and most costly Muslim centre in the country.

Conclusion

Most mosques established by Muslim immigrant communities have prioritised themselves as religious places for religious practice and preservation, and have built community services around this to a greater or lesser degree. In most cases, these community services are designed and targeted at Muslim communities, where need is perceived to be the greatest, and have tended towards social service-type provision. The Salaam Centre, however, will offer a different kind of community space, with an emphasis on recreation and cultural expression. Perhaps most significantly, these facilities are intended to be used by the wider population, and to emphasise this a multifaith room is included on the first floor of the building. There is no 'mosque' as such, according to the religious criteria of the community, but a prayer hall where congregational prayers will be established.

It is this reordering of the hierarchy of religious and non-religious spaces, and the associated narrative of 'inclusivity', that sets the Salaam Centre apart from the majority of mosque buildings in Britain. The religious practice element of the centre, according to its own rhetoric, can be read as being spatially and conceptually secondary. Although the centre is intended to be 'open to all', it is expected that it will be used mostly by members of its own community as a faith-based social space. Nevertheless, it will still represent a significant shift in the conception and creation of Muslim social and religious space in Britain, where religious identity through lifestyle and culture take up a significant role alongside religious practice.

5 Cambridge Mosque, Mill Road, Romsey Town, Cambridge (in progress, 2017)

In 2011 a planning application was submitted for a purpose-built mosque on Mill Road in Cambridge, a thoroughfare that forms a geographic focus for the city's Muslim communities.[10] The new mosque was to replace the Abu Bakr Mosque within a mile of the new site, a former chapel converted in 1984 that was now too small for the expanded congregation. The site was purchased by the Muslim Academic Trust, a charity led by Yusuf Islam (formerly Cat Stevens). The secretary of the trust, and leader of the commissioning team, is Tim Winters, also an English convert to Islam and a Cambridge academic, who is a prolific writer on aspects of British Muslim culture.

In the new mosque's design statement, Winters articulates a critique of mosque design in Britain and positions Cambridge as something of an antidote to what is presented as an uninspiring architectural heritage. Winters describes these 'first generation' buildings as 'cheap but vast barns to keep the rain from the heads of worshippers, with scant attention paid to architectural nuance'.[11] He makes the point that while generational shift within Muslim communities brings with it new aspirations, 'a newer generation, both more educated and more reflective about religion, is growing restless'.[12]

The question of style that has dogged mosques in Britain from the earliest examples reverberates here in Cambridge, as Winters writes:

> Mosque design has historically reflected the local cultures of the Muslim world. A mosque in Java bears no resemblance to a mosque in Bosnia, or a mosque in Senegal. And with Cambridge Muslims claiming such a diversity of origins, it was far from clear what the chosen idiom should be.
>
> A hybrid seemed inevitable, and one with local references. But if mosque design has historically reflected local culture, how could British architecture figure in the shaping of the Cambridge building? One could quarry the past, and build a Gothic or a Palladian mosque. The dangers of pastiche would be immense. So, too, would be the potential alienation of the mosque's users, unused to the religion's heritage and its particular notion of the sacred.[13]

An international design competition was held to select the design proposal for Cambridge, with submissions varying from 'brutalist concrete ... [to] Star Trek futurism, replicas of medieval Syrian buildings, and revivals of Victorian architecture'.[14] The winning design, approved in 2012, was by Marks Barfield Architects (Fig 7.22), a prominent British firm (best known for the London Eye), which had cut its teeth on Islamic projects for Yusuf Islam in north London.

The design competition enabled different visions of a contemporary mosque to emerge through shortlisted entries by 5th Studio and Mangera Yvars Architects (Figs 7.23 and 7.24). Their schemes both presented ideas of the mosque that were a radical departure from known and recognised forms. They were not the first architects to do this; in the Muslim world, contemporary mosques that do not obviously reflect traditional design, or that re-present traditional form in new ways, have been built for some decades. For Mangera Yvars Architects this new approach to the mosque came from a belief that mosque architecture 'should not be concerned with typological representation but instead should consider the ethereal qualities of Islamic space – for example, the use of light, colour, geometry and calligraphy'.[15] These proposals adopted a form-led response to the site, where its layout and context influenced the proposed building's shape and character, and took priority over symbolic representation, which is effectively absent.

From the outset, Marks Barfield situated the design scheme more literally within the narratives of Islamic architecture (and in this they differed from the other two shortlisted architects). They explained their concept by referring to descriptions of Islamic architecture as the 'architecture of the veil', where beauty lies in the inner spaces which are not visible to the outside.[16] This idea of an inward-facing building enclosing a courtyard is further legitimised with reference to the first mosque, that of the Prophet Muhammad in Madinah, which established this typology. This concept is adapted in the Cambridge design into the idea of the mosque as a calm oasis, again evoking imagery from medieval Arab imaginations. The architects are aware, however, of local context, and raise the question of 'what an English mosque should look like and how it should be adapted to English culture'.[17]

Fig 7.22
Visualisation (2011) of the proposed Cambridge Mosque, which gained planning approval in 2012. The prayer hall, with its golden dome, can be seen on the far right, and the main entrance, with the garden opening onto the street, is to the left.
[By kind permission of Marks Barfield Architects/ CGI by F10 Studios]

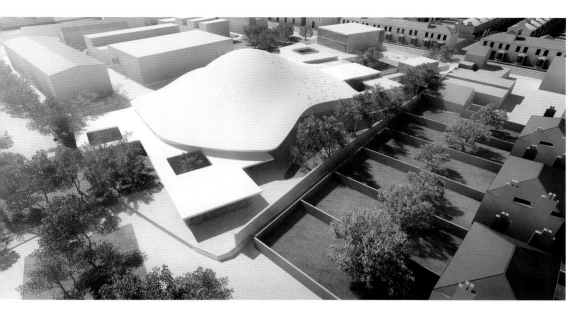

Fig 7.23
The 2009 shortlisted
competition submission for
the Cambridge Mosque by
Mangera Yvars Architects,
a fluid and informal shape
without traditionally
recognisable Islamic
references.
[© Mangera Yvars
Architects]

What sets Cambridge apart from the wider genre of British mosques is this very question, which does not seem to have been raised in any other mosques across the country. While a handful might be seen to be dealing with the challenge of an architectural response to local contexts, the existential question of what makes such buildings English has never been verbalised as explicitly as here.

The architects set out to address this by attempting to 'synthesise the essential application of geometry with Islamic and English

Fig 7.24
*Visualisation of the interior of the main prayer hall of the 2009 Mangera Yvars competition entry for the Cambridge Mosque.
[© Mangera Yvars Architects]*

heritage'. The plan of the new mosque was inspired by a 13th-century drawing of a garden, evoking the image of a calm oasis which the Cambridge Mosque was imagined as being. From this the architects derived the idea of the garden, or the orchard with lines of trees. The mosque is therefore organised with a grid of structural 'trees', 'evoking the 14th-century English innovation of the fan vault', and 'the concept of the oasis is reinforced across the whole site with over 60 new trees creating a permeable green edge around the new building' (Fig 7.25).[18]

The proposed building's geometry is arranged as a sequence of spaces from the front of the site to the rear, to culminate in a large square prayer hall (Fig 7.26). At the front, a landscaped garden will mediate between the street and the building (Figs 7.27 and 7.28). A modestly proportioned gilt dome, internally decorated with geometric tracery, will be placed off-centre in the prayer

hall towards the mihrab – an arrangement reminiscent of Andalusian Islamic architecture, for example the Mezquita in Cordoba (8th–10th century), where the dome is not a large central feature but a smaller one placed closer to, or above, the mihrab. Like traditional mosques, the Cambridge Mosque will be mostly laid out over a single floor, with the atrium and portico being two storeys high and the prayer hall three. The whole building will be enclosed with a brick skin patterned with diamond-shaped profiled brickwork in a light buff Cambridgeshire brick, so materially tying the building in to its context.

The mosque was designed in conjunction with Professor Keith Critchlow, an expert in sacred and Islamic art and founder of the organisation Kairos, which promotes the traditional values of art and science. He founded the Visual Islamic and Traditional Arts School in 1984, which eventually became the Prince's School of Traditional

Fig 7.25
Marks Barfield Architects'
2011 proposed ground-
floor plan for the
Cambridge Mosque,
showing a square prayer
hall set on the Qibla axis
which is accessed through a
garden followed by a
covered courtyard space.
[By kind permission of
Marks Barfield Architects]

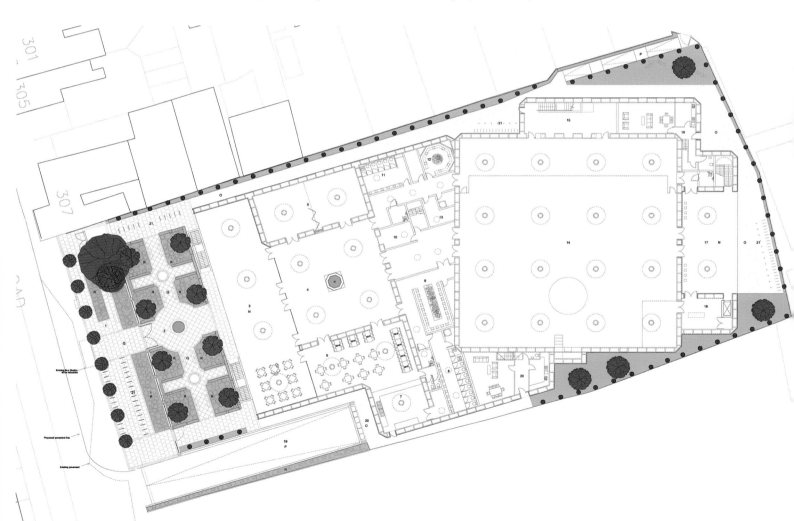

Arts. His colleague at the school, Emma Clark, an expert in traditional Islamic gardens, was engaged to design the garden for the mosque.

Critchlow's collaboration with and influence on the architect David Marks is of long standing, as he had been Marks's tutor in the 1980s. Geometry and its hidden structures underlying art and architecture have therefore been a passion that informed the practice's work. Cambridge was the first mosque Marks Barfield designed, and given this interest in the traditional practices of geometry, it follows that the firm's proposal was founded on such principles. David Marks's idea is that Muslim architecture has a long history and lineage, and that contemporary Islamic architecture in Britain should continue this. The way to do this is to draw from the principles of past architecture, and use these to generate new original forms. As Marks emphasises, the meaning of 'original' is 'from the origin', indicating an emphasis on the continuation of traditional processes to make contemporary space.[19]

This is a very different approach to the past, to history and to Islamic architectural heritage from the replication of the forms and symbols that have been implemented on British mosques from the 1980s. Marks Barfield pursued what could be considered a scholarly approach to historical process, to create a building conceived as an expression of English Muslim architecture. The traditional Islamic process of making art and architecture is being used contemporaneously to generate a new form.

The proposed mosque for Cambridge, therefore, marks a step change in the narrative of British mosque design. First, it is not a building conceived and commissioned by immigrant Muslims, as most mosques have been, but rather one where the committee is multi-ethnic and includes white English Muslims. Perhaps this cultural background has prompted the project to ask what an 'English mosque' should be. The response to this question is not a building that moves away from traditional Islamic architecture and visual culture, or that reinvents the

Fig 7.26
Visualisation (2011) of the main prayer hall of the proposed Cambridge Mosque: Islamic patternwork is abstracted into an organic network of beams that emerge from columns to form the roof structure.
[By kind permission of Marks Barfield Architects/ CGI by F10 Studios]

mosque to develop a new English form, but on the contrary one that sees itself as having traditional Islamic roots in a more intrinsic rather than symbolic way. The architects and commissioners have drawn attention to the use of local brick, with the diamond-shaped patterns referencing the decorations found in the domestic architecture of Cambridge. Although Winters states that the building will be 'strongly modern in inspiration and temper',[20] its bearing will be historical in its proposed final form. It will be within this structure from the past that architectural innovation will take place, mainly through the materiality of the façade and the treatment of the interior columns.

Conclusion

Through asking a series of questions about design and cultural identity, the proposed Cambridge Mosque attempts to position itself as both an Islamic building and an English one. It therefore overlaps with the new historicist mosque genre through its reliance on an interpretation of traditional Muslim architecture, and suggests a new one where forms are reinvented for an English context. That the mosque asks these questions is a consequence of how it has been commissioned. The client body and process of procuring a design has conformed to professional norms, with architects selected through an involved and protracted process of design proposals and consultations. Design, and the right designer, therefore, have been of fundamental importance. This has largely been due to the involvement of Tim Winters, who has been described by David Marks as an inspirational and sophisticated client.[21]

The centrality of design and a commitment to finding the right architect have been common denominators in projects that have resulted in buildings that explore the idea of the mosque in contemporary Britain. These projects have also been characterised by a determined and often artistic client, with Regent's Park Mosque (*see* pp 133–47), the Ismaili Centre (*see* pp 148–55) and the Muslim Cultural Heritage Centre (*see* pp 121–7) being notable examples. The Cambridge Mosque, therefore, illustrates a potential trajectory for mosques where design and architecture can be central to the project from the start.

New visions

These case studies show that by the early 21st century mosques were being built and imagined according to a new set of narratives. Muslims were exploring new cultural identities as a generation of British-born Muslims became active in the making of religious and cultural space, introducing new conceptions of Muslim architecture and bringing new procurement practices to the creation of mosques.

Much new mosque development by this time was being carried out through the upgrading or replacement of existing mosque facilities that were not sufficient to accommodate increased congregations and not able to provide services in the way that communities needed. Mosques that had grown from a local to a regional scale were becoming ambitious social and cultural institutions, providing a wider set of resources to Muslim communities that were now multigenerational and multi-ethnic. These communities were also much more complex than their predecessors who had established the first mosques in the 1970s and 1980s, as they were more culturally diverse, including both indigenous English converts and converts from other backgrounds. These visions went further than meeting the immediate needs of creating prayer space, and had started to imagine larger social, symbolic and aesthetic objectives.

Fig 7.27 (opposite top) Visualisation (2011) of the Mill Road front elevation of the new Cambridge Mosque with the centrally placed main entrance reached through a garden fronting the street. [By kind permission of Marks Barfield Architects/ CGI by F10 Studios]

Fig 7.28 (opposite bottom) Visualisation (2011) of the view from the inner courtyard of the proposed Cambridge Mosque looking towards the main entrance and garden that opens onto Mill Road. [By kind permission of Marks Barfield Architects/ CGI by F10 Studios]

8

Surveying the landscape –
130 years of the mosque in Britain

When Abdullah (William) Quilliam started his mosque at 8 Brougham Terrace in Liverpool in 1889 for his growing company of Muslim converts and cosmopolitan émigrés, little did he know that his would be the first of some 1,500 mosques to emerge across the country over the next 130 years. These buildings would come to furnish the religious and architectural history of Britain with a new social and visual culture.

From the early maritime communities of Cardiff and east London in the mid-20th century to mass migration and mosque building following decolonisation, the patterns of mosque establishment show certain similarities. Muslim immigrants settled in inner-city areas of Britain to fill post-war labour shortages, and as the communities and their families grew, the need for religious and cultural practice and education became apparent. Through collective efforts, mosques were established to cater for this need, usually starting as simple house conversions, with some evolving into larger purpose-built centres as the decades progressed.

Most British mosques have evolved organically. In some places they have been fashioned from existing buildings, which are often found in awkward configurations and on restricted sites. These mosques, particularly in their early forms, were very much improvised spaces, deploying an array of layouts and solutions to the task of creating a place of worship from a given building or site. Elsewhere, mosques had to fit themselves within the existing fabric and context of their urban setting, which in inner cities was most often an industrial urban landscape, 'characterised by regular streets, long street blocks, standardised plot sizes and repetitive two-storey terraces'.[1] This need for the mosques to fit into awkward sites and/or into existing urban topography has resulted in forms and aesthetics unprecedented in Muslim architectural history. The need for Islamic signification, in whatever rudimentary and immediate form it could be achieved, resulted in an aesthetic character of assemblage that came to be seen by many as pastiche and was considered unsophisticated. Later mosque architecture that was better resourced attempted to redress this through more exact replication of examples of historic Islamic architecture.

The genealogy of mosque design in Britain started with the conversion of domestic space, with the converted house serving as the most rudimentary form of mosque. Generally with such examples the street scene remains largely unaltered, with the mosque being signified with little more than signage or decoration applied to windows. In more elaborate cases, the house would be embellished with elements such as minarets and domes, as with Bradford's Jamia Mosque on Burnett Place (*see* p 250) and the Masjid Ghausia in Dewsbury (Fig 8.2). Nevertheless, alterations and significations aside, the mosque in these cases remains in essence a domestic building, situated accordingly within its urban context.

Fig 8.1 (opposite)
The Suleymaniye Mosque in east London was built by the local Turkish Muslim community in the late 1990s. It provides a religious school to train imams as well as a dining hall, kitchen and other community facilities. The low dome and needle-style minaret is characteristic of traditional Ottoman architecture, which identifies its Turkish origins. [Author]

Fig 8.2 (below)
The Masjid Ghausia, Warren Street, Dewsbury – a house mosque which has had a minaret added to its front façade to signify its new religious use. [DP143510]

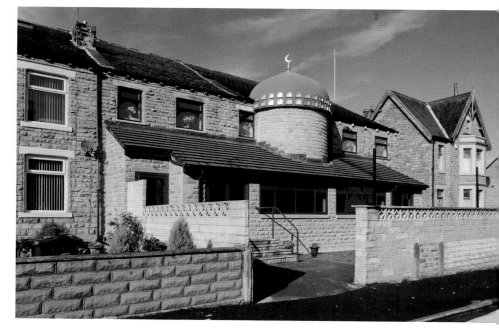

Mosques that are formed through the conversion of non-domestic buildings present a more varied Islamic architectural landscape than house conversions. Non-domestic conversions range from warehouses and factories to public houses, cinemas and churches, and the variation in the typology of the existing building directly impacts the form of the adapted mosque (Fig 8.3). The adaptation and signification of the mosque again vary widely, from subtle signals such as signage or window embellishment, to more architectural features such as the introduction of minarets or domes, whereby the building is almost completely transformed. Often with warehouse conversions the body of the building is left unaltered and a new frontage is constructed onto which Islamic identification is applied. Bristol Jamia Mosque is an example of this type of complete conversion, where a 19th-century chapel has had its pitched roof replaced with a dome and acquired a minaret, so that the line between a converted building and a new build becomes blurred (see pp 63–7). Similarly, Kingston Mosque began as a social club very much in the idiom of local domestic architecture, was converted into a mosque and gradually adapted one alteration at a time until it was transformed into an amalgamation of vernacular and Islamic elements (see pp 84–8).

The non-domestic conversion, therefore, has a wider range of manifestations than the house conversion as it encompasses a wider range of building types. One characteristic across all types of conversions is the iterative nature of the process of mosque-making. Often a series of proposals and planning applications occur over a period of years, some implemented and others not. The proposals are determined by the ever-changing needs of the Muslim community and congregation. In most cases the number of worshippers is continuously expanding, so necessitating the continuing extension of the premises. Such piecemeal development is also a reflection of the financial ability of the mosque, whereby funds are not available in one tranche at the outset but are collected as the project progresses. The development of the site is therefore carried out as funds become available, and as needs become apparent. It is the nature of community funding which leads to mosques being built iteratively. This may sound problematic; however, it serves its own purpose in that the building can adapt to a community's evolving needs. It is often the case that the community, represented by the mosque committee, amends the mosque design while it is being built. What emerges, therefore, are buildings very much self-designed and in many ways self-built, especially where the builders are members of the community or are known to them, as is often the case.

The purpose-built mosque has traditionally been the final stage in the development trajectory. However, not all house mosques evolve into larger conversions or purpose-built centres; many remain as house conversions serving very local congregations. Howard Street Mosque in Bradford is a good example of a house mosque that has remained a house, even though it has been extended into adjacent houses in the terrace (see pp 59–62). For this mosque, embedded within streets of terraces in the inner city, moving to another location would have meant becoming disconnected from its congregation, hence the houses were converted to such a degree as to enable them to permanently serve a large Muslim community. However, nearly every purpose-built mosque began life in an earlier form, as either a house or other conversion.

A few mosques were built before the advent of mass Muslim immigration in the 1960s, scattered across the country and disconnected from a shared social history. Fazl in Southfields served

Fig 8.3
The Islamic Centre of England, Maida Vale, London: a good example of a historic listed building that was converted into a mosque in 1998 with little external adaptations. The original building was constructed in 1912 as a cinema and had been subsequently reused as a dance hall and bingo hall before becoming a mosque. [DP132066]

the Ahmadiyya in London (*see* pp 35–43), while Yemeni seamen built in Cardiff (*see* pp 52–6). The Raza Mosque in Preston (*see* pp 101–3) and Jamia Mosque in Coventry (*see* p 259) were among the first purpose-built mosques of the post-Partition immigrants. From here the number of mosques began its exponential rise, starting with the conversions from the 1960s and 1970s, and leading to the rise in numbers of the purpose-built mosque from the late 1970s.

As with all the mosque types discussed so far, the siting and location of purpose-built mosques was dependent on the land that was available in inner-city areas. This land was often post-industrial plots, or existing mosque premises in a converted building that was to be demolished and rebuilt. Invariably the site for the mosque was awkward, perhaps resulting in an uncomfortable relationship with the Qibla. The layout of the mosques built, therefore, varied considerably as each dealt with the particularities and constraints of its plot. Two main types of layout have

emerged: the purpose-built mosque that follows the scale, style and character of the streetscape in which it is situated; and the mosque that stands apart as a landmark, impacting and altering the urban landscape. Noor-ul-Uloom, Small Heath, Birmingham, is a good example of the former, situating itself politely on a residential corner site (*see* p 264), while north London's Harrow Central Mosque represents the latter, a new building looming alongside the former house mosque and forming a significant presence in the town centre (*see* pp 250–1).

Whether the mosque is integrated within the streetscape or set apart as a landmark, a common architectural language has emerged across the mosque landscape and remained remarkably consistent, namely the inclusion of the minaret, dome and arch. Almost all purpose-built mosques have incorporated these elements in some form, whether as integral symbols in a new design such as at Regent's Park (Fig 8.4 and *see* pp 133–47), or as elements applied to an existing building

Fig 8.4
The south-eastern side of Regent's Park Mosque, with the Qibla wall of the main prayer hall visible behind the foliage. The design of this mosque demonstrates the importance of the architectural symbols of the dome and minaret, which were incorporated into a broadly contemporary design approach.
[Author]

such as at Kingston (*see* pp 84–8). Only a few mosques have articulated their purpose and identity through other, perhaps more nuanced, Islamic signifiers, such as the Muslim Cultural Heritage Centre in west London (*see* pp 121–7), the first Alice Street Mosque in Cardiff (*see* pp 52–6) and the Shahporan Mosque in Bethnal Green (*see* pp 217–19). Most mosques have strived to ensure that traditional elements are adhered to in some form.

The role of mosques in the migration and settlement of Muslim communities

Prior to the arrival of families, anecdotal accounts describe religious practice among male Muslim migrants, often living collectively in shared houses, as lax or non-existent. One Pakistani immigrant in Dewsbury narrates:

> We're very grateful to Allah for keeping our children on the path of Islam. They haven't gone away from their culture or their religion, unlike myself, when I came over to England there was no mosque in England; there was no way of telling when … we have to fast … We were quite isolated … so we just used to celebrate Eid whenever we could.[2]

Another formative experience narrated by early immigrants, also formally documented, is the prevalence of racism and associated discrimination. Such racism was enacted across a range of spheres, from housing policies to employment practices, to daily experiences on the street. Policies and experiences led to the geographic clustering of Muslim communities in certain urban areas. These areas of high Muslim population became the locations for mosques, which in turn attracted more Muslims to the area, leading to what some academics have called the 'Islamisation of space'.[3] Racism and exclusion also left immigrants in a cultural no-man's land, suspended between a home culture from which they were disconnected and were in danger of losing, and a host society that excluded them completely. As families were reunited in Britain and children were born indigenously, the prospect of such alienation for the next generation was a cause for deep concern. This was allied with the cultural distance immigrants felt towards majority White social practices, whereby the 'West' was imagined as 'materialist, exploitative, licentious, and

at once, godless and Christian'.[4] It was the lack of a religious infrastructure to maintain and transfer traditions and values that served as a significant motivation for the establishment of mosques, where religious ritual and education could be enacted, and religious practice could be transferred and maintained.

Mosques in Bradford established by the first generation of immigrants from South Asia have been described as

> vehicles for the dynamic reconstruction of tradition and culture so as to advance subaltern group interests in contexts of rapid social change … [providing] an important space – for first generation immigrants especially – to resist assimilation, navigate social exclusion and organise self-help … [by] creating continuity of experience in terms of institutional form, religious rituals and specialists, and social relationships.

This process and the role of community institution-building is not exclusive to Muslim immigrants: 'Many first-generation peasant and working-class immigrants, from East European Jews to Irish Catholics, have adopted this same strategy of survival in Britain.'[5]

However, it is important to note that the mosque is not the only, or indeed the primary, way in which 'Muslim space' is constructed. The mosque is just one part of a matrix of Muslim practices which does not require any judicially claimed territory or formally consecrated or architecturally specific space.[6] This means that the mosque is a component within a network of Muslim practices, such as prayer, language and food, that together constitute Muslim culture and identity in Britain (Fig 8.5). Within this matrix the mosque fulfils a symbolic role, transmitting a range of messages from presence to permanence, and also serves to replicate a religious and social institution familiar to immigrants from their places of origin.

The mosque in Britain does not, however, simply represent the relocation of a religious institution from a 'home' culture into a new 'Western' one, but also serves as a transforming social and religious mechanism within Muslim discourse. In many cases mosques in Britain, although having their origins in ethnic and culturally bounded communities, have inevitably become multicultural through the sheer pressure of Muslim demographic change, and thereby have become spaces which combine plural Muslim religious practices from different parts of the world. They therefore serve as hubs for a globalising Muslim community, and instigate a shift from culturally homogenous forms of religious practice that may be found in the place of origin of one ethnic group. This delinking of the mosque from cultural forms of religious practice has been identified as a characteristic of diaspora mosques in the 'West'. For example, 'In the United States, the Islamic Society of North America ... has particularly urged Muslims to overcome ethnic customs in favour of a shared normative practice ... [Here] Muslims strip away centuries of innovation and succeed in getting to the essence.'[7]

Accordingly, diaspora Muslim communities settled in the 'West' have been described by academics as 'border populations',[8] and are seen to constitute a wholly new potential for the evolution and development of Muslim cultural practice. This new practice has emerged from the new realities in which migrated Muslim populations have found themselves, where they are minorities within majority non-Muslim societies, ruptured from the cultural trajectory of their homeland and forced to address new relationships alongside globally diverse Muslim communities.

Although denominational differences do exist within Muslim religious practice, they are less overt and less structured than in, say, the landscape of Christian architecture. The two main branches in Islam are the Sunni and Shia traditions, which have distinct forms of practice and liturgy; they also have separate mosques, although members of each community will worship in each other's mosques. Shia Islam is more formally organised into branches representing schools of different imams, such as the Ismaili or the Bohra, and each branch tends to form a particular community with its own mosque. Within the Sunni tradition there are various schools of thought, but none so overt that they necessitate separate places of worship. Within the South Asian Sunni tradition, the two main schools of thought are the Deobandi and the Barelwi, which originate in India and reflect the Muslim religious landscape of South Asia itself. The issue of denominational difference tends to be played down by mosques in Britain, who emphasise that such differences are of only nominal importance.

There are a number of factors that have led to the multiplication of mosques in Britain, alongside the simple fact of growing Muslim populations. Denominational difference has played a role, as has place of origin, nationality and culture. To a greater or lesser degree, mosque

congregations are also culturally influenced, with those from similar religious or ethnic backgrounds tending to attend mosques that reflect that make-up. In larger towns and cities, however, congregations are increasingly multicultural, with Muslims who are more recent immigrants from other Muslim regions, such as Somalia, North Africa and Iraq, settling in an area and attending the existing mosque there. In some cases, newer Muslim immigrant communities have established their own mosques, for example in London for the Somali community in Mile End and Nigerian Muslims in Camberwell.

It is necessary to note that among this array of ethnic and religious divergences there is an underlying commonality in liturgy and theology that ultimately serves to unite diverse approaches. As one theologian points out, 'the form of the prayer is something we all essentially agree on. We also acknowledge the same scriptures and rules of tajwid ... No other religious community is blessed with such unity, and given that we have nothing like the Vatican to impose it on us, this looks a little like a miracle.' This commentator goes on to identify that differences do, however, exist and are manifest in the design and decoration of the mosque itself: 'Braelvis [Barelwi], Deobandis, Traditional Sunnis, Salafis, Ja'faris and many others often announce their control of our spaces very stridently ... Egotism and nasty tribal prejudice mean that when you enter one of our mosques for the first time, you will soon notice something hanging on the wall, or around the mehrab, that either includes or excludes you.'[9]

Fig 8.5
Muslim prayer and mosques are among a range of religious and cultural practices that constitute Muslim life and identity.
[DP035269]

Mosque design and its discontents

Examples of religious denomination influencing design can be seen when comparing Deobandi and Barelwi mosques. While there are of course exceptions, if generalisations can be made they would be that Barelwi aesthetics lean towards decoration and expressive aesthetics, whereas the Deobandi tend towards austerity and simplicity. For example, the mihrab at Leytonstone Mosque (Deobandi) is a plain arrangement of two types of marble (*see* Fig 3.24), compared to that at Ghamkol Sharif in Birmingham (Barelwi) which is set within a full wall of green onyx hung with framed photos of religious sites, large calligraphy and banners (*see* Fig 4.21). Minbars also vary considerably, with those in Barelwi mosques often being more ornate and expressive, while in Deobandi mosques they can be a simple short timber staircase.

This difference in aesthetics may be linked to theological approaches, where the Barelwi emphasise emotional attachments to religious guides as well as the Prophet Muhammad, and see decoration, along with more demonstrative rituals involving music and singing, as a means to express this. The more functional Deobandi perspective, where emphasis is on the correct form of ritual and its enactment, translates this into a design language with less adornment and flourish. It is an approach shared by the Lewisham Islamic Centre (*see* pp 214–17) and the Salafee mosque in Brixton (*see* pp 96–9), which demonstrates an exceptional form of austerity, with no wall decoration or calligraphy, no mihrab, and a plain timber staircase as a minbar. The

mosque representatives at Brixton were determined that a mosque did not need these embellishments, neither domes nor minarets.

Visual cultures from the places of origin of Muslim communities in Britain also influence the expression of their mosques. With the majority of the British Muslim population originating in South Asia, it is Indian Mughal styles that are largely replicated. For example, the converted church of Brent Mosque had limited scope for Muslim signification, the only possibility being a series of smallish domes at key locations (*see* pp 89–96). These domes were designed as replicas of the Jamma Masjid in Delhi, in the distinct Mughal style of the onion dome with spire. Again, the Deobandi/Barelwi distinction in design approach can be discerned here, where it is the Deobandi mosques that are more likely to move away from Indian references, even when communities originate in South Asia. For example, with Leicester's Jame Mosque a North African Fatimid language was chosen (*see* pp 202–6). This can be compared to the Mughal-shaped dome of Preston's Raza Mosque, a Barelwi mosque which is also adorned with fluttering green flags and coloured lights (*see* pp 101–3).

Mosques serving communities other than from South Asia differ in their design approach, and reflect the traditions of their places of origin. This is particularly evident in Turkish community mosques, which embrace Ottoman architectural and aesthetic heritage. The Aziziye Mosque, in Stoke Newington, has transformed an Art Deco cinema by fully tiling the front façade with traditional Ottoman-style tilework (Fig 8.6 and *see* p 257). The nearby Suleymaniye Mosque is marked out by its distinctly neo-Ottoman needle minaret (*see* Fig 8.1).

There are, of course, exceptions, and design sources do cross over as Muslim communities in Britain become more diverse and, with generational change, potentially less tied to places of origin and their attendant visual cultures. Harrow Central Mosque, although a South Asian Barelwi mosque, has been designed in the style of an Ottoman mosque, with a flat dome and needle minaret (*see* pp 250–1). The designer was of Muslim Indian Gujarati heritage, and the mosque committee was made up of members originating from India and Pakistan, so there were no Turkish links as such. The language was perhaps, therefore, a simple matter of choosing an Islamic architectural idiom acceptable to all. Although Sheffield Islamic Centre is a Barelwi mosque, the commissioners, who were British-born of

Fig 8.6
Decorative tiling on the façade of the Aziziye Mosque in north London. With Muslims from many different countries, Britain's mosques reflect a diversity of Islamic architectural histories.
[DP132024]

Pakistani descent, were clear that their design language should originate in the Middle East and North Africa, as such stylistic approaches were closer to their own aesthetic tastes (*see* pp 188–94). Perhaps this is also a case of British-born Muslims wanting to demarcate their cultural expression from that of their parents' generation, as a demonstration of the forging of new cultural identities that are not fixed geographically according to origin, but rather according to ideas and affinities.

Architects have also played a key role in the evolution of mosque design in Britain. Atba Al-Samarraie, originating from Iraq, and Najib Gedal, from Libya, have brought design influences from these regions. Gedal's Shahjalal Mosque in Manchester (*see* pp 127–31) references the Malwiya minaret of the Samarra Grand Mosque, while Al-Samarraie affirms that his designs are based on his memories of Baghdad. The emergence of Muslim mosque designers over the last 20 years has introduced the idea and influence of authorship to British mosque design. Al-Samarraie, for example, on occasion convinced mosque committees that the designs they might have commissioned were inadequate expressions of Muslim architecture, and was able to persuade them through his knowledge of the field, and the added credibility of being Arab-speaking and originating from a country central to Islamic history. He has thus been able to revise mosque designs, bringing to them his own evocatively Muslim architectural language.

Ahmed Eliwa, an Egyptian, was another designer who competed with existing design schemes to offer what he considered more accurate or authentic expressions of mosque architecture. His minarets and embellishments were realised at Maidenhead (Fig 8.7 and *see* pp 107–14) and Gloucester (Fig 8.8 and *see* pp 114–18), the minarets being near copies of a medieval Cairene example. He also presented the same minaret, along with a complete redesign, for the proposed East London Mosque in the early 1980s (*see* pp 155–67). This highly ornate and decorative brand of Islamic architecture has its origins in Fatimid Egypt.

The result of these myriad influences and forms of expression over the decades of mosque building in Britain is an architectural landscape where references to Islamic architectural history are mimicked in various ways. In earlier post-1960s mosques, such as Raza and Wimbledon, the architecture seemed to reflect historical examples as found in the community's places of origin,

in those cases India and Pakistan. This association between place of origin and architectural style became looser with later mosques, and a more eclectic mosque style emerged with more generic Islamic references. By the 21st century, the mosque in Britain, and Europe, had become an architectural genre of increasing architectural and sociological debate in which it was broadly

Fig 8.7
The free-standing minaret of Maidenhead Mosque, an elaborate and expressive feature which punctuates an otherwise unremarkable edge-of-town landscape. [DP148061]

Fig 8.8
*The front façade of the
Jama al-Karim Mosque in
Gloucester: a decorated
brick façade and minaret
form a landmark presence
in the local area.*
[DP148028]

characterised as the architecture of homesickness, of 'imitation culture' or 'self-Orientalism'.[10] At its more vociferous end, the debate drew some strong reactions, with the output of mosque architecture described as 'a kind of barbarian Orientalism' and 'garish syncretism', designed by 'underpaid jobbing architects' who are dimly recalling Muslim culture in the subcontinent.[11]

Historian of Islamic architecture Dr Yaqub Zaki (formerly James Dickie) claims that the design process for some mosques is as follows:

I know the way these architects work; they are commissioned by the mosque committee, and the mosque committee consists of the cash and carry walla, the take-away tycoon, who don't know the first thing about mosques. So what they do is they take out the Yellow Pages, they pick out [an architect] quite arbitrarily, the man comes for a meeting with the mosque committee and the mosque committee are all contradicting each other, so he gets no proper guidance whatsoever. So he [the architect] goes to the library, takes out one or two books on Islamic architecture, picks a feature from here and feature from there and combines them, and the result is an inconsistent mish-mash. These people tend to rely on identity symbols to make a building resemble a mosque, ergo a mosque has a dome, well not every mosque has a dome; ergo a mosque has a mihrab, well Prophet's Mosque had no mihrab ... Then another identity symbol is minaret ... If you have an onion dome, you can't have with it an Egyptian minaret.[12]

Mosque design – between aesthetics and identity

In 2002 the architectural critic Jonathan Glancey, writing in *The Guardian*, asked: 'Why are there no great British mosques?' He considered Woking Mosque as the only real expression of a credible Muslim architecture in the country, with the mosques that followed failing to reach criteria of architectural merit, often being 'no more than brick boxes with minarets and domes applied like afterthoughts ... Why are the new mosques ... so determinedly glum?'[13]

Glancey identified the changed demographic of Muslim immigration post 1960 as a primary reason for the resulting mosque design. He noted that in the early 20th century Muslim life in Britain, and in particular the Woking mission, had been a 'meeting of high minds, with great learning and a degree of wealth and culture', whereas after 1960 the Muslim demographic was overwhelmed by rural immigrants needed to provide cheap labour. Poverty, therefore, is one of the root causes of 'poor mosque design', and Glancey notes that Britain's mosques 'raise their domes, minarets and crescents over some of the poorest quarters of our oldest cities'.[14] However, it is not only a question of finance. Glancey quotes an architectural academic on the subject who proposes that aside from money 'there is the question of cultural transference ... It will take ... perhaps another 10 or 15 years for the architecture of the British mosque to develop a clear and sophisticated vocabulary of [its] own.'[15]

This was followed in 2007 by another article in the same paper, which similarly lamented the lack of architectural merit of modern British mosques. David Shariatmadari complained that 'despite the huge number of new mosques being built, few reach beyond the level of flimsy imitation'. Like Glancey, Shariatmadari identified lack of money as a core reason for poor quality, observing that 'there's no central institution like the Vatican bankrolling mosque construction, and a relative shortage of mega-rich Muslims'. However, he also points to a lack of architectural aspiration as a limiting factor, stating, 'More important though is a failure of imagination, the result of many community leaders' thoroughly conservative outlook. Changing, letting fresh ideas in, might seem like losing touch with your roots.'[16] Shariatmadari makes a salient connection here between the architectural expression of the mosque and the religious identity of the community that builds it, relating religious conservatism to architectural timidity.

This tendency of commentators to correlate the design of a mosque to the cultural outlook of the community that builds it is explored in the work of Dutch anthropologist Oskar Verkaaik. He notes that the architectural critique of Europe's new mosques condemns 'neo-traditionalist mosques ... for being cheap and inauthentic replicas of religious architectural styles', and through this critique the view of Islam as an 'inert tradition, both socially and architecturally'[17] is put forward. Verkaaik states:

New mosques are evaluated in a modernist tradition as works of art. This tradition demands a building to be innovative, autonomous, and the expression of the architect as artist. Most of them are found wanting and condemned as mere copies ... [they are] taken to be expressions of a continuing loyalty to the fatherland and a failure to integrate in Western society. A non-traditionalist design is favoured as either an expression of successful integration or an instrument thereof.[18]

New mosques, therefore, are evaluated as expressions of Muslim culture, society and belief; critiques of them are not simply about design. Inherent within these critiques is a 'disapproval of the role and place of migrant Muslims in European societies. It assumes an almost one-to-one relationship between mosque design and degree of social integration ... [serving as] a reliable indicator of whether or not the Muslim community in question performs its citizenship.'[19]

The question then arises as to what actually is the nature of the relationship between the design of the mosque and the cultural identity of those who have built it. To begin to address this question, the mosque needs to be understood as being situated within a network of complex social dynamics in which immigrant communities are finding their identities and attempting to assert their rights.

One of the key motivating factors for the establishment of mosques was the preservation and transference of religious tradition; it could be said that they were by their very nature 'conservative' institutions. The communities faced discrimination and exclusion in all spheres of their lives in Britain, from housing, to employment, to public space, and the mosque served as the only safe communal space for such groups. Under these circumstances, it might not have been appropriate for the mosque to explore new architectural frontiers as such an endeavour would have presented visual languages that were unfamiliar to its users. Instead the mosque was required, visually, to denote the familiar typologies that Muslims could recognise, and from which they could gain some self-recognition and comfort. As the architectural historian Peter Guillery notes, 'Imaginative architecture is a luxury, not just because it tends to cost money, but because it arises from cultural confidence whereby it isn't felt necessary to make a basic statement about identity. Simple signification, never mind aesthetic quality, comes first.'[20]

This requirement for signification, as this book has shown, has not been a straightforward process for Muslim communities in building their mosques. The case study of Brent Mosque (see pp 89–96) shows how the mosque community struggled to find the appropriate way to resignify the church building. From the very first proposals, the exterior was to be altered to denote that this was now a Muslim building. The proposed designs oscillated between the sophistication and complexity of Latif Siwani's

Fig 8.9
The minaret and entrance gateway of Ghousia Mosque in Peterborough, one of a series of mosques designed by Atba Al-Samarraie which sought to reproduce a more authentic Islamic architecture.
[DP147362]

Fig 8.10
The marking out of the mihrab for a new mosque in Bethnal Green, London, which is being built to replace an existing mosque housed in temporary buildings. Decision-making in mosque design is a collective and negotiated process between members of the mosque committee and the design and construction team.
[Author]

latticework (*see* Fig 3.42), to a proposal to completely replace the church with a crude and simple building with the generic Islamic elements of a dome and minarets. The latter seemed to be a rushed alternative after Siwani's more nuanced design failed to attract funding from the congregation.

Similar processes of stylistic indeterminacy can be seen on a number of other mosques surveyed here. The East London Mosque, for example, had several schemes prior to the eventual John Gill design, which presented approaches from the highly contemporary to the literally historicist (*see* pp 155–67). And the Yorkshire-based architect Atba Al-Samarraie has shown, with his Bilal Mosque in Leeds (*see* pp 170–4) and Ghousia Mosque in Peterborough (Fig 8.9 and *see* pp 179–85), how he has been able to persuade mosques to adopt, as he calls it, a more authentically Islamic architecture rather than the nondescript versions they would otherwise have settled for.

The visuality of the mosque has been one of the fundamental strategies through which Muslim communities have made their presence in Britain known. Delivering a mosque that their congregation approves of is the priority for a mosque committee, not whether it is seen as progressive or worthy within the architectural or design establishment. Visually, therefore, the mosque needs to symbolise its identity quickly and easily to as many of its users as possible, which means, in essence, replicating known and popular images of mosques from around the world. Through their architecture, Muslim communities have sought to articulate their identity to themselves as well as to wider society. For example, with Suffa-Tul-Islam in Bradford (*see* pp 207–11), when the committee wanted a building that spoke unequivocally of being 'a mosque', they were demarcating what a mosque should look like for themselves and other Muslims, as well as what wider society should perceive a mosque to be. This historicist period of mosque building can therefore be seen as an attempt to aesthetically conclude, for the benefit of Muslims and non-Muslims, what a mosque actually is.

Mosque design – an anthropological view

There is an alternative way of thinking about mosques in Britain and Europe, other than as simple visual representations of cultural identity or as demonstrations of cultural authenticity. This more anthropological approach looks beyond the mosque as an architectural object, and sees it as part of a more complex array of cultural practices that diasporic Muslim communities perform as they settle into new environments.

The condemnation of the traditional mosque as 'an expression of deplorable homesickness or misplaced melancholia' fails to grasp the idea that melancholia for social minorities is 'a mechanism that helps [them] (re)construct identity'.[21] To deny mosque commissioners this vehicle, therefore, could be seen as an 'attempt to deny them a social identity'.[22]

Furthermore, this anthropological perspective is used to challenge the discourse where the mosque is a 'material symbol' of social or religious behaviour, and an expression of 'an already existent identity'. Instead the mosque, insofar as it is the 'production and consumption of a building', is 'not so much an expressive as a creative process'. Viewed as such, the bringing into being of a mosque becomes an 'intimate engagement with form [which] enables people to gain knowledge and reformulate identity'. This is in contrast to the 'representational paradigm of contemporary mosque critique', referring instead to a process whereby the creation of material objects 'help[s] us identify with these objects and ... form an identity of ourselves on the basis of our identification with the object'.[23]

This is a very significant repositioning of the way in which the mosque as a piece of architecture is considered. Instead of it being read as the representation of a pre-existent Muslim culture which is being transplanted from some other place, the anthropological approach demands that the physical making of the mosque is seen as an inherent part of the way in which immigrant Muslim communities construct their identities anew in their new homelands.

This is a process whereby Muslim communities engage with architectural form, 'vis-à-vis religious tradition, European society, their memories of their places of origin, their future aspirations, their relation to God, their place in the world'.[24] Therefore, the act of making the mosque is a performance that the community engages in to establish its own dynamics and relationships to each other and the outside world (Fig 8.10). The replication and reuse of Islamic architectural symbols from history, rather than being the ill-considered application of the past, is instead a statement of where that group sees itself, and its relation to the wider world, and is part of the process of becoming for minority communities.

This process can be seen enacted in the iterative, and ad hoc nature of most mosques established in Britain from the late 1960s to the end of the 1990s, such as Leytonstone (*see* pp 76–81) and Kingston (*see* pp 84–8). The replacement of one design with a succession of others, for example at the East London Mosque (*see* pp 155–67) or in Maidenhead (*see* pp 107–14), each perhaps wildly different from the previous, shows the mosque struggling to find an appropriate architectural form. Each of the different designs enables the committee to react

and position itself, informing its sense of identity, how it sees itself and how it wants to be seen.

The paradigmatic shift that the new historicist mosques of the late 20th and early 21st centuries represent, such as Bradford's Suffa-Tul-Islam (*see* pp 207–11) or Leicester's Jame Mosque (Fig 8.11 and *see* pp 202–6), is that the building is now pre-designed professionally, and then implemented on site. This represents

Fig 8.11
The Jame Mosque, Leicester, completed in 2010, was one of a new generation of mosques from the late 1990s onwards which pursued a coherent historicist style in their architecture.
[DP137457]

the modernisation of mosque-making, brought about through the professionalisation (a generational shift) of procuring mosques. This handing over of mosque design from the committee to the design professional has enabled the mosque to be conceived as a piece of architecture before it is built. The use of professional designers has empowered the committee with the tools to conceive of the mosque as a coherent and complete historical object, as replicative of buildings from an Islamic past, rather than to try to assert a new and contemporary architectural language.

The new religious landscape and the town-planning process

The trajectory of mosque design and architecture over the 20th century has seen a parallel evolution in the way in which the town-planning process understands and deals with this new building type. Conventional planning discourses have developed since the mid-20th century to regulate the built environment. The mosque, as an expression of the architecture of minority communities, presented a challenge to the cultural assumptions on which these discourses were based.

A 2004 study by the geographer Richard Gale of three mosques in Birmingham shows how the treatment of mosque proposals through the planning system was transformed over a period from the 1950s to the 1990s.[25] The first example tells the story of Birmingham Central Mosque (*see* p 259), initiated in the late 1950s. As the mosque was situated within a regeneration area, the planners required it to 'integrate' with the overall identity of the newly constructed neighbourhood. This led to a requirement for the materials of the new mosque to be a brick matching the adjoining shopping centre and flats. Accordingly, on its completion in 1975, 'the building became a stylistic hybrid, signifying simultaneously its relation to its local context and to traditions of mosque architecture'.[26] While the mosque had been built with a large central dome, the application for a minaret in the 1980s elicited the council's position on Islamic aesthetics: they approved it on the basis that the design was 'elegant and well proportioned, [forming] a good foil/contrast with the main domed building'.[27] A public debate also ensued over the use of this tower to broadcast the adhan (the call to prayer), which the council eventually allowed with restrictions on the number of times per day it could be transmitted, and its duration.

The opposition was founded on the notion of Islam as an alien culture, which should not be permitted to find full expression in an English city. Architecture therefore became a vehicle through which social tensions existent within society were articulated and mediated.

By the 1990s, however, with a new understanding of multiculturalism becoming prevalent in the city council, the Birmingham Central Mosque had been reinterpreted as a landmark, marking a change in its perception from a 'controversial element of a regeneration scheme, [to] a celebrated icon'.[28] This shift was part of a wider repositioning of the council's self-identity through an increasing recognition of the 'contributions made to the economy and civic administration by different sectors of its ethnically and religiously diverse population'.[29]

The second mosque in the study, the Jame Masjid in Handsworth, involved similar discussions over the inclusion of a dome and minaret. When the proposal was presented to the council in 1978, the chairman of the planning committee stated that he had received confirmation from the mosque that it was prepared to remove the dome and minaret from the proposal, to 'make the proposal more sympathetic to the design and architecture of the adjoining shops'.[30] This discussion demonstrates the council's attempts to curtail the impact of mosques on urban space.[31]

The third mosque reviewed in the study was the Ghamkol Sharif Mosque in Small Heath (*see* pp 118–21), completed in 1996. By now Birmingham had been rebranded as a multicultural city, which resulted in observable changes in the planning process. With this mosque, for example, the council intended to make the building visually prominent so that it could serve as a landmark and represent Birmingham as a multicultural city. The council did, however, still stipulate the material palette, so dictating a degree of vernacularisation in the design.

The message of this investigation into these three Birmingham mosques is that there has been a shift in the way mosque proposals have been treated by the planning system, from ambivalence or hostility in the 1970s and 1980s, to endorsement and acceptance in the 1990s. Accordingly, the meaning of the building has transformed from being an alien intrusion to being a symbol of cultural diversity. The ability of the planning system to respond to diverse cultural needs has been questioned, and the system has been shown to be adaptable in its conception and understanding of these new building types and aesthetics. The examples in this book corroborate Gale's study by showing the transformation of mosque architecture over 30 plus years. Whereas mosques in the 1970s and 1980s were required by planning regulations to demonstrate the use of vernacular architectural references and materials to temper any Islamic forms, the mosques of the first decade of the 21st century have gained approval as full-blown representations and replications of historic Islamic architecture.

The road ahead

The examples of new and forthcoming mosques presented in Chapter 7, such as Bethnal Green's Shahporan Mosque (Fig 8.12), demonstrate that a diverse set of narratives for mosque-making has started to emerge. This has been driven by social change within Muslim communities, alongside better availability of resources and skills, and has led to an increased diversity in the types of mosque that make up the Muslim religious landscape in Britain, from the small scale to the large. Many mosques that were first established as rudimentary conversions of existing buildings became unfit for purpose due to limitations of size and layout. These mosques were then remodelled, extended, or replaced entirely

with a new larger purpose-built mosque, either on the same or sometimes on a nearby site.

With the growth of Britain's Muslim population from just over 1.5 million in 2001 to 2.7 million by 2011, the pressure on existing mosque facilities became intense. The redevelopment of mosques provided new opportunities for Muslim architecture to find expression, as the by now better resourced and organised Muslim congregations consciously used design and aesthetics as a means by which to represent and identify themselves.

So mosque development has continued apace and is showing a diverse range of expressions, from small-scale conversions to the transformation or replacement of existing mosques into major landmark structures. Mosques continue to transform the religious and urban landscape of Britain's towns and cities. They are established largely by immigrant Muslim communities and their descendants, and they are emerging in previously unseen forms, mostly within areas of historic Muslim settlement, but also in new areas, as Muslim populations disperse. These mosques are driven by new social narratives, and in some cases they explore new architecture, and expand their activities. It is a process of evolution and growth which, near the end of the second decade of the 21st century, can be seen as the next phase of the British mosque.

Fig 8.12
The Shahporan Mosque in east London adopts a contemporary approach to traditional Islamic art in the design of its new wing, while the original mosque in the historic house (on the left of this photograph) has been retained and refurbished.
[Author]

Fig A1.10 (left)
The Ashrafia Mosque in Bolton (before its demolition and rebuilding in 2016–17) was in a converted Sunday-school building which was unaltered on the exterior except for the addition of two small minarets. [Author]

Fig A1.11 (below left)
Interior of the Ashrafia Mosque in Bolton (before its demolition and rebuilding in 2016–17): the existing fabric had been retained alongside the new elements of the mosque. [Author]

The mosque is a converted early 20th-century chapel, built in a distinctive castle-like style with suggestions of Arts and Crafts influence. The interior of the church remains largely intact and the upper gallery, with its original timber panelling, is now used as a women's prayer hall (Fig A1.12).

Fig A1.12 (below)
The Shah Jalal Mosque, Cardiff, established in 1988 through the conversion of a former chapel. [Author]

levels to include prayer halls to accommodate up to 700 worshippers, funeral facilities, and teaching accommodation for 200 children. Construction started on site in May 2016, with completion planned for December 2017 (Figs A1.10 and A1.11).

3 Shah Jalal Mosque, Crwys Road, Cathays, Cardiff, 1988

While there were already two mosques in Butetown (see pp 45–56), established by Yemeni communities, the Shah Jalal Mosque was set up by the newer and growing Bangladeshi population of the city.

Fig A1.13 (right)
The Taiyabah Mosque
and Islamic Centre, Bolton,
moved in 1988 to the
converted buildings of a
former Congregational
Sunday school.
[DP143420]

Fig A1.14 (right)
The ablution facilities of
the Taiyabah Mosque and
Islamic Centre.
[DP143415]

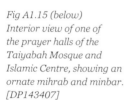

Fig A1.15 (below)
Interior view of one of
the prayer halls of the
Taiyabah Mosque and
Islamic Centre, showing an
ornate mihrab and minbar.
[DP143407]

4 Taiyabah Masjid and Islamic Centre, Blackburn Road, Bolton, 1988

The original Taiyabah Mosque was established in a converted warehouse in Canning Street, Bolton, in 1967. With the growth of the Muslim community, largely from the Bharuch district of Gujarat, the mosque purchased the Victorian buildings of a former Congregational Sunday school (Fig A1.13).

The complex comprises a series of imposing red-brick buildings. The interior spaces were varied in size and character, with a considerable amount of timber panelling. Original features have been left largely intact, showing how institutional and religious buildings can be adapted to Muslim use with minimal alterations, and how the character of such spaces can be retained with a new use (*see* Fig 1.17 and Figs A1.14 and A1.15).

5 Wembley Central Masjid, Ealing Road, Wembley, London, 1993

The mosque is the conversion of a former Non-conformist chapel dating from 1904, built in an Arts and Crafts style. A series of proposals has been considered, intending to introduce traditional Islamic typologies such as courtyards and fountains, but the building has remained unaltered in its exterior. The main hall itself has simply been cleared and reused as the main prayer hall (Figs A1.16 and A1.17).

Fig A1.16 (left)
Wembley Central Mosque
is a former early
20th-century
Nonconformist chapel that
was converted into a
mosque in 1993.
[DP183213]

Fig A1.17 (below left)
The main prayer hall of
Wembley Central Mosque.
[Author]

Fig A1.18 (below)
Leeds Grand Mosque was
established in 1994 through
the conversion of a brutalist
1965 Catholic church.
[DP34003]

6 Leeds Grand Mosque, Woodsley Road, Leeds, 1994

This mosque is the conversion of a Catholic church, the Church of the Sacred Heart, built in 1965 in a brutalist style as one of a series of churches in Leeds that moved away from 'traditional brick idioms to steel, concrete and glass'.[1] A large glazed box-like baptistery was placed at the west end to bring light into the building, and the nave spanned 23 metres, with the choir on a gallery at the west end (Fig A1.18).

The church was acquired and converted by the Muslim community in 1994, and its conversion into a mosque was aided by the fact that the Qibla was aligned to a long side wall in the main prayer

Fig A1.19
The ground-floor prayer
halls of Leeds Grand Mosque.
[DP34007]

hall. A simple mihrab has been placed in the centre of this wall, formed of carved arabesque plasterwork wedged between the concrete structural columns (Fig A1.19).

The mosque is entered alongside the former baptistery, which now serves as a glass-curtain-walled lobby area that is used for overspill prayer space when the main hall is full. The former chancel has been partitioned to form a further worship space or classroom, the former chapels either side of it house the administrator's office, and the former choir gallery is reused as the women's prayer space.

Fig A1.20
The Jumma Mosque, Batley
Carr, was established in
1960 through the conversion
of a storage building.
[DP185876]

c Conversions from public buildings and other building types

By the end of the 20th century, the vast majority of Britain's mosques were converted buildings, either houses, former places of worship or other types of building. These other conversions were from an array of building types, from cinema halls, to fire or police stations, to offices, to banks and so on. They ranged in scale and in the degree of alteration that had been carried out. Some were almost unchanged externally, except for perhaps some elements of decoration or signage, while others had Islamic architectural icons applied to radically alter the visual presence and identity of the building.

The vast array of examples of mosques formed through conversions of such buildings shows the diverse approaches and priorities of Muslim communities in establishing mosques across the country.

1 Jumma Masjid, Bradford Road, Batley Carr, Batley, 1960
2 Green Lane Masjid, Green Lane, Birmingham, 1979
3 Aziziye Mosque, Stoke Newington Road, Stoke Newington, London, c 1985
4 Islamic Centre of England, Maida Vale, London, 1998

1 Jumma Masjid, Bradford Road, Batley Carr, Batley, 1960

The first mosque in the mill town of Batley was formed through the conversion of a single-storey narrow storage building. Built from local stone, it was clad in pink marble and an impromptu minaret was added to a prominent corner (Fig A1.20).

2 Green Lane Masjid, Green Lane, Birmingham, 1979

This distinctive building was acquired by a Muslim community and converted into a mosque in 1979, prior to which the mosque had operated in two terraced houses in nearby Alum Rock. The building was formerly a Free Public Library dating from 1893 and a Public Baths from 1902.

When the library and baths moved to a new site in 1977, the local authority sold the buildings to the mosque. The spaces lent themselves to community uses, with the swimming pool hall being converted into a sports and assembly

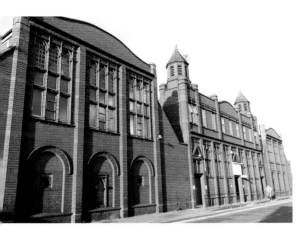

Fig A1.21 (far left)
The Green Lane Mosque in Birmingham was formerly a public library and swimming pool; it was converted into a mosque in 1979.
[Author]

Fig A1.22 (left)
The street façade of the Green Lane Mosque, which has been retained without any exterior alterations.
[Author]

Fig A1.23 (below left)
The main prayer hall of the Aziziye Mosque, which was formerly a cinema auditorium (see the frontispiece for a photograph of the minbar).
[DP132041]

Fig A1.24 (below)
The Aziziye Mosque in north London was a former cinema built in 1914, which was converted into a mosque in the 1980s.
[DP132023]

hall. Adaptation work has continued since the building was first acquired, to provide facilities for worship and for the community as needs have developed (Figs A1.21 and A1.22).

3 Aziziye Mosque, Stoke Newington Road, Stoke Newington, London, *c* 1985

The Aziziye Mosque in north London was originally built in 1914 as a cinema, the Apollo Picture House. It was designed in a mock-oriental style popular at the time for cinema buildings. In the 1980s the local Turkish Muslim community acquired the building.

It was gradually converted. Initially the cinema hall itself was used as the prayer hall, complete with sloping floor. Eventually the building was comprehensively refurbished, with a new main prayer hall constructed in place of the cinema hall (*see* Fig 1.8), and the exterior clad in Iznik tiles (Fig A1.23 and *see* Fig 8.6).

The original design of the building complemented its conversion into a mosque, with the oriental styling finding ready resignification as a mosque. In a way that is traditional to mosques in the Muslim world, commerce is found attached to the mosque, with a grocery store and restaurant on the ground floor (Fig A1.24).

Fig A1.25
The Maida Vale Picture
House in 1920. It was
converted into the Islamic
Centre of England in 1998.
[BL25078]

Fig A1.26
The main prayer hall of the
Islamic Centre of England.
[DP132086]

4 Islamic Centre of England, Maida Vale, London, 1998

The Islamic Centre is in an imposing and distinctive building, erected as the Maida Vale Picture House in 1912. The most distinctive features are the rectangular towers flanking the entrance bay, each crowned with a dome (Fig A1.25 and *see* Fig 8.3).

After a varied history – in 1949 it became the Carlton Rooms Dance Hall, and in 1965 a casino

and bingo hall – the building was purchased by the mosque in 1997. It had been listed in 1991 as a 'rare example of a virtually unaltered early picture house'.[2]

The Islamic Centre carried out a few careful internal alterations to enable it to be used as a mosque. These were mainly cosmetic, such as the concealing of statues at the top of columns in the main prayer hall, and the addition of calligraphic features. It stands as a fine example of how an Islamic aesthetic language can be introduced sensitively to a historically significant interior (Fig A1.26 and *see* Fig 1.18).

d Purpose-built mosques

Purpose-built mosques have been seen in Britain since Woking Mosque was constructed in the 1880s (*see* pp 26–35). However, only a handful had been built by the late 1970s. It was in the last two decades of the 20th century that purpose-built mosques went up at a significant rate. By the end of the century there were estimated to be around 200.

It was through the building of the mosque from the ground up that the fullest expression of a Muslim architecture in Britain could emerge, as Muslim communities were able to explore their own visions for representing their identities and aspirations in architecture. These examples demonstrate a range of approaches.

1 Jamia Masjid, Eagle Street, Foleshill, Coventry, 1957
2 Birmingham Central Mosque, Belgrave Middleway, Highgate, Birmingham, 1975
3 Glasgow Central Mosque, Mosque Avenue, Gorbals, Glasgow, 1984
4 Jamea Masjid, Clarendon Street, Frenchwood, Preston, 1984
5 Leicester Central Mosque, Conduit Street, Leicester, 1994
6 Jamiyat Tabligh-ul-Islam (Bradford Central Mosque), Darfield Street, Westgate, Bradford, 2000
7 Baitul Futuh Mosque, London Road, Morden, Surrey, 2003
8 Noor-ul-Uloom Mosque, St Oswalds Road, Small Heath, Birmingham, 2004
9 Masjid-e-Shah Jalal (Bangladeshi Islamic Society), Ellers Road, Leeds, 2004
10 Anjuman-e-Jamali Markaz, Syedna Way, Lidgett Green, Bradford, 2008
11 Masjid e Tauheedul Islam, Bicknell Street, Blackburn, 2010

1 Jamia Masjid, Eagle Street, Foleshill, Coventry, 1957

This is one of the earliest post-war purpose-built mosques in the country. It was built in 1957, an unadorned single-storey brick building on a site that had been cleared of five terraced houses. In 1962 plans were prepared for the extension of the mosque, construction for which started in 1966. The building was further extended through the 1970s, and in the 1980s the onion-shaped dome and twin minarets, along with further embellishments, were added. In 2015 a front extension was built to provide a room where the deceased could be prayed over.

This is an early example of a mosque iteratively built by post-Partition South Asian immigrants, and a prime example of a place of worship self-built by its congregation. It was designed by the mosque committee, and physically built through the volunteering of the community. The evolution of the mosque also shows the enduring desire of the congregation to communicate its identity through the application of symbols derived from Mughal Islamic architecture, suggesting the importance to the community of maintaining symbolic connections to places of origin (Figs A1.27 and A1.28).

2 Birmingham Central Mosque, Belgrave Middleway, Highgate, Birmingham, 1975

Birmingham Central Mosque (*see* p 259) incorporated conventional motifs and symbols borrowed from Islamic architectural history, namely the dome and minaret, and came to be seen as a landmark structure. As with many purpose-built mosques to come, it was built incrementally, as funds were raised, with minarets added some years after the main building (Fig A1.29).

Fig A1.27 (left top)
The Jamia Mosque, Coventry, is one of the earliest examples of a post-World War II purpose-built mosque. [Author]

Fig A1.28 (left bottom)
The main prayer hall on the ground floor of the Jamia Mosque. [Author]

Fig A1.29 (below)
Birmingham Central Mosque, which opened in 1975, was one of the first generation of post-war landmark mosques. [DP137782]

Fig A1.30
The main prayer hall
of Birmingham Central
Mosque.
[DP137781]

Fig A1.31
The main entrance of
Glasgow Central Mosque,
an ambitious interpretation
of traditional mosque
architecture.
[DP143533]

The interior of the main prayer hall is plain and unadorned, with a circular beam and chandelier to represent the dome from within (Fig A1.30).

3 Glasgow Central Mosque, Mosque Avenue, Gorbals, Glasgow, 1984

This was the first purpose-built mosque in Glasgow, and was completed and opened in 1984. It is a large mosque in a prominent location on the bank of the River Clyde, and has served as a landmark in the city.

It has a distinctive design language, in which traditional Islamic architecture is interpreted in a postmodernist idiom. A glass faceted dome is positioned above a large glazed entrance portico formed in concrete. A series of concrete ribs project on the façades with smoked-glass glazing behind to let light into the prayer hall (Fig A1.31).

In common with other landmark Muslim buildings from the late 1970s and through the 1980s, such as Regent's Park Mosque and the Ismaili Centre, both in London (*see* Chapter 5), Glasgow Central Mosque sought to interpret traditional Islamic architecture in a contemporary way (Figs A1.32 and A1.33).

4 Jamea Masjid, Clarendon Street, Frenchwood, Preston, 1984

The Lancashire mill towns were the destination for significant numbers of immigrants from northern Pakistan and Gujarat in India in the 1960s and 1970s. Preston, Bolton and Blackburn consequently acquired large Muslim populations, who quickly established religious institutions. Today these towns have some of the highest concentrations of Muslim residents, and mosques, in the country (*see* pp 270–1).

The Jamea Mosque in Preston was designed by Thomas Hargreaves, who ran a successful northern practice with George Grenfell-Baines

before the latter went on to found the Building Design Partnership (BDP) in 1961. Hargreaves was in his later years at the time, and had said that if there was one building he would like to design, it would be a mosque. Like many mosques of the period, it started life as two converted houses on the same site, subsequently demolished to make way for the new building.

There is no dome and no single minaret – the Islamic identification is contained in four small spire-minarets along the front façade, and a crescent motif over the main entrance. Hargreaves layered the front façade with Forticrete blockwork, a recessed layer of which is riven. The building carries overtones of a medieval castle, with square turrets, stepped buttresses and battlements (Fig A1.34).

Completed in 1984, Hargreaves' mosque reflects contemporary postmodernism, which may have influenced the metaphorical strategies he employed, mixing references of English medieval revival with an Islamic twist.

With post-1960s Muslim immigration and the mass mosque building that followed, this mosque stands out as one of the few that continued the approach of London's Regent's Park Mosque (*see* pp 133–47) and the South Wales Islamic Centre in Cardiff (*see* pp 52–6), not relying on literal translations of Islamic architectural history, but instead exploring an idea of what the mosque is and could be in a new British context.

Fig A1.32 (above left)
The upper women's prayer gallery of Glasgow Central Mosque, overlooking the men's prayer hall.
[Author]

Fig A1.33 (above)
The main men's prayer hall of Glasgow Central Mosque.
[DP143529]

Fig A1.34
The Jamea Mosque, Preston, a mid-1980s example of a mosque that reinterpreted traditional Islamic architecture.
[Author]

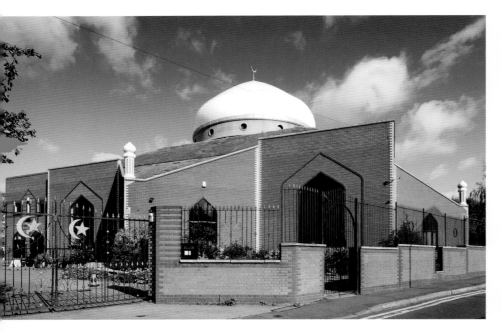

*Fig A1.35 (above)
Leicester Central Mosque,
a landmark building
constructed over a
period of six years.
[DP137471]*

*Fig A1.36 (above right)
The richly decorated
mihrab of Leicester
Central Mosque.
[DP137466]*

*Fig A1.37 (below right)
Bradford Central Mosque,
a landmark mosque close
to the city centre with
strong references to
Ottoman architecture.
[DP143427]*

*Fig A1.38 (below)
Detail of the stalactite ceiling
in the main entrance portico
of Bradford Central Mosque.
[DP143426]*

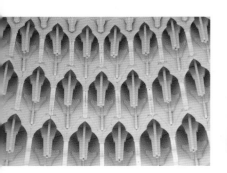

5 Leicester Central Mosque, Conduit Street, Leicester, 1994

Leicester Central Mosque started as a house mosque on Sutherland Street in 1968 (*see* p 262). In 1986 the mosque organisation, realising the need for larger premises, bought a 1.35 acre (0.55ha) plot of land, close to Leicester train station, from the local council.

Construction of the Central Mosque started in 1988, and the first phase, completed in 1994, was a large prayer hall to accommodate 1,500 worshippers (*see* Fig 1.7). Further phases included a basement ablution area, ground-floor reception and offices, and a women's gallery with ablution facilities (Figs A1.35 and A1.36).

6 Jamiyat Tabligh-ul-Islam (Bradford Central Mosque), Darfield Street, Westgate, Bradford, 2000

This mosque is located close to the city centre, and is built with Ottoman references as well as more generic Islamic languages. The mosque has a long and protracted history, a more elaborate scheme having been proposed prior to that approved and built (Fig A1.37).

While the interior remains plain, considerable craft has been undertaken in the dome and the entrance portico, both of which have replicated traditional decorative motifs (Fig A1.38).

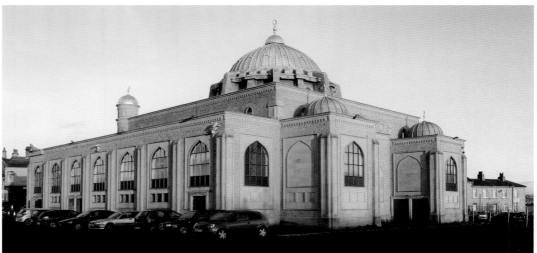

Fig A1.39 (left)
The interior of the Baitul Futuh Mosque is restrained and simple, with a large central dome and floor-to-ceiling windows.
[DP148081]

7 Baitul Futuh Mosque, London Road, Morden, Surrey, 2003

This is cited as the largest mosque in Europe by its founders, with a capacity of some 6,000 worshippers. It is the centre of the Ahmadiyya community, who also constructed London's first purpose-built mosque (and Britain's second), Fazl, in 1926 (*see* pp 35–43).

This mosque also has community facilities, including a library and sports halls. The community facilities are housed in the main part of the building, a former dairy whose chimney was adapted into the site's tallest minaret. The mosque section was a new-build element at the end of the converted dairy (Figs A1.39, A1.40 and A1.41).

Fig A1.40 (below)
The Baitul Futuh Mosque, Morden, is a new building that is part of a larger religious complex.
[DP148084]

Fig A1.41 (below left)
The library of the Baitul Futuh Mosque complex is in a converted building on the site.
[DP148079]

8 Noor-ul-Uloom Mosque, St Oswalds Road, Small Heath, Birmingham, 2004

This mosque lies within a densely populated residential neighbourhood, and is characteristic of many mosques that serve as local facilities. Prior to this building, the mosque was accommodated within a converted shop and flat on the same site. This was redeveloped into the purpose-built facility, following a common development trajectory for purpose-built mosques – the redevelopment of an existing mosque site that had become inadequate for the community's needs.

The building closely follows the language and grain of the existing urban context, forming a corner block that joins two streets and using red brick and tiled, pitched roofs. It is only the placing of two minarets on the corners of the building that definitively characterises it as a religious place (Fig A1.42).

9 Masjid-e-Shah Jalal (Bangladeshi Islamic Society), Ellers Road, Leeds, 2004

This mosque is in the inner-city ward of Gipton and Harehills, with a Muslim population of approximately 20 per cent, and a working-class area characterised by densely packed terraces of back-to-back housing.

The Bangladeshi Islamic Society was formed in 1978 and converted two houses in Ellers Road into a mosque. As the local Bangladeshi Muslim population grew, the house mosque could not accommodate the congregation, and was replaced in 2004 with a purpose-built mosque at a cost of around £800,000.

Architecturally the mosque completes the end of a terrace of back-to-back houses, with a minaret positioned at the corner defining the point where the streets meet. It forms a corner block and provides a local landmark within otherwise fairly uniform streetscapes. The scale mediates a transition from the two-storey houses to the taller minaret and dome structure, and the materials also reflect local brick and stone banding. The minaret is capped in a green plastic dome, on a hexagonal base with keyhole-shaped profiles, mimicking a chattri. Decorative gables, somewhat Dutch in style, pick up the rhythm of the terraced house gables on Ellers Road. Internally, the mihrab and minbar are elaborately designed.[3]

This is a new mosque that is physically embedded into the urban landscape. It carefully follows the existing scale and character of the locale, and makes itself prominent while remaining aware

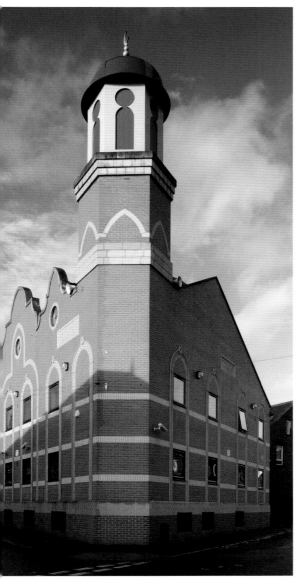

of its context. It is a different type of new-build mosque from the landmark structure that aims to stand autonomous of its surroundings (Fig A1.43).

10 Anjuman-e-Jamali Markaz, Syedna Way, Lidgett Green, Bradford, 2008

This mosque is for the Shia Bohra community, who are a minority group tracing their origins to Fatimid Egypt. Because of this historical lineage, the Bohra mosques built in Britain take on the aesthetic language of this period of history. Here motifs from medieval Cairo are carefully replicated, with stepped battlements, a square minaret and pointed-arch windows.

The mosque follows a trend that emerged in the late 20th century, where new mosques attempted to fully replicate previous Islamic architectures, without any concessions to modern or contemporary aesthetic cultures (Figs A1.44 and A1.45).

11 Masjid e Tauheedul Islam, Bicknell Street, Blackburn, 2010

This is a large mosque in an inner-city area of Blackburn with a high percentage of Muslim residents (*see* Fig 1.1). Although it is a local mosque, as the local Muslim population is large, it is a substantial building and intensively used. It is interesting to note how the mosque has

Fig A1.44 (top) Anjuman-e-Jamali Markaz introduces a new architectural language alongside more traditional buildings. [Author]

Fig A1.45 (above) Anjuman-e-Jamali Markaz, Bradford, attempts to replicate the 11th-century Fatimid architecture of North Africa. [Author]

Fig A1.46
Masjid e Tauheedul Islam, Blackburn, is a local landmark mosque which serves a neighbourhood with a high concentration of Muslim residents.
[DP143574]

Fig A1.47
The main prayer hall of Masjid e Tauheedul Islam.
[DP143577]

occupied as much of the site as possible with an elongated octagonal plan, with central dome. This model could be traced to the Dome of the Rock in Jerusalem completed in 691 CE, which is considered one of the first examples of Islamic architecture. However, it could also be that there was no overt historical reference intended but rather that the octagonal plan enabled the maximum use of the site and enabled one wall to be oriented towards the Qibla (Fig A1.46).

Internally the building is elaborately finished, with marble-lined walls, decorated ceiling tiles and calligraphic lighting features in the main prayer hall (*see* Fig 1.5). It also generates some energy from solar thermal technology. Both in its elaborate interior decoration and in the use of new technologies, this mosque offers exemplary facilities in this part of the city (Fig A1.47).

Appendix 2

Maps prepared as part of the English Heritage/Historic England research project show-ing mosque locations in three key urban locations overlaid with the density of the Muslim population and levels of deprivation (*see* p 16).

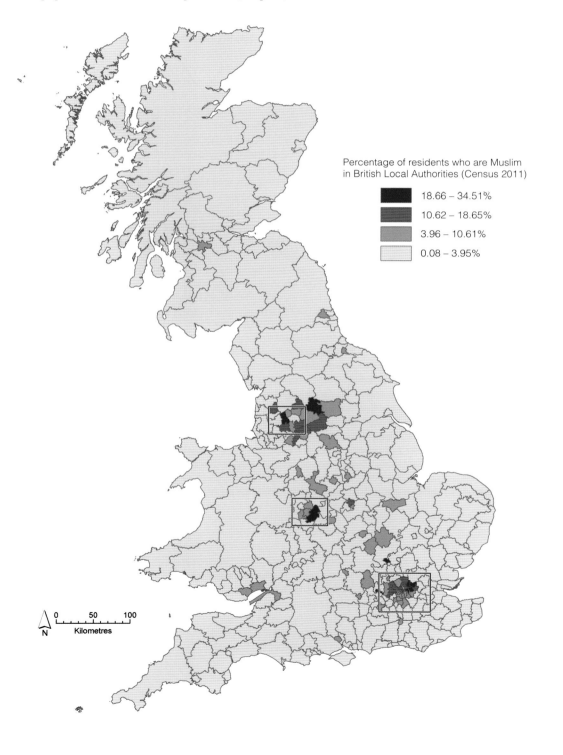

Percentage of residents who are Muslim
in British Local Authorities (Census 2011)

■	18.66 – 34.51%
■	10.62 – 18.65%
■	3.96 – 10.61%
□	0.08 – 3.95%

0   50   100

Kilometres

N

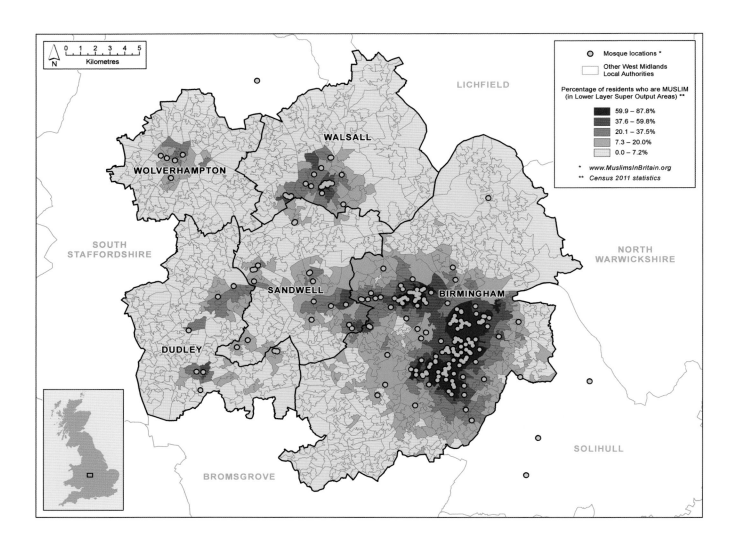

Fig A2.1
Mosque locations in Birmingham and parts of the West Midlands, overlaid with the density of the Muslim population.

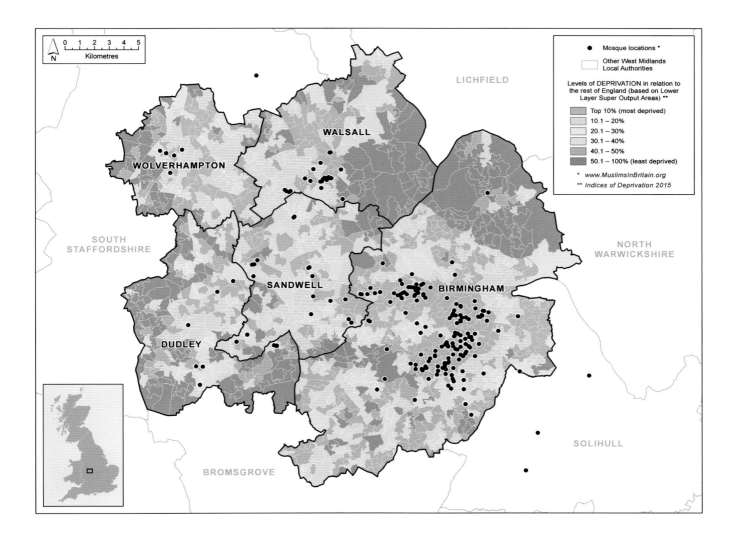

Fig A2.2
Mosque locations in Birmingham and parts of the West Midlands, overlaid with levels of deprivation.

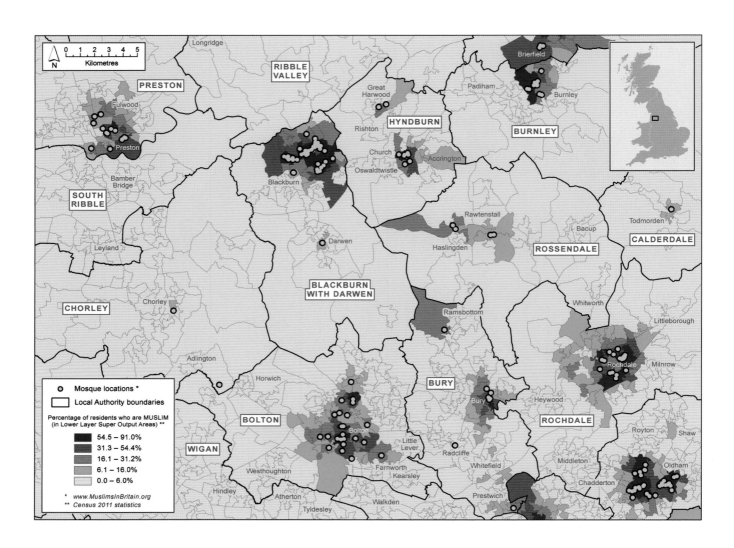

Fig A2.3
Mosque locations in southern Lancashire and parts of Greater Manchester, overlaid with the density of the Muslim population.

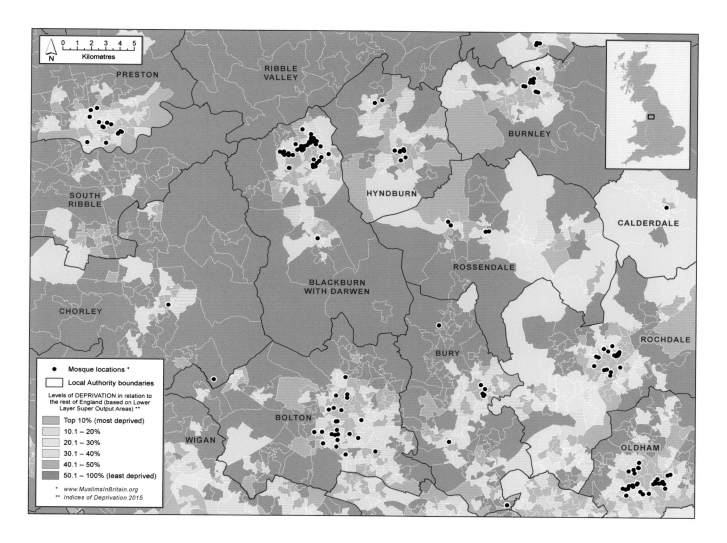

Fig A2.4
Mosque locations in southern Lancashire and parts of Greater Manchester, overlaid with levels of deprivation.

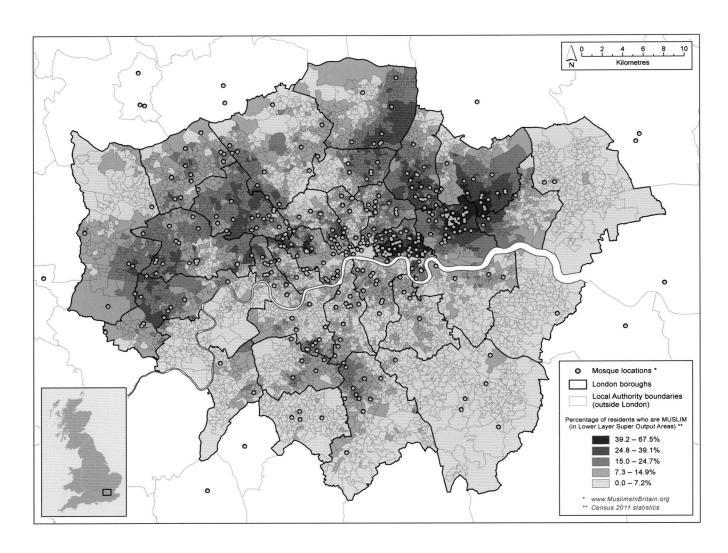

Fig A2.5
Mosque locations in Greater London, overlaid with the density of the Muslim population.

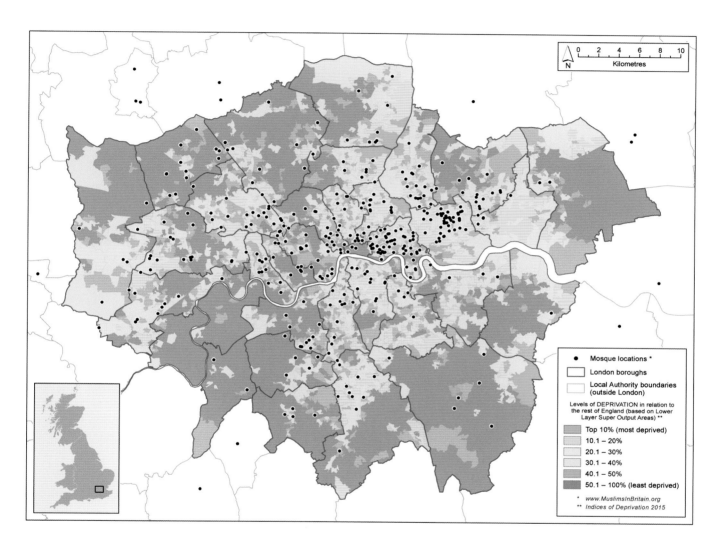

Fig A2.6
Mosque locations in Greater London, overlaid with levels of deprivation.

The legend within the figure reads:

- Mosque locations *
- London boroughs
- Local Authority boundaries (outside London)

Levels of DEPRIVATION in relation to the rest of England (based on Lower Layer Super Output Areas) **

- Top 10% (most deprived)
- 10.1 – 20%
- 20.1 – 30%
- 30.1 – 40%
- 40.1 – 50%
- 50.1 – 100% (least deprived)

* www.MuslimsInBritain.org
** Indices of Deprivation 2015

Glossary

Abbasid
The third Islamic caliphate to succeed the Prophet Muhammad, which ruled from North Africa to modern Iraq from the 8th to the 16th centuries.

Ahmadiyya/Ahmadi
An Islamic movement founded in 1889 in Punjab, India, by Mirza Ghulam Ahmad (1835–1908), who claimed to have been divinely appointed as the promised 'Mahdi' (messiah or renewer) of Islam, foretold by the Prophet Muhammad. Since his death the community has expanded into a global movement through a programme of missionary work. In 2005 it was estimated to have around 20 million adherents.[1] Ahmadi religious practice is essentially in line with majority Sunni Islam; however, because of their belief in the divine appointment of Mirza Ghulam Ahmad, they have been declared by some mainstream Muslims as heretics, which has resulted in cases of discrimination and persecution.

Barelwi
An Islamic movement founded by Ahmad Reza Khan (1856–1921) in 1904 in the north Indian town of Bareilly, said to be a reaction against Deobandi influence in that it promoted a Sufic type of Islam traditional to South Asia. It is thought that the majority of Muslims in India and Pakistan adhere to the Barelwi movement.

Bohra *see also* **Dawoodi Bohra**
An Ismaili sect within the Shia branch of Islam, with its origins in western India. Bohra is an adaptation of the Gujarati word *vahaurau,* meaning 'to trade', and encompasses a Sunni minority as well as the better known Shia majority. In the 16th century there was a split in the Bohra community between the followers of Da'ud ibn Qutb Shah and Sulayman, who both claimed leadership. The followers of Da'ud came to be known as the Dawoodi Bohras, with the seat of their leadership residing in Mumbai. The followers of Sulayman are known as the Suleymani Bohras, with their leadership in Yemen.

chain migration
The process by which immigrants from a particular town or locality follow others from that same place on a migratory journey to a new place of residence. It may be facilitated by organised or semi-organised networks of agents who identify employment opportunities and assist with travel and accommodation. The encouragement and assistance of preceding migrants is fundamental to the establishment of chain migration networks.

chattri
Literally meaning 'canopy' or 'umbrella' in Urdu, these are small architectural features consisting of a dome supported on columns, which are usually used to mark the corners, roof or entrances of major buildings. They originated in Rajasthani architecture of the 6th century and later became a standard feature of Mughal buildings.

Dawoodi Bohra *see also* **Bohra**
A sect within the Ismaili branch of Shia Islam. They follow a Shia Islam of the Fatimid Imamate of medieval Egypt and are concentrated mostly in Pakistan, Yemen and East Africa.

Deobandi
A Sunni Islamic movement founded by a group of Indian scholars in 1866 in the north Indian town of Deoband, where they established their first Islamic seminary, the Darul Uloom Deoband. The movement is described as having developed as a reaction against British colonialism and as an attempt to preserve and revive correct Muslim practice. It is therefore seen as being a revivalist movement in opposition to the Barelwi practice of Islam in South Asia.

dhikr
Devotional acts of remembering God, usually through the repetition of short phrases or prayers, and usually associated with Sufi religious practice.

Eid al-Fitr/Eid al-Adha
The two major festivals in the Muslim calendar. Eid al-Fitr is a prayer and day of celebration that marks the end of Ramadan, the month of fasting. Eid al-Adha is a prayer and celebration that marks the end of Hajj, the annual pilgrimage to Makkah.

Fatimid
An Ismaili Shia caliphate that ruled across North Africa from the 10th to the 12th centuries.

imam
The leader of a Muslim prayer when it is performed in congregation.

Ismaili
The second largest Shia community in the Muslim world after the Ithna'ashari (Twelver) branch. The Ismailis were followers of Ja'far al-Sadiq's second son, Ismail, while the Twelvers followed his third son, Musa. The Ismaili evolved various branches through time including the Nizari and Mustali.

Ithna'ashari (*also known as* Twelvers)
The largest branch of Shia Islam. The two major Shia branches emerged after the death in 8th-century Madinah of the Prophet's descendant Ja'far al-Sadiq, who had developed Shia theology and jurisprudence. The Shia Ithna'ashari are communities of Shia Muslims originating in the Indian subcontinent, mainly in the states of Gujarat, Maharashtra, Rajasthan and Hyderabad. Following migratory patterns prevalent among communities on the west coast of India through the 19th century, many members of the Ithna'ashari community settled in East Africa.

iwan
A rectangular hall or enclosed courtyard for gathering which can serve as a room in itself or/and as an entranceway to a larger or more significant space, traditionally built with a vaulted roof and enclosed on three sides where one side would be left open, though often it would be fronted by a ceremonial entrance gateway.

jamatkhana
An Ismaili term for community meeting hall. An amalgamation of the Arabic word *jama'a* (gathering) and the Persian word *khan* (house/place), it literally means a place of meeting. The Ismaili refer to their places of worship specifically as *jamatkhanas* and not mosques or masjids.

Jummah
The main weekly congregational prayer for Muslims, held every Friday just after noon in the place of the Zuhr (afternoon prayer).

Ka'ba
Literally meaning 'the Cube', it is located in Makkah and is considered by Muslims to be the House of God, and the most sacred site in the world, the place towards which all prayer is directed. Muslims understand the Ka'ba to be at the centre of the world, with the Gate of Heaven directly above it. It has been rebuilt numerous times since Muhammad, with the current structure – a cuboid made of granite blocks – rebuilt in the 17th century.

madrassa
A religious school.

mahalla
A Bohra term for neighbourhood or community.

Makkah
The city in the Hejaz region of Saudi Arabia in which the Ka'ba is located, Islam's holiest site, towards which Muslims pray. The city is the place of the Prophet Muhammad's birth and where he received his first revelations.

markaz/markazi
A community centre with a prayer space.

mashrabiya
An Arabic term referring to a window with a latticework screen in the place of glass.

masjid
An Arabic term for mosque; it literally means 'place of prostration in prayer'.

Madinah
A city 211 miles north of Makkah, to where the Prophet Muhammad migrated with his followers in 622 CE. It is the second-holiest place in Islam and is where Muhammad founded the first Muslim political city state and where he died and is buried.

mihrab/mehrab
A niche marking out the place for the imam to stand when leading the prayer, and the direction of the Qibla.

minbar
An Arabic term for a series of steps which serve as a pulpit where the imam stands to deliver sermons or other lectures. It is usually a stepped structure and has varied in size and style across Islamic history.

muezzin
The person appointed at the mosque to recite the call to prayer.

Mughal
An empire ruled by a Muslim dynasty over large parts of the Indian subcontinent from the 16th to the 19th centuries.

Qibla
Direction of the Ka'ba.

Quran/Koran
The Muslims' holy book, which literally means 'the recitation'. It is a record of the word of God as it was revealed to the Prophet Muhammad through the angel Gabriel.

Ramadan
The Muslim month of fasting.

Salafee/Salafi
A Sunni Islamic reform movement originating in the 18th century whose adherents sought to return to the authentic religious

practices of the time of the Prophet Muhammad, following the example of the earliest Muslims, the companions of the Prophet Muhammad, who are seen to embody the best Islamic practice.

Shia

One of the two major branches in Islam (the other being Sunni), the split having originated at the time of the death of Muhammad when his succession was contested. The Shia believe that the Prophet Muhammad appointed Ali ibn Abi Talib, his cousin and son-in-law, as his successor, but that his succession was usurped. In 2009 it was estimated that 10–13 per cent of the world's Muslims were Shia.

Sufism

An Islamic practice which emphasises the inner mystical dimension of the religion and aims at the purification of the inner self through religious practice.

Sunnah

The verbally transmitted teachings, deeds, sayings, silent permissions or disapprovals of the Prophet Muhammad which have been recoded to form a canon of religious guidance and instruction. Along with the Quran, understood as the revealed word of God, the Sunnah constitutes the secondary source from which Islamic theology is determined.

Sunni

The dominant of the two major branches in Islam (the other being Shia), the split having originated at the time of the death of Muhammad when his succession was contested. The Sunni believe that the Prophet Muhammad did not appoint a successor, but rather that it was the role of his companions to elect the next leader, which they did by electing his father-in-law, Abu Bakr.

Tariqa

A school or order of Sufism through which the spiritual teachings of that order (which are ultimately understood as being the mystical teaching of the Prophet Muhammad) are transmitted.

Twelver *see* Ithna'ashari

wudu

The ritual ablution that Muslims undertake before prayer. It involves washing of the hands, nose, mouth, face, neck, arms and feet with clean running water.

zawiya

A Sufi place of worship, meeting house.

Notes

Foreword

1   Tanyeli 2014, 32.
2   Ibid, 47.

1   Introduction – mosques and Muslims in Britain

1   English Church Census 2005, www.eauk. org/church/research-and-statistics/ english-church-census.cfm (accessed 14 Sep 2015).
2   Mackay, M 2005 'New study finds mosque goers to double church attendance'. *Christian Today*, 5 Sep 2005, www.christiantoday. co.uk/article/new.study.finds.mosque. goers.to.double.church.attendance/3858. htm (accessed 17 Sep 2011).
3   Ansari 2004, 24 and 26.
4   For the purposes of this book, South Asia is taken to refer to India, Pakistan and Bangladesh.
5   Ansari 2004, 61.
6   Lewis 2002, 14.
7   Ibid, 15.
8   Ansari 2004, 148, quoting from Anwar 1979, 214.
9   Lewis 2002, 16.
10 Ibid.
11 Ansari 2004, 149.
12 Ibid.
13 Ibid.
14 Ibid, 176.
15 Lewis 2002, 18.
16 Ibid, 19.
17 Ibid.
18 Ibid, 343.
19 Ibid.
20 Ibid.
21 Dickie 1978, 16.
22 Petersen 1996, 68.
23 Creswell 1926.
24 Petersen 1996, 188.
25 Ibid, 25.
26 Jones 1978, 161.
27 Ibid, 164.
28 Serageldin 1996, Introduction.
29 Peach and Gale 2003. Sources for their survey: 'Data transcribed by Simon Naylor from manuscript records of the General Register Office Register of Places of Worship, kept at Southport, Merseyside; data published annually in *Marriage,*
Divorce and Adoption Statistics, Series FM2 (London: Office for National Statistics); no separate Hindu data are given in the published records. Our data differ slightly from the published sources because our fieldwork revealed disused sites.'
30 www.muslimsinbritain.org.
31 The research project which resulted in this publication was originally funded by English Heritage's Heritage Protection Commissions (HPC) Programme. Work began in 2010, with Shahed Saleem as the main researcher. In April 2015 English Heritage was divided into the English Heritage Trust and Historic England. Historic England now oversees the HPC.
32 The distribution maps for the project were originally based on data from the 2001 census. They were later updated using data from the 2011 census.
33 The Indices of Deprivation are prepared by the Department for Communities and Local Government. The distribution maps for the project were originally based on data from the 2010 indices. They were later updated using data from the 2015 indices.
34 Peach and Gale 2003.

2   The first mosques

1   The Ahmadiyya movement was founded by a local preacher in northern India near the end of the 19th century. Mirza Ghulam Ahmad was born in the city of Qadian in 1835. At the age of 59 he declared himself the Mahdi, the promised messiah foretold by Muhammad, and the metaphorical second coming of Jesus, who would come during the last days to revive the religion of Islam and lead the Muslims (for the official website of the Ahmadiyya Muslim Community, *see* www.alislam.org/ introduction/index.html). By the time of his death in 1908, the Ahmadiyya estimate that they numbered 500,000 members globally (interview with Imam Rasheed, imam of Fazl Mosque, 28 Mar 2011) and they had embarked on a programme of propagation and expansion that continues to this day. The Ahmadiyya are considered heretics by some orthodox Muslims because of the messiah status attributed to their spiritual founder. In 1914 there was a
split in the movement and the Lahore Ahmadiyya were formed. Their ideological difference with the Ahmadiyya was that they did not believe Mirza Ghulam Ahmad to be a prophet, but rather as the Mahdi and a reformer.
2   Geaves 2010, 64.
3   Ibid.
4   Ibid.
5   Ibid, 77.
6   Ibid.
7   Ibid.
8   Ibid.
9   Ibid.
10 The National Heritage List for England entry for 8, 9 and 10 Brougham Terrace, West Derby Road, Liverpool (list entry 1062583).
11 Cannon, J 1964 'Woking Mosque'. *Surrey Today*, Dec 1964, 24.
12 Nairn and Pevsner 1971, 165.
13 Entry for Chambers, Irish Architectural Archive, Dictionary of Irish Architects 1720–1940, www.dia.ie/architects/ view/132 (accessed 7 Mar 2013).
14 Peter Guillery (of the Survey of London), pers comm, 2 Nov 2011.
15 Ansari 2002, 7.
16 Salamat 2008, 26.
17 *Surah Fatihah* – the opening chapter of the Quran, which is recited during each of the five daily prayers.
18 Salamat 2008, 26.
19 Ibid.
20 Ibid, 24.
21 Ibid, 62; *see also* note 1 above.
22 *Daily News*, 29 May 1922, as quoted in Salamat 2008, 37.
23 *Woking News and Mail*, 2 Jun 1922, as quoted in Salamat 2008, 39.
24 Woking Mosque website, www. shahjahanmosque.org.uk/history-mosque/ history-mosque-part-3 (accessed 12 Oct 2011).
25 Office of National Statistics Census 2001, Woking.
26 Ansari 2002, 14.
27 Salamat 2008, 59.
28 Woking Borough Council (WBC) planning file 18152 and 18612.
29 WBC planning file 18612, letter from James Hanson, quantity surveyor to Woking Urban District Council (UDC), 5 Nov 1964.

30 WBC planning file 18339.
31 WBC planning file 18339, letter from James Hanson to Woking UDC, 16 Jul 1964.
32 Salamat 2008, 64.
33 As quoted in Salamat 2008, 65.
34 Salamat 2008, 64.
35 WBC planning file 28718.
36 WBC planning file 74/777.
37 WBC planning files 82/660, 82/289 and 83/47.
38 Salamat 2008, 72.
39 Ibid, 66.
40 WBC planning file 1999/0628, letter from the Shah Jahan Mosque to WBC planning dept, 27 May 1999.
41 WBC planning file 1999/0628, decision date 3 Oct 2001.
42 Interview with Imam Rasheed, imam of Fazl Mosque, 23 Mar 2011.
43 Willey 2006, 455.
44 'Moslem mosque for Southfields', *South Western Star*, 2 Oct 1925, cutting in 'Fazl Mosque' file at Wandsworth Local History Library at Battersea.
45 Ibid.
46 Naylor and Ryan 2002, 45.
47 Anon 1926a.
48 Anon 1926b.
49 Kadish 2011, 175.
50 *South Western Star*, 8 Oct 1926, 5, quoted in Naylor and Ryan 2002, 50.
51 Anon 1926b.
52 *The Builder*, 8 Oct 1926, **131** (4366), 558.
53 Naylor and Ryan 2002.
54 Naylor and Ryan 2002, 50.
55 Interview with Imam Rasheed, imam of Fazl Mosque, 23 Mar 2011.
56 Naylor and Ryan 2002, 46.
57 Ibid.
58 *South Western Star*, 8 Oct 1926, 5, quoted in Naylor and Ryan 2002, 46.
59 'First mosque in London', *The Times*, 2 Oct 1926, 7, col A.
60 'The first London mosque', *The Times*, 4 Oct 1926, 11, col C.
61 Ibid.
62 Ansari 2008, 51.
63 Ibid.
64 Naylor and Ryan 2002, 51.
65 Ibid.
66 London Borough of Wandsworth (LBW) planning file 2010/0486, planning committee report, 14 Jul 2011, 42.
67 Naylor and Ryan 2002, 52.
68 Ibid.
69 LBW planning file W/98/0555, refused 5 Aug 1998.
70 LBW planning application 91/W/109, refused 16 Dec 1991.
71 LBW planning file 2010/0486, planning committee report, 14 Jul 2011, 42.
72 Baitul Futuh website, www.baitulfutuh. org/community/index.shtml (accessed 4 Sep 2011).

73 LBW planning file 2010/0486.
74 LBW planning file 2010/0486, decision notice, 15 Jul 2011.
75 LBW planning file 2011/4853.
76 'Cardiff Council Minutes: 1896–7', *Cardiff Records: Volume 5*, ed John Hobson Matthews (Cardiff, 1905), 238–61, www. british-history.ac.uk/report. aspx?compid=48196 (accessed 20 Aug 2011).
77 Ibid.
78 'The History of Cardiff's Suburbs: Butetown and Cardiff Bay, incorporating Tiger Bay and the docks', www.cardiffians. co.uk/suburbs/butetown_and_cardiffbay. shtml (accessed 22 Aug 2011).
79 Ansari 2004, 39.
80 Ibid, 35.
81 Ibid, 36–8.
82 Neil Evans, quoted in Gilliat-Ray 2010, 37.
83 Alison Benjamin, 'Mixed metaphor', *The Guardian*, 14 Mar 2001, www. theguardian.com/society/2001/mar/14/ guardiansocietysupplement5 (accessed 17 Nov 2015).
84 Howard Spring, quoted in Halliday 2010, 18.
85 Gilliat-Ray 2010, 36.
86 Ibid, 33.
87 Interview with Dawud Suleiman of the South Wales Islamic Centre, 25 May 2011.
88 Gilliat-Ray 2010, 33.
89 A Sufi religious order started by Sheikh Ahmad al-Allawi in North Africa in the early 20th century.
90 Lawless 1993.
91 Gilliat-Ray 2010, 33.
92 *South Wales Echo*, 7 Jan 1955, cutting held in 'Muslim/Mosque' files at City of Cardiff Local History Archive files.
93 Lawless 1993.
94 Lawless 1995, 231.
95 *South Wales Echo*, 7 Jan 1955, cutting held in 'Muslim/Mosque' files at City of Cardiff Local History Archive files.
96 City of Cardiff planning file BC/133198, approved, 11 Nov 1938.
97 Ibid.
98 City of Cardiff planning file BC/33848, conversion of existing houses to mosque, Jun 1939, rejected.
99 Lawless 1993.
100 City of Cardiff planning file BC/34485, temporary mosque, Mar 1943, approved.
101 City of Cardiff planning file BC/35865, Nov 1946, approved.
102 City of Cardiff planning file BC/34302, proposed private mosque at rear of private garden at 17 Maria Street, Aug 1941, approved.
103 City of Cardiff planning file BC/34311, Sophia Street, proposed alterations for proposed temporary mosque, Aug 1941, approved.

104 'Rival Moslems fight in Cardiff mosque', *South Wales Echo*, 23 May 1955, cutting held in 'Muslim/Mosque' files at City of Cardiff Local History Archive files.
105 City of Cardiff planning file BC/34658, 34–35 Maria Street, house mosque, May 1944, approved.
106 City of Cardiff planning file BC/35583, Bute Street, Jul 1946, approved.
107 This site was next to a community centre called the George Cross, which was reported as having been built on the site of the very first Bute Street mosque that was bombed during the war – interview with Dawud Suleiman of the South Wales Islamic Centre, 25 May 2011.
108 Tom Davies, 'End of the road for mosque that faced wrong way', *The Sunday Telegraph*, 29 May 1988, cutting held in 'Muslim/Mosque' files at City of Cardiff Local History Archive files.
109 Interview with Sheikh Muhammad Abdul Dahir, imam at Noor-el-Islam Mosque, 25 May 2011.
110 Ibid.
111 Cardiff City Council planning file 09/01786/C.
112 Noor-el-Islam Mosque website, www.noor-el-islam.org.uk/donate-2/ (accessed 8 Oct 2011).
113 Ibid.
114 Lawless 1993.
115 'Rival Moslems fight in Cardiff mosque', *South Wales Echo*, 23 May 1955, cutting held in 'Muslim/Mosque' files at City of Cardiff Local History Archive files.
116 City of Cardiff planning file PA/29518.
117 City of Cardiff planning application 1967/29518, erection of new mosque. This was the file for the original approval of the new-build mosque, and Webb's 1971 letter enquiring about a possible extension to the mosque was within this file although it came after the scheme had been approved.
118 City of Cardiff planning file PA67/29518, letter from J D Evans of Osborne V Webb and Partners to city planning officer, Cardiff City Council, 4 Jan 1971.
119 City of Cardiff planning file 78/2096, drawings stamped by the council on 10 Dec 1978.
120 Interview with Dawud Suleiman, South Wales Islamic Centre, 25 May 2011.
121 City of Cardiff planning application 1979 79/544, demolish existing mosque with retention of existing dwelling and provision of new mosque, approved 19 Jun 1979.
122 Interview with David Davies and Chris Llewelyn, of Davies Llewelyn and Jones LLP, Architects, 23 Nov 2013.
123 City of Cardiff planning application 1981, PA/81/1067, amendments to planning permission 79/544, approved 22 Jun 1981.

124 *The Guardian*, 9 Jan 1984, 3, cutting held in 'Muslim/Mosque' files at City of Cardiff Local History Archive files.

125 City of Cardiff planning file PA/81/1067, letter from A Huw Griffiths of Davies Llewelyn and Jones to City of Cardiff Planning Department, 14 Jul 1987.

126 City of Cardiff planning file PA/81/1067, letter from Alun Michael JP MP to Roger Knight, city planning officer, Cardiff City Council, 22 Oct 1987.

127 City of Cardiff planning application 89/767, proposed new community centre 1989.

128 City of Cardiff planning application 08/202, alterations and extension to the existing Islamic Centre, 2008.

129 City of Cardiff planning application 08/202, design and access statement submitted by Davies Llewelyn and Jones, Nov 2007.

3 Adaptation and transformation – a new era of mosque-making

1 Ansari 2004, 158.

2 www.muslimsinbritain.org (accessed 9 Jun 2015).

3 From Office of National Statistics (ONS) 2001 and 2011 census data.

4 Census analysis carried out by Serena Hussain and Ceri Peach, University of Oxford, and provided to the author.

5 Interview with Muhammad Ibrahim of Howard Street Mosque, Bradford, 20 Jul 2011.

6 McLoughlin 2005, 1046.

7 Ibid, 1054.

8 Alam 2006, 14.

9 McLoughlin 2005, 1051.

10 Ibid, 1050.

11 Ibid.

12 Ibid.

13 Lewis 2002, 56.

14 The National Heritage List for England entry for 1–31 Howard Street, Bradford (list entry 1067743).

15 Bradford City Council (Brad CC) planning file 79/4/04542, observations by chief engineer, 10 Jul 1979.

16 Brad CC planning file 79/4/04542, report and recommendation.

17 Brad CC planning file 79/4/04542, local plan observations by D Webb, area planning officer.

18 Brad CC planning files 94/1847/LBC and 94/01443/FUL.

19 Interview with Khaleel Ahmed of Bristol Jamia Mosque, 23 Mar 2011.

20 Bristol City Council (BCC) planning application 78/01050.

21 BCC planning history for Bristol Jamia Mosque, Green Street: 1979 Raising attic roof – planning file 79/04669/U_S; 1998 Extension to provide mortuary and additional rooms – planning file 98/00936/F; 2000 Alterations to sloping roof to raise into a flat roof and installation of windows to side and front – planning file 00/00400/F; 2000 Raising the sloping roof to a flat roof to provide extra floor of accommodation to the eastern side of the mosque – planning file 00/00072/F; 2010 Construction of a single-storey extension and a disabled access ramp – planning file 10/00976/F.

22 Willey 2006, 465.

23 Tower Hamlets Final Local Implementation Plan for approval 2005/06 to 2010/11 Main Volume 1-1.

24 The National Heritage List for England entry for Brick Lane Jamme Masjid (list entry 1065278).

25 Survey of London 1957, 178–84 (www.british-history.ac.uk/survey-london/vol27/pp178-184; accessed 1 Feb 2016).

26 Survey of London 1957, 199–225 (www.british-history.ac.uk/survey-london/vol27/pp199-225; accessed 1 Feb 2016).

27 Ibid.

28 London Metropolitan Archives, Information Leaflet Number 61: *Huguenot Society of London Publications*.

29 Survey of London 1957, quoted in Museum of London Archaeology Service (MOLAS) Historical Appraisal of Jamme Masjid, 35 Fournier Street and 59–64 Brick Lane, Jan 2004.

30 Survey of London 1957, 199–225 (http://www.british-history.ac.uk/survey-london/vol27/pp199-225; accessed 1 Feb 2016).

31 Ibid.

32 Ibid.

33 Survey of London 1957, 225, quoted in MOLAS Historical Appraisal, Jan 2004.

34 Revd Joseph Nightingale, quoted in Survey of London 1957, 199–225 (http://www.british-history.ac.uk/survey-london/vol27/pp199-225; accessed 1 Feb 2016).

35 Survey of London 1957, 199–225 (www.british-history.ac.uk/survey-london/vol27/pp199-225; accessed 1 Feb 2016).

36 Ibid.

37 Survey of London 1957, quoted in MOLAS Historical Appraisal, Jan 2004.

38 Ibid.

39 Ansari 2011, 58.

40 London Borough of Tower Hamlets (LBTH) planning file 95/00016.

41 Interview with Tom Berndorfer, DGA Architects, 10 Jun 2015.

42 LBTH planning file PA/04/00673, decision date 30 Jan 2006.

43 LBTH planning file PA/04/00672, condition No 8, 30 Jan 2006.

44 LBTH planning file PA/09/01200, approval of detail report, 25 Sep 2009.

45 www.stjohns-leytonstone.org.uk (accessed 20 Oct 2011).

46 Ibid.

47 Ibid.

48 Ibid.

49 London Borough of Waltham Forest (LBWF) planning file 1967/0112.

50 LBWF planning file 1973/1024.

51 www.stjohns-leytonstone.org.uk (accessed 20 Oct 2011).

52 Interview with Iqbal Patel of Leytonstone Mosque, 20 Jan 2011.

53 LBWF planning file 1978/0157.

54 LBWF planning file 1978/0157, planning report to committee, 1 Aug 1978.

55 LBWF planning file 1978/0157, letter of objection from P Maddy, 17 Mar 1978.

56 LBWF planning file 1978/0157, letter of objection (objector not named).

57 LBWF planning file 1978/0157.

58 LBWF planning file 1978/0157, planning report to committee, 1 Aug 1978.

59 LBWF planning file 1978/0157.

60 LBWF planning file 91/1068, planning decision notice, 16 Jun 1993.

61 LBWF planning file 91/1068.

62 LBWF planning file 91/1068, planning application supporting statement from Boyer Planning, 6 Jan 1992.

63 Ibid.

64 LBWF planning file 91/1068, Bushwood Area Residents Association letter of objection to planning application 91/1068.

65 Ibid.

66 LBWF planning file 91/1068.

67 LBWF planning file 91/1068, planning report to planning committee, 22 Jul 1992.

68 Ibid.

69 LBWF planning file 91/1068, letter from director of planning LBWF to chief executive LBWF, 25 Nov 1993.

70 Bewley and Ibrahim-Morrison 2008, 5.

71 Ihsan Mosque website, www.muslimsofnorwich.org.uk (accessed 29 Jun 2015).

72 Interview with Uthman Ibrahim-Morrison of Ihsan Mosque, Norwich, 26 Jun 2015.

73 ONS census 2011.

74 www.muslimsinbritain.org entry on Norwich mosques (accessed 1 Jul 2015).

75 Royal Borough of Kingston upon Thames (RBKT), planning file 23239, statement by Mubarak Ali at planning appeal, refused 4 Nov 1980; Department of the Environment (DoE) planning appeal T/APP/5022/A/81/02154/05, appeal allowed, 12 Oct 1981.

76 Ibid.

77 This subsequently proved not to be the case, and the mosque had to submit a Change of Use application in 1980 (23239), which was refused by RBKT planning committee on 4 Nov 1980 but won at appeal on 12 Oct 1981 (DoE planning appeal T/APP/5022/A/81/02154/05).

78 RBKT planning file 23239, statement by Mubarak Ali at planning appeal, refused 4 Nov 1980; DoE planning appeal T/APP/5022/A/81/02154/05, appeal allowed, 12 Oct 1981.
79 RBKT planning file 23239, planning report, 22 Oct 1980.
80 RBKT planning file 23239.
81 DoE planning appeal T/APP/5022/A/81/02154/05, 3 Sep 1981.
82 RBKT planning file 99/03426, Agular, S 'Residents oppose Muslim tower plan', cutting from local newspaper in planning file (name of paper, date and page number unknown).
83 RBKT planning file 27174, refusal, 7 Sep 1983.
84 RBKT planning file 91/0728/FUL, decision, 5 Jul 1991.
85 RBKT planning file 94/3109/FUL, 28 Mar 1995.
86 RBKT planning file 96/3460/REM.
87 RBKT planning file 96/3460/REM, decision, 13 Feb 1997.
88 RBKT planning file 99/03426/FUL, decision, 31 May 2000.
89 RBKT planning file, 99/03426/FUL, planning officer report to committee, 31 May 2000.
90 RBKT planning file 99/03426, Agular, S 'Residents oppose Muslim tower plan'.
91 RBKT planning file 99/03426/FUL.
92 RBKT planning file 00/03366/FUL.
93 Brent Heritage/Cricklewood, www.brent-heritage.co.uk/cricklewood.htm (accessed 19 Mar 2011).
94 *VCH* Middlesex 7, 242.
95 *A History of Cricklewood Congregational Church*, Sep 1927, 3 (pamphlet published on the 25th anniversary celebration of the church).
96 Ibid.
97 Cherry and Pevsner 2002, 127.
98 Ibid, 58.
99 Ibid.
100 *A History of Cricklewood Congregational Church*.
101 Ibid.
102 *VCH* Middlesex 7, 243.
103 London Borough of Brent (LBBr) *Local Area Agreement Story of Place 2008* quoted in LBBr *Core Strategy – adopted 12 July 2010*, 7, brent.limehouse.co.uk/portal/planning/cspo/adopted_cs?pointId=1253569#document-1253569 (accessed 2 Dec 2015).
104 LBBr planning file M7245.
105 LBBr planning file M7245, letter from Latif Siwani to chief planner at LBBr, 5 Aug 1980.
106 LBBr planning file M7245, architect's notes, GRC or GRP.
107 LBBr planning file 83/0368, application, 17 Mar 1983.

108 LBBr planning file 83/0368, case officer notes (handwritten).
109 Ibid.
110 LBBr planning file 83/0368, officer report to planning committee, 11 May 1983.
111 Ibid.
112 LBBr planning file 96/0228, application, 14 Feb 1996.
113 LBBr planning file 01/2445.
114 LBBr planning file 01/2455, planning committee report, 26 Mar 2002.
115 Bewley and Ibrahim-Morrison 2008, 10.
116 Ibid.
117 Ibid.
118 Brixton Mosque Website, www.brixtonmasjid.co.uk (accessed 11 Nov 2011).
119 London Borough of Lambeth planning file 01/020907/FUL.

4 Building mosques – new identities, new architecture

1   Preston City Council planning application 06/1980/0952.
2   Spurrier, A 'Unique Muslim mosque opened', *Lancashire Evening Post*, 21 Dec 1970, cutting in 'Muslim' file at Preston Harris Library, Preston.
3   London Borough of Merton (LBM) planning file MER298/71.
4   Interview with Mohammed Hassan (d 2010), former chairman of Wimbledon Mosque, 19 May 2010.
5   LBM planning file MER 1332/73.
6   Haider 1996, 36.
7   LBM planning file MER1332/73, approved 31 Jan 1974.
8   *Qarz-e-Hasna* is a term that appears in the Quran and is translated into English as a 'beautiful loan' (Yusuf Ali) or a 'goodly loan' (Marmaduke Pickthall). It is described in the Quran as being a loan to God, and the Quran says that 'he will double it to your credit and he will grant you forgiveness' (chap 64 verse 17). Mosques have used this concept to implement a system of borrowing money interest free from members of the community, which is then paid back, usually once the mosque is built. Mosques with *Qarz-e-Hasna* loans outstanding will continue to fundraise once they are completed and operational to pay off these debts.
9   LBM PA/MER/654/77, 19 Aug 1977.
10 LBM PA/MER/654/77, letter from Mr Monckton, planning officer, to Jack Godfrey-Gilbert (JGG), 4 Oct 1977.
11 LBM PA/MER/654/77, 7 Oct 1977.
12 LBM planning file DC 122/10052.
13 Interview with Mohammed Hassan (d 2010), former chairman of Wimbledon Mosque, 19 May 2010.
14 LBM planning file MER478/83.

15 LBM planning file MER 103/84.
16 LBM planning file MER 672/85.
17 Rondeau 1995, 71.
18 Simms *et al* 2005, 1. The New Economics Foundation argued that this retail-driven transformation was depriving such towns of their diversity, compromising a sense of place and belonging and 'pulling apart the rich weave of natural systems upon which our livelihoods and the economy depend' (Simms *et al* 2005, 5).
19 Maidenhead Mosque Archives (MM archives – uncatalogued), JGG response to local planning authority observations, *c* 1976.
20 MM archives (uncatalogued).
21 Royal Borough of Windsor and Maidenhead (RBWM) planning file 408584, letter from residents to planning committee chairman, 3 Jul 1978.
22 RBWM planning file 409606, officer report, 11 Jun 1979.
23 MM archives report E60/78, minutes of council meeting, undated but referred to elsewhere as 21 Sep 1978.
24 RBWM planning file 409606, letter from Miss M Wright (planning officer) to JGG, 21 Sep 1979.
25 MM archives, JGG notes from meeting with mosque, 5 Jan 1979.
26 MM archives, letter from RBWM planning officer to JGG, 11 Jan 1979.
27 MM archives, JGG notes from meeting with mosque, 5 Jan 1979.
28 Ibid.
29 MM archives, JGG letter to Maidenhead Mosque, 15 Jun 1979.
30 Ibid.
31 RBWM planning file 409606, notes from meeting between JGG and planners, 11 May 1979.
32 MM archives, letter from JGG to Mr Habib-ur-Rehman (chairman of mosque), 23 Oct 1979.
33 MM archives, letter from JGG to Mr Habib-ur-Rahman, 6 Sep 1979.
34 MM archives, letter from JGG to Mr Habib-ur-Rehman, 23 Oct 1979.
35 Ibid.
36 RBWM planning file 411185.
37 RBWM planning file 411185, architects' panel report, 6 Jun 1980.
38 RBWM planning file 411185, architects' panel report, 1 Jul 1980.
39 RBWM planning file 411185, architects' panel report, 8 Jul 1981.
40 RBWM planning file 411185, Ahmed Eliwa elevation of minaret, 24 Jul 1981.
41 RBWM planning file 411185, notes by Vincent Dowling of the architects' panel, 28 Jul 1981.
42 Short 1925, 136.
43 RBWM planning file 411185, notes by Vincent Dowling, 5 Aug 1981.

44 RBWM planning file 411185, letter from Reginald Hyne, architects' panel, to chief planning officer, 11 Aug 1981.

45 RBWM planning file 13/02447/FULL, approved 26 Nov 2013.

46 www.localhistories.org/gloucester.html (accessed 12 Jan 2012).

47 Interview with Yaqub Banti and Ayub Miah, founder members of Jama al-Karim Mosque, Gloucester, 17 Sep 2011.

48 Office of National Statistics Census 2001.

49 City of Gloucester (CoG) planning file 12265/01, application form, 6 Jul 1981.

50 CoG planning file 12265/01, comments from civic design committee, 28 Jul 1981.

51 CoG planning file 12265/02, application form, 18 Mar 1982.

52 'Work starts on city's new mosque', *The Gloucester Citizen*, 14 Dec 1982, 5.

53 Interview with Yaqub Banti and Ayub Miah, 17 Sep 2011. ('Al-Karim' is one of the 99 names of Allah and means 'The Generous', and 'Jama' can be translated as 'place of', so Jama al-Karim Mosque can be translated as 'Place of The Generous'.)

54 Interview with Ghalib Hussain, Al Haj Fazalilahi, Mohammed Saleem Akhtar, members of Ghamkol Sharif Mosque committee, 19 Mar 2011.

55 Muslim Cultural Heritage Centre archives, full appraisal *c* 1993–4.

56 ONS Census 2001.

57 Interview with Ali Omar Ermes, 18 Mar 2013.

58 Moulvi Mohammed Faizul Islam, 'A chronicle of the Shahjalal Mosque of Manchester', *Janomot*, 14–20 Feb 1997, 30.

59 Ibid.

60 Ibid.

61 Manchester City Council planning file 077256/FO/2005/N2.

62 Interview with Najib Gedal, 20 Jan 2012.

5 Making Muslim landmarks and institutions

1 Ziauddin Sardar, 'Review of *The Infidel Within*', *The Independent*, 10 Oct 2011, www.independent.co.uk/arts-entertainment/books/reviews/the-infidel-within-muslims-in-britain-since-1800-by-humayun-ansari-561666.html (accessed 9 Nov 2015).

2 Ansari 2011, 5.

3 Ibid, 13.

4 *The Times*, 5 Jan 1911, quoted in Ansari 2011, 6.

5 Ansari 2011, 1.

6 Ibid, 7.

7 Ibid.

8 Ibid, 8.

9 Ibid, 10.

10 Ibid, 11.

11 Ibid.

12 Ibid.

13 Ibid, 14.

14 Tibawi 1981, 196.

15 Ansari 2011, 14.

16 H Ansari, pers comm, 16 Sep 2011.

17 Tibawi 1981, 197.

18 Ansari 2011, 15.

19 Ibid, 17.

20 Ibid, 18.

21 Letter from Syed Hashimi to A S N Anik, Aug 1930, quoted in Ansari 2011, 18.

22 Ansari 2011, 19.

23 Ibid, 22.

24 Ibid, 27.

25 Tibawi 1981, 198.

26 Ibid.

27 Ibid, 200.

28 Ansari 2011, 26.

29 Tibawi 1981, 205.

30 City of Westminster (CoW) planning file AR/TP/81101/W, minutes of meeting between Mr Richardson and CoW planning office, 1 Oct 1962.

31 Ibid.

32 Ibid.

33 CoW planning file TP720 item 35, letter from Richardson and McLaughlan to CoW planning office, 17 Sep 1963.

34 Ibid.

35 Ibid.

36 'Dome and low minaret for mosque', *Daily Telegraph*, 28 Sep 1965, cutting in CoW planning file TP720.

37 Anon 1964.

38 CoW planning file TP720, letter from Godfrey Samuel, secretary of the RFAC, to LCC architect, 14 Apr 1962.

39 CoW planning file TP720, memo from LCC chairman's secretary, to the architect to the Council, 24 Apr 1964.

40 CoW planning file TP720, letter from J Rogerson, Ministry of Housing and Local Government, to Sir William Hart, clerk of the LCC, 5 Jun 1964.

41 CoW planning file TP720, letter from CoW planning dept (authored as 'Architect to the Council') to Secretary, Ministry of Housing and Local Government , 15 Jul 1964.

42 CoW planning file TP103218/W.

43 CoW planning file TP720, 'Conditions of competition, erection of the proposed new Central London Mosque' – the design brief issued by The London Central Mosque Trust Ltd 1968.

44 Ibid.

45 Anon 1969, 988.

46 Windsor 1977.

47 Ibid.

48 Frederick Gibberd & Partners, Design Statement, Nov 1983.

49 Anon 1969.

50 Mars 1977.

51 Anon 1977, 144.

52 Mars 1977.

53 Sharp 1978.

54 Ibid.

55 *Radio Times*, 6–12 Aug 1983, cutting in the RIBA cuttings file for Frederick Gibberd & Partners.

56 Daftary and Hirji 2008, 166.

57 Known as the Arnould ruling, it was tried by Sir Joseph Arnould; *see* Daftary and Hirji 2008, 194.

58 Dahya 1996, 123.

59 Ibid, 124.

60 Ibid, 120.

61 Ibid, 111.

62 Ibid, 112.

63 Ibid, 126.

64 Ibid, 131.

65 Aga Khan IV, Prince Shah Karim Al Hussani, speech at the inauguration of the Ismaili Centre, Houston, Texas, 23 Jun 2002, Institute of Ismaili Studies, Aga Khan Development Network, www.akdn.org/Content/666 (accessed 27 Jun 2015).

66 Aga Khan IV speech at the foundation-laying ceremony of the Ismaili Centre, Dubai 13 Dec 2003, Institute of Ismaili Studies, Aga Khan Development Network, www.akdn.org/speech/594/Foundation-Laying-Ceremony-of-the-Ismaili-Centre-Dubai (accessed 27 Jun 2015).

67 www.theismaili.org (accessed 5 Dec 2011).

68 Ibid.

69 Aga Khan IV speech at the inauguration of the Ismaili Centre, Houston, Texas, 23 Jun 2002.

70 Davey 1999.

71 Spring 1979.

72 Sutherland 1983.

73 Pawley 1983, 34.

74 Ibid.

75 Anon 1983, 4.

76 Ibid, 5.

77 Ibid, 4.

78 Ibid.

79 Pawley 1983, 35.

80 Ibid.

81 Williams, A & Partners 1984, 38.

82 Sutherland 1983, 11.

83 Ansari 2011, 18.

84 Ibid, 22.

85 Ibid, 19.

86 Ibid, 23.

87 Ibid, 19.

88 East London Mosque (ELM) Archives, 'Proposed East London Mosque', funding leaflet 1975.

89 ELM Archives, funding letter from S M Jetha, chairman of ELM Trust (ELMT), 14 Dec 1967.

90 Ibid.

91 ELM Archives, 'Proposed East London Mosque', funding leaflet 1975.

92 ELM Archives, letter from Ahmed Eliwa to S M Jetha, chairman of ELMT, 15 Jun 1982.

93 Ibid.
94 Ibid.
95 ELM Archives, letter from Eliwa to S M Jetha, chairman of ELMT, 21 Jul 1982.
96 Ibid.
97 Interview with Choudhary Muenuddin, formerly of the ELMT, 7 Dec 2011.
98 ELM Archives, letter from John Gill Associates to Mr Muenuddin of the ELMT, 20 Sep 1982.
99 ELM Archives, letter from Eliwa to S M Jetha, chairman, ELM 15 Jun 1982.
100 ELM Archives, 'Whitechapel Muslim Project' document accompanying John Gill Associates drawings 1982.
101 Ibid.
102 Ansari 2011, 69.
103 Ibid.
104 Ibid, 70.
105 Ibid.
106 ELM Archives, London Muslim Centre mission statement, promotional literature, 2001.
107 LBTH planning file PA/02/01764.
108 LBTH planning file PA/09/00159.
109 Interview with Moshe Winegarten, trustee of the Federation of Synagogues, at Fieldgate Street Great Synagogue, 25 Jun 2015.

6 New century, new historicism

1 Hussain 2008, 18.
2 Ibid, 3.
3 Ibid.
4 For example 'Community cohesion, a report of the Independent Review Team' chaired by Ted Cantle, UK Home Office, 2001.
5 Morey and Yaqin 2011, 36.
6 Heathcote 1997.
7 Ibid.
8 Al-Samarraie, pers comm, 8 May 2013.
9 The site was within the 'University Action Area', a Comprehensive Development Area, and was shown for redevelopment in Phase 1 of the plan, over one to five years.
10 Edinburgh City Council (ECC) planning file R/643/175/70, report on application for commercial and shopping development, applicant Archibald Bennet & Co Ltd.
11 ECC planning files 2636/80 and 2625/80, permission dated 27 Mar 1981, application dated 19 Dec 1980, agent Ian G Lindsay & Partners.
12 ECC planning file 08-9AY, application dated 10 Jul 1983, permission dated 16 Jan 1984.
13 ECC planning file 08-9AY, case officer report, 30 Nov 1983.
14 ECC planning file 1583/86/35.
15 ECC planning file 1583/86/35, case officer report.
16 ECC planning file 1583/86/35, planning notes, 21 Jan 1987.

17 Ibid.
18 Ibid.
19 Ibid.
20 Ibid.
21 Fehervari 1989, 26.
22 Ibid.
23 Al-Bayati 1993, 13.
24 Antoniou 1986.
25 Al-Bayati 1997.
26 ECC planning file 1583/86/35, planning notes, 1 Jul 1987.
27 Al-Bayati 1997.
28 Interview written response by Al-Samarraie, Jan 2012.
29 Ibid.
30 Ibid.
31 Interview with Nawaz Khan, Sheffield Islamic Centre, 8 Feb 2012.
32 Ibid.
33 Sheffield City Council (SCC) planning application 98/699P, recommendation sheet, 26 Aug 1998.
34 SCC planning application 03/02079/FUL, design and consideration statement, 9 Jun 2003.
35 SCC planning application 03/02079/FUL, urban design and conservation, design review meeting, 1 Jul 2003.
36 Ismailite – *Encyclopædia Britannica Online,* www.britannica.com/EBchecked/topic/296133/Ismailite (accessed 3 Feb 2012).
37 Bohra – *Encyclopædia Britannica Online,* www.britannica.com/EBchecked/topic/71729/Bohras (accessed 5 Feb 2012).
38 http://www.malumaat.com/archives/jamaat/europe.html (accessed 1 Feb 2012).
39 Northolt Industrial Estate, HC Deb 03 Jul 1992, vol 210, cc1139–46 *from* http://hansard.millbanksystems.com/commons/1992/jul/03/northolt-industrial-estate (accessed 9 Nov 2015).
40 Aliasger Jivanjee, pers comm, 2 Feb 2012.
41 Ibid.
42 http://thesplitlabs.com/research/bohra-mosques-in-gujarat (accessed 6 Feb 2012).
43 Aliasger Jivanjee, pers comm, 2 Feb 2012.
44 Ibid.
45 Leicester City Council, planning file 20080419.
46 Little Horton Lane, Conservation Area Assessment, Bradford City Council 2004.
47 www.suffatulislam.org/#/history/4541036774 (accessed 24 Feb 2012); interview with a representative from Suffa-Tul-Islam, 9 Sep 2012.
48 www.suffatulislam.org/#/vision/4541036773 (accessed 25 Feb 2012).
49 Interview with representative from Suffa-Tul-Islam, 9 Sep 2012.
50 Ibid.

7 New narratives

1 Aberdeen City Council – planning reference for change of use to mosque 120484; for alterations and extensions to existing building 121740; for alterations to façade 141199.
2 London Borough of Harrow (LBH) planning file P/1953/10.
3 LBH planning file P/2377/08, date of refusal 24 Jul 2009.
4 www.thesalaamcentre.com (accessed 7 Jul 2012).
5 Ibid.
6 LBH planning file P/1953/10, design and access statement 132091B, Mangera Yvars Architects, 20 Jul 2010, 5.
7 Ibid, 32.
8 Ibid.
9 www.thesalaamcentre.com, promotional video (accessed 7 Jul 2012).
10 Cambridge City Council (CCC) planning file 11/1348/FUL.
11 CCC planning file 11/1348/FUL, design and access statement for proposed mosque on Mill Road, preface by Tim Winters, 4 Nov 2011.
12 Ibid.
13 Ibid.
14 Ibid.
15 Email from Antonio Callejon of Mangera Yvars Architects to the author, dated 26 Feb 2013.
16 CCC planning file 11/1348/FUL, design and access statement for proposed mosque on Mill Road, Marks Barfield Architects, 4 Nov 2011.
17 Ibid.
18 Interview with David Marks, Marks Barfield Architects, 18 Apr 2013.
19 Ibid.
20 CCC planning file 11/1348/FUL, design and access statement for proposed mosque on Mill Road, preface by Tim Winters, 4 Nov 2011.
21 Interview with David Marks, Marks Barfield Architects, 18 Apr 2013.

8 Surveying the landscape – 130 years of the mosque in Britain

1 Nasser 2003, 8.
2 Metcalf 1996, 9.
3 Eade 1996, 217.
4 Ibid.
5 McLoughlin 2005, 1060.
6 Metcalf 1996, 3.
7 Ibid, 10.
8 Ibid.
9 Murad 2009.
10 Verkaaik 2012, 164.
11 Murad 2009.
12 Interview with Dr Yaqub Zaki (formerly James Dickie), 21 Sep 2010.

13 Glancey, J 2002 'Why are there no great British mosques?' *The Guardian*, 17 Jun 2002, www.theguardian.com/culture/2002/jun/17/artsfeatures.religion (accessed Jan 2009).
14 Ibid.
15 Mohsen Mostafavi, quoted in Glancey 2002.
16 Shariatmadari, D 2007 'Modern mosques are as bad as Barratt homes', *The Guardian*, Art & design blog, 3 Aug 2007, www.theguardian.com/artanddesign/artblog/2007/aug/03/modernmosquesarethereligio (accessed Oct 2015).

17 Verkaaik 2012, 164.
18 Verkaaik 2011, 3.
19 Ibid, 4.
20 Peter Guillery (of the Survey of London), pers comm, 5 Feb, 2012.
21 Verkaaik 2011, 7.
22 Ibid.
23 Ibid, 8.
24 Ibid, 9.
25 Gale 2004.
26 Ibid, 21.
27 Ibid, 22.
28 Ibid.
29 Ibid.

30 Ibid, 27.
31 Ibid, 26.

Appendix 1

1 Minnis with Mitchell 2007, 39.
2 The National Heritage List for England entry for Mecca Social Club Carlton Rooms, Maida Vale (list entry 113102).
3 Minnis with Mitchell 2007, 66.

Glossary

1 'Breach of Faith'. *Human Rights Watch* **17**, (6), Jun 2005, 8

Bibliography

Alam, M Y (ed) 2006 *Made in Bradford.* Pontefract: Route

Al-Bayati, B 1993 *Basil Al-Bayati: Recent Works.* London: Academy Editions/Ernst and Sohn

Al-Bayati, B 1997 'Attributes a designer ought to have in order to design the house of God'. *Alam El Benaa,* (193), Aug 1997, 6–9

Ameer Ali, Syed 1891 *The Spirit of Islam or The Life and Teachings of Mohammed.* London: W H Allen and Co

Anon 1926a 'Mosque at Southfields'. *The Builder,* 8 Oct 1926, **131** (4366), 564

Anon 1926b 'London's first mosque'. *Building,* Nov 1926, **1** (8), 371

Anon 1964 'The Regent's Park Mosque'. *Country Life,* **135** (3496), 5 Mar 1964, 488

Anon 1969 'Just what Nash would have liked'. *Architects' Journal,* **150** (43), 22 Oct 1969, 988–90

Anon 1977 'The London Mosque'. *Architectural Review,* **162** (967), Sep 1977, 144–7

Anon 1983 'East meets west in Kensington'. *Concrete Quarterly,* (139), Oct–Dec 1983, 2–7

Ansari, H 2002 'The Woking Mosque: A case study of Muslim engagement with British society since 1889'. *Immigrants & Minorities,* **21** (3), 1–24

Ansari, H 2004 *'The Infidel Within': Muslims in Britain Since 1800.* London: C Hurst and Co

Ansari, H 2008 'Making transnational connections: Muslim networks in early twentieth-century Britain' *in* Clayer, N and Germain, E (eds) *Islam in Inter-war Europe.* London: Hurst and Co, 31–63

Ansari, H (ed) 2011 *The Making of the East London Mosque, 1910–1951: Minutes of the London Mosque Fund and East London Mosque Trust Ltd* (Camden Fifth Series Vol 38). Cambridge: Cambridge University Press

Antoniou, J 1986 'Basil Al-Bayati, interview'. *Architectural Design,* **56** (12), 16–23

Anwar, M 1979 *The Myth of Return: Pakistanis in Britain.* London: Heinemann

Bewley, Shaykh A and Ibrahim-Morrison, U 2008 'Islam in Norwich: English beginnings and Caribbean roots'. Unpublished essay, Ihsan Mosque, Chapelfield, Norwich

Cherry, B and Pevsner, N 2002 *The Buildings of England: London North West.* New Haven and London: Yale University Press

Creswell, K 1926 'The evolution of the minaret'. *Burlington Magazine,* **48**, Mar 1926, 134–40

Daftary, F and Hirji, Z 2008 *The Ismailis: An Illustrated History.* London: Azimuth Editions in association with the Institute of Ismaili Studies

Dahya, B 1996 'Ethnicity and modernity: The case of Ismailis in Britain', *in* Barot, R (ed) *The Racism Problematic: Contemporary Sociological Debates on Race and Ethnicity.* Lewiston, NY: Edwin Mellen Press, 106–38

Davey, P 1999 'Hugh Casson 1910–1999'. *Architectural Review,* **206** (1232), Oct 1999, 37

Dickie, J 1978 'Allah and eternity: Mosques, madrasas and tombs', *in* Michell, G (ed) *Architecture of the Islamic World: Its History and Social Meaning.* London: Thames and Hudson, 15–47

Eade, J 1996 'Nationalism, community, and the Islamisation of space in London' *in* Metcalf, B (ed) *Making Muslim Space in North America and Europe.* Berkeley: University of California Press, 217–33

Fehervari, G 1989 'Faith in tradition'. *Building Design,* (940), 9 Jun 1989, 26–27

Gale, R 2004 'The multicultural city and the politics of religious architecture: Urban planning, mosques and meaning-making in Birmingham, UK'. *Built Environment,* **30** (1), 18–32

Geaves, R 2010 *Islam in Victorian Britain: The Life and Times of Abdullah Quilliam.* Markfield, Leicestershire: Kube Publishing

Gilliat-Ray, S 2010 *Muslims in Britain.* Cambridge: Cambridge University Press

Haider, G 1996 'Muslim space and the practice of architecture', *in* Metcalf, B (ed) *Making Muslim Space in North America and Europe.* Berkeley: University of California Press, 31–45

Halliday, F 2010 *Britain's First Muslims: Portrait of an Arab Community.* London: I B Tauris

Heathcote, E 1997 'Company profile – Bullen Consultants: Mosque design in a multicultural society'. *Church Building,* (47), Sep–Oct 1977, 22–3

Holod, R and Khan, H-U 1997 *Mosques in the Modern World: Architects, Patrons and Designs Since the 1950s.* London: Thames and Hudson

Hussain, S 2008 *Muslims on the Map: A National Survey of Social Trends in Britain.* London and New York: Taurus Academic Studies

Jones, D 1978 'The elements of decoration: Surface, pattern and light' *in* Michell, G (ed) *Architecture of the Islamic World: Its History and Social Meaning.* London: Thames and Hudson, 144–75

Kadish, S 2011 *The Synagogues of Britain and Ireland: An Architectural and Social History.* New Haven and London: Yale University Press

Lawless, R 1993 'Sheikh Abdullah Ali al-Hakimi'. The British-Yemeni Society (website) article, http://www.al-bab.com/bys/articles/lawless93.htm (accessed 18 Oct 2015)

Lawless, R 1995 *From Ta'izz to Tyneside: Arab Community in the North East of England in the Early Twentieth Century.* Exeter: University of Exeter Press

Lewis, P 2002 *Islamic Britain: Religion, Politics and Identity Among British Muslims,* 2 edn. London: I B Tauris

McLoughlin, S 2005 'Mosques and the public space: Conflict and cooperation in Bradford'. *Journal of Ethnic and Migration Studies,* **31** (6), Nov 2005, 1045–66

Mars, T 1977 'Barefoot in the park'. *Building*, **233** (6994), 15 Jul 1977, 48–9

Metcalf, B (ed) 1996 *Making Muslim Space in North America and Europe*. Berkeley: University of California Press

Minnis, J with Mitchell, T 2007 *Religion and Place in Leeds*. Swindon: English Heritage

Morey, P and Yaqin, A 2011 *Framing Muslims: Stereotyping and Representation after 9/11*. Cambridge, MA: Harvard University Press

Murad, A H 2009 'Praying for the mosque'. *Emel Magazine*, (53), Feb 2009, 32

Nairn, I and Pevsner, N (revd by Cherry, B) 1971 *The Buildings of England: Surrey*, 2 edn. London: Penguin

Nasser, N 2003 'The space of displacement: The making of Muslim South Asian places in Britain'. *Traditional Dwellings and Settlements Review*, **XV** (1), 7–21

Naylor, S and Ryan, J 2002 'The mosque in the suburbs: Negotiating religion and ethnicity in South London'. *Social & Cultural Geography*, **3** (1), 39–59

Pawley, M 1983 'Cross-cultural centre'. *Architects' Journal*, **178** (48), 30 Nov 1983, 32–5

Peach, C and Gale, R 2003 'Muslims, Hindus and Sikhs in the new religious landscape of England'. *Geographical Review*, **93** (4), Oct 2003, 469–490

Petersen, A 1996 *Dictionary of Islamic Architecture*. London: Routledge

Rondeau, B 1995 *Wimbledon Park: From Private Park to Residential Suburb*. Wimbledon: self published

Salamat, P 2008 *A Miracle at Woking: A History of the Shahjahan Mosque*. Chichester: Phillimore

Serageldin, I with Steele, J (ed) 1996 *Architecture of the Contemporary Mosque*. London: Academy Editions

Sharp, D 1978 'Faith in design'. *Building*, **235** (7044), 7 Jul 1978, 65–9

Short, E 1925 *History of Religious Architecture*. (Facsim edn Kessinger Publishing 2003)

Simms, A, Kjell, P and Potts, R 2005 *Clone Town Britain: The Survey Results on the Bland State of the Nation*. London: The New Economics Foundation

Spring, M 1979 'Islamic architecture turns to modern and traditional designs'. *Building*, **237** (7105/37), 14 Sep 1979, 16

Survey of London 1957 *Volume 27: Spitalfields and Mile End New Town*. London: Athlone Press/University of London for London County Council

Sutherland, L 1983 'Ismaili Centre, an architectural no man's land'. *Building*, **245** (7316), 4 Nov 1983, 11

Tanyeli, U 2014 'Profession of faith'. *Architectural Review*, **235**, 32–47

Tibawi, A L 1981 'History of the London Central Mosque and the Islamic Cultural Centre 1910–1980'. *Die Welt des Islams*, **21** (1), 193–208

VCH Middlesex 7 1982 *A History of the County of Middlesex: Volume 7, Acton, Chiswick, Ealing and Brentford, West Twyford, Willesden*. Oxford: Oxford University Press for Institute of Historical Research, University of London

Verkaaik, O 2011 'Designing the "anti-mosque": An anthropological approach to contemporary mosque design in Europe', unpublished draft

Verkaaik, O 2012 'Designing the "anti-mosque": Identity, religion and affect in contemporary European mosque design'. *Social Anthropology*, **20** (2), 161–78

Willey, R, 2006 *Chambers London Gazetteer*. Edinburgh: Chambers

Williams, A & Partners 1984 'Ismaili Centre'. *Building*, **246** (7331), 24 Feb 1984, 35–42

Windsor, P 1977 'Islam comes west'. *The Architect*, **123** (8), Aug 1977, 27–30

Index